BIGFOOT CHRONICLES

A RESEARCHER'S CONTINUING JOURNEY

MIKE QUAST

UNTOLD PUBLISHING

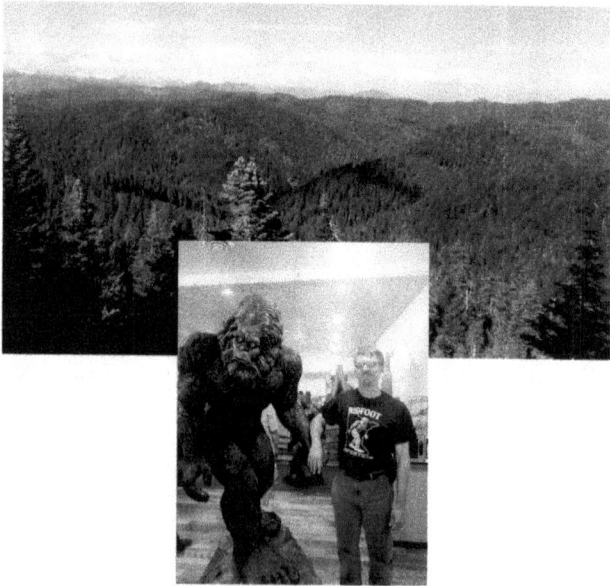

To report Bigfoot encounters in the state of Minnesota or for further information the author may be contacted at mqstk@aol.com.

CONTENTS

For Sarah W, aka Cleo, 1975-2018. You were not a believer, my friend. Now that you have crossed to the realm where all truths may be known, I hope you have become a knower. And for all the witnesses everywhere.

INTRODUCTION

As I begin to write this, I am in the days surrounding my 50th birthday, a major turning point that often makes people look back at what we hope will be the first half of our lives if we would like to try and live to be 100, which - because why not? - I would like to shoot for. My father's mother made it to 103, but it keeps me humble to remember that he himself passed away at 61.

My first 50 years consisted of me growing up on a dairy farm in Minnesota in an area where I was able to appreciate nature and the privilege of being able to observe wild animals and then being led to an interest in art and writing and studying those things in technical college, but ending up with a career in menial labor jobs mostly involving cleaning up after people. I currently work as a custodian in a school, which comes with a halfway decent benefits package and lets me maintain a certain level of comfort, but it is definitely not the passion in my life.

Since my earliest memories, I have had an unending fascination with the paranormal and supernatural. UFOs and aliens, ghosts and psychic phenomena, monsters and cryptozoology- all of these things have always called to me in a way that didn't seem to require any kind of specific trigger but just kind of seemed to be a natural part of me, and as a kid, I devoured every book I could get my hands on involving those subjects. I have often wondered how important it was to maintain this level of interest that at the age of eight in 1976, I happened to have my very own sighting of Bigfoot.

While on a Sunday drive with my family in the summer of that year in the forested area around Strawberry Lake in Becker County, Minnesota, I saw a tall black object standing beside the blacktop road about a hundred yards ahead of us that I at first thought was a burned and blackened tree trunk about seven feet tall, but in a few seconds, it suddenly walked away from the roadside on two legs and disappeared into the woods. Why I was the only one in the car who saw it is something I have never understood, in spite of Native Americans who would eventually tell me that I alone was meant to see it and that it was invisible to my parents and sister.

I immediately knew that what I had seen could not have been a bear since they do not walk for any great distance on two legs, nor was it likely to have been a man in a costume since if he was trying to scare people, I would have thought he would have let our car get a lot closer before disappearing. My eight-year-old self knew instinctively that I had just seen a Bigfoot, one of the huge hulking manlike/apelike hairy creatures that are alleged to inhabit North America. Even at that young age, I understood that many people scoffed at the idea of such things existing but that thousands of sightings over the years argued otherwise.

My interest continued all through elementary and high school, and after I graduated in 1986 I determined to start investigating Bigfoot reports in my home state of Minnesota. Though my studies told me that the majority of reports came from states like those in the Pacific Northwest and a few other hot spots around the country, there were a few recorded for Minnesota and I used those as my starting off point.

Over much time I would eventually discover that what had been recorded in books was just barely scratching the surface and that Minnesota was just as much a hotbed of Bigfoot activity as any of those other more famous states like Washington or Oregon or California or Ohio or Pennsylvania or Florida. I had thought that my own sighting had been a freak occurrence, but I came to understand that hundreds of other people in my state had seen similar things. My database of reports grew bigger and bigger over the years as I started to network with other investigators, sharing information and collecting the reports they'd gathered on top of the ones I'd uncovered myself. It was almost as big a thrill to realize that other people were doing this same work as it was to meet with Bigfoot witnesses and hear their eyewitness accounts of what they'd seen.

I had a level of notoriety in the 90s as my name became known to the other members of the Bigfoot community around the country, and I decided to delve into the world of self publishing. In 1990, I produced a book entitled 'The Sasquatch in Minnesota,' and then a follow up the next year called 'Creatures of the North: The New Minnesota Sasquatch Encounters,' which were really cheap projects banged out on typewriters and containing hand-drawn illustrations as well as black and white photos. I also launched the monthly newsletter 'The Sasquatch Report' which was just as amateurish a job but ended up garnering quite a few subscribers and lasted for several years. It was a fun time, my 20s, bolstered by my frequent forays into the Minnesota wilderness in the physical search for the creatures that fascinated me, sometimes leading to dangerous encounters with rough terrain or wild animals or even sinister people. I took it all in stride as being the price one pays for this quest, with the payoff being the actual physical evidence I occasionally found.

In 1996, I did an updated combination of my first two books entitled 'The Sasquatch in Minnesota- Revised Edition,' and then in 2000, I did a very unique project called 'Big Footage: A History of Claims for the Sasquatch on Film' in which I used my artistic skills to do recreations of all the various photos and films of Bigfoot that people claim to have captured over the years. I could never do that book today, as the Internet has produced scores of supposed Bigfoot videos far too numerous to be included in one volume, many of which are fake.

But the real evidence was out there if only one would look for it.

In exploring areas with reported Bigfoot encounters I have found the creatures' tracks well over a dozen times now and I have even had the priceless experience of hearing what I believe to have been Bigfoot vocalizations, a crazy wailing cry from such a powerful pair of lungs that the woods practically shook with it. I have found trees and branches broken and arranged in such weird and dramatic ways that it almost has to be done by something with intelligence and great strength rather than just a natural happening.

At one time, I felt that the term "Bigfoot" sounded too silly and cartoonish to be a name for a real animal and preferred to use the name "Sasquatch," which is thought by many to be a Native American word. It is actually a name coined in the 1950s by a white man named J.W. Burns who was a teacher on an Indian reservation in British Columbia and who took various tribal names he was hearing for the wild men of the woods and combined them into the word "Sasquatch." Since my earlier days as a researcher and investigator, I guess I have softened a bit, and with the massively widespread use of the term "Bigfoot," I have let it grow on me and come to embrace it.

Bigfoot is real. I have seen one, I have heard them, I have seen their tracks, and the other traces they leave upon the land. I have interviewed witnesses who have described seeing things that are so amazing they put my own brief experiences to shame. The fact that these things go on year after year, not only in my home state of Minnesota but all across North America, without the creature ever being proven to be real is absolutely madding to me, and I have taken it upon myself - as have many others - to try and be the one who proves that these things exist.

Why do I do this when the rewards are so few? I do it not only because of my own experiences, which I know to be true but also for all of those other witnesses and all of our experiences that have been utterly ridiculed by skeptics. I don't mind people being skeptical in a general sense, but I do mind when people who are simply telling what they have seen are cut to pieces because of it. Just picture this for a moment. You see something incredible that changes your world-view of what is real and what isn't, and you decide to tell people about it. If people don't believe you, they are really telling you one of three things.

One - No, you didn't really see that, and you are lying to me.

Two - No, you didn't really see that, and you only think you did because you are crazy and have extreme hallucinations.

Or three - You didn't really see that because you are so stupid that you can see a normal animal or an old tree stump and think that it is a Bigfoot.

Imagine being given that treatment by people you have always loved and trusted, just because you tell them you have seen something. I feel for all those people because I am one of them. I endeavor to keep on striving to prove that Bigfoot is real because if the day comes when that becomes proven, then all who have ever been ridiculed for saying that they have seen them will be vindicated. That means more to me than I can possibly say.

Having said that, I would like to introduce to the Bigfoot field a friend who has not rejected my belief in and experiences with Bigfoot. His name is Dean Opsahl, and we have been close friends since the first grade. For several years he has been my unofficial partner in my search, accompanying me on many a wilderness foray even though he is actually an agnostic when it comes to Bigfoot, on the fence as to whether the creatures actually exist but finding the subject intriguing enough to be involved. We argue about the various aspects of the subject all the time, spirited debates about what makes for a justified motivation for pursuing it, what impact final proof would have on society and many other things, but our partnership endures, and we truly have fun together whenever we are out in the field. Dean is my best friend, and he will be mentioned here and there in the stories that follow.

I have also taken on a special project of attempting to document every single Bigfoot report in the state of Minnesota for all time. I know that is impossible and that I will never succeed in getting them all, but I intend to come as close as anyone ever can. To that end, I have searched every published and online source that I've been able to find as well as collaborating with other Minnesota researchers on a personal basis in order to add their information to that which I've collected myself to assemble the most comprehensive list of Bigfoot repots for the state that anyone has ever assembled.

I will present that list of reports as an appendix at the end of this book, and the total number of reports promises to be astounding. In this book, I will present a memoir of the continuation of a Minnesota Bigfoot researcher's 30-year journey since the publication of my last books, as well as my thoughts and observations on other aspects of the whole Bigfoot field.

There is a chapter on the Minnesota Iceman case, which actually has only a tenuous connection to the state but which I felt it my responsibility to investigate, and also one on the famous California Patterson-Gimlin film which I am fascinated with and have delved into because of my deep interest in Bigfoot photos and films even though I am an outsider. I hope you, the reader, will both enjoy this account and be able to learn something.

Dean Opsahl with Mini-Bigfoot friend.

1

IN MEMORIAM

I wanted to begin by honoring the memory of a few people involved in the Bigfoot field in Minnesota, that have sadly passed away since my last book came out. We've lost so many big names now on the national and international scenes - John Green, Rene Dahinden, Grover Krantz,

Bernard Heuvelmans, John Bindernagel, and others - it feels as if all the great sages are leaving us. I had some level of correspondence with most of them, and I feel their loss, but the handful of names I will share here were people I knew in person and will always hold a special place in my heart.

ED & NOVA TRIMBLE

My second book, 'Creatures of the North: The New Minnesota Sasquatch Encounters' published in 1991, was mostly based on the experiences of this wonderful man. He first came to my attention when he reported to the Minnesota Department of Natural Resources in December

1990 that he had found what appeared to be Bigfoot tracks on his property in Clearwater County near a tiny community called Zerkel,

15 miles south of the slightly larger town of Bagley (population 1,400). The DNR referred him to me, and after receiving a four-page handwritten letter from him complete with drawings of the tracks he'd found, I drove up to the area, located his home, and knocked on his door.

Ed was 76 years old at that time and lived with his wife Nova on a rather ramshackle little farm in the midst of a vast series of rolling wooded hills, very near the White Earth State Forest and an area locally unofficially known as the Buckboard Hills, a major wilderness region where logging and hunting were common.

Ed and Nova welcomed me into their home with warmth and friendliness on that winter day and impressed me from minute one with what genuinely nice and decent people they were. Being in their golden years, they were retired, but Ed had worked as both a farmer and a truck driver and had lived in Iowa but had spent the most time doing what he loved the most working in the Minnesota wilderness as a professional animal tracker and trapper. His knowledge of predators like wolves and bears rivaled that of any zoologist.

He even had a bit of a dubious attitude toward certain scientific experts who he saw as refusing to accept what people like him who actually lived upon the land know from personal experience, such as the fact that mountain lions are still native to Minnesota. In his deep but soft voice, he regaled me with stories that made me come to know that if there was anyone in a position to know what they were seeing when Bigfoot tracks turned up, it was him.

Ed was staying very active in his retirement with various projects, from becoming a commercial beekeeper and producing honey to doing various environmental landscaping work around his property, including creating hybrid trees and taking charge of water sources by building earthen dams to form a large manmade pond a couple of hundred yards from his house.

It was just offshore on that frozen pond where the tracks first appeared, pressed into the snow atop the ice. To his trained eye, they instantly had to be bipedal, but not human, something that he said left him "stupefied." He had always had a vague awareness of the

Bigfoot subject and had even had several mysterious experiences over the years that had made him wonder about it, but here now was what seemed undeniable evidence that two creatures- one larger and one smaller- had walked across his pond on two legs.

He was referring to them as "Mama" and "Junior." And with Ed being the unique character that he was, it didn't seem to be enough that he had found Bigfoot tracks. They had to be markedly different from any other such tracks ever found.

The tracks on the pond were not human-like in shape but rounded, with the smaller set being slightly oval-shaped and the larger being nearly circular, but each showing two large toes and three tiny ones that left impressions only about the size of a dime with what looked like impressions of hair growing underneath the toes. In size, they were not massive, both less than nine inches in length and approximating the size of bear tracks but showing no claw impressions.

What was this? As bipedal creatures, they fit within the realm of Bigfoot, but their feet were like nothing ever seen before. It caused a level of controversy within the Bigfoot field when I wrote about it, some researchers insisting that it could not be Bigfoot and not seeming to care that even if it wasn't, it was still something extremely cryptozoological that deserved to be studied, especially when the tracks appeared again in March 1991 when Ed estimated that he saw up to 2,000 prints meandering around his property in the snow.

Over the next few years, I visited Ed's place several times, and now and then, the tracks would sporadically turn up. There came a point where he and even some of his neighbors began to also find the more familiar human-like tracks that are normally associated with Bigfoot, and a scenario began to evolve that suggested that the traditional Bigfoot existed here alongside some kind of subspecies that had a completely different kind of foot. Ed became very active in researching the subject and collecting stories from the area, and it turned out that there had been several sightings over the years that sounded like any other Bigfoot reports I had ever heard. This area and, in particular, the Buckboard Hills became my primary focus as a

Bigfooter in the 90s, and I made some track finds there myself. One night while camping on Ed's property, I had the priceless experience of hearing what I believe were the crazy high-pitched screams of two Bigfoot creatures calling to each other, terrifying me to no end.

Since I was a young fledging Bigfooter then and Ed was a venerated woodsman, I suppose it was only natural that he would become a mentor to me, and I learned much from him. He accompanied me on hikes through the woods several times, during which he would try and educate me about the different kinds of trees and other such things, eventually becoming amused with how I seemed to only want to stay focused on Bigfoot.

One memory that stands out in my mind is how we were once making our way down a trail that had a flooded patch, and after he skirted it fairly easily on one side, I was struggling to do the same on the other and he said, "If you fall in, I'm gonna laugh at you." I could only respond, "Yeah, and I'll deserve it too." This was on a foray that he and I made into Itasca County together to investigate reports there that turned up some of the best Bigfoot evidence I have ever documented involving wooden highline poles attacked by something that tore large pieces off of them and left teeth marks up to seven feet above the ground that clearly came from a mouth bigger than a bear's.

I guess all things must wind down and have their end. As the mid-90s passed, the activity on Ed's property seemed to wane. I still continued to do searches in the Buckboard Hills until a huge thunderstorm with hurricane-force winds struck the region in July 1995 and felled over a million trees. After that, the Bigfoot activity in the Buckboards seemed to stop. I didn't see Ed for a long time but we exchanged letters from time to time, and he told me that his wife Nova was having health problems and had to be moved into a nursing home in Bemidji and that he had moved into an apartment there to be near her and was no longer on the farm.

I wish I could recall the date now in the late 90s when I last saw Ed, when he showed up unexpectedly one night at my apartment building in Moorhead after Nova had passed away, and he had insisted on transporting her himself to be cremated in Fargo. The cremation was to take place the next day but he needed a place to stay for the night, and I gladly allowed him into my home. After all he had done for me over the few years that I knew him, it was the least I could do.

I will always remember him and Nova as sharing a true love story, as he told me that not only was she the first girl he had ever kissed, but she was also the first that he had ever held hands with.

I lost track of where Ed ended up after that sad time but in the spring of 2002, a college student named Beverly Brandenburger produced a research paper for school on the subject of Bigfoot in Minnesota, for which she had interviewed me online.

She informed me that she had learned that Ed had since followed Nova into the great beyond. I have told myself that what should one expect when befriending the elderly but that the friendship will be short. One fond memory I have is how when I turned Ed on to some of the Bigfoot literature, he decided to contact the famous Canadian researcher John Green both by letter and by phone, and the two enjoyed a long-distance friendship for a time. I'm so glad I was able to get those two old men together, both of them gone now.

Ed was my "Old Man of the Woods," and I really miss the guy.

Ed Trimble displays his honeybees.

MARK HALL & TIM OLSON

In the summer of 1989, when I took some vacation time to go on a Bigfoot fact-finding tour of southeast Minnesota I looked up the cryptozoologist Mark A. Hall in the Twin Cities suburb of Bloomington. Mark was a veteran researcher and a virtual human storehouse of knowledge, with a huge book collection dominating his apartment.

For a living, he was a government employee who worked for the Department of Agriculture and the Customs Service, but his passion was cryptozoology which he researched as a mostly under the radar figure, never becoming really famous in the field but providing much information to it. In addition to his interest in Bigfoot, one of his best-known writings was the book "Thunderbirds: The Living Legend," which chronicled accounts of the seemingly impossibly giant birds that have been sighted across North America.

He was a close personal friend and collaborator of one of the celebrities in the cryptozoological field, Loren Coleman, who continues to soldier on. Mark suffered on and off with cancer in his last years and died in September 2016 at age 70.

When I met Mark, we chatted in his apartment for a while on the Bigfoot subject in general and about how keyed up I was at the time about just having met the keeper of the Minnesota Iceman Frank Hansen earlier that day (more on that in a later chapter).

He then suggested that we drive over to meet with his friend Tim Olson who lived nearby, a fellow Bigfooter. I will always remember Tim as being on the younger side even though he was six years older than me. He was living at that time in Bloomington with his father, but he also had roots in northern California where his mother lived, having attended college in Arcata at Humboldt State University in the region where the term "Bigfoot" had first been coined and where the famous Patterson-Gimlin film had occurred in 1967.

For a time out there, he had worked with Rich Grumley of the California Bigfoot Organization. Mark, Tim, and I had a very spirited discussion of all things Bigfoot while sitting around the kitchen table in Tim's dad's house. It led to Tim becoming my Bigfooting partner for several years.

Tim and I only did field investigation together for one brief period in Minnesota in the summer of 1990 in which we camped in the Chippewa National Forest and then ended up actually finding some Bigfoot tracks in an area called Vergas Trails, but after that, he became my co-editor of the "Sasquatch Report" newsletter that I published for several years.

Before long, he moved back to California where he lived with his mother, and I remember very long phone conversations with him when he would call from there. He loved to talk.

In 1995 when I felt that I had run out of fresh ideas for the newsletter, Tim took it over as lead editor and managed to keep it going for another couple of years.

Tim suffered from epilepsy and was plagued by frequent seizures that took the form of extreme fainting spells in which he would just suddenly blank out and fall heavily onto his back.

I witnessed several of them. They were scary, but within a few minutes, he would always come out of it and regain his composure. However, he was also a very devout Christian and often talked about his faith and how it was the thing that saw him through his illness. I remember him talking about how when he would go on Bigfoot expeditions into the California wilderness, he would wear a bicycle helmet to protect his head from rocks in case he suffered a seizure and fell.

Tim died unexpectedly on February 3, 2015, when he was at home in Areata and suffered a seizure in his bathroom, falling and hitting his head against the bathtub. He was 52. He was a dedicated Bigfooter and a really good person.

Miss ya, man.

Tim Olson.

Tim Olson.

2

KETTLE RIVER

WHEN "FINDING BIGFOOT" COMES TO TOWN

The cable network Animal Planet first appeared on American television in 1996, a channel whose theme was that every program they aired would have something to do with animals.

Amidst the many wildlife specials and shows about humorous pets, there was one show that quickly took its place as the network's flagship series - 'The Crocodile Hunter" starring Steve Irwin, the operator of Australia Zoo in Queensland. Most people will remember him as that extremely charismatic chap in the khaki shorts who loved animals as much as he loved people and was never afraid to get up close and personal with even the most dangerous of creatures.

I remember being one of his many fans, but in retrospect now, I also remember always having the thought, "Something is gonna get that guy someday." When it happened in September 2006, it was not in the way I had imagined. He was killed by a stingray while filming underwater, stabbed in the heart by its poisonous barb. I had assumed it would be something with teeth, most likely a croc or a shark, but the culprit didn't matter. Steve knew the dangers every time he got close to wildlife, and he accepted them, but it was an extremely sad episode for anyone who values the environment and a horrible tragedy for his family and everyone else who loved him.

It was left to Animal Planet to decide how they were going to go on after the death of their major star. Their choices in the decade-plus since then have been a mixed bag. One of my favorite shows they've produced has been "River Monsters," beginning in 2009 and chronicling the adventures of the British extreme fisherman and biologist Jeremy Wade as he travels the world searching out little known but deadly and toothy denizens of the world's waterways.

Part of what I enjoy about the show is that it sometimes touches on the realm of cryptozoology, and it does it respectfully. But alongside quality shows like this, the network has also delved into the realm of "mockumentaries," shows that are made to look real but which the credits explain is actually fiction meant as nothing but entertainment.

The most notorious of these has been "Mermaids: The Body Found," which aired in May 2012, a show that told the story of scientists that had discovered that mermaids were real and had found the remains of one, complete with convincing video evidence. It was 100% fake, but to this day, there are people who still buy into it in the same way that people were convinced that 'The Blair Witch Project" was real. Mockumentaries are usually one-off specials, but there was at least one series called "Lost Tapes" that did the same thing, a found-footage show presenting fictional stories of various cryptozoological creatures as if they were true.

In May 2011, into the Animal Planet arena stepped a show entitled "Finding Bigfoot." Like most Bigfoot enthusiasts, I was thrilled that such attention was being given to the subject, but time would tell just exactly what kind of show it would be. One thing it did was to introduce some new words into the English language- "Squatch" (both noun and verb), "Squatchin'" (verb), "Squatchy" (adjective), etc. It definitely had a sense of humor about itself but was absolutely not a mockumentary.

It ran for an impressive 11 seasons, ending in May of 2018. "Finding Bigfoot" followed the exploits of a four-person team traveling North America and even sometimes venturing into other regions of the world, checking out places where Bigfoot-type creatures have been reported.

It was largely formulaic, consisting of them coming into an area and holding a public meeting in which they invited the locals to share their stories, then zeroing in on a few of those stories they selected to focus on and investigate at the places where they occurred, augmenting them with computer-generated animations of what was reported to have happened.

The episodes always ended with the team geared up with night vision equipment and two-way radios out in the woods attempting to lure Bigfoots to them by making loud imitations of Bigfoot sounds. Sometimes they found nothing, and sometimes there seemed to be credible sights or sounds to suggest they might actually be close to their quarry, with the emphasis on making it all as scary as possible.

On rare occasions, they actually thought they had captured audio or video evidence of Bigfoot. But in spite of the wealth of good information this show brought forth, I think I am hardly alone in what my overall opinion of it turned out to be.

I think that "Finding Bigfoot" was not a good name for the show since they were clearly not interested in actually finding one of the creatures. Even in the episodes in which they found truly tantalizing evidence, it ended with them packing up and moving on to the next location rather than staying and continuing to search the most promising areas.

Actually finding Bigfoot would mean an end to the show, and so they continued on with the same formula as all the "Ghost Hunter" shows that populate cable tv. Having said that, however, I should add that I understand what happens once someone is locked into a Hollywood contract.

I'm sure that each of the team members separately would be thrilled to be the one to make that ultimate discovery, just not on the show. I do appreciate "Finding Bigfoot" very much for the number of reports it brought to light.

Time now to introduce the team:

Matt Moneymaker founded the BFRO (Bigfoot Field Researchers' Organization) in 1995.

It is the largest and most extensive organization of its kind and hosts a website that catalogs many hundreds of reports across North America. He has hosted many expeditions in areas far and wide for BFRO members, but he has his share of critics who complain that he will only network and share information with paying members of the BFRO. I suppose that makes his last name rather ironic.

I don't begrudge him, though, for the work he's done in bringing the Bigfoot subject powerfully into the public eye. He is a burly, long-haired, and bearded guy with a charismatic personality who acted as team leader on the show.

Cliff Barackman came across as the most sensible and no-nonsense member of the team. He is known as a Bigfoot researcher who spends as much as 200 days a year out in the field and was often portrayed as the voice of reason on the show. He also has a friendly and engaging demeanor that makes him one that anyone seeking information on Bigfoot is highly recommended to seek out.

James "Bobo" Fay is a big man who was often used on the show in reenactments of Bigfoot sightings to stand in the same spot where the Bigfoot was in order to determine its size.

He was also the comic relief character, making frequent jokes. He and Barackman are friends who investigated Bigfoot reports together well before the show came into being.

And finally, there was Ranae Holland. I will call her what she is -- the token skeptic. She is a field biologist who says her father was fascinated by Bigfoot when she was a child and that that is largely what brought her to her position as the member of the "Finding Bigfoot" team that found the subject interesting but wouldn't accept that the creatures really exist until she saw absolute proof. She was the foil against which the other three members bounced off. In almost every report they investigated, she tried to rationalize some non-Bigfoot explanation.

Having delved into things a bit myself, I feel it my responsibility to report that a source I will not name told me that after talking to

Ranae, he knew that she is, in actuality, a Bigfoot believer and only played the part of the skeptic on the show because the script required her to. I can neither confirm nor deny that allegation.

I mean Ranae no ill will, but on a humorous note, I just have to say that since I first began watching the show, I have referred to her as "Velma" because she kind of looks like the character by that name from the Scooby-Doo cartoons. The way the team toured the country in an SUV even calls to mind the Mystery Machine, just without the dog.

All in all, I am glad that the show came to be because it did a good job of getting the word out to a wide audience that might not otherwise ever know that Bigfoot is seen all across America.

After all, your average Joe doesn't normally seek out books or films or websites on the subject on a casual basis, but almost everyone channel surfs and will eventually run across the show. I wondered how long it might be before the team came to Minnesota.

It wasn't long. The fourth episode of the show's second season aired on January 15, 2012 and was set in a part of Minnesota where I'd never been, the Kettle River area in Carlton County, about 50 miles southwest of the major city of Duluth. The river flows through a region of farmland and small towns, but it is not exactly like the prairie farmland where I grew up in west central Minnesota.

Rather, it is peppered sporadically with dense woodland and swamps that cover many square miles, and as I discovered from watching the show, it was the scene of a series of dramatic and fascinating Bigfoot encounters between 2008 and 2010 that I instantly wanted to learn more about. I made three trips there in 2013 and 2014, twice by myself and once with my partner Dean, and was able to flesh out some of the information given on the show a bit farther and also to get a feel for the kinds of subtle changes that are often made when true stories are brought to television.

What first called attention to the area was a report by BFRO member Andy Pieper who made a tantalizing audio recording on September 13, 2009, that became officially known online as the "Minnesota Howls." Pieper is also a member of a Minnesota-based group known as the Sasquatch Research Association (SRA) and is an avid investigator.

The recording is of wolf howls that seems to have something else joining in, a deeper and throatier howl that sounds distinctly un-wolflike. Pieper appeared on the show to present the recording, after which the team members debated whether or not it sounded like only wolves.

Typically, only Ranae thought that it did. The show moved into the town meeting they held on August 22, 2011, indicating that it was in the small town of Tamarack, which is a few miles north of where all the reports featured occurred. The meeting hall was jampacked with up to 200 people on a hot summer day in sweltering conditions, the local people evidently feeling that the subject was important enough for them to show up and endure the heat.

When Matt Moneymaker asked for a show of hands from anyone in the crowd that had seen Bigfoot, an astoundingly large number of hands went up. I remember hearing commentary on the episode that described it as one of the biggest returns they had ever had.

I would eventually learn, however, that some clever editing had been used. The meeting did not actually take place in the town of Tamarack but at a rural meeting hall called the Lakeside Community Club a short distance outside of town, which confused me when I first came to the area because there was a building in town that at first seemed to fit the bill.

Admittedly, that was partially my mistake. However, there was also some deliberate deception, not a big deal, really, but still something that struck me. I was told that two questions were asked at the meeting, the first being how many people had seen a Bigfoot and the second being how many people knew of someone who'd seen a Bigfoot. What was featured on the show was the first question being asked, but the hands then being raised were actually the response to the second question, which were much more in number.

It's mildly shady, but that's Hollywood for you. There was also the fact that the narrator for the show described the location as being northern Minnesota "near the Canadian border."

There is about 130 miles of Minnesota north of Kettle River before one reaches Canada. Much more important, though, were the stories shared at the meeting. I know there were many more than were actually featured on the show, but the ones told were all quite incredible.

A young blonde woman with glasses and a ponytail named Kristy Aho stood up and told her story of what marked one of the earliest occurrences of Bigfoot in the area, and she spoke with such conviction that she really impressed me. Her husband Dale was a logger who was often away on jobs, and he wasn't there, so it fell to her to describe what they and their children had seen.

On a day in September of 2008, they had all been out in the woods on an ATV four-wheeler sharing the experience of Dale hunting partridge, stopping at various spots where Dale would walk into the bush to try and flush out his quarry. At one such spot, he flushed out something much more than that. A huge black hairy creature suddenly stood up from out of the bushes where it had apparently been bedded down, its height estimated by different members of the family as anywhere from 7 1/2 to eight feet, and took off on two legs through the woods at a run passing within full view of Kristy and the kids as they waited on the ATV.

What Kristy stressed the most were how its footfalls made the ground shake, driving home how massive a beast it was. "I seen it run by probably 15, 20 feet from where we were sitting," she said. "And the ground shook when it run. It was just boom, boom, boom." Dale was present after the town meeting when the team went with the family to the sighting location, and as he so often did, Bobo went to stand where the creature had stood to establish its size.

This resulted in the conclusion that it had been even bigger than first thought, perhaps as tall as nine feet. The team judged it a solid sighting, but it was not the only one the family had had.

Nearly a year later, in July 2009, the family had a second sighting while driving at night in their pickup truck. In their headlights, they first saw red eyeshine about 200 feet away that then approached them and formed into a Bigfoot creature that they thought seemed even somewhat bigger than the earlier one, swaying back and forth as it walked. They retreated from the encounter when the children started crying from fear.

Even more contact with the creatures was suggested when Kristy spoke at the town meeting and said, "My husband has seen them, probably a family, several times, but he is not here tonight to talk about his experience."

The Kettle River, between the towns of Kettle River and Moose Lake.

The Lakeside Community Club where "Finding Bigfoot" held their town meeting.

On my last visit to the area, I had the brief pleasure of meeting Kristy Aho. By then, I had been in contact by e-mail with Cliff Barackman from the "Finding Bigfoot" team since he has a website and makes himself fairly available, and he told me that since the airing of the show the Ahos had stopped speaking publicly because there had been a lot of trespassing on their property by people that had seen it.

I tracked down where they lived and knocked on the door there around mid-morning, a rustic place with several large pieces of logging equipment scattered about.

Dale was apparently again away on a job, but I could hear the kids running around inside just before Kristy came to the door. She was a bit bedraggled, not yet put together for her day, and I felt bad about disturbing her but was also somewhat excited to meet this woman who had so impressed me on television.

I told her that I was a Bigfoot researcher and was in the area for the weekend and wondered if she would be willing to talk because I wasn't about to intrude without permission. I had a map with me and asked if she would be willing to point out on it exactly where their first sighting had occurred, but she said, "Well, I really can't do that because it wasn't actually our property," and that they had decided to just not talk about the whole thing anymore.

I thanked her for her time, and as I left, she smiled and told me, "Good luck!" I will never forget that encounter, a very sweet woman who came to regret having appeared on "Finding Bigfoot." The next report of note came from another young woman, Jenna Wilenius, a nurse who lived part-time with her parents near the town of Kettle River, a bit south of where the Ahos' experiences had occurred.

Jenna enjoyed running for exercise, which is what she was out doing on June 12, 2010, when she had a frightening encounter. She had jogged two miles down the gravel road from her parents' house, her dog running with her, and on the way back, the dog began to act nervous. When Jenna took a glance behind her, she saw a towering black hairy creature standing at the edge of the treeline beside the road, watching her.

After hearing Jenna's story at the town meeting, Matt and Ranae met with her at the location of the sighting. "I didn't know how to react," Jenna said. "I was in shock. I just kept running. I was talking to my mom, I was saying this wasn't a bear, it wasn't a human, it's like a mixture of the two. And she's the one who said, 'well, it's gotta be Bigfoot then.'"

She indicated that the creature had stood as high as a certain tree branch that protruded out a bit, so Ranae went and stood at that spot and raised a stick into the air until it reached that height. Combining her own height, the length of her arm, and the length of the stick,

Ranae delivered her assessment -- it came out to a height of 11 feet. One of the lasting images from this episode of "Finding Bigfoot" that has stayed with me is of Jenna gazing up at the top of that stick in wonder and saying, "That's uh... that's tall."

Ranae went on to give her usual skeptical argument. "After being at the location and hearing the witness' story," she said, "I think this is a misidentification. I mean, I'm runnin', I'm movin', and I'm freaked out, I could definitely blow something out of proportion."

"That's true, that's true," Jenna replied but then stuck to her guns. "But I know for sure that's what I saw... I definitely think it was Sasquatch. There's no question in my mind now, definitely not."

Matt had a different opinion than Ranae's, saying, "I found Jenna to be a very credible witness. She's not the type of person to make up something like that. What she saw was a real animal and probably a sasquatch."

The spot where Jenna Wilenius saw a Bigfoot while jogging, shot from where the creature was standing.

When I made my own trips to the Kettle River area, I hoped very much to be able to meet Jenna and do my own interview with her. She seemed like an extremely nice and innocent young soul, a quirky redhead with a somewhat odd but charming lisp in her voice, and I think it would have been interesting to spend some time with her, but by the time I figured out exactly where the location was I had learned online that she had gotten married and was living in the Minneapolis/St. Paul area. Not only that, but her parents had moved away as well, and their property was vacant when I finally visited in 2014, but I did make contact with a neighbor of theirs who lived just down the road from them named John Gran, and he turned out to be a major source of information and a Bigfoot witness himself.

John was a town board supervisor in his early elderly years who lived on a quite impressive piece of property beside the Kettle River, with a wonderfully landscaped backyard featuring a manmade pond where he allowed me to camp. The show featured him for only a few seconds in sound-byte form, speaking at the town meeting about some of what he had observed, but without identifying him. That was a shame because he was very much a part of the full story surrounding Jenna's sighting, living halfway in between her parents' house and where she saw the creature.

Not giving him a more prominent role was even more surprising since I learned that it was in that same backyard, he gave me access to where the entire cast and crew of "Finding Bigfoot" had set up camp while they were filming the episode. He talked about what a big production it was. The show makes it look like just the four-team members driving around the country by themselves in an SUV, but of course there are many other people and vehicles involved. There are cameramen, sound and lighting technicians, and even a helicopter that provides the many aerial shots that are seen on the show.

John told me that on June 13, 2010, the day after Jenna's sighting, he was driving past her family's house at about 11:05 AM, pulling a lawnmower on a trailer when he saw a huge dark figure standing beside their garage, apparently watching the house and standing about the same height as the garage eave, perhaps a little over eight feet. In the quick glimpse he got of it, he could see that it had a black body with a lighter face and long legs. He wanted to stop to get a better look but found it difficult with the equipment he was pulling. The next day he made a point to drive by at the same time to make sure that it hadn't been some kind of optical illusion, and there was nothing there.

John had two other experiences during the time of Kettle River's Bigfoot episode, and I apologize for having lost track of whether they occurred before or after Jenna's sighting, but they were very close in time to it. He was sleeping one night in his very nice screened-in porch when he was awakened by a sound coming from down his driveway.

He described it as a loud throat clearing type of sound, far louder than a human could make. When I asked him what he thought it was he said, "Oh, I immediately knew it had to be a Bigfoot," because the activity in the area was well known by that point, and the sound was just so unlike anything he had ever heard before.

As a result, he put up a trail camera in his back yard just a few yards from the bank of the river which picked up one photo of what he believed to be eyeshine of the creature continuing to prowl around the area. He and his wife searched for that photo when I asked if I could see it, but unfortunately, they were not able to remember what they'd done with it.

John took me out and showed me the sighting locations, his own and Jenna's. He stood on the same spot where Ranae Holland had stood to mark where Jenna's Bigfoot had been, and when I saw it up close, I realized that the line of trees there was rather thin and that just on the other side of them was another neighbor's residence. It seemed to me that the show might have filmed the area in a way that made it seem wilder than it was, being careful not to show just how many residences there was along that road.

In walking the roads, however, and taking in all the surrounding scenery, I saw that much of the area that Jenna's run had passed through consisted of wooded pasture land through which the river flowed, plenty of cover for a large creature to have used to watch Jenna and follow her until it came out to show itself by the roadside.

The fact that it turned up the next morning in her yard watching her house deeply disturbed me. It seemed to indicate that the creature had taken an interest in her and not only stalked her all the way home but staked the place out later. What its interest in her might have been is a matter of frightening speculation, which I'm sure Jenna must have had her own worried thoughts about. It is indeed fortunate that nothing else ever came of it, and odd that the show didn't cover it.

John thought that Jenna, in her excitement, had overestimated the creature's height, pointing out to me that a very slight rise in elevation in the road might have affected the angle at which she was viewing it. He stated with conviction that the thing he saw standing next to the garage was far short of 11 feet tall. He then gave me permission to enter the deep woods behind his place and encouraged me to seek out some deer hunters' tree stands that were nearby.

I ended up sitting in one of them for quite some time a few hundred yards from the scene of Jenna's sighting as dusk approached, and when I heard a distinct twig snapping sound nearby and then further sounds of an animal approaching it was a tense and exciting moment. It turned out to only be a deer, but getting to shoot video of it as it passed directly underneath my tree stand seemingly oblivious to my presence was an amazing experience. If only it could have been a Bigfoot!

John Gran stands at the spot where the creature from the Jenna Wilenius sighting stood.

The Wilenius home, where John saw a Bigfoot standing beside the garage the day after Jenna's sighting.

John Gran's back yard, where his trail camera captured possible Bigfoot eyeshine and where the "Finding Bigfoot" crew set up camp.

John's screened-in porch from which he heard a Bigfoot vocalizing as it prowled the area.

That experience happened on my third and final trip to the area. On my second when I was with my partner Dean, I don't know what was in the air, but for some reason, we saw deer in huge numbers literally all over the place. I remember driving past pastures filled with cattle and

Dean remarking, "Calm cows -- that means no Bigfoot is around." But there were also herds of deer out in those pastures just mingling with the cows as if it was the most natural thing in the world. At one point, we had to stop for a little half-grown fawn crossing the road, and when he came to a fence leading into a pasture, I thought we were going to get to see him leap over it, but he was so small that he ducked underneath it instead.

I wish I had gotten that on video. Matt Moneymaker made much of the large deer presence in the area, pointing out how there is strong evidence that Bigfoot preys on deer.

A dairy farm just up the road from John's place and from Jenna's sighting was the home of two brothers by the names of Robert and Roger Siltanen, who reported that in September 2010 they had been hearing strange growling and whining sounds around their property, and then one night their dogs were barking wildly at something in a plowed field which made them go out to investigate the next day. They were expecting to find bear tracks but instead found about 75 manlike footprints but much bigger, with a gait of 42". They made plaster casts which were shown in the local media, but Cliff Barackman told me that the BFRO suspected them of being hoaxers and cautioned me not to have anything to do with them, so I didn't.

While walking the roads at night though I did pass by their place and learned by the sounds I heard that in addition to cattle, they also had a flock of peacocks, not a common animal to find on a farm. The Siltanen brothers were both rather grizzled looking characters with long beards who appear for a few seconds on the show at the town meeting without any comment or inclusion of their story.

I got the impression that they tried to cash in on the real activity going on in their area with fake tracks, but have no personal knowledge to confirm that. "Finding Bigfoot" often tended to pick three main reports to focus on per episode, and their third one this time around after the Aho and Wilenius sightings was that of Lorraine Tomczak, an elderly lady whose report gave this episode its title. It was called "Peeping Bigfoot" because it featured her story of a creature peering into a window.

The exact date of this sighting is unclear, but it was in that same summer of 2010 as the Jenna Wilenius and John Gran experiences. The spot was also within two miles of where the "Minnesota Howls" recording had been captured by Andy Pieper the year before.

Lorraine and her husband Greg were driving on an excursion to the nearby town of Moose Lake, which is the only community of any real size in the area (population about 2,750) when they spotted two cars pulled over at the edge of the gravel road they were on. They slowed down, wondering if it was some kind of police situation, but as they did, they saw a huge black hairy upright creature a short distance off the road, peering into a window on a yellow trailer house

23

in an area of a few sparse trees and tall grass in broad daylight. The other cars that had pulled over both contained young men who have never been identified, and the four people just sat in wonderment watching this giant beast.

After a few moments, it took off running, crossing the road into nearby woods, and disappeared from view.

The trailer house where Greg and Lorraine Tomczak saw a Bigfoot looking in the nearest window.

On the show, Cliff Barackman went with Lorraine to the site. In my e-mail contacts with him he confided to me that though she was a very nice lady, she also had a rather foul mouth and swore like a sailor, so a certain amount of editing was necessary to feature her words on air. In particular, she made some comments on the size of the creature's male anatomy. (Sorry folks, but that's just funny.) She showed Cliff the window it had been looking through and said that not only was its head as high as the top of the trailer, which Cliff measured as about nine feet, but also that the head from top to chin equaled the expanse of the eave, which was 19-20".

That's a big head! "Yeah, he was huge," Lorraine replied. "I never saw such a huge thing in my life." Cliff commented, "Looking in windows is a very commonly reported behavior by sasquatches, and it was no surprise to hear that the ones in this area do the same thing. These sasquatches are looking in windows because they're wondering what's going on inside.

Obviously, this big male sasquatch has had some kind of positive reinforcement in the past. There was something interesting inside some window at some point to make it start doing it on a habitual basis."

It was on my second visit to the area that Dean and I located this site. The trailer house was vacant and abandoned, and I never heard anything about whose land it was on, but as it was just off a main road, it was easy to do a little illegal trespassing as long as it was kept short. I did my own measurement with a tape measure and confirmed Cliff's finding for the height of the creature.

Though it was reported by the Aho family that there was a family of creatures in the area, I had the impression that it was the big male that was mostly being seen and that the estimates of its height at anywhere from 7 1/2 to 11 feet were clarified here as being right around nine feet tall. During my third visit to the area a few months later, I visited the trailer again and decided to try the door. It was unlocked, and when I looked in, I could see that it was completely trashed and that the ceiling was even caving in.

When I let go of the door and let it slam shut, I suddenly heard the sound of a multitude of mice squeaking and scurrying around. That was a little on the disgusting side, but it gave me the thought that perhaps that was why the Bigfoot was there -- to feed on mice. I think it's as good a theory as any.

I also traced the route of the creature's retreat from the site and found that on the opposite side of the road it was said to have crossed was a barbed-wire fence. I asked Cliff about that, and he said that it had crossed the fence in one stride without having to jump over or breaking through the wire, a feat that has often been attributed to Bigfoots when encountering fences.

On the other side of that fence was thick woodland, and in driving around the area, Dean and I realized that it was a solid block of woods of about a square mile in size, whereas the tree cover in the rest of the area was sporadic. This one large expanse of woods caught our attention, and was rife for speculation.

The fact that the Bigfoot seen by the Tomczaks had fled into it made me say, "He ran home." It was all private land which meant that we could not trespass there, but it was in my third visit to the area when I met with John Gran and learned about the Jenna Wilenius sighting that I got to penetrate that square mile at least a little and had my experience sitting in the tree stand.

There were many sightings in the Kettle River area for a couple of years, not all of which I have managed to document. All I know of are featured in this book's appendix. When I first arrived in the area on my first visit, I stopped into a cafe in the town of Tamarack and asked the waitress if she knew anything about the show and the Bigfoot subject.

While first seeming surprised that I had any interest in the tiny little town at all, she then related that she certainly knew about the show and that I should visit the small grocery store nearby because the couple that ran it had been at the town meeting and had some information. She also said that a friend of hers in Automba (the township containing Kettle River) insisted that Bigfoot sometimes came into his yard and scared his dog. "Automba's the place to go for Bigfoot," she said.

When I stopped into the grocery store, I found what I thought was the funniest old married couple, the husband being very stoic, unemotional, and even a little rude, but the wife being happy and bubbly and eager to talk. It was even funnier when I rewatched the "Finding Bigfoot" episode and spotted them in the crowd at the town meeting, both of them still acting in the exact same way.

Their daughter was also at the store, and between the three of them, they told me that though they hadn't encountered Bigfoot themselves, they knew an elderly woman in the area who had heard a "godawful sound" outside her house and then found that something had stripped all the fruit off of her apple tree.

These were stories that came to me simply from stopping into a cafe for a cup of coffee and asking a few simple questions. However, after my final visit, I came away with the strong impression that the creatures were no longer in the area. John Gran was of the same opinion, telling me, "They're gone."

I also visited the somewhat larger town of Moose Lake and stopped into their police station, where they were well aware of the show but responded to my question about whether they ever got Bigfoot reports by saying, "We don't, but the County Sheriff does." But when I e-mailed the Sheriff's Department I got a reply from the Sheriff herself, who said rather curtly that she had no knowledge whatsoever of Bigfoot.

It was a discrepancy, one that suggested the Sheriff did not want to acknowledge the subject. Where had the creatures gone? A possible answer brings us full circle back to Andy Pieper, the man who produced the "Minnesota Howls" recording that first turned the "Finding Bigfoot" team on to the Kettle River area. As I mentioned earlier, in addition to being a member of the BFRO, he is also one of the main organizers of a Midwest-based group called the Sasquatch Research Association whose website does not give its members full names and refers to him only as "SRA Andy."

When I discovered this in 2014 through web surfing, I found that they had just posted information on an area near Cloquet, a town not far from Duluth located just under 50 miles northeast of Kettle River. They were planning an expedition in an area of private land-based on a report by an anonymous bowhunter in 2012.

The man and his family had been hearing strange howls and tree knocking as well as finding tree breaks in the area he hunted in since the fall, leading up to a frightening encounter he had on December 7th. Just after 6 AM, as he walked toward his tree stand in the dark predawn he noticed a tree that had been broken and twisted over to cross the trail he was on, and then heavy footfalls on the frost-covered ground in the woods began to keep pace with him, stopping just after he would stop to try and listen. He reached his stand, climbed up into it and readied his bow and arrow to watch for deer once the sun came up, the time now being about 6:25 AM.

A moment after he turned off his flashlight, he heard a very loud tree knock only about 20 yards behind him, a scary thing to hear at any time of day but doubly so in the dark, and then in the same instant, the sound of something big and heavy running through the woods broke out from another position nearby, snapping branches and heading toward the point of the first sound. Apparently, there were two large somethings out there, and at that point, the nervous hunter decided to turn around and turn his flashlight back on.

I love the line he gives in his narrative about what happened next, the description of what has been felt emotionally by so many Bigfoot witnesses over so many years.

"When I clicked on my light, my whole life as I know it changed forever."

What he caught for the briefest of instances in his flashlight beam was a glimpse of a large hairy upright creature turning away from the light and quickly disappearing behind a tree. He did not see its face, just a portion of its body from shoulder to waist with an arm hanging down, yet that alone was enough for him to state that it changed his life forever.

It is an immediate process of going from being either a total unbeliever or at least an agnostic on the creatures' existence, moving straight past the level of believer and going instantly to an absolute knower.

The man contacted the SRA and gave them access to the property, where they found several tracks and tree breaks to suggest that the creatures were still in the area. A year after the hunter's sighting on December 9, 2013, a man listed as "SRA Jim" had a major footprint find while driving through the area when he saw a line of tracks in the snow crossing the road, coming out of one remote wooded area and going into another.

He was not equipped to follow up on them too thoroughly but noted that they were 18-19" in length with a stride of up to six feet. I never heard whether the SRA's 2014 expedition into the area had made any major finds.

Dean and I visited there in 2015 in general reconnaissance mode, finding that there was very little state forest land where we could explore without landowner permission and without the bowhunter's name, there was little else we could do.

But with the proximity in time and distance to the Kettle River reports, it made us wonder if the creature or creatures encountered by the bowhunter just might have been from the same group seen by the Ahos and the Tomczaks and Jenna Wilenius, with at least one big male standing nine feet tall. If they were the same ones then it speaks of a nomadic lifestyle, roaming from area to area based on conditions known and understood only by them. These reports occurred relatively near but not within the huge expanse of the Superior National

Forest where a permanent population of such creatures would be expected.

Obviously, it is all just speculation. But it's frustrating too and makes me feel, as a researcher, as if I have become very good at finding places where Bigfoot WAS a few years ago but isn't anymore. Such is the nature of this quest.

But this series of reports also gave me an important lesson about whenever a show like "Finding Bigfoot" gets involved. We live in the age of "reality tv," and we have to take it for what it is. Even if it is a non-fiction show covering real events, there are bound to be a certain number of tweaks and adjustments that reshape the actual events to make them look the way the producers want them to look. This happened at Kettle River, and it would not be the only time "Finding Bigfoot" visited Minnesota.

I'll close this chapter with a smile, recalling that at one point in the episode, the team sent Bobo out on his own to camp in the area and look for evidence, but what he found the most of were Minnesota's infamously fierce mosquitoes that plagued him the entire time and made him vow eternal hatred for them. It would be a recurring theme for him whenever the team revisited the state, used for comic relief. I share your pain, Bobo. I've dealt with those damned bugs my whole life.

Bobo also had the quote for this episode that I think has become kind of iconic for the team's trademark nocturnal night vision searches. The team was so excited about making a find in this area that it led him to become overcome with emotion and yell, *"Come on, you hairy bastard!"*

ADDENDUM

While I was putting the finishing touches on the appendix for this book, I discovered that an additional incident had occurred in this area on September 3, 2015, involving a mysterious trail camera photo, and also that people in the Kettle River-Moose Lake area during the earlier outbreak of Bigfoot activity had attached an affectionate name to the big male that was seen so many times. They called him Carl since this was Carlton County. (Shades of Nessie at Loch Ness, I suppose.)

Some people on a fishing trip to the area placed a trail camera along the road near the the cabin they were staying in near Moose Lake, apparently just for the fun of seeing what they might pick up on it. Unlike most such cameras that operate via either motion or heat sensors, this one was set to snap a picture every five seconds. I can't imagine perusing the thousands of shots this would result in, but nevertheless, in addition to the many shots of passing vehicles, there was also one of a bear running across the road in the far distance.

Then, on the Friday morning in question at 7:07 AM, a mysterious dark upright figure appeared in only one shot, standing close to the roadside not very far in front of the camera. Whatever it was had to have rushed into the frame and then out again within a ten-second window. The figure is very indistinct, but comparisons were made later with people standing at the same spot that established its height at only around four to five feet.

I could just barely imagine a bear running in, standing upright for an instant, then running out again, but it does not seem to have the short hind legs of a bear. In addition, there is what looks like a large object sitting at the figure's feet with some kind of long and thin protuberance extending up and forward from it.

To me, this suggests a human carrying something in and setting it down for a moment but doing so and then disappearing within ten seconds seems unlikely. The photo is indeed a mystery. It was equated with the earlier Bigfoot reports, but whatever it shows, it is definitely not Carl.

3

CHIPPEWA NATIONAL FOREST

In my early years of Bigfoot research in Minnesota, I never in a million years would have thought that the smaller of the state's two national forests- second to the Superior up in the Arrowhead region- would become a hotbed of activity and a promising area to search with an optimistic hope of making a major find.

Back in those days, I only had a few reports on file for the Chippewa National Forest and my few forays into it had made me think of it as a place that was indeed a wilderness area but was also so populated that one couldn't venture far without blundering onto private property.

I was camping there in 1990 with Tim Olson, and we decided to go for a nocturnal hike on a very dark night, so dark in fact that we could not tell that what we thought was a side road we turned on was actually someone's driveway. We were just starting to make out the shapes of buildings, fuel tanks, and so forth around us when out of the pitch darkness came a harsh male voice informing us -- *"Get outta here right now, or I'll put a slug in ya!"* Needless to say, we quickly departed the scene.

My opinion would change drastically in later years when I realized that with patience and further exploration, the Chippewa did turn out to have more extensive remote areas, with the system of roads winding through it and the presence of people never a great distance away meaning that you could always be hopeful of finding help if you got into trouble.

The forest lies in the great Central North region of Minnesota, in the midst of that entire upper third of the state that is practically one giant unbroken wilderness, established as a national forest in 1902 and comprised of 666,623 acres in Itasca, Cass, and Beltrami counties.

The main headquarters is in the town of Cass Lake, where signs upon entering the town proclaim "Where Eagles Soar," and indeed the forest has the largest population of bald eagles in the country, with golden eagles also being frequently seen. Other ranger stations are found in the towns of Blackduck, Deer River, and Walker, the latter of which is well known for an annual Classic Rock music festival called "Moondance Jam" and draws huge crowds every year with nationally known bands and solo acts who are perhaps past their prime but still know how to rock and roll.

The Native American presence in the region is unmistakable, with the tribe whose name the forest bears being a driving force -- the Chippewa, who are also known as the Ojibwe.

Of the half dozen or so largest lakes in Minnesota, two of them lie in the Chippewa -- Leech Lake in the south and Lake Winnibigoshish (just Wini for short) in the north, with Highway 2 passing between them. Some popular landmarks lie along that road. One is the Big Fish Supper Club, a building made to look like a giant northern pike with its entrance lying inside the gaping toothy mouth, a photo op waiting to happen if there ever was one. It has appeared on postcards and was even briefly shown in the movie "National Lampoon's Vacation."

A few miles east of the Big Fish in the tiny Native village of Bena is another iconic landmark, the Big Wini Store which was built in 1932 and has stood mostly unchanged since then. The red, white, and blue general store and gas station has a few small cabins for rent around it that cater mostly to fishermen, since the surrounding lakes attract throngs of them. Only one other business operates in Bena, a cafe, with the rest of the town consisting mostly of trailer houses and dirt roads, the population being just over a hundred. The town sits right up against the forest, with no buffer at all between it and the wilderness.

Chippewa National Forest entrance and map showing its location in Minnesota.

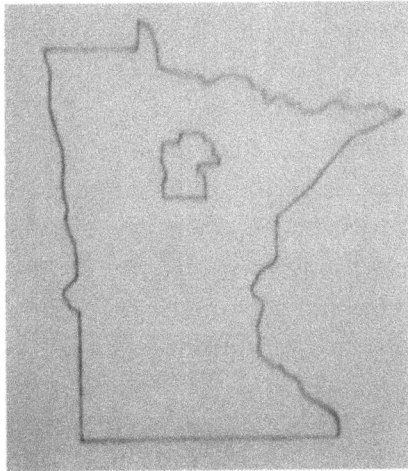

The famous Big Fish Supper Club, and the author standing in its mouth.

It was just a couple of minutes drive east of Bena, where on June 7, 2006, the Chippewa National Forest declared its place as the central Bigfoot hotspot for the state of Minnesota. On that day just before noon, 29-year-old road grader operator Cory Frazer was working the Six Mile Lake Road at a snail's pace of only around two miles an hour when he looked down from the high vantage point of his big Caterpillar machine and caught sight of some large tracks in the gravel at the roadside just off Highway 2.

It was his second pass along the road that morning and the tracks had not been there the first time. Cory first thought they might be bear tracks, but upon closer examination, they were human-like, each 15" long, two to three inches deep with 15-18" between them, and about 30 in number. He estimated from their depth that they must have been made by something weighing five to six hundred pounds.

It's hard to say what makes some reports start a fire while others don't, but in this case when Cory went public with his find, it caused a sensation in the area, and throngs of people came to see the supposed Bigfoot tracks. Inevitably this caused the tracks to not last very long, being wiped out one by one within days by vehicles and by people treading upon them.

But the tracks would end up having a profound effect on two of the local people that were able to examine them, fascinating them and inspiring them to form the Northern Minnesota Bigfoot Research Team. These two men made excellent plaster casts of the tracks, and in the aftermath of the incident they would become known as the place to go to report encounters with Bigfoot in the area.

They were Bob Olson, then 57 years old, a mechanic with his own auto body shop in the town of Deer River, and Don Sherman, then 53, a facilities manager for the Cass Lake Indian Services Hospital. The story of the tracks appeared widely in the local print media and was even covered on tv news out of Duluth.

Whenever a report causes such excitement, it is common for people in the area to come forward with past experiences and also for witnesses to new incidents now knowing that they are not alone and feeling some level of safety in divulging their stories. This happened quickly in the Bena area following the finding of the Six Mile Lake Road tracks.

The site of Cory Frazer's track finds, shortly beyond the railroad.

Two weeks later, on June 20th, a 67-year-old Ojibwe woman was driving toward the White Oak Casino in Deer River to do some gambling sometime after 11 PM. This might seem late, but just like their counterparts in Las Vegas, Indian casinos are open 24/7. Deer River lies about 20 miles east of Bena, and just over halfway between the two along Highway 2 is a very tiny community known as Ball Club, which she had just passed when she saw an upright brown hairy creature about eight feet tall standing on the right side of the road, looking like it was about to cross the road toward Ball Club Lake.

An older report also came out from the previous year. In June 2005, another elderly Ojibwe woman named Thelberta Lussier was on a sad journey, on her way to tie up some loose ends as her husband had just passed away in a nursing home, and she and her adult daughter were driving near Bena, once again along Highway 2 at about 4:30 PM. when something first thought to be a deer was seen at the side of the road ahead of them.

As Thelberta slowed down it suddenly stood up and raised its arms, a creature about seven feet tall covered in dark brown hair and having a pointed head. When the car was about 60 feet away, it turned, and with one large stride beat a hasty retreat away from the road and into the woods. Thelberta screamed, waking her daughter beside her, who'd been napping, but the daughter just missed seeing the creature.

That same month, yet another woman driving on Highway 2 near Bena saw a brown-haired creature standing near the railroad tracks that parallel it and had a seemingly spiritual experience, saying that the creature seemed to "look into her soul" and made her start to cry.

A few years previously, a rather high-profile sighting came to light because of who one of the witnesses was. William Bobolink, a venerated elder and spiritual advisor to the Leech Lake band of Ojibwa, lived with his daughter and son-in-law a mile west of Bena and in the fall of 2002 the three of them had all seen a Bigfoot outside their home. Watching through a window, they watched it standing at a clothesline about 30 feet from the house, which only came up to its stomach, attesting to its huge size. Almost playfully, they said it was fingering the clothespins on the line and spinning them around.

When the creature realized it was being watched, it walked away. It's a wonderfully whimsical story, backed up by the testimony of a highly respected member of the community.

Native stories abounded in the area and another community that seemed to be a center point for them was the small village of Inger located 18 miles northeast of Bena along the Bowstring River. It seemed to be such a hotbed that in April of 2006 when researcher Bob Olson heard about tracks found along Pine Grove Road near Inger, he had a hunch that if he were to drive slowly along that road with his window open and keep his eyes glued to the roadside that he would have a good chance of finding something.

His hunch proved correct, and he ended up making a cast of a footprint that appeared misshapen or crippled, measuring 14" long by seven inches wide. I first came to Bena exactly one month after the famous track find of July 2006 to have a look around. After having spoken briefly on the phone to Bob Olson, I had gotten directions to the location, which I found to be just a bowshot off of Highway 2.

It was sandwiched in between the railroad tracks and an underground high-pressure gas line that runs through the area, and while I was there, a train passed and loudly blew its horn. It did not immediately seem like an area where a Bigfoot would be found, but while I was at the site, I did note a large patch of flattened grass where all the curious onlookers had parked their vehicles.

The Six Mile Lake Road then led off into what was for me unexplored wilderness, so off I went. I quickly learned how wrong I had previously been about the Chippewa National Forest, for though this section did have a few cabins and fishing resorts, it was a truly wild area, thick bush for mile after mile. Six Mile Lake itself (which is not six miles long as I first thought but is apparently named because it lies six miles from the headquarters of the Leech Lake Indian Reservation) is central to the area.

All in all, it struck me as an excellent habitat for Bigfoot, even though it was only a few miles from the famous Big Fish Supper Club and other touristy sites. I immediately knew I would want to return to explore this area many times. A few months after my visit on September 30[th,] a 16-year-old boy named Everett A. was hunting west of Ball Club near the Mississippi River when he too saw a Bigfoot walking in a low swampy area.

It looked at him but then just kept walking, but he was frightened enough to run all the way to Highway 2, where he hitched a ride home and vowed that he would never go hunting again. That vow was short-lived; however, as just a week later, he was once again out in the woods, where he was tragically killed in an accidental shooting. To some in the area, this lent weight to the idea that to see a Bigfoot was an omen of ill-fortune.

Reports continued to accumulate in the general area, several of which were related in newspaper articles or online sources, and for a couple of years, I made forays there exploring and searching for evidence. It wasn't limited to the woods south of Highway 2 but also extended to the north. Just across from the famous 2006 track site was a road known locally as the "Wini Dam Road," as it led to a spot where the Mississippi River flows out of the huge Lake Winnibigoshish through floodgates on a large concrete dam where there is a popular picnic ground and fishing spot.

That stretch of road also became known by rumor as a Bigfoot hotspot with several sightings by people driving along it. About three-quarters of the way between Highway 2 and the dam is a gravel road leading a few miles west into the woods toward a place along the Wini shoreline called Tamarack Point.

Off to one side from this road is a small fishing resort and picnic ground, and at the very end of it is a campground where I and a female friend of mine (who does not wish to have her name used) briefly stopped on the afternoon of June 28, 2008. I had no earthly idea what was about to happen. We were on a typical weekend excursion hoping to hike, search for Bigfoot evidence, and camp for one night, and we were checking out the campground to evaluate it, but unfortunately the weather had turned on us, and there was a constant drizzling rain.

I had had high hopes for this trip, but I remember standing there looking around as the light rain poured down with no signs of letting up, and the dampness was spawning swarms of mosquitoes that seemed as if they could have carried us away and realizing that it just wasn't going to work out.

We made the decision to abort the mission and head for home, and I was in a foul and irritable mood. My friend was driving, and as we headed back up the road in her minivan, I was in the passenger seat with my head bowed, half sulking and half studying a map that rested in my lap.

Suddenly my friend slowed down and brought the van to a stop. I looked up, not toward the windshield but at her, and just said, "What?" I found that she was staring straight ahead with a blank look on her face, and she said in a near monotone, "Something just crossed the road up there."

Of course, once I looked forward, whatever it was that she had seen was gone, and in an extremely odd moment we both had to shake ourselves out of our respective mental states in order to speak intelligently about what had just happened.

She said that she had just seen a tall black-figure about seven feet tall as solidly built as a football player in full pads cross the road a short distance ahead of us, swinging its arms but walking so smoothly that it almost appeared to be gliding, crossing the road in what seemed to be an impossible two strides.

Though she knew we were there specifically to look for Bigfoot, she seemed so in shock that she was not entirely ready to admit that that was what she'd just seen. She was an extremely spiritual and rather New Age type person (and I might as well admit at this point-so am I), and she actually said, "It was either a Bigfoot or a spirit of some kind."

I will never forget the feeling I had of jumping out of that van and peering into the woods in the pouring rain where I suddenly had reason to believe that I had just missed out on having my second Bigfoot sighting of all time by mere seconds, anxious and hoping that I would be able to spot it again through the drenched woods. Things can easily get confused in such moments, and either my friend misspoke, or I misunderstood her as to which direction the figure was going.

It went right to left, but for some reason, I thought she first said it went left to right. To the right was a hiking trail, and to the left was solid woods. I first thought that it had come out of difficult terrain and on to a more open space, but it was actually just the opposite. There seemed little else we could do in those circumstances, so what I did was to set up the trail camera that I had with me a short distance down the hiking trail before we continued on with our journey home.

When collected later, the camera did not show anything. Another camera did, however, at another rainy time just over a year later, on October 24, 2009, and this turned out to be another story that captured major local media attention.

The small town of Remer lies about 25 miles southeast of Bena and Six Mile Lake. It is bigger than Bena but not by much, its population being around 370, yet this does result in its having many more thriving businesses. One of the many bodies of water in the area is Shingle Mill Lake seven to eight miles east of town, where Tim Kedrowski and his sons Peter and Casey had a hunting area where they'd set up a trail camera.

At 7:20 PM on the evening in question something passed in front of that camera and into the realm of instant controversy. The photo taken appeared widely in newspapers and on tv, showing a tall, dark upright something walking through the frame from left to right. It very much lacks definition for the most part and the bottom of its legs flares out very oddly, almost like bell bottoms.

Many people commented that it looked to them like a hunter in a gilly suit or some other kind of camouflage, though the figure does not appear to be carrying any weapons or anything else. One thing I took special note of when studying the picture is that hand is visible at the end of the right arm, and it looks unusual, dark but shiny, possibly skin but just as possibly a glove.

Like the masses, I am skeptical of the photo, but Bob Olson and Don Sherman of the Northern Minnesota Bigfoot Research Team stated that after investigating the story and determining that a comparison with the trees in the picture put the figure's height at about seven feet that they believed it to be a Bigfoot. There was also the testimony of two elderly men who were staying in a hunting shack nearby on the night in question who told the Kedrowskis that during a visit to their outhouse at around 2 AM, nearly seven hours after the picture was snapped, they heard strange squealing sounds coming from the area where the camera was. I believe it's a mystery for the ages. To me, it doesn't look like a Bigfoot, but it doesn't really resemble anything else that makes sense either.

The reports continued and garnered enough media attention that, in time, they attracted the attention of the "Finding Bigfoot" team -- Matt, Cliff, Bobo, and Ranae -- enticing them into making their second visit to Minnesota, the first having resulted in the fourth episode of their second season back on January 15, 2012.

This second venture produced the ninth episode of their sixth season, airing on the oddly similar date of January 18, 2015. It was

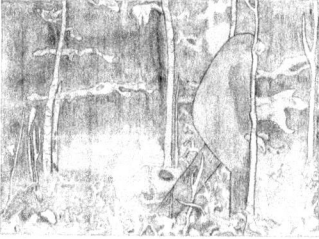

Artist's rendering of the Kedrowski trail cam photo.

entitled "Bigfoot Basecamp." The report that peaked the team's attention was a track find that occurred at the Maple Ridge Resort just off Highway 6 near the town of Bigfork on March 3, 2013.

The resort is located along what is known as the Turtle Lake Road but is actually on Hatch Lake, a nice looking operation with a couple of log buildings making up the office and the owners' home surrounded by several small cabins where guests can stay. The track incident happened in the offseason when there were no guests, and the ground was still covered in snow.

The resort's owner Lyle Enger said that at about 10 PM, his two dogs began acting strangely, scratching at the door and wanting to be let out, but once outside, they shied after only about 15 seconds and ran back inside. When he went out with a flashlight to look around, he found that a long line of bipedal human-like footprints 16" long had crossed the frozen lake and come ashore to meander about the resort, the stride varying at different points but often reaching an astounding eight feet, evidently a running gait. The prints led directly past some of the cabins, indicating that their maker was not afraid to come close to human dwellings.

The "Finding Bigfoot" team, visiting in the summer indicated that they had asked Lyle to mark the location of each track, and he had done so by planting little orange flags in the ground to show where each print had been.

What I absolutely do not understand about this episode is how in the world he was able to do that just from memory, marking the exact spots for hundreds of footprints. Skeptical Ranae agreed with me on that, pointing out that they could not rely on Lyle's memory being accurate.

One thing I should mention before I continue the story is that since viewing this episode of "Finding Bigfoot," I have taken the time to drive to the Maple Ridge Resort while on expeditions in the area two or three times, and each time I have found no one around.

The office was open, I walked in and looked around, finding the registration desk and a little gift shop area, but despite hanging around for quite some time waiting for someone to appear, no one ever did. I even knocked on the door of the owner's house next door to the office, but still no results.

The only members of the family I have gotten to meet so far are the two dogs who first sensed something amiss, who were hanging around the property just being big friendly dogs. None of my visits were at the height of the summer tourist season, but it still seems very odd that a business would be left consistently unattended like that.

Lyle Enger was there for the "Finding Bigfoot" crew, though, and after telling them that other Bigfoot reports had been occurring around the area he offered them a cabin he owned on another property to use as their base -- hence the episode's title, "Bigfoot Base-camp." The show seemed to infer that this site was fairly close to the resort, but it and the rest of the spots where they investigated for the rest of the episode were actually around Leech Lake thirty to forty miles away.

For several days the team stayed at the cabin, surrounding it with cameras as they explored the neighboring woods, with Bobo continuing his humorous feud with Minnesota's mosquitoes. They got excellent wildlife footage but no sign of Bigfoot. They did, however, get Bigfoot stories aplenty when instead of their usual town meeting, they hosted a barbecue at the cabin and invited any locals with experiences to come and share food and conversation.

Bob Olson and Don Sherman were both in attendance and appeared for the first time on the show as part of the crowd but without being identified.

The team checked out a couple of sightings at the places where they'd occurred and then ended the episode with one of their trademark night time searches in which they used a small flying drone equipped with a night vision camera to try and catch sight of a

Bigfoot from the air, but without success. The episode was good for keeping the area in the public eye.

But who could have known what was coming next? The grand-daddy of all Bigfoot sightings in the Chippewa occurred on July 5, 2016, when a young Native man named Sammy Cleveland, living in Bena, was spending an evening bass fishing on Six Mile Lake, just off of one of the very few pieces of private land in the area that was owned by his family.

As I found when I began to look into the story, Sammy is an impressive man. He is an MMA (Mixed Martial Arts) fighter, and I found a video online of one of his fights that took place at one of the area's Indian casinos. As I watched the two shirtless opponents rain punches and kicks upon each other, I noted the series of tattoos on Sammy's chest, appearing to me to look like Indian shield symbols arranged in a semicircle to look like a large necklace.

Sammy won the fight, and it added much to my image of him as I learned about the sighting he had while on the lake. (I should mention that I did attempt to meet Sammy in person to interview him, but though people in Bena were friendly and directed me to the trailer house where he was living with his grandmother, when I knocked on the door there, no one would answer even though I could hear people moving about inside. Native communities are often very private, and one just has to accept that.)

He was fishing from his canoe a short distance down shore, from the boat launching site on the property and was casting away from the shore when his line accidentally flipped over in the opposite direction and made him turn toward shore, where he suddenly saw an enormous bipedal hairy creature at the water's edge, crouching in the shallows and doing something in the water with its hands.

It's been surmised that he probably overestimated its size when he described it as looking to him to be ten feet tall, but even if it was slightly shorter, it must have been truly massive to generate such an estimate. Even more shocking is the fact that it was covered in white hair, and Sammy compared it to a polar bear. Though not completely unknown, sightings of white Bigfoots are rare. The vast majority of them being dark in color, and if a white one of this size exists in the Six Mile Lake area, it is surprising that Sammy appears to be about the only one to have ever reported seeing it. Even if one imagines a species with hair that turns white in the winter, as some small mammals do, this sighting occurred in the middle of summer.

Sammy was amazed by what he saw, but being the fighter he is, he reacted by trying to scare the creature off, shouting at it and striking at the water and at the side of his boat, but it stayed put and continued to do whatever it was doing along the shoreline. Incredibly, the accounts that I have for this sighting state that he then sat in his canoe and simply observed the creature for as long as two full hours. As Bob Olson would later comment to me, "If he'd had a camera, he'd be a millionaire."

Bob Olson with his collection of Bigfoot casts displayed at his auto body shop.

The spot where Sammy Cleveland's Bigfoot sighting occurred along the shore of Six Mile Lake.

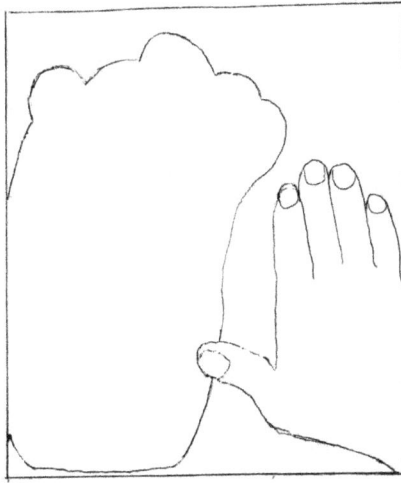

Sketches showing differences in footprint shape in Sammy Cleveland's video footage.

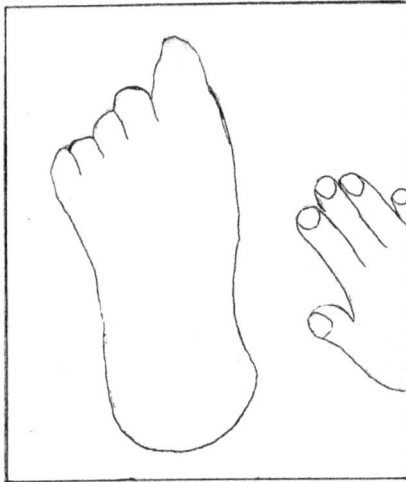

Exactly what the creature was doing for such a long time is unclear. Possibilities include washing something in the water or foraging for food, but Sammy did not report seeing it raise its hands to its mouth as if eating anything. It was late in the evening, and darkness began to fall as he watched, and he eventually began to row back toward his boat launching site.

When he did the creature stood and began to walk along the

shoreline, keeping pace with him as if it was determined to keep him from coming ashore. This tense standoff finally ended, however, when a relative of Sammy's arrived as planned to pick him up, and headlights bathed the scene.

At that point, the creature finally fled into the woods. I first became aware of this sighting a short time later when I was working on the list of Minnesota reports that appear in the appendix of this book, and I simply entered the search term "Recent Minnesota Bigfoot Reports" into YouTube. It showed me a video that Sammy shot the day after his sighting when he returned to the scene with a camera, not showing the lake but searching the swampy woods on the shore that the creature had disappeared into to see if he could find any evidence to back up his story.

The video is about four minutes long and consists of Sammy narrating as he surveys the area, never showing his face. He begins by describing how he was 30 or 40 yards out into the lake the evening before, then says, "I'm a little nervous, got my machete" and shows the large bladed weapon in front of the camera.

His language is peppered with profanity as he notes how he can see clearly well-worn animal trails through the bush and deer tracks, but when he first comes across the tracks of the Bigfoot from the night before, he is taken aback. "Holy (blank)!" he exclaims a couple of times. "Somebody needs to get over here. Look at this, guys. I can't (blanking) believe this."

He questions whether viewers of the video can see toes in the first print as he believes he can, then puts both his hand and his foot down next to it for size comparison and intones, "Ooh, I'm freaked out, dude!"

As he sees more he says, "And then, to make it worse, there's that (blanking) perfect print, and then five feet away there's another one that got in the deep mud that ain't so clear... there's another one that's water-filled, he sunk, he was (blanking) heavy."

He then puts his hand down a second time next to another print to show the size and excitedly says, "I gotta go investigate this, man. This is serious. I'm pumped, man. Like whoo, look it, there's another one on land." He almost stumbles as he goes to examine a print in solid ground. "It's so thick in here, almost fell off.

Sorry about my language, but this is crazy. He must have stepped over this log and then put his foot here, this is a (blanking) footprint, right here." For a third time, he puts his hand down to indicate the print's dimensions. "And then it goes up into here... it's dry land up here, but he sunk way in, his heel sunk way down in there. And this is a monster track.

If I was to put my foot in there, it'd be like, it would just swallow my foot whole. That is nuts." He then turns to the side to show a worn trail through the woods and continues, "But look at this, you can just see where he walked right through there, five-foot strides. No other track and thing at all, there's no way that anybody (blanking) fabricated this story. I guarantee you, I seen a Bigfoot last night. I was 20 yards away.

And he was not scared. Holy (blank), I gotta get outta here before I get eaten alive." There the video and narrative ends, and apart from the one discrepancy of Sammy saying at the beginning that he was 30-40 yards away and then at the end saying it was only 20 yards, his emotional reaction to what he is seeing makes for quite a compelling experience while watching it.

His anxiety is palpable, a true testament to the effect seeing a Bigfoot can have on a person. The long five-toed tracks seen in the waterlogged forest floor do not give any suggestion of fakery, being on a surface where such would have been extremely difficult, if not impossible. I did notice one thing that intrigued me, that being that the two clearest prints that Sammy put his hand down next to appeared to be of similar size but otherwise looked completely different.

The first showed the toes spread out in a crescent shape, while the second had them angling sharply down diagonally from the big toe. This made me wonder if there might have actually been two creatures present, and that if the one seen by Sammy in his canoe had a mate hidden back in the woods that might have been why it was so intent on not letting him come ashore, acting protectively.

However, when I shared this theory with Cliff Barackman from the "Finding Bigfoot" team through e-mail, he assured me that a living and flexible foot can vary widely in the impressions it makes in the ground and that he believed it was only one creature present for Sammy's sighting.

At the very least, I think it rules out fakery, as fake wooden feet attached to a hoaxer's shoes have a cookie-cutter effect and result in every print looking identical. I respect Cliff's opinion but think the matter remains in question, and Bob Olson agreed with me. It was in the late summer of 2016, just weeks after this sighting, that I made another venture up to the area and finally sought out and met both Bob and his partner Don Sherman.

I arranged to meet Bob at his auto body shop on the outskirts of Deer River, which I found to be half that and half the Bigfoot Central headquarters for the region, his office containing a display on one wall of various plaster casts of Bigfoot footprints collected from the area since 2006, most of which were of better quality than any I had ever made. I must confess that I was downright giddy, for after my years of research in Minnesota, this was like Disneyland.

I found Bob to be an extremely engaging and friendly guy, and we sat for a couple of hours discussing the subject. He was in his late 60s but looked younger, being even more old school than myself when it came to technology and had little to no Internet presence but kept his record of paper report forms and photographs in various binders and boxes.

In a later visit, I would learn that he also investigated UFO and ghost reports in the area and had much documentation of those as well, but during our first meeting, we mainly stuck to the Bigfoot subject. I was surprised and elated when I described the project I was working on of trying to compile a list of every known Minnesota report for all time and he offered to let me borrow his big box of report forms and make copies of them.

I assured him that I would mail the box back to him as soon as possible, to which he humorously replied, "Well, you damn well better!" It made me laugh, and of course, I stuck true to my word. Bob gave me directions to the site of the Sammy Cleveland sighting, located along the shore of Six Mile Lake. He said to just look for the little blue fire number sign since it was the only piece of private property out there, but he assured me that it would be ok if I explored it.

He also urged me to stop and visit his partner Don Sherman, who had more of a connection to the sighting than he did. Not long afterward, I would learn that Don was a friend of Sammy's and was actually present when the YouTube video was being shot, having been the first person Sammy called to report the sighting. I was surprised that Don didn't chime in on camera, but he did make one very impressive plaster casts of one of the prints, as classic a Bigfoot cast as anyone will ever see.

I do not know its exact dimensions, but it looks 14-15" long. On my way west from Deer River and my meeting with Bob toward the sighting location I passed through the tiny community of Ball Club, which is not really a town though its residents might take offense at that.

It is just a few homes and one convenience store, next door to which lives Don Sherman, having moved there from Cass Lake since the Bigfoot mania had first broken out in 2006. Unlike with Bob, I had no appointment to meet him but showed up cold, and happened to see him in his backyard.

He was wearing a cap with what I recall as some kind of Bigfoot-related logo on it, and on the back deck of his house rested what appeared to be a fresh plaster footprint cast. When I introduced myself, Don wasn't exactly as engaging as Bob had been, and seemed to only want to talk to me at arm's length. I can understand that since I was a complete stranger just dropping by.

As we got into the subject, at one point, he cut in and asked me if I had spent significant time in the woods as if he didn't want to deal with someone who was just a city boy. In his early 60s, I kind of got the impression that he viewed me as a young novice even though I was nearly 50 myself. (Though, I'm happy to say that like Bob, I look younger than I am.) He did warm up to me a little, though, and ended up sharing some fascinating information with me.

He first played for me a recording he'd made of what he believed were Bigfoot howls joining in with wolves just as had earlier been documented down in the Kettle River area, and then told me his theory that he thought Bigfoot might actually work together with wolves for hunting purposes just as prehistoric man did before they domesticated wolves to create modern dogs.

In spite of that, it was a much shorter visit than I'd had with Bob, but Don also described how to get to the Cleveland sighting location. I thanked him and moved on, eager to get there, and said I would be in touch again. That ended up happening the next year when I had a much longer and more involved visit with him in his house during which he was much more open with me than before, and ended up doing the same thing Bob had done in letting me borrow and make copies of his big box of reports.

Bob and Don are a perfect partnership, a melding of the white and Native races that makes just about any Bigfoot witness in the area comfortable enough to seek them out and share their experiences. I wish there was more of that, and they are both really great guys. I had my own time in the sun, so the speak, as the main Bigfoot investigator in Minnesota back in the 90s and early 2000s, and I would be thrilled to resume that role should I make a significant discovery, but for now, I am happy to pass the torch on to men like them.

So, to get back on track, I arrived at the site of Sammy Cleveland's sighting. After the famous track find of 2006, I was excited at the prospect of the Six Mile Lake area still being viable ten years later and a possible "hot spot." It was odd how this single piece of private property lay amidst the great expanse of national forest, but it appeared to be a sort of getaway place where the family would camp and fish.

After a couple of minutes' walk down the approach, there was a pile of debris where a small trailer house had stood but had been demolished. In looking around I found where a latrine had been dug into the ground, and at the lakeshore, there was Sammy's canoe cached and waiting for its next use. Bob Olson had told me that the spot where the tracks were found was "about a five-minute walk into the woods" to the left of the boat launch site, and the directions were good.

There was a clear trail to follow through the thick bush, and as I started down it with the lake on my right, I found that there was a strange land feature, a ridge slightly taller than myself that lay along the lakeshore for as far as I could see. It was instantly obvious that the creature Sammy saw would have had to have climbed over it to get to the water, and back over it again to make its escape. I also noticed with great interest an area where some ferns had been smashed down flat to the ground, obviously by something of great weight passing through, something that deer with their tiny hooved feet would not do.

This was over a month after the sighting, so it made me wonder if Sammy's creature might still be visiting the area. When I found what I estimated to be the approximate site where the tracks had been found, there was nothing but wet and spongy ground to be seen. I didn't know if I had the exact spot, but it didn't matter. I wanted to put up a trail camera in this place, and anywhere would do. As I found a good spot and was setting it up, I suddenly heard the voices of a couple of fishermen in a boat on the other side of that strange ridge that blocked my view of them, and also their view of me, which I was thankful for since I knew I was on private property. I don't like doing that, but

I'd been assured by Bob and Don that it would be all right. Nevertheless, I did my work and made my exit as quietly as possible. A week later, on August 20, 2016, my intrepid best friend and partner Dean made a rare solo venture and drove up to the site to retrieve the camera with directions I provided.

Instead of walking into the lakeshore as I'd done, he drove his car all the way in, and just as he was getting out he heard a sound off to his right in the woods that startled him, something moving about and breaking brush. Now he may not want me to include the incident in this book, and he downplayed it significantly after first telling me about it, but he did not have a gun with him that day as he usually does in the woods, and the sound scared him to the point of getting back in his car and taking off without retrieving the camera.

Dean is a country boy like me and has heard the sound of deer bounding through the woods many times. In spite of his later protests, it struck me that whatever he heard that day had such an effect on him, giving him a feeling of danger. He called me the next day to tell me about it and wanted to go back to the place together right away, which we did, gun at the ready this time.

When we got to the approach to the site, I wanted to walk in quietly but instead, he drove in at rather high speed and said, "No, if there's anything in there I want to take it by surprise." It was a dramatic moment, and I held a camera at the ready. But typically, we found nothing. We explored the woods in the area where whatever he'd heard the day before had been but found no tracks of any kind in the wet spongy ground. We retrieved the camera, which turned out to have taken no pictures in a full week. We left empty-handed that day, but with much food for thought.

I remembered the signs of well-worn trails that Sammy had noticed while filming the place the day after his sighting, and I also noticed as Dean and I were making our way to the camera that the flattened ferns I'd seen a week before had risen back up so as to show no trace of an animal passing, so I did some quick intellectual math in my head. If flattened foliage in this setting did not last for a week, then there was no way that the crushed ferns I'd seen were left over from the sighting over a month before, which at least suggested the creature might still be around.

But the sign did last for at least a day or two, which made it just frustratingly weird that Dean and I didn't find a single animal track of any kind in the spot where he'd heard the frightening sounds one day earlier, not even deer tracks.

As I puzzled over it, I asked Dean if he thought it could be possible that what he'd heard might have been moving through tree-tops rather than on the ground, but he seemed to think that a strange question and an unlikely one. Though not a disbeliever in Bigfoot, he is a natural skeptic and is not quick to believe, but though he denies it, I personally believe that during that episode, he joined the club and heard a Bigfoot less than a hundred feet from him, probably the same one that Sammy saw.

We will never know.

I returned to the place not long after, equipped with high rubber boots so that I could wade out into the shallow water along the shoreline and walk exactly where Sammy's Bigfoot had walked. It is always an awesome and intimidating feeling standing where you know these creatures have stood, and I've done it several times, but this time seemed especially so.

One thing I took particular note of was that I was seeing frogs in the water all around me, which made me wonder if feeding on them might have been the reason why the creature was there. But then again, as I said before, Sammy did not report seeing it raising its hands to its mouth, so a mystery remains as to why it would have simply crouched there in the shallows with its hands in the water for two hours.

I saw some raccoon tracks in the mudflats along the shore, but no Bigfoot evidence. I did make one other find that day in a nearby spot that left me scratching my head. The sighting location is located about four miles out along a rough forest road that stretches east out of the town of Bena. About one mile out from the town is a corridor that's been cut through the forest where the underground gas line in the area passes through and crosses the road.

I decided to hike that corridor a bit, first heading north and finding that it soon ran into a swampy area. South of the road, it went much farther, and after a few hundred yards, I suddenly came upon a dead fox lying in the grass near a large shrub. It was recently dead, with very little odor of decay and only a few insects on the body, which was lying flat on its left side with its legs curled beneath as if in a running position.

In trying to guess how the animal had died, I noticed a mushed-up area of hair on the right side of its neck about the size of my hand that clearly looked like the hair had been wet and then dried in the sun, just in that one spot. Other than that, there were no marks on the body at all, no torn flesh, not a drop of blood to suggest that the fox had been savaged by some larger predator.

I decided to feel along its spine, and when I came to the neck, I could no longer feel it even when pressing into the soft flesh of the nape, suggesting that the neck might be broken. So what to make of this? As I pondered it, it looked for all the world as if something with a mouth about the size of my hand had bitten down on this poor animal's neck almost gently, just enough to snap the spine and kill but not doing any further damage, then laid the body down gently in the position I found it in. No bear, wolf, or cat did that. They would have torn the body to pieces.

Why a Bigfoot would have had cause to kill the little fox without eating it, I have no idea and I do not count this as Bigfoot evidence, but I do wonder about it, and it is one more mystery in an area already haunted by mysteries.

The next major event in the Chippewa saga actually coincided with the Sammy Cleveland sighting when just a couple of days later the town of Remer -- near where the trail camera photo that had received so much media attention had been snapped -- launched their first annual Remer Bigfoot Days weekend festival and began advertising themselves as 'The Home of Bigfoot."

It was a town-wide celebration, with picnics and food stands, sporting events, all manner of gifts for sale, etc. as well as informational talks and sales of Bigfoot souvenirs to provide fun as well as education on the subject. It drew huge crowds as most such small-town celebrations tend to do, but unfortunately, I did not happen to learn of it until it was over and would only come to experience it in its second year the next summer.

When I heard about it, I was instantly reminded of how the town of Crookston in northwest Minnesota (population 7,800) had briefly billed themselves as "Bigfoot Capital of the World" in 1995-96 even though as far as I was able to determine, there was only one report anywhere near the town, a track find in 1981.

Crookston insisted that they were treating the subject seriously even though it was obviously being done mainly to bring in tourist dollars, and after heavy media exposure, they did sell a ton of Bigfoot souvenirs. A prominent restaurant in town hired a taxidermist to create a huge hairy Bigfoot statue that spent time welcoming patrons both outdoors beneath the place's sign and indoors in their entryway.

Once the attention had died down, and the town decided to let it go, I was contacted by nationally known cryptozoologist Loren Coleman who was seeking to acquire the statue for the Cryptozoology Museum he operates in the state of Maine. I directed him where to go and today it does indeed reside in the museum, Crookston's dubious claim to being a Bigfoot hotspot at an end. But now it was Renner's turn, and with the plethora of reports surrounding them, their claim had much more merit to it. Honestly, I think just about any town in the region could have done the same thing with just as much legitimacy but to each their own.

Still, when the festival attracted the attention of "Finding Bigfoot" and they came to shoot their third Minnesota episode, only a year after their last one, they first came in with a skeptical air. It was the seventh episode of their ninth season, airing on February 12, 2017, and entitled "Bigfoot Town."

As they drove into the area, Bobo commented to the rest of the team, 'There's no way this place is The Home of Bigfoot.' That's like me proclaiming myself the fittest man in America. I gotta go straighten these people out. There's no way they're The Home of Bigfoot.' We all know it's Willow Creek in northern California, it has been for 50 years."

As soon as they got to Remer, however, the team met with city councilman Mark Ruyak, who had come up with the idea for the festival. He pointed out that in addition to the many reports in the area in the present day, the postmaster William P. Remer for whom the town was named back in 1904, had reported seeing giant foot-prints in the area.

He also explained that calling the town "The Home of Bigfoot" was meant to convey the message that it was a place where anyone with experiences to report could feel at home and could come to share their stories without fear of ridicule. Bobo and the rest of the team seemed to like that explanation, and the rest of the episode proceeded in the usual way.

They linked up at first, not with Bob Olson and Don Sherman, but with another couple of Minnesota Bigfooters, Abe DelRio and Michael Hexum of the Minnesota Bigfoot Research Team, which, if you are paying attention, is very close to the name used by Olson and Sherman, the Northern Minnesota Bigfoot Research Team. I believe there may have been some minor controversy there for a time, and I noticed that on their report forms, Olson and Sherman host the heading "Northern Minnesota Research & Field Investigations" and also the phrase "Searching for Bug-Way-Jinini," a local Ojibwa name for Bigfoot. DelRio and Hexum were new faces to me, the former being a younger and energetic guy, muscular and with a buzz cut, and the latter being older and rather grizzled looking and having had a sighting as a teenager way back in 1970.

They and other members of their team had been investigating reports throughout Minnesota and went out with the "Finding Bigfoot" crew early in the episode to a supposed hotspot near Remer where they heard possible Bigfoot sounds during one of their patented night time searches.

The original two-man Northern Minnesota Bigfoot Research Team, however, was not relegated to nameless cameos in this episode as they'd been before, and when it came time to collect stories from the locals, Don Sherman was front and center with the fresh footprint cast he had made only the day before beside Six Mile Lake at the scene of the Sammy Cleveland sighting, about 20 miles northwest of Remer. This truly did not seem to be scripted, and with such a recent sighting of such an impressive nature, the team decided to devote a major segment of the episode to Sammy's sighting.

First, they visited the scene with Sammy and Don, which was exciting for me watching the episode and seeing the footage of them being in a spot where I had followed shortly thereafter in their foot-steps. Then after dark, based on what I tend to think was a bit of a leap in logic on Matt Moneymaker's part in speculating that the huge white Bigfoot seen by Sammy probably prowled that lakeshore every single night; they did their final night search there with Matt and Bobo out in the lake in a boat and Cliff and Ranae onshore, all armed with their traditional night vision gear.

As usual though, the creature did not do them the honor of making a return appearance. So ended the third and final Minnesota episode of "Finding Bigfoot." There will be no more, as after seven years on the air, the series wrapped with a finale episode on May 27, 2018 that focused on Willow Creek, California, which, as Bobo insisted, will always be the true "Home of Bigfoot."

Matt, Cliff, Bobo, and Ranae may not have had success in finding Bigfoot at Six Mile Lake, but someone else claimed to do better the following month. That was the She-Squatchers, the newly formed all-female group of Bigfoot researchers who were based out of various locations in Minnesota, and all claimed some level of psychic ability that aided them in their quest.

On August 20, 2016, they were exploring the Six Mile Lake area intending to have their very first overnight excursion in the woods. Amazingly, this happened to be the very same day that my partner Dean had his encounter at the Sammy Cleveland site with a sound in the woods that intimidated him into leaving without retrieving the trail camera he'd come to collect. The area is extensive but not so much so that Dean didn't have a chance of running into the ladies, but as it happened he did not, and in any case, we had not even heard of them yet at that time.

Team members Stephanie Ayers, Jen Kruse, Kimberly Juarez, Katie Sonmor, and Mario Schmidt were present that day for the finding of some possible Bigfoot tracks at a location that I have the impression was not in the vicinity of the Cleveland sighting, but later that evening while driving the stretch of road along the lake's southern shore very near to the sighting location, their psychic intu-itions led them to stop and set up camp and explore the woods there after dark.

That night they claimed that they heard something large approach them through the woods, something they never saw but which then began throwing rocks in their direction. They could tell that the rocks were not meant to hit them but were soaring up and over the treetops and merely landing near them. It was a typical rock-throwing incident such as many Bigfooters have reported over the years from all across America, but this one may have been unique in how its witnesses came to be there.

I first became aware of the She-Squatchers on a day in February 2017 when I foolishly took my car (which was hardly an all-terrain vehicle) into the Six Mile Lake road system for some late winter exploration. The winter had been fairly mild, so I was hoping the roads wouldn't be too bad, but as it turned out, I quickly got the feeling that I was an idiot for being there that early in the year and that it was only by the grace of my guardian angel that I did not get stuck in the snow and made it out safely.

When I got home, I was told by friends that this group called the She-Squatchers had just been featured on the evening tv news and that they had held two town meetings that day -- one in Mahnomen, which is near the Buckboard Hills in Clearwater County where I did much of my Bigfooting in the 90s, and the other in Bena, which I had just passed through on my way home.

In fact, their meeting there was in progress at the local cafe as I passed by, and if I had known about it in advance, I definitely would have stopped in. They called their meetings "Bigfoot Banters," friendly gatherings where they were able to collect several reports from the local people.

In studying their website, I found that the next Bigfoot Banter was to take place at the Home, Sport, & Family Show in the town of Thief River Falls (population 8,570) in northwest Minnesota on April 8th, and as I was well into the project at that time of assembling the comprehensive list of all known Minnesota Bigfoot reports that appear at the end of this book, I resolved to drive up and meet with them and see if they would be willing to share information. I attended the Banter and took notes on the few stories that were shared there, and afterward I introduced myself.

The group member I ended up sitting down and talking with and who I've had the most contact with since was one of their main organizers, Jen Kruse. How shall I describe her? She is without question, quite a character. Approaching middle age and with very long flowing brown hair, I think I can safely describe Jen as one of the most New Agey people I have ever met. That is not at all a criticism in and of itself since I fall under that umbrella myself and so do many of my friends. But though she has a keen interest in Bigfoot, I found that she associated the subject in her mind with a vast array of other paranormal areas that she seemed more interested in talking about.

We had a long talk, most of which consisted of her describing her experiences with elemental beings, dimensional gateways, and parallel universes. Now, these are all things that I have an interest in myself, and I want to be very clear about that, but the reason I was there that day was a hundred percent focuses on Bigfoot and on gathering information to complete my list and I found it downright impossible to keep Jen on the subject. She eventually had to go and rejoin her teammates, but we traded contact information, and in the following weeks, I found her to be the type who is always extremely busy and always wants to get together and talk more but just can't seem to find the time.

I would see the She-Squatchers again on July 8, 2017, when Dean and I both attended the Second Annual Remer Bigfoot Days festival. Having missed the first one, I was happy to find that the town was continuing it as a new tradition. It was quite the spectacle to behold, being very clear that the whole little town had embraced Bigfoot as its community mascot.

Jena Grover and Jen Kruse of the She-Squatchers.

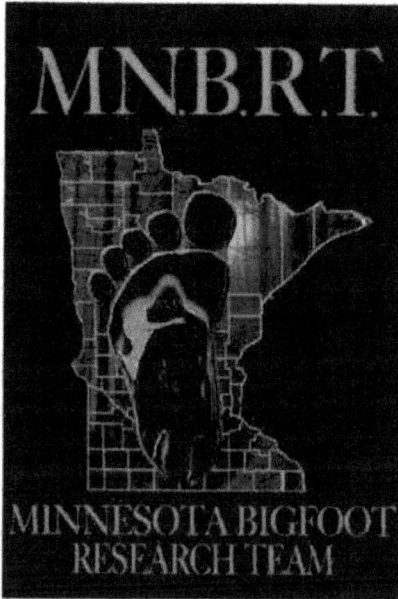

The logo of Abe DelRio's Minnesota Bigfoot Research Team.

The author at the Remer Bigfoot Days festival.

Entrance to Remer, "Home of Bigfoot."

A display in Remer's Bigfoot Gas and Gifts.

The author with an amazing statue on display in
Remer's Bigfoot Gas and Gifts.

Signs upon entering city limits welcomed visitors to the Home of
Bigfoot. There were Bigfoot statues and larger than life wooden
cutouts here and there, as well as businesses named after the creature
such as the Bigfoot gas station and gift shop. There were Bigfoot
burgers for sale at the various food stands and events such as the
Bigfoot flea market, Bigfoot basketball, Bigfoot barbecue contest, and
the Bigfoot 5k run.

I knew that Willow Creek in California had celebrations like this
but what a thrill it was to see it now happening in my home state, just
a weekend of happy, goofy fun with a serious subject at its heart. Scattered amidst the more lighthearted aspects of the event, there were
information booths, displays of plaster footprint casts from the area,
and a stage, where presentations took place on the variety of Bigfoot
reports that surrounded Remer.

I don't know if I agree with them calling themselves the Home of
Bigfoot because I think just about any town in the surrounding
region could make the same claim and have just as much to show for
it, but it was as good a place as any. I had met for a second time with

Bob Olson in Deer River just over a week earlier and he had indicated that he and Don Sherman would be in Remer as they had been the year before when the "Finding Bigfoot" crew had been there and I expected them to be giving a presentation, but for some reason, not only was that not the case but they didn't seem to be there at all.

Who was there, giving talks up on the stage in the town center, were the Minnesota Bigfoot Research Team led by Abe DelRio, and the She-Squatchers. Both teams gave good talks and shared both their own experiences and those of other witnesses that they invited to come up on stage, with me sitting in the audience furiously taking notes.

Dean and I had managed to find the She-Squatchers earlier while out and about the streets of Remer and had already had some discussion with them, and we knew that they had another of their famous Bigfoot Banters planned for later in the afternoon, their second one at the cafe in Bena. However, I had another item on my agenda for the latter part of the day that precluded me from attending, so I asked Dean if he would go in my place, which he did.

It was also one of the reasons why I did not stick around to introduce myself to Abe DelRio and his team. I wish now that I had, but months later, I would end up meeting him in a most unexpected setting very far away from Remer. As it turned out that late afternoon and evening, Dean attended the ladies' Bigfoot Banter in Bena, but surprisingly, this time, no one else showed up, so it ended up being a visit between just him and them. Dean has a certain charm about him and an ability to do well with just about anyone, so he seemed to really hit it off with the She-Squatchers.

They talked mostly about older reports we already knew of, and Dean wasn't able to pick up any new information, which the team seemed to be keeping close to the chest. The visit ended well and he received a hug from one of them as they were saying their goodbyes.

My mission in the latter part of that day was to revisit a site I'd been turned on to in a meeting I'd had several days earlier on June 26th with Bob Olson. At that time, he'd told me that the most recent sighting he knew of in the area was from only two weeks before, when two women in a car had seen a Bigfoot leap across the blacktop of Highway 6 about a half hour's drive north from his home base of Deer River near a place called Talmoon.

This was one of those typical tiny roadside communities that are not really towns but are just made up of a few buildings with some type of legal designation. As I would come to realize later Talmoon happened to be practically in the backyard of the Maple Ridge Resort where "Finding Bigfoot" had come to film their second Minnesota episode in response to the tracks found there.

But on June 26, 2017, after my meeting with Bob, I drove up just to check it out and look for trails to explore. I found what looked like a good one about two miles north of Talmoon, parked my car at the roadside and hiked in.

What I found began what I considered to be a whole new chapter in my research. Before I describe it, however, I need to keep myself humble by including some words by a Bigfooter named Hugh Phillips that he posted online to Facebook and which were then quoted in the June-July 2018 issue of the Bigfoot Times newsletter published by Daniel Perez.

Phillips was complaining that the Bigfoot field seemed to have been taken over by publicity hounds and attention seekers wanting to make a quick buck. He wrote: "The field is overrun with 'researchers' who truly make you cringe when you hear the word 'researcher,' as half of them can't even spell the word. They go out into a fairly wooded area with their cell phones and film 'tree breaks' and 'stick structures' that anyone familiar with the woods can tell are totally natural in scope...

They litter YouTube, many claiming to find 'activity' on a daily basis. If they are finding activity on a daily basis, they are hoaxing or simply ignorant; take your pick. Not trying to be harsh, but it is absolutely making a mockery of us all... we were close to having science take a look at this subject, but for now... we are further away than ever and moving further away each day."

I need to remember those words to keep things in perspective for myself, because for nearly a year in repeated visits to this trail north of Talmoon, I found what I felt were possible signs of Bigfoot activity on a level that I had never seen anywhere else, much of it consisting of what seemed to me to be inexplicable tree breaks and stick structures exactly like the ones referred to by Hugh Phillips that no matter how hard I tried to dismiss them, did not seem to have a natural explanation.

I will not bog this chapter down in minute details about them and my extensive speculations about them, but will just mention a couple of things that struck me the most. (There will be more about stick structure evidence in Chapter 6.)

Several times I found healthy trees eight to nine inches thick snapped like matchsticks and fallen over, oftentimes blocking the trail and always broken at about waist-high level above the ground. I know that strong windstorms can snap trees, but when that happens, there are many, not just one here and one there.

Sometimes these trees had fallen in ways that it seemed they should have gotten caught up in the upper canopy and not reached the ground but somehow had done so anyway as if they had help. The way in which the breaks were always the exact same height above ground made me imagine something with extreme strength standing there and snapping those tree trunks and then lowering many hundreds of pounds of weight in a controlled manner.

I also found tree branches that were pulled down from opposite sides of the trail to cross it in the middle, snapped just enough to not spring back up but not enough to separate completely from the trees. These, along with the fallen trees, seemed to be attempts to block the trail, and though they were not nearly actual insurmountable barriers, they seemed to carry the message "Keep Out." Needless to say, the wind does not snap branches in opposite directions, especially not just in one spot.

There were other things I found along that trail over the months, such as truly weird arrangements of sticks that seemed unlikely to have fallen the way they were naturally and also a palm-sized patch of deer hide that something had placed inside a hollow stump.

Once while I was placing a trail camera in the area, I heard what had to be a very thick tree limb snapping some distance away, really loud, the kind of sound that makes one wonder what in the world might be responsible. I count some of the things that I found in this place as possible Bigfoot evidence, but I try to stay impartial and am not insistent about them. However, they would all be much more of a gray area for me had it not been for the actual Bigfoot footprints that I also found on that trail.

June 26, 2017, saw my very first visit to the trail near Talmoon. It went a few hundred yards through fairly light woods until it opened up into a vast clearing where a logging operation had been, with the ground plowed up and the soil mixed with sawdust and wooden debris-strewn about everywhere.

I have seen so many of these logged areas over the years, and they are at the same time a sad thing to see but also an excellent setting to look for animal sign. I was startled by a deer that I spooked just after entering the clearing as it bounded away, something that would happen more than once while visiting this site. When I got to the far end of the logged area, the trail ran into a solid wall of forest with the point at which the trail entered it having an appearance that made me label it "the doorway."

After I continued on through it, the trail began to get a little rougher with a roller coaster type terrain, harsh dips with muddy water at the bottom that had to be carefully negotiated, but after just a few minutes of that, I came to another clearing of sorts. This one was filled with short brush and wildflowers, quite a lovely little scene really, and as I was exploring it, I found something that made me think I just might not be imagining things in the odd tree breaks and stick structures I was seeing.

I almost stepped on it, but as I was looking down I suddenly caught sight of some very clear toe impressions in the mud. As I knelt down to examine it, I made out the impression of a print that was not quite complete but seemed to fill out the space made by a five-toed foot with a somewhat pointed heel and measuring about eight inches long. I put my fingers in those toe impressions, eliciting a feeling I have had only a few other times when finding Bigfoot tracks.

This one was small, and as I pondered it, I told myself that the only other thing this could be was a bear track, and that if it was, it was from an adult bear, but if it was from a Bigfoot, then it was a juvenile.

I knelt there for a long time staring at that impression in the mud, telling myself that I needed to be impartial and trying to convince myself that it might be a bear track. But I couldn't do it. There was absolutely no trace of claw marks, and every time I'd ever seen bear tracks before the claws were unmistakable. And then, for further vindication, I looked two feet further on and found another print identical to the first that still showed not a hint of claws.

On another visit to the Talmoon trail, four months later, on October 28th, I came to retrieve a trail camera I'd left at the site, at which time a light blanket of snow had fallen on the area although it wasn't terribly cold, making for a rather lovely winter wonderland setting. Tree signs were particularly bizarre that day. When I came to the clearing where I'd found the tracks in June, as God as my witness on that same stretch of trail within 50 feet of the first spot I found another one.

Despite the slight cold, the mud was not frozen, and just as before, I almost stepped on the single track that was there waiting for me, clear toe impressions and that little pointed heel just as before, the eight-inch long track of a young Bigfoot. I started to wonder if this little juvenile just wasn't wise enough yet to stop stepping in mud in the middle of the trail and leaving tracks.

I also had the thought that if I continued to find its tracks over time, they should grow. On another visit to the trail on May 6, 2018, I found another possible track in sawdust in the wide-open logged area. The toes seemed more splayed than before, with a more prominent big toe, but otherwise, it looked similar to the earlier tracks, and sure enough, the length was now close to ten inches.

Either it was made by a different creature, or the little one I'd discovered had grown in the nearly one-year period since my first visit.

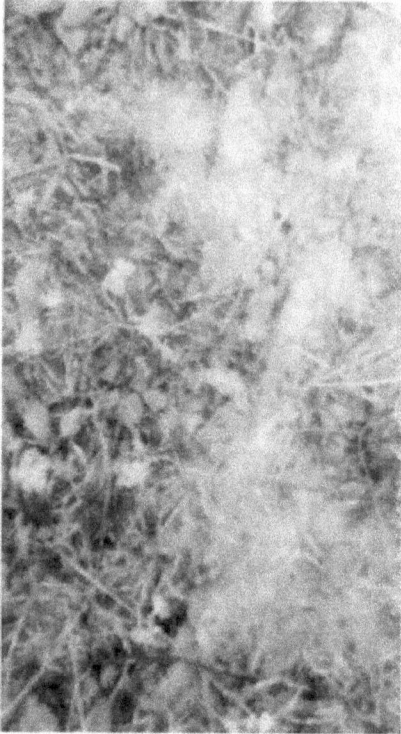

Two shots of the juvenile Bigfoot track found on the Talmoon trail, with glove to give scale.

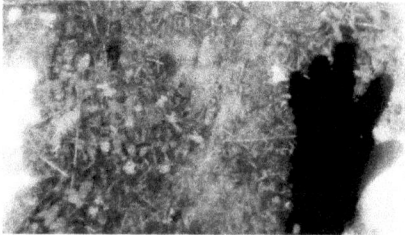

A lone healthy tree, snapped like a matchstick.

Branches bent down to block the trail in opposite directions.

As the 2018 Remer Bigfoot Days festival was approaching, I heard of yet another dramatic incident that had occurred on February 19th of that year in which two men driving on Draper Tower Road, about ten miles south of Remer, had reported witnessing a Bigfoot apparently having a temper tantrum and hurling large logs up in the air as high as treetop level, where some of them became lodged in the trees. I searched that area while nearing completion of this book but did not find any tangible evidence. However, once while doing so, I heard what sounded like large rocks being banged together in the woods from a far distance away, loudly and unmistakable, repeating about five times.

I do not count it as a Bigfoot report, but it was intriguing. The years 2016-2018 turned out to be enormously exciting for me in the Chippewa National Forest and a time of regenerated interest in the region. The reports from earlier years were obviously not just isolated incidents, and a permanent population of sasquatch definitely seems to be in residence.

Bob Olson and Don Sherman continue to investigate reports in the area, as does Abe DelRio and his team. The She-Squatchers, however, have gone through some discord amongst their ranks having to do with the sharing of information and have split into two separate teams. Jen Kruse maintains the name "She-Squatchers" and now leads that group, while former leader Stephanie Ayers has formed a new team called the "SquatchHERS," both of them still being all female.

I became aware of this while attending the ParaCon, an annual paranormal convention held at the Shooting Star Casino in Mahnomen, Minnesota, on October 14, 2017. It was the famous cryptozoologist Loren Coleman who first explained the situation to me during my first ever meeting with him after years of occasional correspondence between us, and he shared with me some new Minnesota Bigfoot reports he'd collected from visitors to the convention.

It was he that the Shes cited as their inspiration since he had once stated that perhaps it might be a female group with their gentleness and empathy that might have the best chance of finding Bigfoot, and now he and they all happened to be at this convention together.

As for the Shes and their disagreements I have to say that it vexes me since personally, I was never able to get either faction to go into very much detail on the stories they'd collected when I tried to enlist their cooperation in my project of assembling a complete list of all known Minnesota reports.

Some investigators share openly while others choose to keep things close to the chest, and while I would like for there to be a free exchange of information throughout the Bigfoot community one cannot dictate how everyone should feel about it. Just a week after the ParaCon, I traveled to California, where I was blessed to meet Cliff Barackman from "Finding Bigfoot," and since I knew he'd met the She-Squatchers in Remer, I asked if he remembered them, but he said he didn't since he and his crew had met over a thousand people there at the Bigfoot Days festival, but when I told him about their situation, I remember he had an amused reaction something along the lines of, "Oh, a fracture in a Bigfooting group? Shocking!"

To be fair and honest, I should add that the She-Squatchers do maintain a website on which they share their own personal encounters, and also that Jen Kruse did share with me a little information she had on sightings in the Ulen, Minnesota area from the "Prairie Sasquatch" chapter of this book, but it is the stories they collect from local people during their Bigfoot Banter meetings that remain confidential. I have always been perfectly fine with witnesses remaining anonymous and even keeping the exact locations of their experiences private, but in those cases I still always hope to be able to just document the fact that the events happened.

The Shes have not seen eye to eye with me on this, and I know that they have collected stories that do not appear in my comprehensive list, making it incomplete. Meanwhile, the trail cameras that my friend Dean and I have deployed may not have captured an image of Bigfoot as of yet, but they have hardly come up empty.

In 2017, we had them both on the Talmoon trail and along a trail just off Six Mile Lake, only about a tenth of a mile from the site of the Sammy Cleveland sighting where a giant white Bigfoot is supposed to prowl. We have captured many deer pictures at both sites, and a small to medium-sized black bear at Six Mile. But our most significant photographic find so far has been to capture two nocturnal images of mountain lions, one at each site. This is an animal that wildlife officials will not admit is indigenous to Minnesota, insisting that any sightings of them are either mistaken identifications or rare occurrences of them straying into the state.

We have put up trail cameras just to see what was out there and with that minimal effort have captured two images of mountain lions in two spots about 30 miles apart. That seems to suggest that there must be a lot of them out there, and that alone feels like a significant discovery. It's a nice reminder that things the experts say are not there can be found to actually be. I'm not going to settle for it, though. Bigfoot is the end goal, the Chippewa National Forest is a boiling hotbed of activity, and the hunt will continue.

| A deer at the Talmoon site, and a bear at Six Mile Lake.

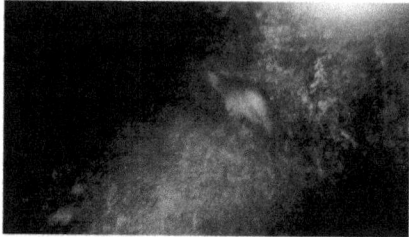

Mountain lions - Above: Six Mile Lake. Below: Talmoon.

4

PRAIRIE SASQUATCH
BIGFOOT IN UNEXPECTED PLACES

W hat constitutes a wilderness? I live in the metro area of Moorhead, Minnesota, and Fargo, North Dakota, where even though we are surrounded by concrete and steel and thousands of people, there are pockets of wildness and a functioning ecosystem where wild animals thrive, due largely to the fact that the two cities lie on opposite sides of the Red River of the North. Animals I've seen in town include deer, raccoon, beaver, fox, various birds of prey, and flocks of wild turkeys that often turn up in peoples' yards or in city streets like they don't have a care in the world.

There is such a deer population in the wooded areas along the river, in fact, that an annual urban hunting season (archery only, no guns) is allowed. Even large animals, like moose and bears have made appearances here.

I grew up in farm country in Minnesota, where there are small towns scattered here and there, with miles of flat open country in between taken up mostly by family farms with their vast croplands and pastures for livestock. Amidst this rural industrial region are sporadic small patches of woods and swamps as well as many lakes and streams where wildlife is abundant.

Many kids here and in other typical Midwestern rural areas grow up learning to hunt, fish, and trap within easy walking distance of where heavy machinery works fields that feed the nation. A couple of hours' drive north from farm country brings one to the heavily forested upper third of Minnesota, where the word "wilderness" really comes into play.

Here you are surrounded by green towering trees for as far as the eye can see, with the towns being fewer and farther between, but still with a system of roads that provides easy access for hunters, fishermen, or campers. Predators like bears, wolves, and mountain lions that only make rare freak appearances farther to the south are common here.

If one considers true wilderness to be an area that is so remote that you can trek through it for days without crossing a road or seeing any other sign of civilization, that too can be found in Minnesota up in the northeast Arrowhead region and Boundary Waters Canoe Area. You must truly be prepared for visiting such places, where any number of dangers can be encountered. When I first entered the Bigfoot field, it was only the second two of these four types of wilderness areas that I gave any serious consideration to when it came to searching for the creatures.

They are widely known as forest dwellers, needing remote country with plenty of cover in which to live out their lives mostly hidden from mankind. Imagine my surprise and confusion, then, when over time, I began to hear of Bigfoot reports that came from unforested areas where there was only sporadic cover and where farming and other industries were close by.

It seems to make no sense, but one thing I've learned about the creatures over the years is that they are full of surprises and will always challenge what you think you know about them. I received a letter from witness Guy N. about a sighting he and a friend had in October 1995 northeast of the town of Hawley in Clay County, which is only about a 20-minute drive from my home. The two men were duck hunting before noon in an area made up of grasslands, sporadic bogs and small groves of trees, and farmland, hardly an area where one would expect Bigfoot to turn up.

They suddenly saw a large black upright form at a distance of about four city blocks that they could tell was not a moose nor a bear, standing over six feet tall. It began to run, swinging its arms, traveling up a small hill and then down again, moving easily through thick high grass that the men would later find they had difficulty passing through. The creature then ran across a gravel road down which a car was coming, and the driver had to brake to a hard stop to avoid hitting it.

After the creature passed, the car drove slowly on, and Guy wrote that he studied the news that night and in the following days with an expectation that the driver would have reported what he'd seen, but there was no mention of it. Perhaps that should not have been so surprising since he and his friend didn't report what they'd seen at the time either. When I took a look at the sighting location, I was perplexed. It was so open, not what I would have called a wilderness area, and all I could think was that perhaps a Bigfoot making its way cross country would travel at night and bed down by day in whatever small grove it could find, and that the hunters might have flushed it out of its hiding place.

The site was on CRP (Conservation Reserve Program) land, part of a Department of Agriculture program in which farmers are reimbursed for taking areas of their land out of crop production and allowing it to exist in a more wild state to benefit the environment. I didn't doubt the report but wrote it off as an isolated incident.

In 2002, I had some media exposure in the Fargo area, being featured in a newspaper article and then appearing on a local radio show on which I was interviewed about the Bigfoot subject and mentioned the Hawley sighting. I received some new reports as a result, including an e-mail from a woman who wanted anonymity but had a story to pass on.

She wrote: "After reading your article in the Fargo Forum a few weeks ago, my husband told me he may have seen a Big Foot in Keene Township near Ulen, Minnesota, in 1995. He was deer hunting and saw what he at first thought was a huge man. The first thing he noticed about him was that he was not wearing any orange clothes, which is required by law. Then he thought it was way too big to be a man. Also his head didn't look right and his shoulders were too sloped.

He looked away from it for a minute, then looked back and it was gone. He never told anyone about this thinking nobody would believe him anyway. I would be really interested to know about the two duck hunters who saw a Bigfoot north of Hawley around this time." In a follow-up she wrote:

"He says he was about 50 yards away but it was at dusk. The site was just off hwy 33 about 4-5 miles north of 26. Just west of the gravel pit. There is a very big swamp there surrounded by a thick stand of trees."

Now I was intrigued because the town of Ulen is only about 14 miles north of Hawley. Typically duck season is in October and deer season in November, which would put these two sightings only a month apart. I had great trouble picturing the area as harboring a population of native Bigfoots and could only imagine that it must have been the same creature in both sightings, hanging around for whatever reason. But these reports were seven years old, the area in question was made up entirely of private land and so not a place where I could go and just hike around looking for evidence without permission, and so I had little choice but to regard it as a brief episode that had occurred maddeningly close to me but which I could do nothing about.

Large animals do occasionally go astray, I thought, and blunder through areas in which they do not belong. In my own childhood, there was a lone wolf that haunted the area around my family's farm for several months, an area where wolves were otherwise completely unknown. We saw it, we knew that it was there and that it was occasionally preying on livestock. One of our neighbors eventually trapped and shot it for its crimes. It's one of the most exciting stories from my youth and I recalled it as I thought about this apparent wayward Bigfoot that seemed to have briefly found itself in a place where it should not have been.

It wasn't very long afterward that the next bit of information in this episode came in, and I really wish I could pinpoint it on the time-line, but unfortunately, it became part of a massive loss of data that I had when an e-mail account I had had for many years fell victim to a hacking attack and hundreds of messages were permanently lost, leaving me with only my memory of the person who had e-mailed me about other possible Bigfoot activity in the same area as the previous reports.

He briefly described two incidents, the first of which was his own experience of hearing what he believed to be Bigfoot vocalizations in Buffalo River State Park. This park is located about seven miles west of Hawley, just off of U.S. Highway 10, a popular site with both tourists and local people for its hiking trails and swimming area. Like the rest of the region, it is not heavily forested, being primarily a grassland rich in history where plains Indians once made camp along the Buffalo River.

The second report my e-mailer had to relate was an actual sighting of a Bigfoot experienced by his brother-in-law, "who never lies," he assured me, that occurred at a place called Syre, which is not actually a town but just a spot on the map that lies seven miles north of Ulen at the intersection of Highways 39 and 113 and consists of just a few buildings, foremost among them a large grain elevator. My source reported that his brother-in-law had been driving and seen a Bigfoot in the middle of the intersection.

He did not go into much detail beyond that, but I'd been through Syre many times on my way to the much more sensible Bigfoot country up in heavily wooded Clearwater County, and the terrain is so wide open there that I just couldn't wrap my mind around why a Bigfoot would have been there.

The matter rested for a few years until it reared its head again in a powerful way. In June of 2009, an anonymous woman posted a Minnesota report to the BFRO website detailing a major sighting that had taken place on March 4th of that year. The location? Once again, it was near the little town of Ulen. I was amazed. Could a giant ape still be prowling around open farm country after 14 years? Might it only pass through the area occasionally along some kind of migration route? There were many questions, but the report was rich in detail.

The woman stated that her mother lived west of Ulen along the Wild Rice River and that large human-like footprints began appearing in the snow on the property in January of 2007, occurring about every two weeks and always moving from south to north. She still tended to be a doubter until just over two years later when she and her son were approaching the property in a vehicle at around midnight and suddenly saw a huge upright hairy creature standing in the middle of the road just past the driveway. They stopped about 200 feet from it and observed it for two to three minutes in their headlight beam, noting that it stood seven to eight feet tall, was covered in two-tone brown shaggy hair two to three inches long, and was built like a football player.

They did not get a clear look at its face because the lights illuminated it mainly from the chest down and because the whole time it seemed to be looking toward the river about 150 feet away rather than at their vehicle. The sighting ended when they continued on to the driveway and drove down it to the woman's mother's house. She stated that since the sighting, she had become resigned to the fact that such a creature really was in the area but felt no real fear since it had never done any harm.

A BFRO investigator listed as "Chris S." had looked into the report and stated that it seemed very credible to him. I e-mailed the BFRO to see if they might give me contact information for Chris S. but got no reply. I was not that surprised since the organization was somewhat known for not sharing information with non-members. That left me with only one option in how to respond to the report, which was to go to the area and simply drive around and try to pinpoint the site based on land features mentioned in the report. My partner Dean and I spent hours assessing the situation whenever we had spare time over what turned out to be a couple of years, zeroing in on a road just west of Ulen, along which there were a few rural homes and farms.

One of these, we thought, must be the place. I remember one property I came to call "the moose place" since it had a large moose silhouette cutout as a yard decoration, and that no matter how many times I knocked on their door no one ever answered it despite the large number of vehicles parked there that made it look like someone should have been home. An attempt at another home did result in a lady telling me that she had no knowledge of any Bigfoot sightings but that an elderly woman that had lived on a farm across the road from her had recently moved away into the city of Moorhead, so maybe she was the one. A letter to that woman surprised me by actually getting a nice, polite reply, but only to say that she had no knowledge of the matter either and that it sounded like nothing but sensationalism to her.

Dean and I could only shake our heads as we surveyed the open fields and pastures that surrounded the Wild Rice River, with the only sporadic groves of trees and bogs that dotted the area. Could a Bigfoot really live here for years without being seen more often? I wished so hard that I could just set out on foot and explore the area freely as if it was a state forest, but it wasn't. I came to a reluctant resignation that I might have to let this one go unless something new happened. It was a minor thorn in my side -- why drive for hours up to northern Minnesota to look for Bigfoot if there might be one less than an hour from my home?

It was actually as late as August 2015 when I had a random thought about trying a new approach. In the town of Ulen -- population less than 550 -- there is a small museum that today is simply called the "Ulen Museum" but was, until recently, called the "Viking Sword Museum." Seeing the sign with that name and being a lover of martial arts and ancient weapons of all kinds, I remember being bemused at my first visit to the place, not seeing it full of Viking swords as the name implied but instead being a typical collection of rural artifacts from the history of the region.

It turned out that it once hosted a single old sword that a farmer had unearthed while plowing a field in the area in 1911 that was thought for years to be of Viking origin but was eventually revealed to probably be from the 19th century and probably French in its design. The wishful thinking is understandable with Minnesota's heavily Norwegian influences, the Kensington Runestone and so forth, and after all, our NFL football team is called The Vikings.

But anyway, in that late summer of 2015, in between other Bigfoot forays, it occurred to me to pay a visit to that museum and ask the staff if they knew anything about these Bigfoot reports. I know, I should have thought of it much sooner.

Two older men were working at the museum the day I visited, and they smiled a bit when I told them what I was after. They recalled a local man coming in and asking about the Bigfoot subject not long before, and they gave me his name, but they were so amused by the whole thing that they didn't recall the exact nature of his questions and thought he might just have been joking. I thanked them for that information, but I also showed them the BFRO report and asked if they might be of any help in narrowing it down any farther. Thankfully, they were.

They told me to explore the museum (which they let me do for free) while they made some phone calls and asked some sources about the description of the land given in the report, and before long they had a good lead for me. The report described small gravel pits that were near the river, and they had come up with a spot that matched that description even more than the one Dean and I had previously explored. It was another couple of miles to the west, another gravel road with a few homes alongside it.

With new information to go on, I began by contacting the man they had told me about. His name was Earl W., and after I wrote to him, he promptly called me. He was an elderly widower and said that after his wife had passed away, he had tried to occupy the space in his life by getting out more, driving around and socializing, and in so doing, he'd seen something called a "flood apron" on a local bridge spray-painted with graffiti reading "Beware of River Bigfoot" two miles west of Ulen.

It was that that had compelled him to ask about the subject at the museum, together with the fact that it was generally known as gossip in the area that a local woman claimed to have seen Bigfoot. He wouldn't give me her name because he said he didn't want to get involved in the whole thing, and he seemed to be a disbeliever, but he said that if I kept looking around I shouldn't have much trouble finding her. He said he felt like the whole thing was in "another dimension" and implied that he thought the woman was crazy.

Dean and I cruised the new road that the museum had provided, and upon seeing gravel pits next to the river, we were almost certain we'd found the right spot after so much time. It was a rather ramshackle looking place with a trailer house and a few outbuildings at the end of a fenced off driveway. Amazingly, as we drove by, we happened to see a llama -- A LLAMA! -- come walking through the trees down to the riverside.

This promised to be a fascinating inquiry if nothing else. I decided to write down the fire number for the property and use it to find the owner's name online rather than just knocking on the door blind, and when I contacted her she was surprisingly accommodating. After all this time, I had it. This was the place. Sometimes this is how Bigfoot reports are sniffed out.

You have to be a bloodhound.

Joanne S. lived alone on the property, but I gathered she had frequent visits from her friends and relatives. She was probably in her 70s, yet when I pulled into her driveway, she was out doing some gardening wearing shorts and a sports bra with a pack of cigarettes tucked into one of the straps, not your typical grandmotherly type.

There were animals everywhere. Dogs, cats, birds -- and yes, the llama, just roaming around. Joanne seemed pleased that someone new was interested in her story, and she was completely forthcoming with me. There was much more to it than her daughter had posted to the BFRO, and I could tell that she was not crazy.

Eccentric, yes, but not crazy. Joanne confirmed that it was her daughter that had posted the report to the BFRO site, but also said that that sighting, along with the earlier tracks in the snow, were hardly the extent of the Bigfoot activity that had occurred on her property.

The first actual creature sighting had occurred on an evening in the late fall of 2008 when a grandson and nephew of hers saw what came to be called a "teenage" Bigfoot standing 5 1/2 feet tall with dark brown hair walking through her yard. Joanne herself also saw this smaller creature shortly thereafter, running across the yard and driveway.

Tracks also appeared at least twice during that period, five-toed and very large. Instead of estimating the number of inches long the tracks were, Joanne said they made a size 14 shoe look small, and that they crossed a small fence without breaking stride, an occurrence that has often been described for Bigfoot tracks.

Joanne S. points to the spot where her daughter and grandson saw a Bigfoot in their headlights.

The Wild Rice River below the road shown in the above photo.

The ravine behind Joanne's home where the creatures fed on discarded squash rinds.

Joanne indicates the spot where she saw the smaller of the two creatures run across her yard.

There was a small ravine behind Joanne's trailer house in which she sometimes disposed of perishable rubbish and twice there were occurrences of squash rinds being fed on there with blatant Bigfoot tracks everywhere. She also sometimes heard a distant whooping call in the evenings that started out low but then rose in pitch, and finally, a neighbor to the south had a manmade pond that had been stocked with fish that all mysteriously disappeared. These were the events that preceded her daughter's major sighting in 2009.

Joanne had her own version of what occurred that night, some details of which differed from her daughter's. They were the kind of inconsistencies that just kind of make me scratch my head rather than the kind that makes me doubt the veracity of the report. The daughter had described the creature as having brown hair, the sighting taking place around midnight, and said that she and her son felt no fear since the creature did not act aggressively.

Joanne, on the other hand, said that her daughter and grandson had come into her trailer beside themselves with fear and urging her not to go out to get a look at the creature herself because it was so big that they said it had silver hair and that the time was somewhere between 6 and 8 PM. I have no explanation for these differences, but I was struck by one further detail Joanne gave.

She said that as the sighting happened in the early spring, the melting snows had the river in severe flood stage, and she thought that the way the creature kept looking toward the river even though headlights were shining on it meant that it was looking for its child --

the smaller "teenage" creature that had been seen -- afraid for its safety during the flood. It's a nice motherly image to ponder.

Joanne gave me permission to explore her property, but she cautioned me that a huge bear had been seen in the area recently, so I should be on guard. A lot of animals not normally considered native to the area showed up around her place, she said, and a Department of Natural Resources spokesman had told her that she lived along "a very active river bottom."

I explored it extensively, finding probably the densest concentration of what are commonly called "pricker bushes" I've ever seen that leave bundles of tiny thorns stuck to your socks and pant legs, but no Bigfoot evidence turned up. It had been six years after all, and the creatures seemed to have moved on. As I was preparing to leave, I saw the llama sitting down nearby, watching me.

I know very little about llamas. Do they have a mean streak, do they ever trample people? I spoke nicely to the animal as I made my exit, and it didn't interfere with my departure. About half a year later, in early 2016, I had yet another addition to this saga happen in about the most unexpected way I could have imagined. In my community, there are facilities where one can go to donate blood plasma in exchange for money, which is something I have been doing for many years.

You lie back for an hour or so with a needle in your arm and then you get not only some extra spending money but also the satisfaction of helping people. On one particular day when I was donating, a young woman on the bed next to me suddenly spoke to me, asking, "Excuse me, are you a Bigfoot researcher?" I was very taken aback, but when I answered yes, she said she recognized me from some website I had been featured on and that she had a story to share with me.

I guess I got a taste of what it's like to be a celebrity, which is something I've never considered myself, but the story she shared captured my attention. She said that a friend of hers named Tracy S. had had a Bigfoot sighting about two years earlier in Buffalo River State Park while doing a nighttime photography project there.

She'd heard some strange noises, and when she'd moved closer to try and identify the source, she'd seen a Bigfoot fighting with either a wolf or a coyote.

Tracy's friend had no further information on which creature won the fight, what the Bigfoot looked like or anything else, but I thanked her for the information and followed up on it later by tracking down Tracy's Facebook page and sending her an inquiry.

She had many wildlife photos posted on her page, which went along with her friend's story, but as is so typical in trying to seek out Bigfoot witnesses, she never responded to me. That was a shame, since the incident sounded terribly dramatic and deserved to be expanded upon. Naturally, since Buffalo River State Park is so close to my home, I took a drive out there as soon as I had time, in the month of March, remembering my earlier online tipster from years before that had claimed to have heard Bigfoot noises there.

The park is technically open year - round but only in the summer months can you count on finding staff there, and on the day of my visit it was virtually empty of people. I parked my car and set out to walk the trails. And I almost hate to have to report what happened next, but after only a couple of minutes of walking uphill from the parking area, I found what looked for all the world like a barefoot human-like footprint in the black dirt of a gopher mound surrounded by tall grass. It was about 12" long and showed two clear toes with the rest indistinct.

No, I thought, please tell me I am not seeing this. This was ridiculous! I crouched down and stared at it for a long time, trying to convince myself that it wasn't really a footprint, but I couldn't do it. I really had found a possible Bigfoot track where there absolutely should not have been one, and with barely any effort at all. This was wide open grassland a stone's throw from the parking lot and swimming area, with the tree cover that follows the river probably another ten minutes' walk away.

Even if the time of year explained why a creature would venture this close to the developed area, why in the world would it step on the one spot in all that grass where it would leave a footprint? I walked on, hiking the trails that followed the river but did not find any further evidence. Before I left the park, I decided to make a plaster cast of the track, and not having time to wait for the plaster to dry, I came back a day or two later to retrieve it, but when I tried to lift the cast out of the ground, it crumbled and broke into three pieces.

I still have those pieces, they do not look all that impressive, and I do not expect anyone to believe that they represent a Bigfoot track, nor do I fully accept it myself. I came back to Buffalo River State Park that summer when it was officially open and filled with people, mainly so that I could question someone about the sighting. When I approached the ranger on duty in the park headquarters, something very curious happened. As soon as he heard the word "Bigfoot," he threw up his hands and said, "Whoa, DNR can't comment on that!"

I tried to gently press him a bit more, and he said that he had worked in the park for years without ever hearing anything about such things, but his initial reaction surprised me. I had talked with wildlife officials in Minnesota plenty of times before, and they had never been shy about giving their opinions whether pro or con, but never before had I heard one imply that he was not allowed to comment.

A place called the Minnesota State University Moorhead Regional Science Center lies a few minutes drive from the park headquarters but is not actually part of the park, although hiking the trails will bring you right to it. It's a site that hosts a lot of field trips for school kids and boy scouts, teaching them about the environment. I thought I should try and ask about the sighting there as well, but the only new tidbit of information I was given was that if someone was out taking photos at night, it might have been at one of the star parties they host there.

I didn't think that seemed likely since the witness, Tracy S., clearly seemed interested in wildlife rather than in astronomy. I made one more visit to Buffalo River a few months later in the fall to try and hike the full extent of the park's trail system and did a good job of wearing out my feet that day. I found no further Bigfoot evidence, but I did make one dramatic and rather disturbing discovery.

In a remote section far back from the headquarters and swimming areas, I suddenly came across a trail camera attached to a post a few feet away from the carcass of a deer that looked like it had been torn apart by a tiger, bloody ribs protruding from its mangled flesh. I could not tell whether this was a natural kill or whether the deer had been torn open by humans to use as bait, but it seemed instantly clear that the park staff seemed to think there was a predator in the area and they were trying to get pictures of it. I looked nervously over my shoulder as I made my way back to where my car was parked.

I am left perplexed about how and why Bigfoot might show up in open country where it seems absurd that they should be found, but after studying these cases, I do have a theory. It lies in the comment that Joanne had made about the "very active river bottom" she lived in. The Wild Rice and Buffalo Rivers wind their way through this area, rich water sources that cause thick tree cover to spring up all along their length. It's a little odd as you drive across the prairie and from miles away, you can see those thin lines of trees snaking their way across the land, marking where the rivers are.

After much contemplation, I now believe that Bigfoot sometimes follows these rivers, taking advantage of the food sources they provide and thus appearing sporadically in farm country where they would ordinarily never be found. I think that this activity is so hit and miss that attempting an expedition along those rivers would be all but pointless, so I can only hope that another episode happens in this region so close to where I live and that I'm able to hear about it while it is still going on.

A search of my files reveals one final report from this area, and on the timeline, it is actually the first. Larae J. e-mailed me after my media exposure in 2002 and related the following: "When I was a little girl, I lived with my grandparents on a farm northwest of Hawley about 10 miles and I remember my grandfather coming in one morning after chores and talking about these huge footprints in the snow. I would say this was in the late 60s, and he was very concerned because the footprints were very large. I was too chicken to even go outside and look at the time, but wish now I had."

Indeed.

I have one more story to share in this chapter, a series of events that leads me to wonder if not only rivers but also lakes might be an important factor in where Bigfoot can appear, and for me personally, it is the most unsettling of all because it takes place in the very area where I grew up during the first two decades of my life. It also features sightings of an upright creature that is Bigfoot-like but with differences that make it extra strange.

Detroit Lakes is a city of between eight and nine thousand people lying about 35 miles east as the crow flies from the center of the activity so far described here, a tourist city whose population grows much larger in the summer months when people converge there to enjoy the large number of lakes in the area. The Fourth of July is an especially festive time there, as many thousands of people gather to frolic on the beaches and watch fireworks.

While growing up on my family's farm I went to school in a little town called Audubon, a few miles to the west along Highway 10, but it was to Detroit Lakes (or simply "D.L." as it is often called) where everyone went to shop and have fun.

It is farm and lake country, not heavily forested at all but with sporadic small patches of woods, just as in the Hawley-Ulen area. Perhaps I should not have been so surprised to find Bigfoot activity there since the first such case I ever investigated was the legend of the Vergas Trails Hairy Man about a dozen miles to the south, and my own childhood sighting of a Bigfoot had occurred at Strawberry Lake around 20 miles to the north.

The vast forests of northern Minnesota begin only a short drive northeast of Detroit Lakes, but to find creature sightings within the actual city limits was something I was not prepared for at all. In the fall of 2015, I received an e-mail from a young man whose family lived in the Richwood area, which lies midway between Detroit Lakes and Strawberry Lake, informing me that they had had several encounters with Bigfoot-like creatures over several years and wanted to share their story.

Dean and I went and met with the man and his mother at a little eatery in Detroit Lakes, and it was a rather noteworthy occasion as it happened to be the first time that Dean had ever met with witnesses and heard their stories face to face, something I had done many times. They wanted to remain anonymous, so for the purpose of telling their story, I will simply refer to them as John and Mary (nowhere near their real names).

Mary said that in the summer of 2009, a female friend of hers had been driving at night along Willow Street in south Detroit Lakes, where it passes through an area that has a baseball field nearby and also a large industrial water treatment plant right along the street but which is an otherwise undeveloped area dominated by woods on one side of the road and a huge marsh on the other. Suddenly the woman saw an upright hairy figure about six feet tall come out of the woods in front of her car and cross to the marsh side, a hunched over creature that moved in a very gangly manner and had two extremely prominent hooked claws protruding from each hand and foot.

As it reached the far side of the road, perhaps frightened by the approaching car, it leaped up on to a highline pole at the roadside and used its claws to cling to it. In the fall of 2012, Mary related that a second night time sighting of this bizarre clawed creature had been had by her second husband, who she was no longer with by the time she related the story to us in 2015. It had occurred in nearly the identical spot as the first on Willow Street near the water treatment plant, and this time the creature was either chasing or running along with a small herd of deer crossing from the woods into the marsh.

I didn't quite know what to make of these stories. These two sightings took place over three years in a heavily populated area within city limits, with many homes lying along the edges of the woods and marshland in question. If true, it brought to mind images of the thing prowling through peoples' back yards at night rummaging through their garbage cans, a large bear-sized mammal living within a town and being only very rarely seen.

Was it really possible?

Then of course, was the fact that its description was so different from that of a typical Bigfoot. Those two huge hooked claws sticking out of both hands and both feet were, of course, unprecedented and made me think that I might have stumbled upon a cryptozoological mystery never heard of before, even more different than the creatures detected up in Clearwater County in the early 90s by Ed Trimble.

Those I had viewed as a subspecies of Bigfoot, but this weird clawed thing struck me as being similar to only one other animal -- a sloth. Sloths are a Central and South American species of mammal with either two or three toes on each foot sporting large hooked claws but measuring no more than three feet long in size, known for living their lives clinging to high tree branches and being among the most slow-moving of all animals, but in prehistoric times they had a much larger ancestor, the giant ground sloth or Megatherium that was much more robust and active and rivaled modern elephants in size.

Modern sloths are gangly and quadrupedal and can barely move about when they find themselves on the ground, whereas their giant ancestors did so easily and could even stand upright.

Now I was being presented with a story that wanted me to believe that something resembling a miniature Megatherium was seen in the town where I had spent some of my best treasured memories partying as a teenager, something that really played games with my head. It didn't sound like a Bigfoot, but something else.

John and his mother Mary, though, neither of whom had seen the sloth creature themselves, also had other stories from the Richwood area where they actually lived that did sound like descriptions of a traditional Bigfoot. This area is sporadic farms, lakes, and small patches of woods that is populated by upwards of 600 people and isn't what I consider to be a true wilderness, but nevertheless the family's stories sounded impressive as John took Dean and I on a tour of where the various events had happened over the years.

There was a farmstead where John and Mary had lived back in the early 2000s, still owned by the family but vacant now, that lay nestled up against a section of woods. In August or September of 2003, when John was only 13 years old, there was a night when they were awakened by the sound of their dog barking frantically. The animal was tied to a tree just outside the house, and when they looked outside, they were stunned to see a massive form standing behind a larger tree about 30 feet away, an upright creature about eight feet tall covered in dark brown or black hair and with large orange glowing eyes, staring at the panicking dog.

They had the instant impression that the beast wanted to kill their pet, but Mary was too afraid to go outside which left John to display very admirable courage in going out to untie the dog and bring it into the house to safety.

The next site John showed us was his grandmother's house a few miles away, which was also up against a wooded area and had been the scene of several possibly Bigfoot related events, most of which were of the ambiguous type, such as wood knocking being heard in the woods.

But another major sighting had occurred there in June of either 2010 or 2011 (it's sometimes odd how witnesses are only approximate on the dates of such significant events, but so goes the human mind). It involved John's sister, who was, even more, intent on remaining anonymous and declined to meet with us to tell the story herself, so let's call her Beth (again, nowhere near her real name).

On a summer evening near dusk, Beth was standing on the deck of her grandmother's house engaged in an argument with her boyfriend over the phone when she thought she glimpsed a seven to eight-foot dark, hulking figure with glowing orange eyes standing next to a highline pole along the nearby paved road, but in another example of the peculiar ways in which peoples' minds can work she turned away from it and continued with her conversation, assuming she'd just seen some kind of optical illusion. About two minutes later, however, she saw the creature again in a way she could not deny, standing just a few yards across the yard from her with its back to the woods, staring at her.

At that point, she screamed and ran into the house to frantically report to her family members what she'd just seen, and someone with a rifle came outside to look around, but by that time, the creature had disappeared. Beth's grandmother, though she lived at this location that Bigfoot activity revolved around, was a disbeliever and openly laughed at the story, which was traumatic to Beth and a big reason why she didn't want to talk to outsiders about the sighting. Believers within the family, though, especially John and Mary, felt that it was likely the same creature they'd seen seven or eight years earlier that had seemed to want to make a snack out of their dog.

The size and the glowing orange eyes in both sightings seem to support that theory. The color orange is not common in reports of animal eyeshine, and even among Bigfoots, their eyes are usually reported to glow red at night, as do those of many nocturnal animals, whereas animals that usually function during the day, show blue eyeshine when seen at night.

Orange is an anomaly, not completely unknown but very rare. On July 4th, 2014, only a year or so before making the activity known to us, the family was gathered at the grandmother's house celebrating the Independence Day holiday when John ignited some firecrackers out in the back yard at about 8 PM. In the Midwest, in the summer, this time of evening is well before dark, but in a sinister occurrence as if in response to the loud noise a tree a short distance into the woods from the yard was suddenly seen to start violently shaking back and forth.

Then in the late summer of 2015, just a few weeks before Dean and I were contacted, a flock of over 20 chickens on the same property that were kept in a shed at night but which were allowed to free-range during the day fell under attack by some unseen predator and were reduced to only two birds, simply disappearing with no blood or feathers ever being found.

It could be speculated that this suggests something making off with them, not with teeth, but with hands. This was the last incident made known to us in the Detroit Lakes-Richwood episode.

These incidents occurring both in areas where Bigfoot would not normally be expected to appear and also in close proximity to my own childhood sighting have really thrown me for a loop.

It makes it seem as if the creatures are so full of surprises that they might appear just about anywhere. I truly don't know what to do with that information, and these reports are so few and sporadic that

I continue to focus my searches on areas where the wilderness is much more extensive and the reports far more frequent.

As a final anecdote, a year after hearing about the bizarre creature that I will forever refer to as "the sloth," on a summer day in 2016, I parked my car at the baseball field that's near to where those sightings occurred along Willow Street in Detroit Lakes and walked to the location, where I had to ignore the curious stares of passing motorists who must have wondered what I was doing there as I penetrated the woods and explored what was purported to be the creature's lair.

It was probably less than a quarter-mile long and narrow enough that one could have easily fired an arrow through it, and I explored it thoroughly, often looking up to the high treetops to see if I might catch sight of something large nesting up there. But there were no signs of anything unusual, and it seemed hard to believe that something like what had been described could have possibly lived there for so long without being seen far more often.

The marsh across the street was much larger but consisted of a wet bog that would have required special gear to search. I had to just walk away, scratching my head, forever wondering. I know of no similar creatures ever seen in Minnesota or anywhere else.

"John and Mary's" home near Richwood and the large tree where a Bigfoot menaced their dog.

"John" indicates the height of the Bigfoot where it stood beside the tree.

Backyard area at "John's" grandmother's home near Richwood where various Bigfoot activity occurred.

West Willow Street just outside Detroit Lakes, where the "Sloth" crossed the road.

Two shots inside the woods from which the "Sloth" emerged.

Two shots inside the woods from which the "Sloth" emerged.

As the last word for this chapter, we return to the general region of Joanne's story from earlier. The photo above was taken at the end of a farm's driveway along Highway 113 approximately ten miles northeast of Ulen and straight east of the tiny community of Syre. This Bigfoot cutout with eerie glowing eyes added to it stands there to welcome passersby. Is there a story behind it? Might the people living there have had yet another encounter with an out of place Bigfoot in wide-open farm country, or is the figure just placed there for a laugh

A letter I wrote to them went unanswered, so we may never know.

5

RED LAKE
DRAMATIC OMENS

O f all the bodies of water in the Land of 10,000 Lakes, Minnesota's largest is made up of Upper and Lower Red Lakes just outside of what I consider to be the northwest corner of the state in Beltrami County. Both are roughly oval-shaped and are connected in a fashion that forms a long and narrow peninsula between them, their total area encompassing 440 square miles, collectively the 16th largest lake in the United States. I have stood on the eastern shore of Upper Red Lake and marveled at how the north and south shores extend to the horizon and then just disappear, the west shore being beyond the range of sight.

Surrounding this double lake is the Red Lake Indian Reservation, which is a fascinating and complex place for many reasons. It actually lies not on one solid block of land but in a very sporadically fractured series of properties in nine separate counties, but the largest and most populated are those around the lakes themselves.

In the 1930s, there was an effort by the seven different bands of Chippewa in Minnesota to consolidate under the title of the Minnesota Chippewa Tribe. The Red Lake band was the only one that declined, choosing instead to retain their complete independence and aboriginal rights as their reservation lay on their original homeland rather than on the land they were placed on by the U.S. government.

As such, they became the only "closed" reservation in the state, with no private property but all land owned collectively by the tribe. They are the very definition of a tight-knit community, though they do operate the Seven Clans Casino in the town of Red Lake (population around 1,700) on the south shore of Lower Red Lake, in the same way that many Native communities nationwide have hosted such gambling palaces since the 1980s.

For me personally, I wish that land regulations allowed for a freer exploration of the area by non-residents because by all accounts, the Red Lake Reservation appears to be an absolute gold mine of Bigfoot activity. As in many Native communities, there seems to be a mixture of how the creatures are viewed there among the people.

Some take it in stride as a natural and even spiritual thing, but others view it with fear. A shocking series of events began there in 2005 that made local and even national news, with Bigfoot being a bizarre footnote to the stories. On the night of February 6, 2005, a trackway of over a hundred five-toed footprints measuring 17" long and 6" wide appeared in the snow within the town of Red Lake.

They came out of a swampy area, passed through the back yards of several homes, and also crossed a fence to enter the schoolyard of the local elementary school. Sounds like a woman screaming were reportedly heard coming from the swamp as well as dogs barking wildly at around two AM The incident was reported in the media on February 10th complete, with photographs but its inclusion on the BFRO website places its actual occurrence on the 6th.

This appearance of Bigfoot inside city limits was disturbing to the people, who nervously wondered if it might be an omen of bad tidings to come. The fact that the tracks crossed a schoolyard where little children played must have given extra cause for concern.

Several months before this incident, a local teen, 16-year-old Jeffrey James Weise was writing about Bigfoot online. Well known cryptozoologist Loren Coleman related on his Cryptomundo website some of Jeff's musings, including the following post to the "Above Top Secret" forum on June 11, 2004: "Almost everyone I know has a sasquatch story, almost everyone has a person in their family who's probably seen him. At least that's how it is where I live, (on a Reservation in Minnesota). I've asked a few elders about bigfoot, and in my language (Ojibwe), we have a name for him.

I forgot it and barely could pronounce it, but he exists in our neck of the woods, at least I believe he does. I heard a story from my cousin (he works in Tribal Government), he told me that a guy he worked with was out in the forest alone on a fast. He was near a swampy area, and midway through his fast he saw Bigfoot walking through the swamp, reaching down into the water along the way and pulling up a certain type of weed and slinging it over his shoulder. The weed from the swamp he was pulling out was supposedly some kind of herbal medicine used by Native medicine men.

And to feed some of you peoples interest in the possibility of a sasquatch and alien connection? The lake I live by (Red Lake) is one heck of a big lake, and if you sit out at the beach on a clear summer night, you'll see lights over the lake. Everyone says they're UFOs, I believe that too. There was a UFO sighting in broad daylight a few years back, it was over the lake, people said it looked like a metal disc. Anyway, a lot of people were reporting power outages and cars stalling on them around the exact same time. I love living in this lively place."

Jeff seemed enthralled by the tales of Bigfoot that he grew up with. However, there were obviously much darker thoughts in his young mind that had a greater influence over him, for on March 21, 2005 -- 43 days after the appearance of the ominous tracks -- he perpetrated the Red Lake school shooting, one of the worst such crimes up to that time with ten lives lost, including his own and 15 other people wounded.

No one can ever make sense out of such a horrible tragedy, and whatever prompted Jeff Weise to commit it will forever remain a dark secret that he took with him to his grave. In the aftermath, the tight-knit Red Lake community was forced to open up to the veritable invasion of law enforcement, including the FBI that descended upon them in their time of mourning.

In the midst of it all, though, there were some who wondered if the occurrence of the Bigfoot tracks not long before had been a portent of this. The fact that they had crossed a schoolyard in the same town (though not at the same school where the shooting happened) seemed especially ominous. And it was not to be the only tragedy that befell the reservation during the next several months.

Later in 2005, a hunter was lost in the wilderness above Upper Red Lake and was missing for some time. The dog he had had with him was found alive and well, but some articles of his clothing were also located. This is a common occurrence in people who are slowly freezing to death from hypothermia, a psychosis that oddly makes them begin to shed their clothes rather than trying to do whatever they can to get warmer. The hunter's body was eventually found, a casualty of the Minnesota winter.

The next sad and fatal event came a year later when two little boys, brothers just two and four years old, disappeared just before Thanksgiving on November 22, 2006, while outside playing in front of their home. Their family believed they had been abducted, and a widespread search was launched, the case even appearing on the FOX tv show "America's Most Wanted." Just over four months later, however, the family's hopes of finding the boys alive were dashed when on April 1, 2007, their bodies were found in thawing ice on First Thunders Lake only about a half-mile from their home.

Apparently, they had wandered away while playing and fallen through thin ice. What do any of these sad misfortunes have to do with Bigfoot? Nothing on the surface it would seem, but the importance of omens is often significant in Native American culture. Sometimes the appearance of the creatures is seen as a teaching moment of great spiritual weight, but at other times it is met with fear and as a harbinger of tragedy. The Bigfoot tracks found at Red Lake were taken in the latter sense and in the sadness that gripped the community in the wake of all that came next, one can hardly blame them.

I had had an experience north of Upper Red Lake in the Beltrami Island State Forest a couple of years before this great drama played out that ended up going down as one of my most perilous adventures in all my years of Bigfooting. This is a very wild area containing the twin forks of the Rapid River, well removed from the main bulk of the reservation but where scattered areas of reservation, land are peppered here and there, mostly open to any and all activities by sportsmen but with sporadic road signs warning of where one is asked to keep out.

Despite it being one of my best stories, I have never told it in print before because it is so deeply personal to me in some of its details, but I will do so now. In October 2002 I was contacted by a Bigfoot witness named Larry G. from the town of Baudette up along the Canadian border who wanted to tell me about his experiences in the Beltrami Island State Forest in the mid-1970s. He visited me at my home in Moorhead where I recorded the following interview with him:

LARRY G: My name is Larry (G), and right now I'm 55, and back in 1974, I took my son- he was four years old- we went out on the Bankton Trail, and it was in the fall, late fall, there was no mosquitos and the leaves were pretty much down, and we went camping in kind of a sand ridge with Norway pines planted to the right side, and it was... down at the end of the sand ridge was kind of a crick, and just swamp grass and stuff like that. And just brush.

And on the left side was jack pine. We came down the ridge, beautiful evening, had a little fire, a little A-frame tent, and I'd been in Vietnam, so I was used to the night sounds and stuff like that. So we went to bed about ten, ten-thirty, and chit-chatted there for a while, and I was just dozing off going to sleep, listening to the night sounds, little crickets, and stuff or whatever -- and waaaay out on the crick end of things I heard a high-pitched screech that was almost so faint I couldn't hear it, but I heard something. And then I heard it again, and again, and by now, I was wide awake and listening to these intervals, and they were almost timed... ah, scream.

And you could just set your watch by it, it would be a high-pitched scream. And I thought, "What could be making that noise?" And I thought of a screech owl or an eagle, but they don't fly at night. And I thought, well maybe a bull moose in rut. But they beller, different bugle. And I heard it again, and I heard it again- (Imitated scream) -- like that. And it got louder and louder, and all of a sudden, I could hear brush breaking and snapping.

And I cocked my .357 Magnum pistol. And it came into the field, just thundering down the field -- Thump, thump, thump, thump, thump. And another scream. And I had one hand over my boy's head, and I just said, "Don't wake up, don't wake up," and I had my pistol cocked, and I thought I'm gonna get one shot off, whatever this is if it touches the tent.

Anyway, and by the tent, and into the Norway pines, I could hear all these branches snapping -- snap snap snap snap snap.

MIKE QUAST: About how close to the tent do you think it came?

LG: Probably about ten... yeah, it was about ten or twelve feet from the tent. The tent was still there the next morning. About ten or twelve feet from it. Went right by it. And I wish to this day, I'd taken my knife and cut the tent open, took a look-see. I didn't. And another scream, and another scream, and another scream, and fainter and fainter and fainter and fainter, I thought, "What in the world was that?" I had no dealings with Bigfoot before, ever.

Just kind of heard about him. So next— I didn't sleep a wink that night. Next morning, I got up, I got my son up before sunrise. We got into the car, drove to town. I dropped him off at his mom, I went and got my brother, we loaded up to the max with rifles and pistols and came back, and here were these huge footprints. My brother's got a size 13 boot, and he actually put his boot in the print, and it was three or four inches longer than his boot and a couple inches wider than his boot.

MQ: About 14 inches long, you said?

LG: Probably 14 or 15 inches. Or 16, somewhere in there. It was big.

And it was heavy. Like, we stomped twice into the ground, and we couldn't make the depth that that footprint made.

MQ: Could you make out the toe prints?

LG: Yup. You could make it. And it had an arch in the foot -- Perfect prints, all the way -- you could stand right at the tent and see it all the way down the field, the right-left, right-left, right-left.

MQ: Five toes?

LG: Five toes. You couldn't run- it was a perfect human footprint. And you couldn't run and jump from one to the next print. We jumped, and we jumped, and we jumped, and we jumped, and we jumped. And in the Norways, the branches were freshly broke at eight feet high, going through there, the Norway branches. Didn't take any plaster cast, didn't take any pictures, just followed it from where it came out of the crick to back in the Norways there, then we lost it. And we didn't go any farther.

And two years later, my second wife and I were canoeing down the Rapid River- and that's a little further south from where we were, we were on the Bankton Trail, the first time - two years later... it was in the spring, the water was high, it was runoff, and there was no leaves on the trees, we came to this clearing, and there was a cabin there, we had two canoes, there was four of us.

And we parked our canoes, looked around, I went to the back of the cabin, and all of a sudden here was that footprint again. And the grass was going bing, bing, bing, coming up. And I drew my pistol and started scanning the area. Doug (H) came around the corner and he goes, "What's going on?" and I says - I didn't say a word, I just pointed. He goes, "Wow, look at that footprint." And he goes, "And there's another one, and another one." And Henry, he come around the corner of the building, and he said "Don't shoot" and he ran after the footprints.

MQ: You didn't hear anything or smell anything?

LG: Didn't smell anything, didn't hear anything, no. No. So I figured he was standing there watching us, and then ran off.

MQ: Heard you coming, probably.

LG: Yup, probably heard us coming, and he was there. And then in 19 -- that was -- we got in the canoe and we paddled out of there. We got out of there in a hurry.

MQ: Is that cabin used by anybody, or is it-?

LG: Nope, the roof is gone on it.

MQ: It's just ruins?

LG: It's just ruins. Yup.

MQ: Ok.

LG: It's just part of an old, old, old, old logging- either logging or homestead. The whole area's been logged off.

MQ: Do you know if it would even still be there at all now?

LG: Oh, it's still there.

MQ: Ok.

LG: It's still there. I could take you there.

MQ: Mm-hmm.

LG: Yeah. So that winter, in January, Doug (H) and Henry and I decided we're gonna find that cabin, and go look for these footprints in the winter. Cause you can't hide your footprints in the winter.

MQ: Mm-hmm.

LG: So, I think it was January 1st... it was about zero out, and lots of snow. We took off and we drove as far as we could drive, and then we were gonna walk into that cabin. We got about halfway to the cabin, and we spent the night. And during the night, Doug (H) said he heard a scream -- that was so hideous, that he said whatever's out there I don't wanna know, and I don't wanna see, and I'm not going any farther. He's the rough-and-tumble guy that I would'a said would'a not chickened out.

And Henry, he was... he didn't believe in guns, he was an anti-nuke demonstrator in Minneapolis, and ah, kind of a peace and love guy... and he and I were gonna continue on. And I said Henry, you take Doug's gun. Pistol. He says, well, I don't want the pistol. I says, well, take the pistol anyway and wear it. He said, I don't want the pistol! I said, we'll take his pistol and just come along, we'll just go and we'll have two guns. And he didn't want to take it, and he wondered why he should have it. And I says, well, if something's chewing on me, you could be shooting it rather than taking pictures of it. (Laughter.) So he took the gun. But he didn't know how to use it anyway. So the next day we found that cabin.

And there was an animal trail between two cedar swamps, and animals always run the same trail, everything runs on one trail 'cause all the snow is packed down. So I says, let's sleep off to the side of the trail and we'll see what comes down it at night. He said, no, let's sleep in the middle of it. I said, no, let's sleep on the side of it.

And finally... because if there's a pack of wolves chasing a herd of deer, they're gonna come barreling down that trail, and we're gonna be the leftovers, and the wolves are gonna chew on us, so...

MQ: (Laughter)

LG: Ah, we slept in the middle of the trail, and I didn't sleep all night. That was really bad. The next day we looked in the cedar swamps and looked and looked and looked and could not find any tracks anywhere. And finally, we decided that Bigfoot must hibernate in the wintertime. That was the conclusion. Two years later, in 1978, my brother and I were deer hunting between Bankton Trail and Rapid River Trail, and my brother was on a ditch grade out in black spruce-- a big, big black spruce forest-- and he's walking a ditch grade, and all of a sudden, he saw these huge footprints. Now, granted when you step in slush, a print'll almost half double in size.

MQ: Mm-hmm.

LG: You know, it just does that. And he said these were heel and toe, five toes, just looked like somebody took their boot off, and was walking barefoot. And he said there was one huge slush-- perfect print, in the ice, and he said across on the other side was another one. Perfect print. And it was crossing at an angle. And he said when he saw those two footprints, he lost it. He didn't know where he was at. He had it all together up until then. And all he knew was he wanted out of there. And he shot three shots. And I was way out to the road, and

I heard three faint shots, way out there. And I didn't think it was my brother, so I didn't do anything, and I heard three more shots. And I thought, it's gotta be him. And I didn't do anything then, and I heard three more shots, and then I shot three shots, and then he answered back. He said when he heard my shots he was on the run, gettin' out of there. And he came out, and we shot one shot a piece, and then he ran out of bullets, and I was to my last bullet, and I thought do I go back to the car and get more, or do I stay here? I shot my last bullet, and about five minutes later he came out, and told me the story. And... then I'll tell you a little about that Kate (L).

MQ: Mm-hmm?

LG: Little old lady, born again Christian, she had a beautiful garden on the riverbank on the Bankton Trail.

MQ: And what year was that?

LG: Um, um, um... that must be in the 80s, that she saw that. She had a beautiful garden on the riverbank, and one day she was down there, and she said she just had that feeling something was looking at her, and she looked over, and here was something real tall, and black, and hairy.

Standing on two legs, looking at her. And she let out a war hoop-scream, and ran to the house, and she said this thing turned around and the way it came it ran back. Up the river. And...

MQ: It didn't make any noises back at her?

LG: Didn't scream at her, nothing. It was just watching her. And she let out a war hoop, ran up to the house, never finished the garden, never did anything more ever down there. Garden site's still there, but it's all growed over now.

MQ: Did she go into any more detail about describing it, or...?

LG: She just said it was big, black, and hairy, and what surprised her-- she seen tons of bears.

MQ: Mm-hmm.

LG: But what got her was it was on two legs and ran on two legs. And... she died with that same story. (Jump ahead)

MQ: Ok, I'm just trying to pin down how recently things have been going on, you know, to be sure that there's still activity up there.

LG: Mm-hmm. Well, I don't know why they'd go anywhere. After that dramatic interview, I knew that I had to see the area for myself and plan a search to see if evidence might still be found thereafter a quarter-century. In the spring of 2003, I had some vacation time coming up, and on May 17th, I decided to drive up and spend an after-noon scouting out possible camping locations, having no idea what was about to befall me. I found the area of Larry's experiences to be exceptionally wild and thickly wooded, just as he had described it but with the gravel roads passing through it being in good condition and providing easy access. I had fun exploring riverbanks looking for tracks and placed a trail camera along a creek with a pile of fruit I'd brought along as bait.

I found the Bankton Trail he'd described and knew I was close to where his first encounter had occurred, and then I turned on to what was called the Faunce forest road, which eventually led me to a point called Peet's Bridge which crossed the Rapid River. I did not yet realize that this was actually very close to the site of the old ruined cabin Larry had described. Shortly after crossing the bridge, I saw what looked to me like a right turn that had been blocked by a huge pile of dirt that had been dumped there for some reason, while the road I was on looked like it continued on straight.

What happened next happened in mere seconds, and I do not fault myself for it. The gravel Faunce road suddenly turned to dirt, and then to even less than that, and suddenly my tires were spinning and digging into the mud. The right turn I'd just seen was on to a road called the Rapid River road and was where travelers would normally turn at that point, and why there was a giant pile of dirt there to confuse me and block my way I will never know. I ended up a hundred feet or so beyond that point, stuck hard in the mud. I tried rocking the car back and forth to get unstuck but to no avail. This was bad, and I suddenly found myself sitting there saying to myself, "You've got to be kidding me."

Ah, 2003 -- the era when cell phones were still catching on, and not everyone had one yet. I didn't, so I was totally on my own. I got out of the car to survey the situation. Ahead of me was what looked like a wet boggy area, and I mistakenly thought I was still on a road that had become flooded. I had a shovel with me and tried to dig the tires out of the mud, but it was beyond anything I could do.

A sense of dread began to set in. My god, what am I supposed to do here? This was a dense wilderness, not an area where one could at all count on others coming along to flag down for help, and it was late afternoon. I decided to set off walking back up the Faunce road in the hope that someone would come by to help me. I walked, and I walked, and I walked.

I'm not sure how far I ended up going up that road, but as I did, I pondered the gravity of my situation and how grim it was. I was stranded, and there is a sense of hopelessness that comes with that. Night was approaching. What if no one came? I came to a spot where a large pile of logs had been stacked up near the road and sat down there to rest, putting on the headphones of a Walkman I had with me to see what radio stations I could pull in in that remote place.

What emerged out of the static happened to be the song "Angel" by Sarah McLachlan, a favorite of mine that speaks of turning to one's angel for solace in the face of strife. I had an emotional reaction to it, marveling at how that song should come through at that particular moment and admitting that I had become genuinely afraid and bowed my head in prayer. "Please send me someone," I said.

A little while later, after I continued walking, something unexpected and absolutely silly happened. A skunk suddenly stepped out of the grass on to the road about 50 feet ahead of me and began walking along the road in the same direction as me. After it became apparent that the animal seemed intent on following that course indefinitely, I actually shouted into the sky, *"Oh, very funny! I meant somebody HUMAN!"*

I talked to that skunk. I said, "Ok, little buddy, you stay up there, and I'll stay back here and we'll be just fine," not wanting to experience what skunks are most known for. It continued to walk along the road as if guiding me for what seemed like a very unusual length of time, during which I actually came to derive comfort from the fact that at least there was another living thing sharing this experience with me. After a long time, the skunk finally left the road and turned back into the grass where it disappeared, at which point I was sad to see it go and actually teared up a bit, making me realize even further just how rattled I was.

Shortly after the skunk disappeared, I turned back and started heading back toward my stuck car. During that time, evening set in, and darkness fell. I was beginning to be resigned to the fact that I was going to have to spend the night there, and I was scared. I continued to dwell on my earlier prayer for help, and as I walked along the dark road, there came a point where I started to see a peculiar bunch of small points of light appearing along the left side of the road up at treetop level.

What was this? I first thought it must be fireflies, but then realized that it was too early in the year for them to be showing up. As I watched, these dancing points of light then coalesced and formed themselves into one big spherical mass of white light about the size of a basketball that continued to float along the treetops for a few seconds and then just faded out and disappeared.

I stopped and stood there, staring up at where I had just seen this amazing sight, in a strange matter-of-fact state of mind. I suddenly felt no fear, not at my perilous situation and not at the bizarre thing I had just seen, but instead had a sense of calm settle over me because I had a natural realization of what had just occurred.

As sure as I had ever known anything, I suddenly knew that I had just seen my own personal guardian angel and that it had appeared in answer to my prayer to let me know -- calm down, don't worry, I am here, and I have your back, and you are going to be all right and are going to get out of here. I know full well that what I am describing is blatantly supernatural, and though I do not normally like to bring such things into the search for Bigfoot, I cannot deny what I saw, and we are getting into the area of spiritual belief here that

I will not apologize for.

I got back to my stuck car and spent the night in it, during which a drizzling rain began that would last most of the next day, and the ground grew softer, and the car sank in even deeper. I got no sleep that night, and in the morning, I took stock of my situation. As I said earlier, I still thought that I was on a road that was flooded and that it would pick up again if I continued on in the same direction.

When I attempted to do that, I promptly stepped into an area of quicksand, which instantly sucked in one leg with a sensation that felt like some hidden subterranean creature had reached up and grabbed me, pulling me down to hip level in one second. Luckily my other leg was still on solid ground, and I was able to pull out of the muck, and if that hadn't been the case, and if I'd stepped into that quagmire with both feet, then I actually think that I might just not be here today to tell the story, and I don't like to imagine what that kind of death would have been like.

After surviving the quicksand, I still tried to negotiate my way along in the same direction but ended up falling waist-deep into water, in what had looked like solid ground, and I realized that this course of action just wasn't going to work. As I stared off into that direction I had been contemplating, I saw two deer come into view in the far distance, perhaps representing the wildness of the area. As I would come to understand later that route, I had been attempting was not a flooded road, but the entrance into absolutely wild and impenetrable swamp that led after a few miles to the north shore of Upper Red Lake. If I had tried to continue in that direction, I probably would have died. Instead, I looked back at the way I had come with the knowledge of about how far it had been and said out loud to myself, "Well... how long does it take to walk 20 miles?"

It was eight o'clock in the morning when I abandoned the car and started out on my long walk with the light drizzle pelting me, clad in my rain gear and carrying all the items I was not willing to leave behind in bags hanging from my shoulders. Fortunately, I had a jug of water, but the only food I had was one banana leftover from the pile of fruit I'd left at the trail camera the day before. I resolved to walk in half-hour increments, stopping in between to rest for five minutes, but the farther I went, the more often my breaks became and the longer they lasted.

The big boots I was wearing over my shoes became so encrusted with mud over time that they became too heavy to comfortably wear, so I took them off and carried them. At noon, I stopped and ate my banana. There did come the point where I passed where my trail camera was with its pile of fruit as bait, but I opted to just pass by and leave it.

As the day wore on, with me having to will myself to keep putting one foot in front of the other, peculiar mental effects started to wear on me. Every time the wind would rise a bit, I would swear that I was hearing the sound of an approaching vehicle, but it never came true. Meanwhile I worried about just who might come along if one did approach.

The closed Red Lake reservation had a reputation of being unfriendly to outsiders. I had a loaded pistol on me, and the prospect of having to use it in self-defense while all alone in the middle of this wilderness was something I didn't want to think about. If I had wanted to get up close and personal with the area, though, this was definitely my chance. I did not encounter any sign of Bigfoot but found moose tracks in the road and had several occurrences of flushing out both ducks and otters in the water-filled ditches along the road.

Finally, I came out of the forest road system and arrived at what I knew to be a more well-traveled county road. There was a house there, and I knocked on the door, but no one was home, and in fact, the place looked like it might be vacant. I thought that if I still didn't manage to find anyone here, I could at least break into this house to have shelter for a second night. (I would later learn that it was some-one's vacation home, vacant at the time.) It was about 5 PM and I had just spent nine hours walking approximately 20 miles. My feet were blistered, my legs were barely holding me up, my shoulders were wracked with pain from the bags hanging off of them all day, and all in all, I was very aware that as I had aged, I had not exercised enough and kept myself in good enough shape.

Utterly exhausted, I declared to the wind that I was done walking and just collapsed into the ditch beside the road, deciding that I was staying right there until someone came. I think that about a half-hour passed, during which I lay inert and motionless and might have even drifted into momentary sleep before I suddenly heard once again what sounded like a vehicle approaching. This time, however, it was real.

My guardian angel must have still been working for me and sent me the most perfect rescuers I could have possibly wished for. They were a classic Minnesota farm couple of Scandinavian descent in their early elderly years, in a pickup truck on their way to go berry picking. They must have been startled to see me stagger up out of that ditch and flag them down, but when I told them of my plight and asked if they could just take me to a phone, they couldn't have been nicer and gave me a ride to their nearby farm.

They suggested that I should call the local sheriff and let him know that my car was out there, which I did, assuring him that I would see to getting it out as soon as possible. Then I called Dean. Miraculously, though he had a busy and sporadic daily schedule, he was home and had no other commitments, and when I asked him to make the five-hour drive from Moorhead to the little fishing village of Waskish on the east shore of Upper Red Lake to pick me up, he agreed to jump in his car right away and headed out.

Meanwhile, my rescuers continued their generosity, feeding me sandwiches and agreeing to drive me to Waskish even though it was farther away than I had realized. Three times I offered them money for their troubles -- for gas, for the long-distance phone call, and just as a reward for saving me -- but they turned it down flat. I deeply regret that I did not write down their names and cannot remember them after the 15 years that have now passed but on the outside chance that they are still around and should happen to see this book, I want them to know how extremely grateful I am to them for their help and generosity.

They were a true godsend.

I then sat for a few hours in a cafe in Waskish waiting for Dean, where I had supper and explained my situation to the waitress who served me. I ordered a few beers too, which I felt I deserved after my ordeal and helped to calm my nerves. But as I sat there waiting, just as I was starting to feel better, something new and terrible reared its head. It started with the pinky knuckle of my left hand suddenly sinking down into my hand. Well that's odd, I thought, and after I pressed it back into its normal shape, it continued to do it.

Then the other knuckles on that hand started to do the same thing one by one, and then the right hand joined in, and over fifteen minutes or so, I found myself with all of my fingers cramping up into painful and misshapen claws. It was frightening, something I had never experienced before, and I had to clamp both hands down on the edge of the table where I was sitting to get my hands to maintain their normal shape.

Obviously, carrying a pair of boots and a jug of water for nine hours that day had taken a toll and done some kind of damage. I asked the waitress where the nearest hospital emergency room was, and she said it was in the city of Bemidji, but I hoped that would not be necessary.

Closing time for the cafe came before Dean arrived, and they were starting to wind down as I looked out the window and hoped I would not have to wait outside, but he finally came pulling in at the last minute. By then, my hands had relaxed a little and were only cramping up sporadically and I decided to forego stopping at the hospital when we passed through Bemidji, but ever since that day fifteen years ago, I have been subject to occasional recurrences of bad hand cramps and also sometimes in my feet. I must have suffered nerve damage.

Another friend of mine once remarked on this story, "You aged a little that day." I think I aged a lot. The next morning at home I got a call from a forest service agent who had come across my car, as I had left a note in it giving my information and asking anyone who found it to please look for me. I assured him that I was all right.

Dean, as good a friend as anyone will ever have, ended up having to make that long drive twice more over the next few days to help me get my car unstuck. Simply trying a tow rope had no effect. With Dean working a winch in the back that he anchored to trees and me applying a long prybar to the front, we spent several grueling hours at it on the first day moving the car inch by inch. It was stuck so badly that the engine block was dragging in the mud.

We had to give up on the first day when darkness fell, but when we returned the second time, we got it out in half an hour. On the way out, I stopped to pick up the trail camera, which turned out to have captured a few photos of deer and otters.

I knew I would never be able to fully repay Dean for his help in this nightmare, but I bought him a good steak dinner as at least a token gesture.

Five months later, I returned to the place that had tried to swallow me up and explored it without getting stuck, which I think did much for me psychologically in feeling as if I had ultimately defeated it. On that day, I found that a sign had been put up at the site of my accident warning future travelers not to make the same mistake, and I was also able to appreciate some of the marked sites there that spoke of the area's history and how there had been an attempt to settle it in the early 20th century that had failed because the swampy land just wasn't conducive to farming.

There were signs marking where various families' homes had once stood, and I remembered how at one of them when I was on my long walk, I had noted the sign and said to myself, "Well, if it was good enough for them, it's good enough for me," and then plopped down there, with a heavy thud for one of my rest stops.

There was also a small cemetery that I located on a stretch of road that my walk had not covered, and I marveled at how an old couple that had taken part in the attempt at settlement had died just recently and apparently wanted to be buried here in this wild place where they must have had fond memories. As darkness fell, just before I made my way out of the area and headed for home, I even found the old abandoned home of Kate L., the old lady that had fled from her riverside garden after sighting a Bigfoot there.

That is my Red Lake story, a story of Bigfoot and omens and murder and angels and man vs. nature, with even a friendly skunk thrown in for comic relief. I know that as far as survival stories go it does not even begin to compare to what plane crash survivors in the Andes have gone through or any number of other such tales, but for me, it was an ordeal.

I have written of Native American Bigfoot legends in my earlier books and remarked upon their tendency to ascribe spiritual qualities to the creatures, noting that they do the same thing with virtually all the animals of the forest. I think it is only Bigfoot's status in popular culture as a "big hairy monster" that makes people think that it holds some special status as a supernatural being in Native belief.

In a 1999 interview, famous sasquatch researcher John Green responded to a question about his thoughts on Native legends. He responded, "I've never gone into that to any great extent, for this reason -- that in the Indian culture as in nearly all cultures, there is no sharp dividing line between the real and the unreal.

Everything is real. And this was also true of the European culture that we've inherited until the last few hundred years. But now we make an absolute distinction. We put everything on one side of that line or the other. And from my association with it, the key element in this whole thing has been on which side of that line the sasquatch falls on.

So information that you get from a culture where there is no line isn't very helpful." As much respect as I have for Green as a researcher, I have to take some issue with that stance. In my understanding, Native peoples do not distinguish Bigfoot as being a creature that is spiritual in a way that no other forest denizen is. Rather, to them, all animals and people as well take part in a spiritual process.

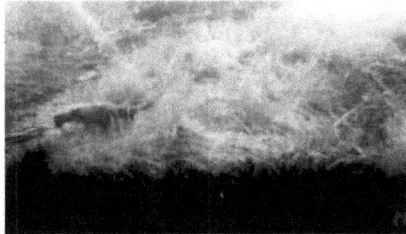

An otter appears on the trail camera in the Red Lake area during the author's ordeal.

For my part, if I'm honest, I can only report that I experienced something absolutely supernatural on the fringes of a reservation that is rumored to be a mystical and mysterious place while I was searching for Bigfoot, which I believe to be a flesh and blood creature that participates in the rhythms of nature in the same way as all other species, but that those rhythms might exist in harmony with others that may not be recognized by science but are known in the heart and soul. If that sounds mysterious and vague, I'm afraid it is simply the best I can do.

6

FORT SNELLING

STICK STRUCTURES AND THE QUESTION OF INTELLIGENCE

I n early 2017, as I was working on the list of Minnesota reports that appear in the appendix to this book, I wanted to be sure that I had everything recent that I could uncover and found YouTube to be a valuable tool. One of the most tantalizing videos I found was entitled "Seven Months of Bigfoot," a documentary posted by Joe Parkhurst, a musician, and Bigfoot researcher living in Minneapolis. Though he had other shorter videos posted detailing some of his searches for Bigfoot evidence many miles away in the northern part of the state, this full-length documentary was a compilation of footage he had shot virtually in his own back yard at

Fort Snelling State Park.

Fort Snelling was constructed in 1819 as a military outpost at the confluence of the Mississippi and Minnesota rivers, around which the Twin Cities metro area eventually grew. Many very well-preserved fort structures still stand in what is now a state park comprising 2,931 acres within the city limits of Minnesota's capital city St. Paul, and also still largely intact is the localized but heavily wooded wilderness area that lies along the courses of the two rivers.

It's quite a unique experience to visit the park, a true wild area complete with herds of deer and many other animals, yet all the while knowing you are surrounded on all sides by the city. The fact that the Minneapolis-St. Paul International Airport is quite close by, and that huge jetliners pass low over the park all day long reminds one of that. Yet in spite of this, Joe Parkhurst was asserting in his documentary, recorded between June 2016 and January 2017, that Bigfoot was present in

Fort Snelling.

In July, Joe and his wife captured some footage on a thermal imager while driving through the park at night just before its 10 PM closing time of what they believed to be two Bigfoot creatures crouching down, with accompanying thermal footage of deer and other animals to show the difference in size and shape to the images in question.

In August, Joe captured another piece of nocturnal thermal footage that became quite controversial among those posting comments on YouTube. It showed the heat signature of a bulky animal of some kind climbing backward down a tree, then continuing to hug the tree as it neared the ground and turning to drop down headfirst and move away on all fours.

Most thought it to be either a raccoon or a bear cub (though I don't think bears are known to live in the park), but Joe did a later size comparison test that seemed to show that whatever it was was considerably bigger than either of those, and he believed it to be a young Bigfoot, which are sometimes reported to move about on all fours. Personally, I'm just impressed that he managed to get thermal imagery of anything after dark in a park that closes at 10 PM since in Minnesota in the summertime, full sundown doesn't occur until after nine.

The bulk of the documentary, however, was of Joe and his daughter Emma exploring the park during daylight throughout the summer and fall and finding a vast variety of evidence, much of which was shown on camera and some of which were just described anecdotally. It included partial tracks, sounds like screams, howls, and growls being heard, skunk-like odors, and most significantly a whole range of very peculiar tree breaks and stick structures that seemed to be practically everywhere.

Areas throughout the park yielded evidence but the heaviest concentration of it seemed to be in an area known as Pike Island. Strikingly, there was also the mention of how Joe's daughter had briefly glimpsed a large brown animal some distance away shaking a tree back and forth, but unfortunately, that was not caught on video.

The last segment of "Seven Months of Bigfoot" was shot on January 2nd in winter conditions, when Joe and his daughter finally found a line of very large and impressive Bigfoot tracks in the snow that dwarfed Joe's boot prints. In following them, they seemed to disappear beneath a pile of forest debris and suggest that there might be an underground lair beneath, but this was not followed up on, seemingly out of safety concerns. So ended the documentary. Partway through the shooting of the production, however, another Twin Cities personality decided to get involved. This was Chris Lapakko, an Internet "talking head" who posted videos about his take on all kinds of subjects and called himself "The King of Earned Media."

In contrast to Joe, who was a bit heavyset, bearded, and unassuming, Lapakko was a younger and slick fast talker with a comedic brashness who was rarely seen not wearing sunglasses. When he saw the videos that Joe was posting he came to Fort Snelling in the late summer to check things out for himself with the clear intention of debunking the whole notion of Bigfoot and to make fun of it, filming everything, of course, to post online. Amazingly though, when he found the bizarre stick structures and tree breaks and even found possible Bigfoot tracks himself along one of the riverbanks, he had to admit that there just might be something to it.

He conducted some experiments in which he partially destroyed parts of some of the structures and then came back later to see if anything had changed, and in at least a few instances, he found that the damage he'd done had been repaired. In one of Lapakko's videos, he actually ran into Joe, and instead of ridiculing him, the two men actually had a spirited conversation about the activity in the park. It was a conversion that really impressed me, and I decided that I just had to go down to what we Minnesotans always refer to as "the Cities" and see the place for myself.

On April 30, 2017, my friend Katelynn Morgan and I drove down to check out Fort Snelling State Park. Though Katelynn has a punk rock look with piercings and tattoos, she is originally an Idaho girl who grew up close to the wilderness and is no stranger to wild things, and she found the idea of going on a Bigfoot hunt to be a fun adventure. My overall assessment of that day has got to be that Joe Parkhurst was not kidding.

The stick structures in the park are absolutely there and not at all hard to find. We spotted the first one just off the road while driving and stopped to examine it. It was a fairly minor one consisting of short branches that had been leaned all around the base of a large tree, the kind of structure that skeptics say can form from branches simply falling by natural means. While examining it, however, we found more that wasn't so easily explained.

A few yards away, there were two trees eight or nine feet apart that had a branch around four inches thick that had been broken off at the exact length necessary for it to be wedged in between them horizontally about 18" above the ground. We stared at this in wonder, for it was obviously not a natural formation but had to have been done by design. As we looked around further, we noticed an odd trail on the floor of fallen leaves that covered the ground that seemed to be leading away from the spot, and upon closer examination, we were able to make out individual tracks. After clearing away the leaves there were what looked for all the world like bare human footprints with partial toe impressions in the dirt beneath, not beyond human range in size, but this was neither a terrain nor the time of year when people would be expected to walk around barefoot. These tracks were slight and subtle and not the kind to show up well in photographs, but they could not be denied.

Katelynn Morgan stands beside an odd arrangement of sticks in Fort Snelling State Park.

That first find was exciting and fascinating, especially since it took such minimal effort to discover it, literally just spotting it from the car window. Our next discovery, though, while exploring the area of the park known as Pike Island that had been pinpointed by Joe as being a Bigfoot hotspot was ridiculously extreme. It was a spot very close to one of the riverbanks that I came to refer to as "the village," a whole array of what were very clearly shelters constructed from branches.

Here there was absolutely no possibility that they were natural formations but a 100% certainty that they were deliberately built by someone or something. There were about a half dozen of them, including teepee like structures tall enough for a man to stand upright inside of them, which Katelynn demonstrated as I took pictures. One of them had flat rocks, which we determined had been collected from the riverbank laid out along the ground leading up to the entrance that looked for all the world like a front walk that leads up to a human family's front door.

There were also structures unlike these shelters, one a thick cluster of large branches stacked in teepee fashion, completely encasing the base of a tree, and another comprised of a huge wall of branches that essentially formed a lean-to.

There was only one conclusion to be made about this discovery- it was either the creation of Bigfoot, or it was man-made. There were literally no other possibilities. It was amazing, stupefying, and with the ease we had in finding it, it was obvious that most visitors to the park must be seeing these things without realizing their strangeness and potential importance.

We continued to explore the area and hiked around in the woods, where we found more evidence in sporadic places. There were large bundles of sticks that had obviously been deliberately assembled and left on the ground in various places. We also found small branches a couple of feet long sticking vertically out of the ground that had been pressed in for some unknown reason. I remember also seeing a slab of concrete that looked like it had come from some construction site just lying in the middle of nowhere in the woods, too heavy for a man to have carried for any great distance and in a spot that didn't seem accessible by vehicle. How did it get there? There were mysteries aplenty.

As if to distract us from the strangeness of what we were seeing, we also ran into a herd of Fort Snelling's deer that are rather famously unafraid of people in this place where they are never hunted. They won't actually let you come up to them and pet them, but they are so used to people that you can get extremely close to them before they move away, and even then they only move off a short distance and continue to look at you. Katelynn and I both found it to be a heartwarming encounter that calmed us down a bit after what we'd just seen. We left the park that day with more questions than answers, and in addition to the photos I took I brought with me one artifact.

At the place I called "the village," Katelynn and I found a very peculiar construct hanging outside one of the shelters. It was about two feet long and consisted of grass and branches woven together to form this bizarre... well, just a thing that looked like some kind of arts and crafts project that a Bigfoot might create if they do indeed do that sort of thing, with no particular meaning evident to a human mind but without question done by something with intelligence.

I wondered if it might be something the young do as a sort of play. There were even actual knots tied in the strands of grass. The moment I saw it I knew that I needed to collect it, and so I have it in my possession now, and hopefully it will come to mean something someday. The weaving of the grass is so complex that I have trouble believing it was done by a human being, and the idea that it was done by simian hands absolutely enthralls me.

A later video by Chris Lapakko explained how he had talked to a staff member at the park and had been told that rangers sometimes conduct programs with kids in which they are taught to build shelters in the woods, but that they are directed to always tear them back down when they're finished. I know that this is all skeptics will need to debunk the entire Fort Snelling episode. Meanwhile, an e-mail that I sent to park headquarters asking a general question about the whole situation went unanswered.

What should we make of all this?

With all the evidence documented by Joe Parkhurst -- the most impressive I personally feel, being the huge tracks in the snow he filmed in January 2017, on top of all his other findings -- I don't think this case can be dismissed. And if Bigfoot truly does build structures like this and even intricate formations that amount to works of art, then I think it speaks volumes about the creatures' intelligence being on a level nearly equal to humans.

Further evidence for this comes in the form of audio recordings that have been captured of the creatures vocalizing to each other in various places all across the country, vocalizations that sound like a language. It is not English, nor is it any Native American dialect or a match for any known language. Rather, unexpectedly, it is what sounds like someone who does not speak Japanese doing their impression of what they think Japanese sounds like, and so it has been dubbed "samurai chatter."

Most recordings of Bigfoot sounds feature more animal-like calls, like howls and screams (like the sounds I've personally heard myself), and I have heard a few recordings of what are alleged to be creatures mimicking actual words in English that I personally believe to be fakes, but the samurai chatter recordings are widespread enough that I tend to think they are genuine and therefore, fascinating.

I've heard speculation by some that the creatures may have picked up on the speech of settlers from various lands over the ages and have come to mimic them as they also sometimes seem to mimic various animal sounds. Another theory has to do with the popular idea that the sasquatch is a survival of the prehistoric ape Gigantopithecus, which is known only from fossils found in China, and that it might have migrated to America via the Bering Strait land bridge that once existed.

If so, is it possible that those creatures once mimicked the voices of early man in Asia, and that those learned sounds have actually survived long enough to still exist in their American descendants all these thousands of years later? It seems incredible. One must consider that Japanese and Chinese are very different languages, and if mimicry really is involved, it seems unlikely that Native American tribal languages would not have entered in over the ages.

But I also can't help but wonder if the creatures simply have an original language of their own that just happens to sound the way it sounds, seeming similar to an Asian style by sheer coincidence. It's an extremely gray area. We do not know for sure how much of the evidence is genuine and how much is not, so we must reserve judgment. But if Bigfoot has the potential level of intelligence that's been suggested then its elusiveness and ability to avoid being proven once and for all to exist year after year becomes a little easier to understand. In a conversation I had with Bigfoot researcher Cliff Barackman of the tv show "Finding Bigfoot" when I met him in California in October 2017, I showed him some of the photos from Fort Snelling and his response was not what I expected.

I want to make it clear that I was absolutely thrilled to meet Cliff, and that I was glad that he was so friendly and engaging, but he had a skeptical opinion on the whole subject of Bigfoot tree structures. His justification was that over the decades, people have observed Bigfoots doing many things, making for quite a detailed image of what their lifestyle is like, but that even with all the tree structures that had been making headlines in recent years no one had ever reported seeing a Bigfoot making any of them, and therefore, he tended to be skeptical of them.

Cliff is an awesome researcher, and I hate to disagree with him, but as I pondered what he'd said it struck me that to my knowledge, no one has ever reported seeing Bigfoots mating or giving birth either (and someone, please correct me if I'm wrong on that), but we're all pretty sure that they do, in fact, do those things.

I feel that I am forced to be non-committal on the activity in Fort Snelling State Park, because I am truly 50-50 on whether it is genuine or not. But if it is, I think it speaks of a level of complex intelligence in the creatures that is truly amazing. Their mere presence in the park would also lend further weight to the idea that Bigfoot follows rivers, even to the point of following them into the midst of a major city.

Katelynn Morgan examines a branch mysteriously wedged between two trees for no apparent reason at Fort Snelling.

Katelynn approaches "The Village."

A teepee-like stick structure

The author sits beside a lean-to structure close to the above shelters.

Katelynn demonstrates how some of the structures are big enough to fit inside of.

The author displays the peculiar object found at "The Village" made from sticks and woven grass.

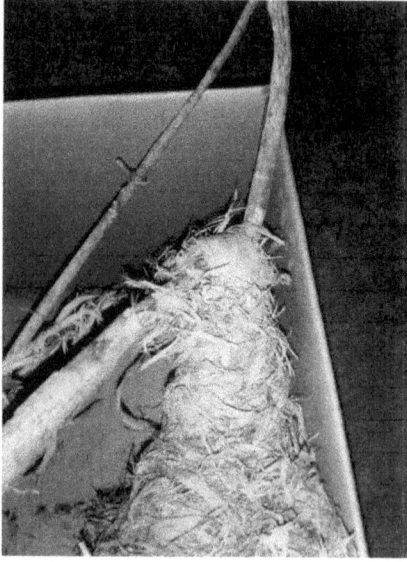

7

SASQUATCH GRAB BAG

NORTHERN MINNESOTA REPORTS IN FAR FLUNG PLACES

You never know where Bigfoot is going to pop up. This is a chapter in which I'm going to share several stories from sporadic places throughout the northern half of Minnesota that I've collected since my last book came out, most of which I've had personal involvement with and all of which I find particularly dramatic. You'll find that the appendix at the end of this book is full of amazing stories, so consider this chapter to be a brief dip into a big pond. I'd like to start with a report that actually was included in my last book but which has always been one of my favorites, and my reason for including it now is that I now have a few photographs of the location that were lacking before, which prevented me from really doing justice to the story.

It occurred in the summer of 1976 within the city limits of Aitkin, a small town of around 2,000 people about 75 miles west of Duluth. I was contacted through a letter by one of the witnesses, B.P., 14 years old at the time of the incident, about what he and his friend R.G. had seen while riding their bicycles along an earthen dike that follows the Mississippi River at the north edge of town. "It was about 8:30 PM," the letter stated, "and we both had to be home at dark, so we took off along the top of the dike for home.

At one particular spot on the dike, there is a large swampy area approximately 300-500 yards across between the dike and a narrow row of trees that border the river. As we rode by this area, we noticed a large brown animal out in the boggy area. We thought it looked like it was digging in the swamp grass or picking it. We watched for about a minute, I guess, it didn't seem to notice us. "Then I hollered at it. It was then I realized it wasn't a bear. It stood straight up and looked our way. It didn't have ears that stick up or a long nose like a bear. Then it turned and took off running, just like a man would, on its back legs, toward the river.

It scared the hell out of us, and we took off riding as fast as we could. I wasn't afraid until it stood up and took off running. We then rode back to my friend's house and told his older brother what we had saw. He didn't believe us, but we rode back down there and didn't see anything. The next day, we went back there, and we were going to walk out there and look for tracks, but that particular area was really swampy. The first step on the very edge was about 6-8" deep in water and muck.

It may have been different where this thing was standing, but I doubt it. It was probably worse, and yet it ran across this stuff like it was dry pavement. I am an avid hunter and have had to cross areas like this before and no way could I run through this stuff like this animal did. It was not a bear. I don't know what it was. But I will never forget it. To me, this was something unexplained. I am not sure what I saw, but I think it was Bigfoot." In a later letter, B.P. added, "...the height I would estimate at between 5'5" and 6'5". The ground was very soggy, and it looked like he was sinking in the mud as it moved.

I said he, not knowing what sex it was, figuratively. It looked rather thick and husky, rather muscular -- maybe 300 pounds. 'The face was hairy, like a full beard and mustache, really full. Long arms that reached to the ground to pull up weeds easily. It was in long weeds, so hard to see legs and tell how long they were.

The location of the Aitkin sighting.

The Mississippi River next to the Aitkin site.

"...The area north of Aitkin is a mostly swampy area, many lakes, rice paddies, and limited agricultural area... A lot of logging north of Aitkin. "I do believe that there could be several families of these creatures that could live in the area and no one would ever see them. The terrain is thick wooded area, swamps, and wild. Perfect cover." It was several years before I was able to view the scene of the boys' sighting, and though it seemed they had overestimated the size somewhat of the swampy area the creature had crossed it was still a very impressive report rich in detail.

Moving closer to modern times, an incident I took part in myself occurred on October 7, 2000, when myself and a friend at the time named Alan Weaver were exploring the area of the Gemmel Ridge forest road in Koochiching County, which crosses Highway 71, east of the Red Lake area and south of the great wild space known as the Big Bog, all of it rich with Bigfoot reports going back to the 1970s. Alan was half Ojibwa on his father's side but looked full-blooded, a highly talented artist but not having grown up with very much knowledge of Native American Bigfoot lore and so curious to see what he might learn in coming with me on some of my excursions to the woods.

We were scouting for a spot to camp for the night and happened to stop at a gravel pit area just off the forest road north of the highway. As we were looking around, we suddenly discovered a curious line of tracks ascending the side of the pit, looking very much like a large man had walked up it on only the foreparts of his feet.

This being gravel, it was not a very stable surface and did not show the greatest detail, but there did seem to be the slight impressions of toes in some of the tracks, and as it was cold enough at the time for there to be a light dusting of snow on the ground at the time it was hardly the kind of place a man would be expected to be walking around barefoot. At one point, there was what looked like a handprint off to the right side of the tracks complete with a thumb, as if the climber had steadied itself there.

Alan Weaver stands before the Gemmel Ridge gravel pit where possible Bigfoot tracks were found. walking around barefoot.

Most curious, though, was a small hole at the very top of the line of tracks that had been dug horizontally into the side of the pit, just below the surface of the ground above. The gravel that had been scooped out was still very evident where it had cascaded downhill.

I stuck my arm into this hole (which when I told Cliff Barackman of television's "Finding Bigfoot" about this find in 2017 caused him to tell me that I was a brave man), and found that I could just barely manage to touch the back of it, making it the exact length of an adult human arm. Our climber, our digger, had been after something here.

Whether or not it had found it, we could not say. Behind the pit was a large expanse of pine forest which could have been harboring just about anything. I found one more possible handprint on the surface near the pit but no further footprints.

Still, our find was such a singularly odd mystery that I couldn't help but equate it with Bigfoot, especially in the area that we were in. It did not seem like something a human would have done, and I could not think of any other suspects. As we camped at the spot that night, however, there was no further activity. The next report comes from less than a year later and was passed on to me by Twin cities cryptozoologist Curt Nelson, involving an incident in a populated area just outside the city of Bemidji in Beltrami County.

This is one of the largest cities and major hubs in the central north of Minnesota with a population of around 14,000 and is well known for its large colorful statues of Paul Bunyan and Babe the Blue Ox, photographed over the years by many thousands of tourists. The city's proximity to the wilderness that lies all around it was well illustrated to me personally, once when I was driving back from a Bigfoot excursion at night and had to suddenly swerve to avoid hitting a deer that seemed intent on using my car to commit suicide in the middle of a highway well within the Bemidji city limits.

Alan walks alongside the tracks in the gravel pit as they approach the hole at the top.

| A closeup of the hole.

In late 2002, Curt turned me on to a sighting in the Town Hall Road area near Alice Lake just north of the city that had occurred in July of 2001. A young woman from the Twin Cities named Amanda K. had come up to check on a vacant house owned by her father and was accompanied by her friend Lisa G. who lived in Bemidji as well as both of their respective male partners.

Apparently, the men were at the front of the house, and it was only the two women who experienced the sighting when they came out the back, which overlooked a low swampy area, as told in writing by Amanda: "My friend and I were leaving my dad's old house, it's in the middle of the woods so normally there are tons of birds and other animals making noise, but we noticed that everything had become completely silent.

All of a sudden, at the bottom of the gully, we hear this crashing sound in the woods. We looked back to see what it was and there was this huge creature standing in the swamp. It was standing on two feet, covered with light brown, long hair. It was shaking the trees, and after we watched it for a second, it took off running through the woods. As soon as it ran, so did we...

Whatever this thing was we saw was standing in a swamp and was able to run through the swamp and the trees... Nobody has ever believed us about what we saw that day, and yet nobody can provide an explanation to us either. We know what we saw, it wasn't a bear, it wasn't a person.

Bears aren't that color, and they don't run through the swamp and forest on two feet. No man could have been that big or able to run like that in 1-2 feet of mucky water and forest." Lisa, the other witness, also provided a narrative: "It was a summer day in 2001, and me and Amanda, and two other people were going into her dad's house to get some of her stuff that was left behind. We were in the house for about 30 minutes or so, and then we had dug around in everything, so we decided to leave.

On the way out the window (me and Amanda were the last out), we heard some twigs snapping in the little swamp in back of her house. When we turned to look, there was a creature that looked quite huge standing erect on two feet, holding on to a tree and shaking it. I was so scared, and the first thing that popped into my head was 'Bigfoot is real! I knew it!' I don't think it could have been a bear because there are no brown bears around here, and this creature didn't have a head shaped the same as a bear, it was more humanly shaped than a bear's head. I didn't stick around much longer after that.

Amanda and I both ran to the car and got in, and locked the doors. I tell myself it was a bigfoot creature because I have always believed in bigfoot, and it looked so much like what I had always envisioned." What I found most interesting about the sighting was the behavior of the creature and how it was shaking the trees as if it was angry or agitated by the presence of the witnesses, though neither woman reported hearing it make any vocalizations.

It was reminiscent of angry behavior by African great apes as well as by Bigfoots in areas throughout North America that have occasionally but consistently shaken trees or even thrown rocks at people, rarely seeming to actually want to cause harm but just trying to intimidate people to go away. Curt asked me if I would be interested in going to check out the location since I lived a bit closer to it than him, so it was in January of 2003, when everything was covered in winter snow, that my partner Dean and I drove up to have a look. We found the Town Hall Road area to have a handful of homes scattered here and there as well as some open pasture land, with significant woods surrounding everything.

When we found the home in question, described to us as a blue trailer house, the first thing we noticed was that there were dogs at properties nearby madly barking at our arrival. If those dogs had been present at the time of the sighting, I would have thought they would have had a similar reaction, but when Curt checked again with the witnesses on that question, they said they had heard no dogs. We found that the property matched the description in the report for the most part, with the swampy area below the house looking more like a frozen pond in the winter with woods on the far side.

In the distance, there was a hunter's deer stand visible, a sign of the thicker wilderness that these woods led into. All in all, by rough estimate, it seemed that Amanda and Lisa must have viewed the creature they saw from a distance of around 50 yards, and it did not seem at all happy that they were there. It seemed a solid sighting, and I was thankful for Curt Nelson for passing it along to me.

Just as I was to another Minnesota Bigfooter, Joe Heinan, in August of 2003 when he also relayed a report to me, which in turn he had received from a Bigfooting couple named Allen and Carrie Donais. Joe lived in the Fargo-Moorhead area the same as me, and I met him a couple of times.

The spot where the creature in the Town Hall Road sighting was seen, shown here in wintertime.

Dean stands on the frozen swamp at the Town Hall Road site.

We never went out into the field together, but he created and operated a website known simply as "Minnesota Bigfoot" that got considerable attention and garnered several new reports from the state. One that happened rather rapid-fire involved a sighting that took place on August 5th, was posted to Joe's site on the 8th and passed on to me, and then followed up on with a visit to the site by myself and Dean on the 26th.

It was quite a hike, as it was to look into a sighting that happened well over 200 miles away near the tiny community of Togo in Itasca County, perilously close to entering the Superior/Arrowhead region. At around 7:30 PM, three women in a car were on their way home from work, westbound on Highway 1 about three miles west of Togo. As they were approaching a place called the Flaming Pine Youth Camp, which was on the left side of the road, they suddenly saw a large creature in the road that seemed to have crossed from the right.

Witness Laura L. related what she and her friends saw: "We were about 400 yards away on a straight stretch when ahead we seen what looked like a very large creature. It was dark brown or black and what appeared to be hair. It was standing on the side of the road looking into the woods. We got to be about 200 yards away when it turned towards us. We did not see any facial features. It quickly took only one step in the ditch, and the next was in the woods. It had a very long leg length because there is about seven feet in between the road and the ditch.

We sped up to look in the woods. It looked as if that area had had some logging done. The only trees for about 150 yards out were about 6" wide, no room for it to hide unless it laid down or something because there was no time even if running to get into the thick woods where we could not see it before we were there stopped in the road and stared into that area for about five minutes before leaving and trying to rationalize what we had just seen. No rationalizing seeing that it was amazing, I seen Bigfoot and I wanna see it again. We are not the only people to see this sighting in the same area."

In a follow-up, Allen Donais related to Joe Heinan, how he had gone to the site and walked through the sighting with the witness Laura and asked her to elaborate on her initial description, coming up with a few minor discrepancies. Allen wrote: 'They came around a sharp corner in the road and could see the creature ahead. The corner was a good 1/4 mile from the creature.

They were within 150 yards or less when it turned to look at them.

She said that it did not turn its head but turned its whole upper body. Did not see the face, but when I asked about distinguishing features, she said it had very thick wrists. Height about 8 ft. Body not real large but athletic looking. She said he looked rather poofy. The area he was looking into is low and swampy, bordering a small lake.

It was not logged but the trees are small stunted poplar. From where she said they were when he walked away into the woods would have taken them about three seconds to drive to the location he entered the woods. There would have been plenty of time for him to get into cover. The small lake was unpopulated except for cabins from the camp.

Also, a camp dumpster is pushed right up to the edge of the woods there. She said that they did not see him cross the road, but I assume he did, from thick 20-year-old pine stand to the lake. I do not know why he would have been standing on the road like that and let them get so close unless someone from the camp was down by the lake or at the dumpster making noise. Then pausing on the road would have been a cautious thing to do. No tracks, lots of deer tracks. Some trails but could have been made by anything. She said someone else from town saw one near there earlier this year."

The site of the sighting near Togo.

| The area the Bigfoot fled into in the Togo sighting.

| A huge fallen tree found near the Togo site.

The description of how the creature turned its entire upper body to look at the approaching vehicle instead of just turning its head was intriguing because the exact same movement is seen in the famous Patterson-Gimlin Bigfoot film. One of the consistent traits in descriptions of the creatures is that they have practically no neck and a chin that rests below the level of their shoulders, so turning their heads to the side as humans do is impossible.

Dean and I only had a limited amount of time to do a cursory search of the area on August 26th, but I returned by myself 18 days later on September 3rd and -- pardon my French – explored the hell out of the place. I knew I was on the fringes of the Flaming Pine, which is a Christian Bible camp for kids, and I didn't want to interfere or disturb them in any way, but I scoured every square inch of ground in the area of the sighting, much of which was a perfect surface for footprints, but I found nothing.

I remember it feeling like a huge letdown, as I had been really optimistic about finding something in those conditions so soon after the sighting, hoping that the Bigfoot visited the area regularly. I found that there was a system of horse riding trails near the camp and as I happened to have a bicycle with me on this trip, I used it to explore them.

I found no Bigfoot evidence there either, but I was greatly impressed by the old-growth forest that made up the area, especially when I came to one particular tree that had recently broken and fallen over. It was so huge that it formed an archway over the trail big enough to ride a horse or even drive a vehicle under. By my estimation this tree was over three feet thick and about 130 feet tall. One doesn't normally find trees quite that big in most of Minnesota, and it gave me an appreciation for just how ancient a forest the Flaming Pine Camp had chosen to establish itself in.

After failing to find evidence in the area, I sent a carefully worded e-mail to the camp, explaining to them that this alleged Bigfoot sighting had occurred virtually in their back yard and that such creatures were not normally known to be dangerous but asking if they had any information on similar observations in the area. I will never know if they had any such info or what their reaction was because they never responded.

Well, c'est la vie. The last report I will include here is one that I had no personal involvement in and have not personally investigated, but it is extremely dramatic and deserves to be looked at in detail. It is made all the more vexing by the fact that two slightly different versions of the story exist from different media sources, and I must admit upfront that I have no explanation for that.

The incident in question occurred in July of 2008 west of the town of Staples, population around 3,000, which straddles the border of Todd and Wadena Counties in the middle portion of the state. It involved a young woman named Amanda Schluttner striking a Bigfoot with her car. The first version of the story was featured nationwide on the History Channel television program "Monster Quest," which described how Amanda had been on the way to visit her boyfriend when the incident suddenly occurred.

"It was just getting dark," she said on the show, "and I was driving down the road, and I was going about 35 and all of a sudden a big black thing just rolled across my vehicle. It was probably like seven feet tall, lot of fur, dark, kind of looked like a bear on two legs but bigger and almost looked like a person at the same time."

The collision threw the creature into a ditch and was witnessed by Amanda's boyfriend Kirk Orr and his brother Matt from their house just a few hundred feet away. In describing what he saw, Kirk reported, "It was pretty big, and it was moving pretty quick on two legs... It was confusing at first. It did kind of look like a bear, but the way it moved and the way it twisted, it looked kind of like a person, but it was too tall and too broad." "Like when you see a football player wearing his gear," Matt added. "It was 8-8 1/2 feet tall." This was a bigger estimate in height than Amanda's. The brothers, both avid hunters, quickly armed themselves with a 410 shotgun and a .30- 30 rifle and went after the injured creature. "It kind of leaned its hand down on its leg," Kirk reported, "then grabbed a branch and started pulling itself back up."

At that point, the brothers fired at the fleeing creature. Kirk felt sure he had struck it in the chest, but it continued to retreat and disappeared into the woods. "Monster Quest" brought in a three-man group to investigate the incident, consisting of Bob Olson and Don Sherman of the Northern Minnesota Bigfoot Research Team and a professional animal tracker and trapper named Gene Hagen. I was so glad to see Bob and Don get this kind of tv exposure, prior to and much better than any that the show "Finding Bigfoot" would ever give them later.

They began with Bob -- an experienced auto body mechanic -- examining the damage to Amanda's car and determining that it seemed completely consistent with the vehicle having struck a large bipedal creature. Some hairs were also recovered from the damaged area for future study. Next, the three men prepared to enter the woods to see if they could locate evidence of the injured creature's passage. 'The creature," Don said, "I believe is dead or died back in the woods and is still back there." Upon entering the woodline, the men quickly located the spot where the creature had supposedly been shot by Kirk Orr.

A clear bullet strike was evident on a tree with no exit mark, indicating that a bullet that may have passed through the creature's body was imbedded in the tree. They cut out that section of the tree to have the bullet extracted later and tested for DNA. That turned out to be their most significant find that day, however, as despite four hours of searching up to two miles into the woods with an accompanying tracking dog and noting what looked like possible evidence of a large animal passing through, they found no further trace of the wounded creature.

Both struck by a car and then shot, it must have been a hardy specimen indeed to have kept going after sustaining that much damage. The scientific analysis of the evidence turned out to be equally disappointing. The hairs collected from the damaged car turned out to be feline and human, and the bullet was successfully extracted from the tree but yielded no usable DNA. These were typical results for "Monster Quest." It was a much better than average cryptozoology show that ran from October 2007 to March 2010, narrated by a man who had a voice identical to the well-known actor Stacy Keach of "Mike Hammer" fame.

Keach has also done narration work, and for a long time, I thought it was him, but it wasn't. It was a man named Stan Bernard, a perfect soundalike. Despite its pretty good production quality, the show, unfortunately, became rather well known for never finding the creatures it sought just as did "Finding Bigfoot," but in fairness, it did have a few successes. In a few of its several Bigfoot episodes, investigators had rocks thrown at them by what were, in all likelihood, actual Bigfoots. In an undersea investigation, the show captured film footage of what may have been the largest squid ever seen, possibly in the hundred-foot range.

Another underwater incident occurred while investigating the Canadian lake monster Ogopogo in British Columbia's Lake Okanagan in which a diver responding to a heat signature spotted by an aircraft suddenly found himself engulfed in a huge upsurge of bottom material that obscured his vision and briefly cut off his communications with the surface that could only have been caused by something very large moving away. Another episode looking into the possible survival of the officially extinct Tasmanian Tiger or Thylacine captured a possible image of just the back of one of those striped beasts along the bottom of a trail camera photo.

So, I think we should give "Monster Quest" credit where credit is due, but success in the Staples Bigfoot sighting eluded them. Now, however, comes the second version of the Staples story that makes things a bit mysterious. When I connected with Bigfooter Don Sherman in 2017, and he allowed me to borrow his collection of Minnesota reports, I found a couple of local newspaper clippings on the incident. These, combined with what Don told me about it personally, make for some marked differences from the version presented by "Monster Quest."

The show had strongly implied that Amanda Schluttner was visiting the Orr brothers at their own home. This new information, however, states that they were meeting up at the home of a couple named Bruce and Marietta Harne, and whereas the show clearly described Amanda as encountering the creature as she was arriving, this second version describes the collision with her car as occurring when she was leaving. I'm perplexed by the Orr brothers grabbing guns if they were not at their own home. Did they borrow guns owned by the Harnes, or did they have their own guns there for what-ever reason? I have not investigated this report for myself, so I cannot say.

This version also states that after the creature was shot, it did not flee into the woods immediately but came toward the brothers, who then retreated into the house. While inside they heard howling sounds, and when they then came back outside, there was the incred-ible claim that they found that a ladder that had been lying in the backyard was now leaned up against the house, and the creature was now up on the roof!

When Kirk took the ladder back down the creature allegedly swung down from the roof via a tree branch and finally ran off into the woods, quite a feat for something that should have been badly hurt. Further howling in the woods, after it had disappeared, was said to sound like there might actually be more than one of them, and more howls were heard by the Harnes in the following days, but no further sightings occurred.

Strangest of all, though, and the biggest departure from the "Monster Quest" version, is that Don Sherman told me in person that the Orrs reported that the upright bipedal creature had a head not like that of an ape or a human but like that of a wolf, with a protruding muzzle. What? In the last several years, a new creature has entered the realm of cryptozoology, largely triggered by a spate of sightings in Wisconsin beginning in the early 1990s but expanding into a whole new fascinating field of study into what have become labeled "dogmen" or even "werewolves," creatures that look for the most part like very large wolves but standing and running upright on only their hind legs. For in-depth study into this field, I strongly recommend the writings of Wisconsin journalist and cryptozoologist Linda Godfrey. She has also delved into the study of Bigfoot but makes a very clear distinction between that and these bizarre canine beasts, which have appeared not only in Wisconsin but throughout the Midwest.

Is it possible that the thing Amanda Schluttner struck with her car was actually one of these and not a Bigfoot? Of special note to me is the part about the ladder. Through my recent studies of Bigfoot I have begun to develop an appreciation for a very high level of intelligence that might exist in them, and grasping the significance and use of a ladder and actually using it to scale the side of a house would definitely be strong evidence of that. The dogmen, the werewolves -- what are they? What level of intelligence might they possess?

Theories on them range all the way from some as yet unclassified animal to literal supernatural shapeshifters, humans transforming into wolves such as they did in ancient legends. As someone who is both a cryptozoologist and a lover of those old legends, it's a lot to take in and to try to process. Speculation could go in almost any direction.

One might even wonder if the reason Kirk Orr's bullet did not kill the creature was that it was not made of silver! We must stay grounded, however. The heavy build and estimated height of up to 8

1/2 feet for the creature does not match the smaller size of the dogmen, being more in line with a Bigfoot, which is what I think is more likely involved in this report. "Monster Quest" did several episodes on Bigfoot, as well as just a couple on the dogmen or "werewolves."

The episode in which this particular report appeared was focused mainly on Bigfoot reports that seemed to be becoming more and more violent, a clearly sensationalistic tactic. Having had just a little exposure to how "reality tv" works with my brushes with "Finding Bigfoot," I have to wonder if the producers of "Monster Quest" collected reports and then spun them off into whatever direction they thought would make for the most entertaining stories, making a decision as to whether this particular report should be included with Bigfoot or with werewolf episodes and editing it to make it fit.

It doesn't mean the reports have no merit, just that they are used by the entertainment industry in whatever way is deemed to bring in the most profit. There are stories galore out there, and probably creatures galore too. We should work hard at finding them rather than settling for them serving as mere entertainment.

8

THE MINNESOTA ICEMAN

O f all the chapters in this book, this will be the one that most blends the Minnesota Bigfoot scene with the nationwide and even worldwide field in general. It involves what by all rational thought should have been absolute proof of the existence of manlike-apelike creatures in our world, providing no less than the holy grail -- an actual frozen corpse of a dead specimen.

Unfortunately, it became mixed up with the world of show business, which resulted in it becoming just another legend, and quite a convoluted one at that. The creature involved has been called by a few different names by different writers, including "Bozo," implying that it was no more significant than a circus clown. But its more well-known name is the Iceman, and more specifically the Minnesota Iceman. Since this strange case was based in my home state, I suppose I saw it as my duty in my early Bigfooting days to look into it. I will share the story here of what I found, what I have come to believe about it, and the opinions of many others who have been involved in the story.

The story revolves around a man named Frances D. Hansen (commonly known as "Frank"), an airman based out of the Air Force Base in Duluth with service during the early Vietnam War and also the owner of a small farm in Winona County in southeast Minnesota. Rather than being a full-time farmer, however, after Frank's military service ended when he was in his mid-40s, he devoted much of his time to being a carnival showman.

Early on, he was touring the carnival sideshow circuit exhibiting an old antique tractor that he owned, a 1918 John Deere "All Wheel Drive" that faced some legal challenges over whether it really was the oldest John Deere model but which Frank won in court, and today the tractor resides in the John Deere Collector Center in Moline, Illinois. But by 1968, he had a new exhibit, the one that would come to define his life. It was a mysterious dead body frozen in a large block of ice inside a glass case, apparently that of a human-like creature slightly larger than a man and covered in dark hair.

Hansen proved to be a consummate showman in the spirit of P.T. Barnum in the way he hyped his exhibit, giving different stories at different times as to where it had come from, and of course capitalizing on the popularity of the Bigfoot subject at that time in America. It was sometimes billed as the "Siberskoye Creature," with the story being that it had been found floating in the sea encased in ice off of Siberia by either Russian or Japanese sailors and that Frank had found it stored in a refrigeration plant in Hong Kong. The exhibit was hugely popular and drew long lines of carnival goers paying a small fee to see it.

Things took a turn in early December of 1968 when a Milwaukee herpetologist named Terry Cullen was at the Chicago International Livestock Exposition. Cullen's primary field of study was reptiles, but he apparently had a general interest in all zoology as he joined the crowd waiting in line to see the Iceman. When he entered the trailer in which the frozen body was housed and took a close look at it, he was thunderstruck. He knew that carnival sideshow exhibits were often phony fabrications designed for nothing more than to rake in peoples' money, but what he was seeing looked real enough that he thought he needed to get word to the world of science.

On December 12th, he phoned Ivan T. Sanderson, well-known biologist and at that time director of the Society for the Investigation of the Unexplained (SITU), who had established himself as an early figurehead in the study of Bigfoot and similar creatures around the world. As luck or perhaps just serendipity would have it; at that time, Sanderson was being visited by the prominent Belgian cryptozoologist Dr. Bernard Heuvelmans, the man who actually founded the term and the science of cryptozoology or the study of "hidden animals."

They decided to travel from the east coast to Frank Hansen's home in Minnesota where the Iceman exhibit was stored, stopping briefly along the way to investigate a recent Bigfoot sighting in Wisconsin, and ended up meeting Frank and being given permission to conduct a rigorous study of the specimen over three days on December 16-18, 1968. The Iceman in its glass case, was housed in a refrigerated trailer just outside Frank's house, and he refused to allow it to be thawed out, but whatever studies the two scientists were able to conduct through the ice was fair game.

What they saw through the ice, which naturally did not give a perfect view, was the body of what they determined to be a male creature covered in dark hair over six feet tall lying on its back with its right arm resting across its lower abdomen and its left arm was thrown up over its head, both hands and both feet appearing somewhat disproportionately large in size. The face looked somewhat apelike while the body was distinctly humanoid in form. There were injuries visible, suggesting how the creature might have died. The raised left arm looked broken, with possible protruding bone in the forearm and some blood in the ice apparent.

A possible wound also suggested itself in the center of the chest, but the face bore the most dramatic damage as the left eye appeared to be missing while the right was hanging out of its socket with blood around it. Sanderson and Heuvelmans naturally went into their investigation of this sideshow exhibit expecting a fake and determined not to be fooled, but over the course of their two-day examination, they came to believe that they were looking at a real body that was not some ancient prehistoric protohuman that had been preserved in ice but a specimen from an extant species that had been recently killed. Both men published their findings soon afterward.

Sanderson was somewhat conservative in his assessment, which was rare for him, declining to classify the specimen but stating "it might constitute a very valuable contribution to knowledge and potentially to a better understanding of primate, anthropoid, and possibly hominoid ancestry." Heuvelmans however was not reserved at all, declaring that he had examined the corpse of a surviving Neanderthal man and giving it the scientific name Homo pongoides or the "ape-like man" and calling for a whole new chapter in the study of human evolution.

Essentially, he was asking people to look at the evolutionary chart most students have seen of the ascent of man and to consider that perhaps while old species gave way to new ones, it might be possible that some of the old ones did not completely die out in the process. Sanderson also contacted the curator of primates at the Smithsonian Institute, John Napier, who expressed some cautious interest in the case.

Quite suddenly, science seemed to be converging on what was promising to be the ultimate proof of Bigfoot-like creatures existing in the world. Frank Hansen, however, was unfortunately not on board with that. He and his exhibit suddenly disappeared for a short time, and when they reappeared, it was at a press conference Hansen called on April 21, 1969, at which he announced two things.

One, he was not the owner of the Iceman but was only exhibiting it for an anonymous west coast millionaire, and two, the Iceman was a man-made, fabricated illusion. He rejected accusations that he had been party to a hoax because he had never insisted that the thing was real. During this same period, there was also talk about how the Iceman now being displayed was not the original, which the mysterious true owner had taken back and replaced with a copy. Slight differences in appearance were indeed noticeable.

Reproduction of photo of Frank Hansen and the phony Iceman from the article '"Ice Man' Not Real, But Murky Mystery is Left," Rochester Post-Bulletin. April 21, 1969.

These things were all the esteemed scientists at the Smithsonian needed to hear. Their Secretary S. Dillon Ripley had previously been concerned enough to contact the FBI out of worry that the Iceman might be human and the victim of foul play, but now he and John Napier and everyone else in a position to do a serious study into the case officially dropped all interest in it.

To confuse the matter even further, two published articles appeared within the next year, both purporting to offer alternate origin stories for the Iceman still being the real thing. In June 1969 a tabloid called the National Bulletin ran the sensational headline, "I was Raped by the Abominable Snowman," concerning a young woman named Helen Westring who claimed to have been attacked by the creature while hunting near the Minnesota city of Bemidji.

In the aftermath of the attack, she was said to have been able to retrieve her fallen rifle and shoot the creature through the eye, killing it. Hansen had then supposedly somehow come into possession of the body. The second article was by Hansen himself, appearing in the July 1970 issue of Saga magazine, entitled "I Killed the Ape-Man Creature of Whiteface." This story described how he had been hunting in the Whiteface Reservoir while on leave from the Duluth Air Force Base in 1963 and had encountered three hairy man-apes feeding on the body of a wounded deer he'd been tracking. When one of them charged him, he shot it through the eye and killed it, causing the other two to flee.

Weeks later, he returned and found the dead creature frozen solid by the frigid Minnesota winter and decided to take it with him, storing it in a deep freeze until his military service was over. This, of course, flew in the face of everything he had stated in his press conference about the anonymous owner and the Iceman being a fake, convincing most people that Hansen the showman was only a huckster telling tall tales to keep the exhibit alive and get people to keep coming and spending their money to see it.

In the 1970s, the Iceman exhibit did a long series of shopping mall appearances, something I personally remember from my childhood when a TV commercial advertised it being on display at the West Acres mall in Fargo, North Dakota, which was only about an hour's drive from where I grew up. Unfortunately, I did not get to go and see it.

In spite of its having been declared a fake people still flocked to see it wherever it went. The last of these showings was in August of 1981, at which time Hansen decided it was finally time to retire it and take it easy since he had recently suffered a heart attack. Nearly two years later, in the spring of 1983, he briefly came out of retirement for one last appearance at a car dealership in Rochester, Minnesota, after which the Iceman officially died.

At that time, it had long since lost most of its appeal to the Bigfoot community. John Napier authored the 1972 book "Bigfoot: The Yeti and Sasquatch in Myth and Reality" in which he admitted to his belief in sasquatch but was firm in seeing no reason to see the Iceman as anything but a fake. By the time of his death in 1987 at age 70, he had also been swayed to believe in the Himalayan yeti, but not in the Iceman. Ivan Sanderson, however, who died not long after all the excitement over it in 1973 at age 62, never bowed to his critics who ridiculed his support of the "hoax" and maintained that what he had examined in a cold, cramped trailer in southeast Minnesota had been made of flesh and blood, not rubber.

Likewise, his comrade, Bernard Heuvelmans, had this to say in 1980 on an episode of the TV series "Arthur C. Clarke's Mysterious World": 'There was no doubt that we were looking at some sort of man. Not homo sapiens, but some sort of strangely hairy man. We were struck by many things, the enormous hands and the enormous feet, and also more especially the features of the face, because it was absolutely unlike any man on Earth. It was obvious that this creature had been killed because the... one eye was completely missing, and the other was hanging out of the socket, and it had burnt all around, so we thought it was probably shot in one eye, and the bullet made the other eye pop out...

From seeing it, there is no question that the Iceman could be a hoax, a faked dummy, rubber dummy or what have you, as they told the press. When you have seen something... We examined this creature for three days, very carefully, and we were very suspicious, I can tell you at the start, but after a while, that was quite ruled out. No, there is absolutely no doubt for me that I have been examining a Neanderthal man, a surviving Neanderthal man."

Heuvelmans stuck firmly to that position until his death in 2001 at age 84. In 1974 after extensive investigation he and Russian researcher Boris Porshnev co-authored a book in French entitled "Le Homme de Neanderthal est Toujours Vivant," which translates to "The Man of Neanderthal is Still Alive." It was a fascinating study detailing his belief that the Iceman was a creature shot and killed by American soldiers in the jungles of Vietnam and then smuggled to the U.S. as part of a criminal enterprise known to have operated during the war that smuggled heroin inside the coffins of slain soldiers.

One of the major hubs used by this drug ring was known to be the airbase at Da Nang, where Frank Hansen served for a time. As further evidence Heuvelmans cited journalist Jim Lucas writing in the New York World Journal Tribune in November 1966 that U.S. Marines in the Vietnamese demilitarized zone sometimes shot at jungle tigers and had also once "shot a huge ape."

No great apes are known to live in Vietnam, so this also persistent rumors Heuvelmans heard about the killing of a "wild hairy man" amounted to his theory that the Iceman had nothing to do with the American Bigfoot but was a specimen of surviving Neanderthals that dwelled in Southeast Asia. Heuvelmans is remembered as a respected elder within cryptozoology, being no less than the man that founded the science and the International Society of Cryptozoology for which he served as president.

Could his theory have merit?

I had yet to even hear of the story of the Vietnam connection when, as a young 21-year- old fledgling Bigfoot researcher, I used some vacation time to go on a fact-finding tour of southeast Minnesota in the summer of 1989 and look into some of the reports in that region. With youthful enthusiasm, one of the stops I planned was to boldly go and track down Frank Hansen and pay him an unannounced visit. The fact that I actually succeeded is something I will always be proud of. Books recounting the Iceman story usually described Hansen as living near the city of Winona, population about 27,000, or the nearby small town of Rollingstone with a population of only around 650.

In seeking out Hansen, my first stop was the Historical Society in Winona, where I found some newspaper articles on him in their archives that described his farm as actually being just outside another little town called Altura, population just under 500 and lying about 14 miles west of Winona. Rollingstone is about six miles northeast of Altura, and I am at a loss to understand why it has so long been identified as the home of Frank Hansen when the true location of his farm, Altura, has never been mentioned.

Upon arriving in Altura, I went to the first business I could find, a small general store, and asked the person working there if he knew where Frank Hansen lived. The young man replied, "You mean Frances Hansen?" and literally just pointed to a small farm visible on the horizon from where we were standing. In a few minutes, I reached the farm and knocked on the door of the house, but no one answered.

Great, I thought, I've come all this way and nobody's home. But as I just kind of lingered around in the front yard for a couple of minutes looking around, a blue car suddenly came speeding down the gravel road and into the driveway. I can't say for sure what make and model it was, but it was definitely several years old and something along the lines of a Gremlin.

Out of that car then stepped Frank Hansen, who came striding up to me, and at the time and still to this day, I couldn't help but think that wherever he had just come from, someone must have somehow tipped him off that some stranger was looking for him and that he wasn't just then happening to arrive home by sheer coincidence. This was before the age of everyone having a cell phone, so I'm not sure how that would have played out.

In any case, he was dressed very casually in jeans and a t-shirt, 66 years old at the time, and he seemed on guard when he first approached me, but when I held up the paperback Bigfoot book I had in my hands open to a photo of him and the Iceman and told him why I was there, a big grin immediately appeared on his face. I was pleasantly surprised at how welcoming he was and willing to talk, and we sat down at a picnic table in front of the house that he said was on the exact spot where Sanderson and Heuvelmans had conducted their famous examination of the Iceman, inside the trailer that he indicated was now sticking partway out of a nearby shed.

I was a complete stranger, yet he told me the whole story, or at least the present version of it. I knew I was talking to a carnival showman and spinner of tall tales, but he acknowledged that, though he said some of the different origins given for the Iceman were based on real events. The story of him shooting the creature himself in the Whiteface Reservoir, for instance, came from a sighting he really did have while hunting there in 1963, though he did not really shoot and kill what he saw.

As to what it was, Frank said, "Maybe it was from outer space, maybe it was Bigfoot, I don't know," but that if I cared to track down his hunting partners, they would attest to his frightened state after the sighting, and he added that the Air Force had it on record that a UFO landing also took place in the area at the same time. I asked him about the Iceman's anonymous owner. He still would not name him, of course, but he said he met him at the 1967 Arizona State Fair while displaying his antique tractor there. He said that when the man introduced himself, "It was a name I recognized immediately," and that it was someone involved in the entertainment industry.

The man told him that he had a specimen in storage that he thought Frank would be perfect for, something he wanted people to see but which he wanted no personal connection to. Shortly thereafter, in Long Beach, California, Frank first laid eyes on the Iceman. The owner said that an agent or employee of his had discovered it in a refrigeration plant in Hong Kong and purchased it on his behalf, and that it had originally been found floating in the sea by Chinese fishermen encased in a 6,000-pound ice block.

The owner was a deeply religious man and thought the creature seemed to go against the theory of Biblical Creation and thus wanted his name kept out of things, but for scientific reasons, he still felt that the public should be allowed to see it and gave Frank permission to use whatever phony advertising he thought would be best to draw crowds. Frank agreed to take possession of it after the ice was temporarily shaved down enough for him to see that it was a real corpse and not a fake.

One of the early ad campaigns was particularly amusing. Frank's tractor display had had a sign reading "Found in the woods of Minnesota," so he simply used the same sign for a while to describe the Iceman. He showed me another sign that he still had in storage on the farm that asked in big lettering, "Is It Prehistoric?" But after some time, in spite of the great success he was having with the Iceman, Frank said he began to worry about getting into legal trouble if the body he was showing turned out to be human, so he returned to California to put a contingency plan in place, having a replica constructed out of latex rubber and hair.

A man often mentioned in connection with this project was Hollywood model maker Howard Ball, who Frank said was the person he went to first but that when he wasn't quite satisfied with Ball's work, he took the replica elsewhere, and the several different model, making companies over the years who claimed to have been the Iceman's creator were, in fact, all telling the truth because they all worked on it. Frank intended to switch the real body with the phony one if he ever felt it necessary.

That time came after Sanderson and Heuvelmans published their accounts of the examination they conducted at Frank's home in December 1968. Frank was quite perturbed by this as he had only allowed them access after they promised not to publicize it, being particularly upset with Heuvelmans, whose article had appeared first. He also told me that what did not appear in either scientist's account was just exactly how they became convinced that the body was real.

To get the best possible view, they had brought in bright lights to hang over the glass- topped refrigerated coffin in which the Iceman lay, and while Frank was away from them for a time, they placed one of the hot lights directly on the cold glass, accidentally causing it to shatter. At that point a pungent odor of rotting flesh rose from the ice, the final proof they needed to be sure that what lay before them was a genuine fresh corpse, leading to great excitement.

Frank said he would never forget what they told him at that point when he reminded them of their agreement not to go public, though he didn't specify which man actually said it. The quote was, "We are scientists first, and gentlemen second." The official version of the Iceman saga, as reported in various publications, has stated that FBI director J. Edgar Hoover informed the Smithsonian that he saw no reason for his Bureau to investigate the Iceman, but according to Frank, he was in fact visited by federal agents from the FBI office in nearby Rochester, Minnesota, after Sanderson's and Heuvelman's findings came out. He stalled them, promising to let them have the specimen examined by experts shortly, but then in the interim, he decided that the time to make the switch had come and did his famous disappearing act, loading the Iceman into a truck and heading out for California in the middle of the night.

Once there, he returned the creature to its anonymous owner and then returned to Minnesota with the frozen replica, which he presented at his April 1969 press conference. He added that as he was in the early hours of his trip west, he was detained for a time by police in Iowa, who never knew what he had in the back of his truck. So the phony Iceman took its genuine predecessor's place on the carnival circuit and continued to draw crowds.

In an ironic twist, Frank added signs reading "Investigated by the FBI," and to throw things off even further, he produced the Saga article stating that he had killed the creature himself in Minnesota. Speaking to me in 1989, he assured me that he no longer possessed either the real or the phony Iceman and that the whole thing was in the past for him, though he was aware of other people who had tried to cash in with their own inferior models and tried to pass them off as the original.

He said he thought of the whole affair as a learning experience that taught him much about his fellow men and that he didn't much care what people thought about it. The mysterious owner, he said, had stated that if he was ever identified, he would take the Iceman out into the Pacific Ocean and dump it. As to his own thoughts on just what the Iceman might have been in life, he said he wondered if it might have to do with what he referred to as the "Hairy Ainu" of Japan, though in that he seemed to have a rather crude assessment of the ancient Ainu tribe who lived in the region where Japan converged with Russia and were sometimes viewed in a very exaggerated way in old folklore due to the fact that they tended to have somewhat excess body hair.

When Frank finished his story, he decided in a very friendly way that our visit was over, and with a smile and a handshake left me with the assertion that if I wrote and published something interesting on the case, I should let him know. Time can fly, and it seems unbelievable now that it was five years before my next contact with Frank Hansen. On September 25, 1994, the NBC television series "Unsolved Mysteries" hosted by actor Robert Stack featured a story about the Iceman that went over the basic story with actors portraying Frank and other central figures.

Terry Cullen was interviewed, giving an expanded version of his role in the case and explaining how he had been so amazed by the exhibit when he saw it in Chicago that he'd gone back several times to try and examine it more closely, his repeated visits seeming to make Frank suspicious. Meanwhile, he was trying to find a qualified expert to come and see it, but he had no luck until an anthropologist from the University of Minnesota finally agreed.

According to Cullen, after the man came out of the exhibit, he seemed in a daze and just muttered "It's amazing" and then walked away without another word. It was after that that Cullen had contacted Ivan Sanderson. (It was interesting to have the U of M included in the story since famous Bigfoot researcher Prof. Grover Krantz who was one of the only scientists to go on record as believing in the creatures went to school at that university and commented in his book "Big Footprints" that if he had walked just a little farther at one particular carnival, he would have been the first scientist to see the Iceman, which he believed was real.) The late Twin Cities crypto-zoologist Mark A. Hall who I had met and corresponded with was also featured on the show, giving his more or less positive opinions on the case.

He took some of the most widely distributed photos of the original Iceman in the 60s, though he seldom got credit for it. I was watching a videotaped piece on the Iceman with him once when he pointed at the screen and said, "I think I took that picture." "Unsolved Mysteries" stated that they'd asked Frank to participate in the broadcast but that he had declined, which didn't surprise me. I wrote about the show in the Sasquatch Report newsletter I was publishing at that time, and a short time later, to my great surprise, I got a phone call from Frank. Someone had apparently sent him a copy of the newsletter, and he had a few comments to make about the whole thing.

He said he had declined to take part in the show because he didn't care for their approach, not because he was being reclusive or had anything to hide. The biggest surprise he had for me, though, was when he said that he had recently been in touch with the Iceman's still anonymous owner, who he had not talked to in a long time. The owner claimed to still be in possession of the body and that it was still frozen and in good condition, and furthermore that he just might consider presenting it to the public once again in the near future. Well, as I write this, now it has been another 24 years, and nothing ever came of it.

A few years later, I got word from an acquaintance who visited Frank that in 1997 that he had a serious accident that nearly took his life. While burning some rubbish, he had reportedly thrown some gasoline on the fire, which exploded and caused him to burst into flames himself. Prompt medical attention saved him, but he was left with severe burns, hindered mobility, and some selective memory loss. He was said to no longer remember me, for instance, but his memories of the whole Iceman saga were still relatively intact. Frank was in his 70s then, surviving what would have been a tough blow for even a much younger man.

A few more years on, in 2002, I was contacted by a trio of heavy hitters from the Bigfoot field who were interested in doing a new investigation of the Iceman by contacting Frank while he was still among the living and wanted to know if I wanted to be involved. They were the esteemed hominologist Dmitri Bayanov of Russia, Canadian researcher Chris Murphy, and California's Alan Berry, who was well known for recording the famous "Sierra Sounds" Bigfoot vocalizations of the early 70s. I was humbled that these men were interested in my counsel when all I had done was pay an unsolicited visit to the Iceman's caretaker when I was a very young and inexperienced researcher and then written about it in some cheaply done self-published books.

Because of various commitments, I had in my life at the time, I told them that I was not able to take part directly in their investigation, but I gave them all the information I had on Frank and wished them well. There is a major new element, though, that needs to be mentioned here before I go on, and that has to do with my own speculation as to who the mysterious and anonymous owner of the Iceman might have been. I can't say that I really wracked my brain over it because there was one and only one suspect that occurred to me, and the more I thought about it, he made perfect sense. The man was said to be a world traveler and to be deeply religious.

Frank had said, "It was a name I recognized immediately," and if I was right, he probably would have recognized the face as well. The man I had in mind was a very famous Hollywood actor who had been involved with Bigfooter Peter Byrne in 1957 when Byrne had acquired a finger from a supposed yeti hand that was held as a holy relic by monks in the Pangboche monastery in Nepal. Byrne has admitted that the finger was purloined through not exactly above-board measures and that he then smuggled it across the Nepalese border into India. He then needed a way of getting it to England for scientific study and met with the actor who was staying at a hotel in Calcutta at the time, convincing him and his wife Gloria to smuggle the finger inside her lingerie case at a time before airport security was as strict as it is today, and polite and proper British officials would never dare to open such a private and delicate container.

The actor was none other than the star of the Christmas classic "It's a Wonderful Life" and so many other movies over so many years - - Jimmy Stewart. At the time, Frank told me he had just been in touch with the owner again in 1994, Stewart was still alive. He died in July 1997 at age 89. I remember very clearly that while I was corresponding with Peter Byrne back in the late 80s, he wrote that he thought he might know where the Iceman was then, but that getting to the bottom of it would involve a lot of time and money, "taking people out to dinner," and so forth. I never got any follow-up to that claim, but I think it is fascinating.

I think that the best way in which I can present what happened next is to present an article written by Dmitri Bayanov entitled "Updating the Minnesota Iceman 2005," which he wrote in response to a request for information on the case by someone named Jim

Burgtorf and then allowed to be posted online. It is long and repeats some of what I've already covered, but it is thorough and provides much detail that Bayanov was nice enough to give me permission to reproduce here in full: "April 20, 2005 "Dear Mr. Burgtorf, "Thank you for your question, for it prompts me to update the old Iceman story and remind younger researchers of it. It is remarkable that the iceman started its 'career' the same year as Patterson's Bigfoot movie.

According to John Napier, 'At the beginning of the summer of 1967' Frank Hansen 'started touring the Iceman' (BIGFOOT, 1973, p. 109). "Both the Iceman and the movie are still officially believed to be fake. But if the film subject is taken now as real by the majority of bigfoot researchers, the Iceman is denied authenticity by most of them, in spite of the fact that the Iceman initially made a louder noise in science than the Bigfoot film. Here is a quote from the article by Magnus Linklater 'Neanderthal Man?', published by The Sunday Times of London on March 23, 1969: "'A strange ape-like creature frozen in a block of ice is providing American anthropologists with one of the most intriguing questions they have faced in recent years. Is it a fraud, a freak, or is it a form of human being believed to have been extinct since prehistoric times? One thing is certain: It has two large bullet-holes in it.

Just as a precaution the FBI have been called in.' "The concluding lines of the article ran as follows: 'Whatever the explanation, a capital crime may have been committed. Accordingly, the FBI has been informed. However fanciful all these suggestions, the anthropological world may be on the verge of one of the most exciting discoveries in the study of man. Dr. Heuvelmans' ape-man might just provide the evidence of a missing link in the evolution of man. Even if it doesn't, it could as great a cause celebre as the Piltdown Man.' "The Iceman owes its 'cause celebre' status to Bernard Heuvelmans and Ivan Sanderson, the founding fathers of cryptozoology, and in part to Boris Porshnev, the father of hominology.

In February 1969, Heuvelmans published, in the Bulletin of the Royal Institute of Natural Sciences of Belgium, a paper entitled, 'Notice on a specimen preserved in ice of an unknown form of living hominid: Homo pongoides.' Later, in 1974, he devoted a voluminous book to the case, 'L'Homme de Neanderthal est toujours vivant' (Neanderthal Man is still alive). "Sanderson committed his findings to paper in the report 'Preliminary Description of the External Morphology of What Appears to be the Fresh Corpse of a Hitherto Unknown Form of Living Hominid' (Genus, Vol. XXV, N.1-4, 1969).

Porshnev's role lies in the fact that Heuvelmans referred to Porshnev's ideas in claiming the present-day survival of Neanderthal man, supposedly evidenced by the Iceman. Porshnev, in turn, dwelt in length on the case in the Russian popular press and asked a very pertinent question: If the Iceman is a model, WHAT is it a model of? "The relevance of this question became especially clear with the publication in FATE (March 1982) of the piece 'The Iceman Goeth,' in which debunkers referred to one Howard Ball, 'who died several years ago' and who 'made models for Disneyland.' 'He made (the Iceman) here in his studio in Torrance (Calif.),' Balls' widow Helen told Emery. 'The man who commissioned it said he was going to encase it in ice and pass it off, I think, as a prehistoric man.' Balls' son Kenneth helped his father build the figure.

He says its 'skin' is half-inch thick rubber. 'We modeled it after an artist's conception of Cro-Magnon man and gave it a broken arm and a bashed-in skull with one eye popped out.' (p.59). "That the Iceman is a model of Cro-Magnon man is sheer nonsense, and the height of anthropological ignorance. There exists no artist's conception even of Neanderthal man as hairy as the Iceman. A 'prehistoric man' of this kind was only posited by Boris Porshnev's anthropological theory, which was not widely known at the time and is not recognized even today.

So the question persists: If the original Iceman is a model, WHAT is it a model of? "But the most crucial question concerns the exhibit's authenticity. There are two episodes in the story that seem to indicate more than anything else that what originally lay in the ice was not a fabrication. In July 1989, Minnesota sasquatch researcher Mike Quast visited and interviewed Frank Hansen at his ranch. In his good book, The Sasquatch in Minnesota' (1996), Mike had this to say on the matter: "'The reports published by Sanderson and Heuvelmans brought an incredible amount of attention Hansen's way, much to his anger because he had insisted on no publicity when he allowed them to examine the Iceman.

He was particularly upset with Heuvelmans, whose report appeared first. "According to Hansen, what does not appear in either scientist's report is just how they became convinced the Iceman was real. To get the best possible view of it, they had hung bright lights over the glass under which it lay, and while Hansen was away from them for a moment one of them placed one of the hot lights directly on the ice-cold glass. It shattered, and a pungent odor like that of rotting flesh rose from the ice. This convinced them that an actual corpse, freshly killed, lay before them.

Hansen will never forget what the distinguished scientists said when he reminded them of their promise not to publicize the story at that point. "We are scientists first," they told him, "and gentlemen second." (He doesn't say exactly which one of them said this.)' (P-144). "Ivan Sanderson, in his report, refers to this important incident in this way: 'The corpse or whatever it is, is rotting. This could be detected by a strong stench- typical of rotting mammalian flesh- exuding from one of the corners of the insulation of the coffin. Whatever this corpse may be, it would seem to include flesh of some kind.' (Genus, p.253). "Why did Hansen insist on no publicity when he allowed the two scientists to examine his exhibit? How could publicity from such examination harm his carnival sideshow business?

And why did publication of the scientists' conclusion that the corpse was real cause the showman's anger? The answer is in Magnus Linklater's words cited above: 'a capital crime may have been committed.' This must have been the reason for Hansen's subsequent actions, maneuvers, and conflicting stories. Let us also note one of his recurring statements that was as little believed as all his other declarations, namely, that the Iceman did not belong to him but to a millionaire in California.

"A second incident indicating the Iceman's reality happened in July 1969 when, after a tour of Canada with his exhibit, Hansen was held up by US customs officials at a border post in North Dakota. The episode was related by Sanderson to Heuvelmans and is mentioned in the latter's book (pp.283-84). Customs demanded from Hansen special permission by the US Surgeon General for carrying the corpse of a 'humanoid creature.' Hansen argued that it was not a real corpse but a 'fabricated illusion' made of latex rubber and offered documents of its fabrication.

That did not impress the officials, who demanded that a piece of the Iceman be taken for examination. Hansen protested, saying this would damage the exhibit. "In desperation he even phoned Sanderson and asked for advice. The latter, thinking that this time Hansen toured the model, advised that the customs x-ray the exhibit, to which suggestion Hansen cried out: 'Impossible! The owner will never allow this!' (My translation from the French- D.B.). (Heuvelmans remarks in brackets that there was no need to inform and ask the owner because x-rays leave no traces).

Hansen then sought by phone the help of the Iceman's owner in California, as well as that of his own Senator in Washington, Walter F. Mondale, subsequently US Vice-President in Carter's Administration. Twenty-four hours later Hansen was released with the Iceman unchecked. "To quote Mike Quast again: 'Some call the Iceman by the name "Bozo," a carnival clown, nothing more.

To most serious investigators now that's all he was- a phony, no more real than a mannequin. He has, for the most part, been written off as a big joke. But the joke is on them, because the Iceman was real.' (p.143). 'At the 1967 Arizona State Fair, he (Hansen) met a man who to this day, he will not name, but he says "It was a name I recognized immediately," and that it was someone connected to the entertainment industry. The man said he had a very interesting specimen in storage in California and asked Hansen to consider taking it on a carnival tour.

Shortly thereafter, in Long Beach, Hansen first laid eyes on the Iceman. "'The man explained that an agent of his had discovered the creature in its frozen state in a refrigeration plant in Hong Kong and that it had originally been found floating in the sea by Chinese fishermen in a 6,000-pound ice block. He was a deeply religious man, Hansen explained, and he thought this creature seemed to go against the theory of creation as told in the Bible, thus he wanted no connection to it.

Hansen agreed to display it, but first, the ice was temporarily shaved down for his benefit and he saw that it was indeed a real corpse, not a fake. "'Hansen was given permission to use whatever phony advertising he wished in order to draw crowds. Stories about "Bigfoot" in the news at that time helped as well, and the display was very popular. (...)

After some time, however, Hansen began to worry that he might get into serious legal trouble if what he had turned out to be a human corpse. So, returning to California, he had a replica manufactured from latex rubber and hair, intending to switch it with the original if he ever had to.' (pp.143-44). "In 1994, Quast got a surprise when Hansen himself gave him a call. 'But the biggest surprise came when he said that he had recently heard from the real owner of the Iceman, who he had not talked to in a long time and didn't even know if the man was still living.

He still wouldn't name him, of course, but he said the owner claimed to still be in possession of the original Iceman and that it was still frozen and in good condition. Also, he might (just might) consider presenting it to the public once again in the near future. Well, that was a couple of years ago. No word yet. (...) The last word, however, belongs to that anonymous owner, who once stated to Hansen that if he was ever identified, he would dump the Iceman in the Pacific Ocean.' (p.146).

"Having read all that, I contacted Mike Quast in 2002 and in April received a letter from him, with the last paragraph reading as follows: 'I have had one theory -- and that is all it is -- about who the anonymous owner of the Iceman might have been. I am not saying that I necessarily believe it as fact, but the only name that comes to mind is the late actor Jimmy Stewart. Hansen said it was someone in the entertainment industry and that when he met him, it was a name he "recognized immediately", and that the man did not want to be publicly identified with the Iceman because of his strong religious beliefs.

I believe Stewart was known as being rather religious, was a world traveler, and he did have some interest in such subjects as he was involved with Peter Byrne and Tom Slick in getting a yeti hand smuggled out of Nepal (according to Loren Coleman's book on Tom Slick). Stewart was still alive when Hansen told me he had just been in touch with the owner, but died a couple of years later. That is the only idea I have come up with... If investigators visit Hansen today, they might try mentioning this theory to him and just studying what his reaction is to the name.'

"I heartily thanked Mike Quast for the information in his book and the theory in his letter, and proposed to Alan Berry to try and verify that theory with a visit to Hansen and one more interview. Alan was too busy to go to Minnesota but interviewed Hansen by phone on April 7, 2002. Here are some excerpts from that interview:
Berry: What do you think the Iceman represented?

Hansen: I can tell you I don't associate it with Bigfoot.

B: You mean if it was real?

H: Yeah... well, I mean if it was real, I would think of it like it might be some kind of early man, but I don't know.

B: What did the owner tell you about where it came from?

H: He was in the business of producing movies, and he (?) was in the Tokyo (?) bay area, and saw a block of ice with this thing in it. He asked the fishermen, 'What do you want for it?' They dickered, and he ended up trading a case of whisky for it. He said he didn't know what it was, just that it was interesting and something his people might use, you know, as a prop. The owner leased space with refrigeration on a ship, and the block of ice with the Iceman was shipped to the U.S.

B: What was the owner's interest in exhibiting the Iceman? "H: Just to see what the public would think of it... what kind of furor or controversy it might create. He wasn't looking for anything out of it himself. He was a religious man. He just wanted to see how people would react if they thought there was really a primitive form of man that came before us in time, you know, evolution and such...

B: What kind of person was the owner?

H: He was very, very religious. He didn't want the Iceman exhibited as anything real, only wanted the public's reaction. Like could it be something almost human from prehistoric times?

B: Who was the owner? "H: I can't tell you, I am under oath. I can just tell you that he was a big name... Anybody would recognize his name right away today even, but he's dead. He passed away.

B: What had become of the body?

H: I tried to take it (the exhibit) into Canada for a show, was stopped at the border. It was the Bureau of Customs, and they stopped me because they thought I was transporting cadaver across the border. It was seized at the border. I explained to them it was just an exhibit, neither man nor beast, but they didn't believe me until a US Senator bailed me out. Because of, who was he, Irene? Well, I was a good friend of him, and had given him a lucrative donation, yes; it was a Senator in Washington. It was through Walter Mondale, the Senator, that they got an order from Agriculture and Forest Products to 'let them go.' After the border incident and with 'all the people' that were after me, I got tired of the whole thing and phoned the owner to take back the Iceman.

It is most important that Hansen confirmed the border incident of which we learned first from Heuvelmans, even though there are certain differences with Heuvelman's words in Hansen's description. Why did he mention Tokyo instead of Hong Kong as the place where the Iceman came from? Was his memory failing?

In September, 2002, Dr. Peter Rubec talked to Hansen on the phone. Here's a quote from Rubec's email to me: 'I did ask Hansen about Jimmy Stewart. There was a fairly long pause, but all he would say was that the owner of the real Iceman (he was fairly emphatic there was a real one) was in the movie industry, and he had died. But he would not reveal who it was.'

I then discussed the matter with Loren Coleman who, when

writing his book about Tom Slick, had contact with Stewart. Loren confirmed to me that the latter was very religious and referred to the opinion of Mark Hall, who had two separate interviews with Frank Hansen in the 1990s: 'It appeared the owner did not value it (the Iceman) in the way many of us would... The true owner of the Iceman did not want to be the one who presented the "missing link" that would undercut the truth of Biblical creation. The owner was interested in seeing peoples' reactions to the "missing link" and so allowed the Iceman to be displayed' (Living Fossils, 1999, p.85). 'Mark Hall senses,' wrote Loren to me, 'that the mysterious owner was a pro-creationist.'

I then addressed Peter Byrne, saying that I've been trying to crack the Iceman riddle in recent years, urging Krantz, Greenwell, and others to do so while Hansen was alive, and continued, in part: 'When I read "The Sasquatch in Minnesota" by your friend and follower Mike Quast, I asked him to help. And he did by supplying information about Hansen, which is not in the book. In his letter he shared with me his opinion and his hypothesis regarding Jimmy Stewart. So the credit for it goes to him.'

Peter Byrne wrote back on August 30, 2003: 'Your hypothesis (I had told him it was not mine- D.B.) concerning an Iceman connection with Jimmy Stewart is very interesting and indeed is one that has surfaced previously, mainly because of my connection with him going back to Yeti and Himalayan days. So, let me talk with some family members and what they have to contribute to it, and then I will get back to you.'

His email of September 4 added this: 'In the matter of the Iceman, these leads definitely need to be examined and followed up; as you say, anything is possible, and actually, there is a faint but persistent rumor in entertainment circles that Jimmy Stewart did have an association of some kind with some large and mysterious animal.' The email of October 30 said the following: 'As of now, I do not have a lot to report. There are, as I said previously, grounds to believe that Jimmy Stewart was definitely connected/associated to/with [a] large animal of some kind; however there are conflicting reports on exactly what it was. This (confliction), of course, could be part of a cover up;

it is my finding that in many cases, families of people who have these associations like to have them brushed under the carpet, so to speak, after they (the finders or investigators) pass away. This was indeed the case with Tom Slick, whose family, after he died, seem to have destroyed all of the evidence that he gathered on the Bigfoot mystery and whose foundation, the South West Research Institute of San Antonio, Texas, now state that they had nothing to do with his BF research when in fact, some of the expense and salary checks that I received when I ran the first northern California Bigfoot project were on the institute's bank account. So it may be the same thing with the Stewart family.'

As of today, I have not heard from Peter Byrne anything more on the Jimmy Stewart connection.

The latest information on the Iceman that reached me comes from Curt Nelson, who on April 11, 2005, emailed me the following:

I live in Minnesota just north of Minneapolis/St. Paul. Hansen, I'd heard (from Mike Quast), was last known to live near the small town of Rollingstone, about 100 miles south of me. I drove down there in February just to see if I might find him (the phone number for Hansen Mike Quast provided was no longer in service). In the town of Altura (a few miles from Rollingstone), I stopped at a bank and went in and inquired about Hansen, about his whereabouts. The woman (a bank teller) I spoke to said she knew where Hansen's home was but that he was gone, that he died two years prior. She said that his wife and son still lived in the area, though, and she looked them up in the phone directory for me. (...)

I went out into the parking lot of the bank and called Mrs. Hansen (Irene) using my cell phone and I reached her. She was not enthusiastic about talking about The Iceman, but she did speak to me for about 5 minutes. (...) She said her husband died with the secret as to the true story on the Iceman [and] that even she didn't know it. She seemed to think that was quite appropriate and she seemed sincere about it. And at least twice she said, in reference to the secrecy surrounding the Iceman, that it was "to protect the innocent ones."

The son is an attorney, and I reached him at work just after speaking to his mother. He was in a bad mood in the first place, I would say, and was just barely polite to me on the subject of his father's Iceman. (I'm sure the Hansen family has been bothered plenty about it over the years.) He told me the second body, the one widely thought to have been an obvious fake, was gone. That it had been cleared out long ago.

I called Mrs. Hansen back again while driving home to ask for clarification on something (can't recall what just now), and she asked me if I knew Roger Patterson. She said she and her husband visited Patterson in California. She just volunteered that, seemingly just to make conversation. She didn't remember anything about the meeting, but it tells me Frank Hansen had an interest in bigfoot. I find that interesting -- that the carnival man showing off The Iceman would look up a man who claimed to have filmed a bigfoot, a man thousands of miles away in California. It suggests to me that Frank Hansen believed what he had might be a bigfoot. (If Hansen's body was a fake, why would he be interested in bigfoot?)

In summary, here is what I took away from my conversations with Irene Hansen and her son: Nothing is final, it is still all a mystery. (...) The son is a lawyer, and if there is a concern about legal issues (the creature might be considered human), he has certainly counseled his mother on how to answer questions-- with no real answers. It seems to me that the simplest truth behind this story was that it was all a hoax perpetrated solely by Frank Hansen. If that were true why, decades later, wouldn't he and now his family just say, forget it, it was just a carnival trick!(?) (...) Please feel free to use what I've told you in any way you like.

Thank you very much, Curt Nelson, for your most important information. It is news to hominologists that Frank Hansen has died. Regrettably, the event passed unnoticed two years ago. I agree with your inferences and conclusions, especially the one concerning Hansen's visit to Patterson in California, which is a big surprise. The news should be verified and discussed with Patricia Patterson. You are right, if the Iceman was a fake why would Hansen be interested in

Bigfoot? He must have been interested in Bigfoot because he was keenly interested in the exact nature of the carnival exhibit he displayed. Was it a human or non-human primate? The very legal status of the exhibit depended on the answer. The leading Bigfoot researchers, such as John Green and Grover Krantz, called Bigfoot an ape, a giant non-human primate. Was it not for this reason that Hansen for a time presented the Iceman as a bigfoot he himself killed during a hunt in Minnesota? The different signs he used for the exhibit in sideshows are also indicative in this connection: 'What is it?', 'Sibserskoye Creature', 'Found in the Woods of Minnesota', 'Is it Prehistoric?'

The question 'What is it?' must have been heavy on his mind when he allowed Sanderson and Heuvelmans to examine his exhibit and asked them not to publicize their findings. Heuelmans' published conclusion that it was the corpse of a killed Neanderthal Man must have alarmed Hansen a lot. From his words to Alan Berry, 'I don't associate it with Bigfoot' and 'it might be some kind of early man', we can conclude that Heuvelmans' verdict stuck in Hansen's mind and determined his words and actions to the end.

Of special interest are Irene Hansen's words that the secrecy surrounding the Iceman serves 'to protect the innocent ones.' This brings up the question: And who are 'the guilty ones'? They can well be inferred from Hansen's own words. First, the Iceman owner who smuggled a corpse into the U.S. and kept it illegally; second, Frank Hansen, who displayed a smuggled dead body without permission; third, ex-Vice-President Walter Mondale through whom Customs got an order to let a cadaver across the US-Canada border.

And who are 'the innocent ones'? Apparently, the families of the guilty ones. They know the truth and for obvious reasons are determined to keep it secret, no matter what detriment to science.

Mike Quast again: 'It is certainly a case that seems to deserve any researcher's undivided attention, for in it we supposedly have what Bigfoot people have sought for so many years: the actual corpse of a hair-covered humanoid' (p.137). I am convinced now that the words 'we supposedly have' could be changed to 'we do have' if not for the fact that the actual corpse is still out of our reach. As I wrote not so long ago, 'The negative impact of indifference on one side, and hidden or open hostility on the other, leaves the tiny number of hominologists little chance to quickly obtain traditionally acceptable biological proof.' The Iceman case illustrates this point with utmost clarity.

Let us note that after Sanderson and Heuvelmans, the case was followed up, and bits of truth gleaned and collected not by scientific institutions, such as the Smithsonian or the International Society of Cryptozoology, whose express task was to investigate such cases, but by private researchers, such as Mark Hall, Mike Quast, Alan Berry, & Curt Nelson. Well, long live private enterprise!

I wish the Stewart connection would finally be established. I wish its confirmation for two reasons. First, to the usual question 'Where is [the] hard evidence?' we'd have a ready answer: 'Ask the Stewart family.' Second, I'd offer Hollywood a scenario of a film, based on facts stranger than fiction, from the scene of getting the body of an ape-man for a case of whisky to the final shots of dumping it in the Pacific Ocean. The story would be the opposite of the Piltdown Man. In the latter, a fake was used to fool scientists. In my scenario, a Hollywood pro-creationist film star makes the anthropological world on the verge of one of the most exciting discoveries in the study of man take a real 'missing link' for a 'fabricated illusion.' The film would be titled, 'The Carnival Cover-up.' Dmitri Bayanov International Center of Hominology Moscow, Russia"

Here ends Mr. Bayanov's excellent and concise update on where the Iceman case now stands. Two more significant events occurred that should be mentioned.

One, as referenced briefly in the article Frances Dean "Frank" Hansen passed away on Sunday, March 23, 2003, at age 80 at the St. Anne Extended Healthcare facility in Winona, Minnesota. He took much with him to his grave.

And two, what appears to be the replica of the Iceman that Frank commissioned to be made by various Hollywood model makers in 1969 was sold online in 2013 on the popular site eBay for around

$20,000 and is now owned by Steve Busti of the Museum of the Weird in Austin, Texas. A very poor and pathetic attempt to replicate a new version of the Iceman occurred in 2008 when two men, police officer Matt Whitton and car salesman Rick Dyer, announced that they had the frozen body of a dead Bigfoot found in the woods of Georgia. Whitton actually lost his job as a cop after it was revealed that the supposed Bigfoot was really nothing more than an ape costume stuffed with animal guts. As a hoax, it was not even a very good one, but it generated national news headlines for a short time.

I believe that the Minnesota Iceman was originally a very real body of a Bigfoot-like creature that came from somewhere in Asia. Perhaps Bernard Heuvelmans' theory that it was killed in Vietnam and was smuggled to America as part of an illegal drug operation is the true story, or perhaps through some other unknown scenario it was a specimen of the Chinese creatures that are known as Ye-Ren or "wildmen." Someone shot and killed it, and somehow it ended up frozen in a giant block of ice. From that point, it very unfortunately got caught up in the American hype machine, which prevented it from becoming the all-important scientific discovery that it should have been. I believe Jimmy Stewart was involved, and though I don't think I was the first person to ever think that I seem to have been credited as the first to actually come out and say it. If that is true, then so be it. If it is not true, then I apologize to Stewart's family for my wrongful accusation.

I do not think there is any realistic chance that the original body will ever surface again, so unfortunately, this is where the Iceman will have to be laid to its final rest.

The former Iceman trailer in storage on Frank Hansen's farm in 1989.

9

THE PATTERSON-GIMLIN FILM

Portions of this chapter are reprinted from my earlier book "Big Footage: A History of Claims for the Sasquatch on Film." In the autumn of 1967, two events occurred that are significant to the story I am attempting to tell here.

First, along a creek in a valley that is set into a series of mountain ridges in the northwest corner of California, on the 20th of October, two cowboys from Yakima, Washington - Roger Patterson and Bob Gimlin - allegedly managed to capture the first and the best film footage of a living and breathing Bigfoot creature, a film that has gone down in history as being either the most significant piece of evidence for the creatures' existence ever or one of the most sophisticated hoaxes of all time.

Controversy, anyone?

In this chapter, I will discuss all the ins and outs and pros and cons and all the different theories and opinions that have sprung up over the decades involving this piece of film, and explain why I believe it to be genuine.

Second, 26 days later, on the 15th of November in St. Mary's Hospital in Detroit Lakes, Minnesota, I was born. I know that in my early formative years, as I began to develop my interest in the Bigfoot subject, the Patterson-Gimlin film made a major impact on me.

To what extent it played a part in my deciding to become involved in the field as an adult I can't say for sure, but it and my own Bigfoot sighting at the age of eight were surely two of the strongest factors. Over the years I have seen and heard more than enough evidence of all kinds to have long outlived the need for either event to have occurred in order for me to be convinced of the reality of Bigfoot, but history is what it is.

Roger Clarence Patterson. He is legendary in the annals of Bigfoot lore, with the film he shot being thought of as the holy grail by most within the field with only a few modern Bigfooters doubting its authenticity. One must wonder what Patterson himself would think of all the attention and controversy his film has garnered had he not succumbed to Hodgkin's Disease at age 38, just over four scant years after the event that defined his life.

We cannot be naive in our views of the kind of man Roger was. He was a jack of all trades from Yakima, Washington - rodeo cowboy, boxer, inventor, promoter, health food enthusiast, an avid outdoorsman, and family man with a wife and children, his wife's name being Patricia which effectively made her "Patty Patterson" - who entered the hunt for Bigfoot when a 1959 article by scientist Ivan T. Sanderson in True magazine captivated him.

He searched throughout the Pacific Northwest, most notably in the pre-eruption landscape of Mount St. Helens, Washington, and in the Bluff Creek area of Del Norte County, California, the birthplace of Bigfoot, and found enough compelling evidence to keep him going over several years in spite of poor finances and the lack of focus that some say he sometimes suffered from.

To be honest, he was not a man one ever wanted to lend money to because you were probably never going to get it back. But he established himself as one of the major Bigfoot investigators in those early days, looking into reports and interviewing witnesses alongside people like John Green and Rene Dahinden, whom he associated with. He probably had no more skill than them or anyone else, but is rather regarded as the man who had one insanely lucky day.

Even schoolchildren interested in Bigfoot know the date by heart now -- October 20, 1967. The previous year Patterson had self-published a book, "Do Abominable Snowmen of America Really Exist?", illustrated with his own very talented drawings, and now with limited funds, he'd come once again to Bluff Creek in response to word that new Bigfoot tracks had recently been seen.

He was working on a documentary film and enlisted the aid of his friend Bob Gimlin, a fellow Yakima cowboy who wasn't even sure he believed in Bigfoot but agreed to go along on the trip for the chance to train some of his horses in rugged terrain. The two had been camping in the Bluff Creek wilderness for several days, shooting scenes of the landscape and hoping to find fresh tracks.

At around 1:20 PM on that fateful Friday, with both men on horse-back and Gimlin leading a third horse to carry supplies, they rode around a large mass of logs pushed up by spring floods and into history. According to their account, the first thing that happened was that the horses panicked and reared, and Patterson's fell over onto its side, crushing a stirrup with his foot still in it.

At some point during those chaotic seconds, the men caught sight of the cause of the commotion, a large black hairy creature crouched on the opposite bank, which immediately stood and began to walk away on two legs, not hurrying but never pausing. It's been suggested that with the creature being familiar with deer, elk, etc., it may not have equated the sound of approaching hoofbeats with man.

Neither man had ever seen a Bigfoot before (though Patterson may have heard the vocalizations of one at least once) yet considering the circumstances, both reacted remarkably well. Gimlin steadied his horse while Patterson managed to pull a 16-mm Cine-Kodak movie camera from his fallen horse's saddlebag even as the animal must have been thrashing around trying to right itself.

I've never seen any other writer mention one little detail, so I'll do it here -- if that horse had fallen on to its other side, the camera would probably have been destroyed and the famous film would never have been captured. Despite his injured foot Patterson then began running toward the retreating creature, filming as he went and shouting to Gimlin, "Cover me!" As Patterson's horse and the pack animal then ran off, Gimlin rode across the creek with his 30.06 rifle at the ready in case the creature attacked, pointing the weapon in its direction but never putting it to his shoulder.

The men had had an agreement that if they ever saw one of the creatures they would not shoot unless absolutely necessary for self-defense. Gimlin would recall later that, if he'd had a rope, he probably could have gotten close enough to lasso it (and what a film that would have made!). Patterson had gotten to within about 80 feet of the creature when it swung around and shot him a glance that made him stop. Later he would describe its attitude as like "when the umpire tells you, 'One more word and you're out of the game!'" but he knelt down and continued to film from a stationary position as it continued on away from him, finally disappearing into the dense forest, at which point the film ran out.

He had captured over 23 feet of color footage (952 frames totaling just under one minute) of the first and only Bigfoot he ever saw in his life. The men decided not to follow the creature. Though their recollections of certain details would vary later, both agreed that its large breasts indicated that it was a female, and they feared it might have a mate nearby. Instead, they reloaded the camera and shot footage of the clear 14 1/2" footprints it had left on the sandy creek bank (footage that was subsequently lost somehow, though excerpts from it have turned up in various places) and made plaster casts of both left and right prints.

After rounding up the horses, they then drove out to civilization (possibly the town of Eureka, possibly Arcata -- accounts vary, and the two are sister cities lying right alongside each other which might have caused confusion) to mail the film by air to Patterson's brother-in-law Al DeAtley, a wealthy Yakima concrete and paving company owner who was married to Patterson's younger sister and sometimes funded some of Patterson's ventures.

They then placed a call to the British Columbia Museum to

inquire as to the possibility of someone bringing in tracking dogs to pick up the creature's trail. The museum, in turn, contacted investigator John Green, who tried in vain to arrange for some scientist to travel to the site before too much time had passed. But Mother Nature had her own agenda. Nightfall found Patterson and Gimlin back at their camp, but a sudden rainstorm and flash flood threatened to wash out the road, and they had to make a perilous retreat out of the woods, luckily deciding to cover some of the creature's tracks with pieces of bark to protect them from the elements before they left.

Accounts describe Patterson as lying in the tent wanting to go to sleep and denying that conditions were that bad until it became blatantly obvious, and then the two men actually ended up having to hijack some logging equipment they found parked along the road out to get their own truck and horse trailer unstuck from the mud so that they could escape. In 2017 when I was in the area for the 50th anniversary of the Patterson-Gimlin film, I experienced what it's like to be in that setting in a hard rain during the day.

I must say that imagining what it must have been like to go through it in the dark of night scares me to no end. One adventure was over, but one of a different kind was just beginning, that of presenting the film to the public and to science. Patterson was anxious to show it to the world, sure he had the proof that had been sought for so long. Al DeAtley was the first person to see the film that millions have now seen.

Soon after, Patterson and investigators John Green, Rene Dahinden, and Jim McClarin viewed it for the first time at DeAtley's home in Yakima. And just what did they see? In the original, the creature is not even as large as the sprocket holes in the film, resulting in a rather anti-climactic effect. In the book "Sasquatch Apparitions" by the late Barbara Wasson, Bob Gimlin stated, "Of course, I thought the film should have been a lot better than that. I thought the film would be very good. I thought you should be able to just pick the flies off its nose, that close."

Subsequent enlargements, however, brought out the images we

all know so well today, not as sharp and clear as a professional wildlife film perhaps, but still striking in their detail. The first seconds are just a furious blur of bouncing motion as Patterson runs and jumps over rough terrain and crosses the creek while filming. He then steadies himself, probably crouching, and we see the creature walking (never running) purposefully from left to right against the autumn forest backdrop, swinging its arms in a smooth bent-kneed stride unlike the bouncy straight-legged walk of a human being.

It is covered with black hair except in small patches such as the face, where grayish skin shows through. The body is massive, proportioned like that of a man but much broader and with muscles that Gimlin compared to those of the horses he had spent his life observing. There is a moment in which the broad back is displayed, and one gets the best sense of how far below the shoulders the head is actually set. Here also are the only views of the feet, with hairless soles and five toes briefly but clearly seen. There is no clear distinction of the other digits, apparently obscured by hair, but the bending of the hand does suggest fingers. Large pendulous hair-covered breasts ("mammary glands" as Gimlin has called them, another animal reference) seem to identify the creature as female, but its head is peaked at the top like that of a male gorilla. Enlargements of the face show a heavy brow ridge, deep-set eyes, a wide nose and no visible ears.

The neck is very short, almost non-existent, and when the creature turns toward the camera in what Patterson thought was a gesture of warning; it turns its entire upper body rather than just its head, for just as with a gorilla, the neck is too short for the chin to pass over the shoulder. This results in the most famous of all the images in the film, frame #352, reproduced countless times on book covers and in at least half the magazine and newspaper articles ever written on Bigfoot, universally regarded as THE official image of the creature- arms wide apart, right leg forward, left leg mostly hidden behind a log, and face directly toward the camera.

From this point, the creature continues on and turns away from the creek bank, gradually disappearing into the forest. There had been a few photographs taken in previous years purporting to show

Bigfoot, but none were very widely known. Patterson's film was definitely the first of its quality and in its potential to sway scientific interest, but John Green and others cautioned him that it would be better for his credibility if he let authorities come to him rather than running all over the country shouting, "Look at this!" But Patterson's enthusiasm proved stronger than his patience.

The first showing for scientists was at the University of British Columbia, where the film caused quite a stir but failed to create the sensation that was hoped for. Showings in other cities raised even less interest, and though Life magazine showed some interest, it quickly dwindled when the American Museum of Natural History assured the editors the film was most definitely a fake after one brief run-through. There was no in-depth scientific analysis of the film, nor did the scientists even seem to think one necessary.

Such creatures did not exist, after all, so why waste time on a film that had to be a hoax? Only primatologist John Napier of the Smithsonian Institute (later author of a popular book on the Bigfoot phenomenon to be referred to shortly) and biologist and paranormal researcher Ivan T. Sanderson (Patterson's original inspiration) paid any serious attention. It was in the February 1968 issue of Argosy, a popular mens' adventure magazine, rather than the more prestigious Life that frames from the film were first presented to the public, with an article by Sanderson entitled "First Photos of 'Bigfoot,' California's Abominable Snowman."

The first amateur investigation at the film site, meanwhile, had been done about nine or ten days after the filming by Bob Titmus, a veteran of the search for Bigfoot in northern California since the late 1950s, who brought his skills as a taxidermist and animal tracker to bear in examining the film creature's 14 1/2" tracks (which had actually first been seen the day after the filming by forester Lyle Laverty, who did little more than photograph them). Titmus made plaster casts of a series of consecutive prints and then followed the trail and was able to determine that the creature had sat down in some ferns in a spot 80 or 90 feet above the creek and 125 to 150 yards from where

Patterson and Gimlin had been excitedly reorganizing, perhaps watching them.

From the depth of the tracks Titmus estimated that the creature must have weighed 600 to 700 pounds. Further insight was made at the film site in June of 1968 by John Green. His idea was to make a comparison film with a large man walking in about the same place where the creature had walked so as to determine its exact physical dimensions. The model used was fellow investigator Jim McClarin, a student at Humboldt State University in Arcata who stood 6'5", just a shade under the height that most serious studies of the film have arrived at for the creature.

Green's conclusions established a height of 6'8", shoulders 34" across, a neck width of 12", and similar massive proportions overall. Perhaps the most significant expert response in America was from Walt Disney Studios, who, in 1969, told John Green that they would not have been able to duplicate the film with existing technology of the time. Another noteworthy opinion was put forth by Hungarian actor and stunt performer Janos Prohaska, who made a career out of playing hairy creatures of various kinds, including apes in film and television in the late 1960s and early 70s and was regarded as being among the best in the field.

When asked about the Patterson film, he stated that he tended to think it was genuine, and that if it wasn't, then the hair seen on the creature would have had to be applied by glue in a process that would have taken up to ten hours. "It looked to me very, very real," he said. "I'm doing this now since 1939, and if that was a costume, it was the best I have ever seen."

However, in the few years marking the first spate of public and scientific attention over the film, no investigator became more associated with it or went to more effort than Rene Dahinden. When American scientists turned a blind eye, he went elsewhere, taking the film both to England and Russia in 1971 to enlist scientists in those countries to take a look and give their opinions. Dr. D.W. Grieve, an expert on biomechanics at the Royal Free Hospital School of Medicine in London, did one of the first well-known studies of the film at Dahinden's behest, and at this time it began to be a major point of argument that Patterson could not recall the exact film speed he had had the camera set for.

He had been filming the Bluff Creek scenery at 24 fps, which was best suited for television, but wasn't sure if he had changed the setting prior to encountering the creature. After carefully weighing the possibility that the film showed a human being in a costume based on the creature's proportions and gait, Dr. Grieve concluded: "My subjective impressions have oscillated between total acceptance of the Sasquatch on the grounds that the film would be difficult to fake, to one of irrational rejection based on an emotional response to the possibility that the Sasquatch actually exists...

The possibility of a very clever fake cannot be ruled out on the evidence of the film. A man could have sufficient height and suitable proportions to mimic the longitudinal dimensions of the Sasquatch. The shoulder breadth, however, would be difficult to achieve without giving an unnatural appearance to the arm swing and shoulder contours. The possibility of fakery is ruled out if the speed of the film was 16 or 18 fps.

In these conditions, a normal human being could not duplicate the observed pattern, which would suggest that the Sasquatch must possess a very different locomotor system to that of man." The analysis by the Russians was even more thorough and delivered an even stronger support for the film's validity. The Soviet Union had its own manlike creature reported to exist in its mountainous wilderness areas, known by such names as Almista and Kaptar, or sometimes as "Snowman" in comparison to the more famous abominable denizen of the Himalayas, and investigators there were beginning to communicate with those in America for insight into the nature and possible relation of their respective creatures.

After numerous showings of Patterson's film by Dahinden in Moscow, researchers Dmitri Bayanov and Igor Bourtsev as well as biomechanics expert Dr. Dmitri Donskoy of the U.S.S.R. Central Institute of Physical Culture subjected it to an in-depth analysis in which they concluded that it was unquestionably genuine. Their points of argument are very complex, but one of the most valuable of their findings was Bourtsev's conclusion of the film speed.

By concentrating on the bouncing in the first moments of the footage, which he reasoned had to correspond with the steps taken by Patterson, he found that if the setting had been 24 fps, then Patterson had been taking six steps per second, which would mean that a man with an injured foot wearing cowboy boots had run faster than a world class sprinter over rough terrain.

A confident conclusion of 16 fps was made, which, according to England's Dr. Grieve would mean that "the possibility of fakery is ruled out." I'll bet that Patterson never thought that herky-jerky bouncing footage at the beginning of his film would end up working in his favor. In the aftermath of his 1971 sojourn to Russia and Patterson's death in 1972, Rene Dahinden would end up spending considerable time in court to secure the legal rights to the film, sharing them with Patterson's widow Patricia until the time of his own death in 2001 at age 70. This often meant little, however, as images from the film have been used countless times in print and on-screen without legal permission, far too many for Dahinden to keep up with.

Less decisive conclusions on the film were reached by the Smithsonian's Dr. John Napier in his 1972 book "Bigfoot: The Yeti and Sasquatch in Myth and Reality." In this book Napier concluded that the sasquatch probably did exist, yet his thoughts on the Patterson film seemed to waffle curiously back and forth for a study that was supposed to bring scientific scrutiny to the subject.

He was of the opinion that the creature's walk was generally consistent with that of a human being, and that its various physical features seemed to combine both male and female primate physiology, a fact that has been noted by other skeptics over the years. The large breasts, for instance, are obviously a female trait, yet the bony crest atop the head is a characteristic of male gorillas and orangutans.

Napier also stated: "The presence of buttocks, a human hallmark, is at total variance with the ape-like nature of the superstructure... The upper half of the body bears some resemblance to an ape and the lower half is typically human. It is almost impossible to conceive that such structural hybrids could exist in nature." Yet after these skeptical comments, he rounded out his section on the film by stating: "...there was nothing in the film which would prove conclusively that this was a hoax.

In effect, what I meant was that I could not see the zipper, and I still can't. There I think we must leave the matter. Perhaps it was a man dressed up in a monkey-skin; if so, it was a brilliantly executed hoax, and the unknown perpetrator will take his place with the great hoaxers of the world. Perhaps it was the first film of a new type of hominid, quite unknown to science..."

All in all, it was a lack of commitment either way. Despite working at the Smithsonian, Napier was English. There came a point where well into the 1990s, people in the Bigfoot field were complaining that no serious American scientific study of the film had so far been done, but this was not really true. Physical anthropologist Dr. Grover Krantz of Washington State University in Pullman, Washington, was another of the celebrities in the field and one of the few scientists willing to state his belief in the creatures.

He studied the film closely and commented on his conclusions both in the early 1970s and in his 1992 book "Big Footprints: A Scientific Inquiry into the Reality of Sasquatch." Krantz had his opponents in the field, however, Rene Dahinden being chief among them, due in large part to his endorsement of certain dubious evidence and his firm stance on insisting that at least one sasquatch needed to be killed to obtain a specimen for study in order to prove the creatures' existence and it appeared that the American study being called for was any besides his.

Nevertheless, Krantz did convincingly address many of the arguments put forth by skeptics of the
film:

- The creature has female breasts yet shows a male crest on its head - Krantz correctly pointed out that the sagittal crest on the heads of male gorillas and orangutans is not really related to gender, but to size. Its purpose is to

187

anchor the massive jaws of these animals, and it so happens that only the males of those species grow big enough to require it. But if a female primate grew to the size of the Patterson film creature, it would very likely have such a crest as well.

- The creature's breasts appear to be hair-covered, whereas the breasts of known primates are generally hairless - Early on, Krantz responded to this rather sarcastically with, "I don't know what the breast of a sasquatch *ought* to look like," and added that the bulge on the creature's chest might not actually be breasts but the laryngeal air sacs that inflate to great size in the throat and chest area in some great apes, particularly the orangutan. But in his book he qualified this with, "Actually, I do not find this to be as likely an explanation as that they are breasts." It is simply a matter of not making broad generalizations about what traits a totally brand new species ought to have.

- The bottoms of the creature's feet are unnaturally light in color - This is common, Krantz noted, even in dark-skinned Africans whose soles simply contain less pigment than other parts of the body. (It is also worth noting that the creature was standing in shallow water when first encountered, and that its necessarily wet feet in the film are the exact same gray as the sand it is walking on, although at some point I read that someone had tried to duplicate this effect at the film site on human feet and been unable to do so.)

- The creature's walk appears human-like and is therefore likely to be that of a large man in a costume - Krantz conceded that the walk is somewhat human-like, which is exactly what we should expect for any bipedal primate. But as pointed out by other studies, the walk does show marked differences from that of man, and Krantz made his most important arguments against the man-in-a-costume theory by simply noting the proportions of the creature's body. With the width of the shoulders and chest, it is simply mathematically impossible for any man alive - no matter how large - to fit into such a costume and still demonstrate the freedom of movement and apparent musculature shown in the film. The differences may be subtle, but there is just no way around them. I feel that possibly because of his controversial nature Krantz failed to really drive this point home in an undeniable manner, but it would be done again years later by someone whose assessment I will conclude this chapter with. Krantz passed away in 2002 at age 70.

The findings of professional scientists like Grieve, Donskoy, Krantz, and others would seem to lend considerable weight to the potential validity of the Patterson film, but support has also come from more controversial sources - some, in fact, that many in the Bigfoot field would much rather do without.

For instance, Jon Erik Beckjord -- an investigator of various para-normal phenomena who operated a cryptozoology museum in California and supported a supernatural origin for sasquatch -- put forth one very unusual theory. What appears to be the creature's breasts in the film, he said, was actually an infant creature clinging to its mother's chest. Almost all serious supporters of the film have denounced this idea with barely a second thought, and even Bob Gimlin emphatically stated that there was no way he and Patterson would have failed to notice something so significant.

It seems to be a matter of peculiar illusions in a few individual frames of the film that gave birth to this view. (I myself see exactly what Beckjord seemed to be talking about, but if he was right, his "infant" would have no legs, and I feel this theory can safely be discarded.) Further wild claims were made by Beckjord in 2000 when he attempted to sell a copy of the film on the Internet, falsely claiming to have the legal right to do so (and for $1 million!) and stated that he had located a metal tube on the creature's arm, suggesting that it may have been "a genetic experiment gone wild, or else an alien."

Enough said.

To further the trend of the old guard slowly dying off, Beckjord passed away in 2008 at age 69. Also in 2008, a bizarre conspiracy theory surfaced involving the film that was endorsed by at least two members of the new guard, Bigfoot researchers M.K. Davis and David Paulides. This is far too complex for me to go into great detail about here, but in a nutshell, it alleged that the film was shot at the tail end of a "massacre," that Patterson and Gimlin were with several other men and that they opened fire on and killed most of an entire family of Bigfoot creatures, with the female seen in the film being the last wounded survivor making its escape.

The evidence put forth for this version of the story consists mostly of a creative interpretation of things seen in the film and in photos taken later at the site, inanimate objects on the ground taken to be bodies, reddish water and leaves are taken to be bloodstained even though the color red is everywhere in the forest in autumn, etc., and computerized color adjustment of the film even being a factor. The theory even includes the respected researcher John Green and alleges that he was involved and took part in a coverup of what really happened. I am saddened that Green was forced to respond to such outrageous allegations in the years before he too passed away in 2016 at age 89.

This is the worst kind of nonsense.

No proof of a hoax has ever been successfully put forth in regards to the film in spite of what people might have heard in popular culture, though many have tried. The 1990s turned out to be a big decade for such attempts. Investigator Cliff Crook of Bigfoot Central in Bothell, Washington offered a booklet entitled "The Abominable Snowjob" to explain why he felt the film must be a fake, mainly consisting of anatomical points already explained by Grover Krantz. Crook later teamed with another prominent Bigfooter, Chris Murphy, to denounce the film by announcing in the Associated Press on January 9, 1999, that a close examination of certain frames had revealed some type of latch resembling a wine bottle opener low on the creature's torso.

Dogged researcher Daniel Perez responded to the charge that same month in the monthly Bigfoot Times newsletter he has been publishing for many years, suggesting certain personality-related reasons why Crook and Murphy would become detractors of the film and adding, "What Chris Murphy claims to see in 'enhanced' frames from Patterson's film, a wine-bottle opener or an ornate latch was not noted by a recent forensic examination of the film by Jeff Glickman." (The study he refers to was an attempt to bring out sharper detail by digitizing the film, carried out by the North American Science Institute in association with the former Bigfoot Research Project headed by investigator Peter Byrne.)

It should be noted that Cliff Crook has promoted photos alleging to show Bigfoot that are very likely fakes, and that in 2004, Chris Murphy produced one of the best Bigfoot books of all time entitled "Meet the Sasquatch," an extremely colorful and richly illustrated volume that fully supports the validity of the Patterson film and shows more frames from it than any other book ever has.

A drastic change of opinion, it would seem. Another attempt at writing off the film as a hoax and one that got a lot of serious attention had occurred in 1997 when movie director John Landis said in an interview with journalist Scott Essman, "That famous piece of film of Bigfoot walking in the woods that was touted as the real thing was just a suit made by John Chambers." Landis had worked with Chambers on the highly successful 1968 film "Planet of the Apes," which used realistic makeup rather than full bodysuits to turn actors into apemen.

The accusation was backed up by Howard Berger of Hollywood's KNB Effects Group. "It was like a gag to be played on the guy who shot it. The guy never knew it was a hoax his friends played on him." Mike McCracken Jr., a makeup artist who worked with Chambers, stated, "I'd say with absolute certainty that John was responsible. A gorilla suit expert, Bob Burns, said that the alleged Bigfoot shows evidence of a water bag in the stomach area- a trick used to make a gorilla suit move like real flesh." (A "trick," however, never even suggested by the several scientific skeptics who have denounced the film in any number of other ways over the years.)

In May of 1996, CNI News had reported, "Harry Kemball, director and screenwriter at Golden Eagle Productions, told 'X' CHRONICLES researchers that he was at the Canwest 16mm film editing room in 1967 when Roger Patterson and his friends put together his Bigfoot hoax on 16mm film... According to Kemball, they all laughed and joked about the rental of the gorilla costume and the construction of the big feet." But here is where the "Hollywood Hoax" theory seems to lose its strength.

Either Patterson faked the film himself, or "the guy never knew it was a hoax his friends played on him." It cannot be both ways, after all. And even many skeptics agree that if the film is a fake the costume is an ingenious creation, absolutely not a common rented gorilla suit. For the record, John Chambers -- who died in 2001 at age 78 -- denied that he had any involvement with the Patterson film, and that is important.

Another very serious attempt to write off the film came on December 28, 1998 when FOX TV aired a special entitled "World's Greatest Hoaxes - Secrets Finally Revealed," which presented alleged films of a variety of paranormal-type events and proceeded to tear them apart. The show was hosted by actor Lance Henriksen, star of the popular FOX series "Millennium" and also well- known from the "Alien" movie franchise, and as I was a fan of his, I could only hope that he was unaware of the true nature of much of what he was paid to say.

Admittedly, most of what was shown on the program actually was fake. A completely ridiculous film of a tyrannosaurus rex lumbering around a park in the middle of London, for instance, though apparently some people actually fell for it. There was also the notorious "Alien Autopsy" film, which has now long since been exposed as a fraud, and some Loch Ness Monster photos that will probably always remain inconclusive.

There was also a lengthy segment on the famous UFO films of

Sweden's Billy Meier, which I happen to support, the debunking of which seemed to rely heavily on the word of his bitter ex-wife. When it came to Bigfoot, three films were presented. A video from Ohio and another purporting to show a Himalayan yeti both suffered from their subjects staying around for far too long to have their pictures taken, as well as foliage in the yeti film that looked curiously American rather than Asian.

But then there was the Patterson film. FOX began by presenting Kal K. Korff, known from the field of UFO study rather than that of cryptozoology. He contended that Patterson's film was most definitely a fake, and as evidence pointed out such things as a line of dark fur running down the creature's back (implication-zipper) and how the bottom of a foot seen in one frame did not match the tracks Patterson and Gimlin said the creature made.

From there, the show moved into a much more serious allegation. Clyde O. Reinke, a rancher and businessman who was once a manager for a film company called ANE (American National Enterprises) in Salt Lake City stated categorically that Roger Patterson was permanently employed by them as a cameraman and that he was assigned to go out and create a Bigfoot film to be used as an attraction that would draw bigger audiences to the company's nature films.

American National did produce a film called "Big Foot: Man or Beast" in 1972 that used the Patterson film, but though Reinke said Patterson's status with the company had always been a closely guarded secret, he produced no documentation to back this up. In other words, there was no paper trail to be found. Reinke also alleged that one Mr. Jerry Romney, a very large man employed as an insurance agent by ANE was the man in the Bigfoot costume, but Romney also appeared on the show and flatly denied this. His walk was compared to that of the creature and very unconvincingly implied to be similar.

Some of it will be repetitive, but I'd like to share parts of an open letter to FOX that I sent them in response to the show. It also appeared in the February 1999 issue of the Bigfoot Co-Op newsletter, and I think it sums up the case quite well: "This is in response to your recent program 'World's Greatest Hoaxes'... "...my reason for this letter is your treatment of the 1967 Roger Patterson Bigfoot film. I have been involved with investigating reports of Sasquatch for many years and treat the subject with great seriousness.

"The other two Bigfoot-type films you showed -- one of an American Midwest area creature and supposedly of an Asian yeti -- are indeed fakes, as are most such films that come in anonymously. But the Patterson film is far from anonymous. Full disclosure of who (and what) Patterson was and of every detail of the filming is a matter of public record.

His film is not a fake, and I wish to present several points to indicate this, for your presentation made it clear that you relied solely on the sources presented for your information and did not take the time to talk to the many qualified people who have worked at analyzing the film over the past 30 years, some of whom knew Patterson personally. "Within the program itself were three relevant points:

"1. The man named as the one inside the alleged 'creature costume' is not elusive and freely consented to your interview and denied the charge. It is one man's word against another, thus canceling each other out. (And when the man's walk was compared to the creature's and said to be clearly similar, that was nonsense. Why, just because he is tall and heavyset? The man showed a straight-legged bouncy walk, as do all humans, while the film creature walks with a bent-knee stride that has been remarked upon by various scientists as being quite unhuman.)

"2. You pointed out how various points on the creature's body just 'look fake,' such as the dark stripe on its back, suggested as being a zipper. Such observations can be made only by qualified zoologists, and even then, no one can really say what traits a totally unclassified animal should have just because other similar types do. The dark strip may very well be just a peculiar shadow effect along the spine anyway. (And in fact, in the 1972 book "Bigfoot: The Yeti and Sasquatch in Myth and Reality" primatologist John Napier of no less than the Smithsonian Institution commented on his analysis of the film and specifically stated that he 'could not find the zipper.'

"Also, your analyst pointed to a frame showing the creature's left foot and said that it could not have made the footprints associated with the film. However, a frame just before this shows a much clearer outline of the creature's right foot, and it matches the prints exactly. Clearly the left foot is simply captured at an odd angle that distorts it.

"3. In your comments on the other two films, you rightly pointed out the obvious human-like behavior of the alleged creatures, how they stuck around to be filmed rather than fleeing like a real wild creature. The Patterson film creature does the exact opposite of this, fleeing from human contact and not reappearing, a fact you did not dwell on. "On now to a number of documented facts on Patterson himself and his film that contradict any claim of a hoax:

"1. By all accounts of many people who knew him -- many of whom do not know each other -- Patterson was a poor man, a jack of all trades and master of none who was almost always in debt.

"2. The camera Patterson used to film the creature -- a Cine-Kodak K-100 16mm home movie camera -- was rented and not even paid for, a fact that subsequently led to a warrant being issued for his arrest.

"3. Patterson had investigated Sasquatch reports and searched for the creatures for six years prior to the filming without any major breakthroughs, had published an obscure book in 1966 ('Do Abominable Snowmen of America Really Exist?') to try and raise funds, and was well known to other investigators in the sasquatch field. In 1967 he was working on a documentary film of his own -- publicly, not in secret -- and was in the Bluff Creek, California area at the time of the filming in response to a call from storekeeper Al Hodgson of nearby Willow Creek, alerting him to fresh footprints recently found in the area. "(Points 1-3 along effectively rule out the idea put forth in your program that Patterson was secretly a full-time employee of a professional film company hired to go out and create a Bigfoot film to increase ticket sales at their nature movies.

Strange, isn't it, that Patterson -- who was dying of Hodgkin's disease at the time -- remained penniless after the filming? And would the company not have supplied him with a more professional model camera? Finally, Hodsgon's call indicates Patterson's spur-of-the-moment trip to Bluff Creek -- it was not planned out in depth.)

"4. After the filming, on the same day (10/20/67) Patterson is documented as having done the following: "A. He mailed the film to his brother-in-law Al DeAtley for processing, not to some professional studio. "B. Next he called the British Columbia Museum to inquire as to the possibility of having tracking dogs brought to the site to pick up the creature's trail. This did not materialize, but he could not have known that it would not. "Neither of these acts would be expected from a hoaxer -- especially the dogs -- unless he wanted to be promptly exposed.

"5. There were at least three forest roads in the general vicinity of the film site down which unexpected travelers might have come at any time -- an unlikely spot in which to stage a hoax. (And incidentally, it is not just a claimed site -- landmarks in the film easily identified it as the spot Patterson said it was, and it has been thoroughly studied by other investigators.

"6. Finally, you totally ignored one of the most important factors of all. While rightly stating that Patterson is no longer living and able to be questioned, you did not even mention the existence of the man who was with him that day, Bob Gimlin, who still resides in Yakimna, Washington. Gimlin has always maintained that they encountered a real sasquatch at Bluff Creek, has never profited from the film at all, and has been offered large sums of money to 'come clean' about the alleged hoax. His answer: 'I'm already telling the truth.' "Your exclusion of Gimlin is all the more odd in that you have interviewed him before for the series 'Sightings' a few years back.

One would think you could have at least used that footage to offer balanced opinions when making such serious allegations about the film. "(It could be claimed that Gimlin was actually the first victim of Patterson's hoax, but this too is discounted by several points. Patterson and Gimlin camped together for several days, making any communications between Patterson and his costumed accomplice very difficult to accomplish in secret, not to mention that Gimlin could have seen the vehicle necessary to bring the costume into the area.

Plus, it was Gimlin's idea to explore that particular stream bank on that afternoon, so how could Costume-man have known where they would be and place himself accordingly? Finally, Gimlin states that Patterson yelled 'Cover me!' as he ran toward the creature with his camera, as Gimlin was holding a loaded rifle, and in the excitement of the moment, there was no guarantee that he would not shoot. Costume-man would have been foolish indeed to risk his life in such a manner, not to mention the risk of being caught and unmasked since both men were riding horses.) "Now I would like to present some of the actual scientific analyses that have been done to vindicate the Patterson film.

Despite what seems to be the popular misconception, most scientists who have labeled it a hoax have never actually done an in-depth study of it but have based their conclusions on preconceived notions that the sasquatch could not possibly exist, therefore the film must be a fake. However..." My letter then went through the findings of Grieve, the Russians, Krantz, and Titmus, adding a few personal comments. Where Grieve had stated, "In these conditions (16 or 18 fps film speed) a normal human being could not duplicate the observed pattern..."

I added that in this context, a large man nearly seven feet tall, as shown on the FOX program, still qualified as a "normal human being." I also added that the film was once studied by experts in the design of prosthetic limbs who found nothing unnatural in the creature's movements. In mentioning how Titmus had followed the creature's trail from the film site and found where it had sat down in the foliage, I pointed out that "Patterson never even hinted at there being any such traces as he would have if they were there but of his own design."

Finally, after quoting Gimlin from an earlier episode of the FOX show "Sightings" on how naturally the creature's muscles had appeared to move underneath the hair, I suggested that perhaps the FOX people should go back and examine their own archives. I concluded the letter: "I wanted to provide FOX with this information in the hopes that if your program is run again you will provide updates and more balanced information.

There have been a number of other such hoax claims made against the Patterson film in the past couple of years -- some of which are completely different and contradict each other -- but they do not and cannot contradict the scientific facts that have been established. It is a peculiar thing that extraordinary claims are always picked apart in minute detail to prove that they could not be, but the second the claim of 'Hoax!' is made, it is accepted without a second thought.

Must not both sides of the argument be studied with equal precision? The trouble in the sasquatch field is that the true facts are readily available only in obscure newsletters and the occasional book that reaches only a tiny percent of the population -- but everyone watches TV. That is why you should fully research every side of any story. As one of your own most popular programs so eloquently puts it, 'The truth is out there.'" I loved being able to quote "The X-Files" at the end of that letter. There is one thing in it that I would like to qualify. I wrote that it had been Gimlin's idea to explore the banks of Bluff Creek on October 20th, not Patterson's. I based that on the account given by psychologist Barbara Wasson in her 1979 book "Sasquatch Apparitions."

Since then it has come to my attention that Gimlin has given the opposite information in other interviews from what he told Wasson, that it was, in fact, Patterson who decided where to go that day. I can only put this down to Gimlin misspeaking to Wasson or Wasson mishearing what he said. I should also point out how I mentioned the forest roads near the film site down which witnesses might have come, and explain that while that was the case in 1967, it is no longer so today.

Those roads have been abandoned and become overgrown and impassable, the only routes to the site now being by foot travel with the nearest road ending about a mile's hike away. I never received a reply from FOX, nor did I really expect one, but I had to wonder if my letter got passed around at all and discussed, or if it just went into the round file. Though I do not in any way claim to be an expert on the Patterson film I think I did a pretty good job on it.

At the time I wrote it, however, I did not yet realize just how much weight had been given by skeptics to the connection between Patterson and American National Enterprises. In 2014, I ended up getting involved in a debate on an online message board about the film that unfortunately devolved into insults and nastiness as such anonymous exchanges often do, and ANE was one of the points being thrown around like ammunition, one of my opponents seem to insist that if Patterson had had any contact with this company at all, then that alone was proof that he was their employee and that his film was a hoax.

This thread also included the ludicrous claims that there was no Bigfoot lore before 1958, and no Loch Ness Monster references before the famous Surgeon's Photo of 1934, and that if there was such a thing as Bigfoot, it should be easily proven because DNA can be easily gleaned from anything that a living thing has brushed against or even from the air that it has breathed. I could only shake my head at some of the ridiculous comments, but I did make a pointed response to a document that was posted that was supposed to be proof that Patterson had been a paid filmmaker for ANE.

I sent a request to the website involved asking permission to quote the thread but received no response, so I will not name the site nor any of the other posters but will just quote myself: "In the assertions made here, I examined the links in post #36... it states that there's a contract showing that Patterson's backers- stated elsewhere as being ANE films -- paid him $37,000 as a cameraman, with a small thumbnail of the contract.

But in the link that shows the contract big enough to read, it turns out that no, it is not with ANE and is not for $37,000. It is an agreement between Patterson and a couple named George and Vilma Radford for them to lend him a mere $850 for the making of the documentary "Bigfoot -- America's Abominable Snowman"... paid on May 26, 1967, and to be paid back within 15 days.

I will concede that this contract is real, even though things written on paper are even easier to fake than Bigfoot tracks. But there is nothing damning in this. The standard story has always included the fact that Patterson was shooting his own private documentary. I did some further reading and found that Vilma Radford sued him when he never paid the money back.

That's no surprise either -- even Patterson's proponents admit he was no saint, and loaning him money was never a good idea. And funny how he had trouble paying back $850 if he had $37,000, and how whether the film is real or fake he shot it on a rented little Cine-Kodak, which he also never paid for."

Patterson finished his documentary "Bigfoot -- America's Abominable Snowman" in 1968 and began to show it in various venues to try and raise funds. Sometime thereafter, he was contacted by Bigfooter and filmmaker Ron Olson whose family was involved with ANE and offered propositions about joining up with them. There is no documentation on paper to show that he ever did so except for making a deal to allow them to use his film in their 1972 doc "Big Foot: Man or Beast," at which time Patterson was near death.

Allegations that he was an ANE employee all along and that the Bluff Creek film was shot as a scene to be used in an ANE movie have been widespread but have nothing to back them up. One would think that the Patterson film had suffered enough slings and arrows at this point, but the biggest onslaught was still yet to come. It reared its head in 2004 in the form of a book entitled "The Making of Bigfoot -- The Inside Story" by Greg Long, with a foreword by Kal K. Korff. I cannot be shy in my reactions to this book. I knew going in that it was an effort at debunking the film and that debunkers always do two things.

One, they begin with a set position that the fact that what they are investigating is phony is a given and then take whatever information they find and twist and slant it to make it fit that assumption. And two, while they will take someone with a fantastic claim and investigate them to no end in an attempt to discredit them, anyone who comes forward saying they have firsthand knowledge of how the claim is a hoax is immediately taken at face value with barely if any effort to investigate and confirm their stories.

I knew that that was what I was in for with "The Making of Bigfoot," but it truly turned out to be the most classic example of both of those things I have ever seen and actually went even farther by being downright insultingly condescending to anyone who believes in Bigfoot. It even brushed off scientists who have thoroughly analyzed the film and concluded that it was genuine with the line "What the hell were they thinking?"

Early on, the book excited me by offering more information on the life of Roger Patterson than I had ever heard or read before, positive things that gave me a whole new appreciation for the man, and I would like to thank Greg Long for providing those details. It described how he was born in South Dakota, how he was the second youngest of six children (four boys and two girls), and how his rancher father had moved the family to the state of Washington after losing everything in the Great Depression.

His father Clarence was also a veteran of World War I who reenlisted when World War II came along and was killed in combat, and Roger himself served two years in the Army in his early 20s at the tail end of the Korean War. As a child, Roger and his brothers were fascinated with acrobatic tumbling acts they saw in Vaudeville shows and trained themselves to do the same, putting on amazing presentations. Because Roger was the smallest in the family, he became a body-builder and grew stronger, faster, and more agile than any of his older brothers and could do handstands and other acts of physical dexterity that were simply incredible.

They all went into rodeo as they entered adulthood. Roger also played football, boxed, and sang country music, all with considerable talent. His skill as an artist was such that his drawings of horses looked almost lifelike. He always seemed determined never to have to answer to anyone to make his living and so never took on a regular job, even after he married and had children. He was extremely innovative and always working on some new idea, including coming up with several inventions. I had always read in the Bigfoot literature that he was an inventor, but never knew exactly what he invented. Greg Long's book supplied that information.

In addition to experimenting with changes to common items like canteens and thermoses, Patterson also invented a rather ingenious training aid for rodeo calf roping, a moving mechanical recreation of a calf's legs that one could practice lassoing. He was also said to be able to build almost anything he could think of with the most meager of resources and created some very fancy looking wagons, which he eventually used to go into business hitching them to both his horses and to Angora goats that he raised and giving rides to children as part of a promotional agreement he negotiated with a Yakima area meat company.

What he was doing just before becoming fascinated with Bigfoot was collecting manure from area farms and selling it to be used as fertilizer. His description as a fly-by-night jack of all trades who was brimming with enthusiasm but who was nearly always on his last dollar was very well fleshed out by the book, and I appreciated that very much.

I was also intrigued by the interviews with Roger's brothers that stated that he had a temper in his younger days and that one of the things that he hated most and could really set him off was anyone that lied to him. He had gotten into fights with people over dishonesty, and was able to pick them up over his head and hurl them.

Despite this, his brushes with the law seemed to have been few. I'd always read that a warrant for his arrest had been issued when he failed to pay the rental fee on the camera he used to shoot the Bluff Creek film, but here I learned that that arrest actually did take place, though through negotiation the charges were eventually dropped. This was the Roger Patterson that I had always wanted to know more about.

After that buildup, however, the book did what it had promised to do from the beginning and proceeded to do an unbelievable hatchet job on the man and make him out to be an absolutely insidious conman. I have to say that throughout the book's narrative, there are many statements along the lines of "it is easy to imagine" or "because this happened, then this and this and this must have also happened." Sometimes there are points made that deserve consideration, but just as often, there are sweeping blanket statements without anything to back them up.

The book goes so far as to imply that any Bigfoot sightings that occurred in the Yakima area must have been Patterson prowling around in a costume. The book references the 1998 FOX special "World's Greatest Hoaxes," which Kal K. Korff took part in, but neither Korff nor Long makes any mention at all of the suspects for "the man in the suit" that the show put forth, a completely different suspect than the one now being supported in the book. The new suspect was Bob Heironimus, a worker for a Pepsi bottling company and an old acquaintance of Patterson and Gimlin living in Yakima who had been 26 years old in 1967 when the film was shot.

It's a very long and involved story, but basically, Greg Long, an investigative journalist who had an interest in Pacific Northwest mysteries got wind that there were rumors and murmurings going on in the Yakima area for years that Heironimus had been the man in the suit in the Patterson film and that he had confided this to various people. In fact, in certain circles it had long been considered common knowledge. (Interesting to note that in certain Hollywood circles it had long been considered common knowledge that John Chambers had involvement, but that hadn't panned out.)

When confronted by Long in December 1998, Heironimus was at first reluctant to talk but eventually decided to cooperate and publicly confess that yes, he had been hired by Roger Patterson and was promised a thousand dollars to wear a Bigfoot costume for the making of the film. His gentlemen's agreement to keep quiet had competed for years with his frustration over having never gotten paid as he watched the film rise to the level of fame that it garnered over the years, leading him to occasionally let his secret slip. Heironimus is known to have passed two polygraphs on the matter, one early on and the other coming later on a very tabloid-esque 2005 TV show called "Lie Detector" on PAX TV.

However, this is countered by the possibility that Patterson might have done the same. In an article entitled "On the Trail of Bigfoot" in the October 1970 issue of National Wildlife managing editor George H. Harrison stated, "Before printing the story and photographs, a National Wildlife editor flew to the west coast to interview Patterson, who believed so strongly in Bigfoot and the photographs he had made that he instantly agreed to take a lie detector test. The results convinced the experienced polygraph operator that Patterson was not lying."

For what it's worth, Wikipedia also states, "Polygraph tests regarding their claims have been passed by both Heironimus and Patterson." Many charges have been made against the true accuracy of the polygraph that keeps its results from being used in court, and it is known that a subject who is overly nervous when telling the truth can fail, while one with little to no conscience can lie and pass. I tend to think of the device as being a useful guide but one which should not be considered the final word on anything. Heironimus claimed that Patterson and Gimlin were co-conspirators in the hoax and that after enlisting his aid, they showed him the costume he would be wearing.

He said Patterson had made it from horsehide and other materials and that it had three main components -- legs, upper body, and head, plus separate hands and feet. After shooting the film at Bluff Creek he said the two men told him to go home to Washington with the costume in the trunk of his car (it was actually his mother's car that he had borrowed) and that they would retrieve it later, and that while at home, some of his family members had seen it. Those family members confirmed that story to Long for the book.

However, another source also weighed in heavily in Long's investigation concerning the supposed costume. A magician and costume maker named Philip Morris in Charlotte, North Carolina stated on WBT-AM radio in August 2002 that he had sold Patterson a gorilla suit and that it was used in the famous 1967 Bigfoot film. In 2003 Long interviewed Morris for the book, getting a story about how Patterson had contacted him in about August of 1967, wanting to purchase a suit. Morris had been designing such suits since the 1950s when an illusion involving a girl transforming into a gorilla was popular among stage magicians, but Patterson reportedly said that he only wanted to use the suit for a prank.

The sale was made, Morris said, and Long viewed this account as a breakthrough in his investigation even though there were major differences with Heironimus' story. The suits sold by Morris were one-piece affairs with a zipper in the back that were made of a synthetic material called Dynel, while Heironimus had described a suit with multiple components made of natural horsehide that stank inside. The book does not seem to recognize any problem with this contradiction, saying only that Heironimus must have been mistaken in thinking the suit was homemade.

Even if both versions of the costume's origin could somehow be true, however, there is a problem with both of them. Both were said to be dark brown in color. The creature in the Patterson film is clearly not brown but black.

There was no mention of a paint job being done before the filming. Heironimus is said to have changed his story over to the Morris suit after the publication of the book, and then later still he told KATU-2 in Portland, Oregon, in May 2004, that in spite of everything else that had been said, the costume maker was actually John Chambers, reverting to the old Hollywood Hoax theory.

A man who changes his story this much can hardly be given a high level of credibility. Heironimus also demonstrated a marked lack of knowledge or memory of the northern California region surrounding the Bluff Creek film site, first describing it as being only a few miles from the town of Willow Creek, which is completely wrong, and then when having Long point out to him that he must be confusing Willow Creek with the smaller town of Weitchpec around 20 miles to the north, his description of how many miles from town the film site was still fell drastically short of the true distance.

To his credit, Long was suspicious about this at first, but then wrote it off as just faulty memory after so many years. Also significant is the fact that the nearest town to the film site is Orleans, not Weitchpec. Heironimus' clumsy descriptions of the area came across as those of someone who had never been there. Long shot video of Heironimus duplicating the walk he said he used while wearing the costume in the film, writing that it "eerily echoed the self-assured stride of the two-legged thing in Patterson's footage."

There is also a photo in that same chapter of Heironimus at age 26, his age at the time of the filming, posing in jeans and a t-shirt with a caption that reads, "Notice his muscular build," implying that he could easily be the man filling out the large bulky Bigfoot costume. I personally find these assessments to be just downright silly. His walk looks unremarkable, and his build looks healthy and in shape but average.

It is also mentioned that Heironimus lost his right eye in a childhood accident and wears a glass eye and a point of light in the right eye of the film creature in a blowup of its face is implied to be evidence of that glass eye. Never mind the fact that light reflects off of real eyeballs too. Phillip Morris provided a picture of the type of gorilla suit he sold to Patterson, and it appeared in the book with assertions that it resembled the creature in the film.

I really can't form any argument against that claim except for the simplest one possible -- No, it doesn't! Morris' costume is shaggy and simple, while the film creature is complex and shows clear musculature. The book postulated that Patterson had removed the face from the costume and added his own homemade mask, but even suggesting a similarity between the costume and the film creature is downright laughable. The book also speaks much about Patterson's brother-in-law Al DeAtley, the man to whom the film was sent for processing immediately after it was shot. DeAtley was the opposite of Patterson financially, being literally a millionaire businessman who sometimes gave his wife's brother money for various projects.

In an interview that he consented to for the book, he said he never believed in Bigfoot, that he had helped Patterson pay for the publication of his book and the marketing of his documentary but had nothing to do with the creation of the Bluff Creek film, and that he had always assumed the film was a hoax but that he went along with it because he saw it as a money-making venture. Family obligations, basically, made him tolerate Roger. Greg Long, however, wrote about DeAtley as if he was some kind of sinister and imposing figure, asserting that "money equals power" and suggesting that people who knew the truth about the film might have stayed quiet over the years because they feared reprisal by DeAtley.

The book actually comes across as practically comparing DeAtley to some kind of mob boss, which I found to be nothing but melodramatic hyperbole. Through it all, though, I have to admit that there were things in the book that educated me and fleshed out the real facts of the case up against the false accusations I believe were being made against it. One of the most significant was the good evidence Long provided about the documentary that Patterson was always known to be filming about Bigfoot before he got the Bluff Creek footage. Some have insisted that it was a professional job being done for American National Enterprises, while others, including myself, still believe it was Patterson's own personal production.

What Long established in his book was that it appears to not have been just a straight-on scientific look at the subject but was also intended to include possible dramatizations or perhaps even fictional vignettes using actors in costumes that were shot in the Yakima area alongside the more grounded footage, Patterson shot of his field investigations in search of Bigfoot. There is evidence that Bob Gimlin and Bob Heironimus may well have been two of the people recruited to play parts in those scenes.

That is all well and good as far as I'm concerned, but once Patterson got his footage of a real Bigfoot at Bluff Creek, his whole life became devoted to only that one piece of film. I do wonder if he really did work at acquiring a Bigfoot costume or even making one himself (or both) to be used in dramatizations in the doc, and if such a costume might have briefly resided in the trunk of Heironimus' car and then been abandoned after Patterson captured the real thing for fear of being labeled a hoaxer.

I also wonder if there might have been people who were slighted over the years by Patterson and his irresponsible ways, especially with money, who might have wanted to jump on the bandwagon once they heard that a major debunking project was being done against his greatest accomplishment just because they thought he deserved it, even in death.

But here, you see, I am speculating. And I want very much not to do that, because it is what Greg Long did a great deal of in forming the conclusions in his book. I don't know what the whole truth is about the human element, but I am convinced by analysis of the film that I will end this chapter with that it has to be genuine.

Unfortunately, I know that people lie and that I am accusing Bob Heironimus of it. I am hardly the first to do so. Sometimes people lie to incredible degrees while looking you straight in the eye and weave vast tangled webs that go on and on, and I speak from personal experience on that. Their motivations are their own. I think Greg Long believed every word he put into his book and that the effort he put into it is to be greatly admired, but that he believed a lot of wrong information.

And that is where I will have to leave "The Making of Bigfoot." For people who have not researched the full story and every competing theory surrounding it, the book can come across as convincing. It reminds me, however, of another field I have an interest in. I am a bit of a true crime buff, with a special fascination for the Jack the Ripper case. This notorious British serial killer prowled the mean streets of east London in 1888 and is infamous for never having been identified.

A vast subculture has been formed by people interested in the case, calling themselves "Ripperologists," and scores of suspects have been suggested over the years, with perhaps a dozen or so being the top contenders. Proponents of their favorite suspects have written extensively on why they think their man was the killer, with tons of scholarly research and historical facts to back them up. Any of the accusations against any of these singular suspects seem to have so much evidence documenting them that they all sound completely convincing.

But of course, they cannot all be Jack the Ripper, which makes it entirely possible that none of them were. I urge people to keep this in mind with any case against the Patterson film, no matter how convincing it might seem, which Greg Long's book is a perfect example of. Ultimately, the year 2017 approached. October 20th of that year was to be the 50th anniversary of the Patterson film, quite the milestone, and as I was about to turn 50 years old myself, 26 days later, the occasion felt especially poignant to me.

For many years I had been subscribing to a newsletter called the Bigfoot Times published by veteran researcher Daniel Perez out of Norwalk, California, and occasionally corresponding with him. Daniel is a no-nonsense kind of guy who is never afraid to speak the truth as he sees it and is also a die-hard champion of the Patterson film.

When I saw him announce in print that he was planning a get-together for any and all who were interested at the film site on the anniversary, I couldn't help but ponder it for a bit and then think to myself, "Why not?" My only other foray into the Pacific Northwest had been a trip I'd made by Greyhound way back in 1989 to visit with famous Bigfoot hunter Peter Byrne in Oregon and I had never been to California before.

If there was ever to be a time for it, this seemed to be it. In 2008 during a vacation to Great Britain, I had had the pleasure of visiting Loch Ness and hoping to spot its famous monster. I didn't, but it was a great adventure nonetheless. Following that with actually being able to stand on the spot where the Patterson film was shot was an opportunity I found I just couldn't pass up. I flew from Fargo to Sacramento, where I rented a car and made what turned out to be a grueling five-hour drive to my destination.

The I-5 to Redding is all freeway through very open country, but once one turns west from there, you are into the forested mountains and an entirely different experience, one that I found I was not ready for. It's not that we don't have wilderness in Minnesota because we most certainly do, but we don't have mountains. I had a hotel booked in the city of Arcata, and the drive between there and Redding was a narrow winding blacktop road the likes of which I had never encountered before.

In this region, it is not simply a matter of cutting relatively straight roads through the forest. Roads here hug the sides of mountains, and mountains are not square. The many twists and turns often made it feel like it wasn't safe to go any faster than 40 miles per hour (and in fact, there are certain spots where speed limit signs warn you to slow down even slower than that for particular curves), but as it turns out, the people who live there and drive those roads all the time are used to it and want to go 70.

This makes for even more perilous driving conditions, and there were times when I had to anxiously wait for one of the pullover spots that are spaced sporadically along the road to let some eager beaver aggressively tailgating me pass by. As I spent time in the area I got better at handling the roads, but it was a drastic adjustment.

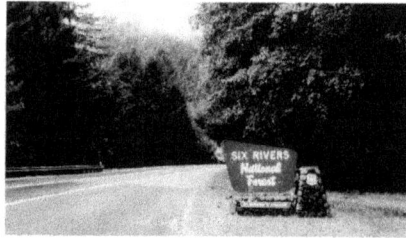

Six Rivers National Forest boundary sign between Arcata and Willow Creek.

China Flat Museum in Willow Creek, home of its excellent Bigfoot artifacts collection.

It grew dark before I passed through Willow Creek, famously known as the Bigfoot Capital of the World, on my way to Arcata, so I didn't get to see much of it except to notice in my headlights that there were several signs in the area advertising the Bigfoot this and the Bigfoot that. I continued on, frazzled by this point by the drive and just wanting to get to my hotel, where I finally arrived in the city of Arcata about 45 minutes later.

This was another big adjustment, as the forest quite suddenly gives way to a huge metro area that is very near the Pacific coast. Arcata has a population of around 17,000, while its adjoining city of Eureka -- the seat of Humboldt County -- is much larger with a population of around 45,000.

Arriving after dark, a total fish out of water and attempting to find my hotel was a challenge, but I managed it and finally got some much-needed rest. The next day was Thursday, October 19th, the day before the anniversary. Early that day I first wanted to go to the coast and see the Pacific Ocean, which I had never seen before. I'd crossed the Atlantic and had walked on its beaches when I'd visited England, but this farm boy from the exact center of North America who grew up as far from any ocean as one can get just had to be able to say that I'd connected with both.

After exploring the beach and watching the crashing surf coming in and imagining that I was probably within just a few miles of great white sharks, I turned my attention back to the east and headed for Willow Creek and the Six Rivers National Forest. The skies were overcast, and the day's forecast called for rain, but the skies had yet to open up. This community of around 1,700 people has a lot to live up to with its reputation of being Bigfoot Central, but it does not disappoint.

There is a Bigfoot Motel, a Bigfoot Steakhouse, and an Ace Hardware store with a huge and magnificent mural painted along its entire length that depicts Bigfoot interacting with people in all the different stages of the town's history. Highway 96 leading north out of town, which I knew to be the road that leads up toward the Patterson film site had a sign designating it the "Bigfoot Highway."

What I most wanted to see, however, was the China Flat Museum in the center of town, which I knew housed an extensive collection of Bigfoot artifacts and memorabilia. As a large bright yellow building with a carved wooden Bigfoot statue, perhaps 15 feet tall in front, and being right along the main road, it is hardly easy to miss but imagine my disappointment to find that it was closed and that its business hours were oddly sporadic unless one made a special appointment. Shrugging that off, I began to explore the town center around the museum and then came across one of the most famous and iconic of all landmarks in Pacific Northwest Bigfoot history - the life-sized redwood carving of Bigfoot created in 1967, the same year that Roger Patterson shot his film, by researcher Jim McClarin.

Whenever I think of McClarin (who I have never had contact with), I remember that he was a student at Humboldt State University in Areata where my late friend and Bigfooting partner Tim Olson also attended. Seeing his famous wooden statue now was a special thrill. It was much smaller than the one in front of the museum at about eight feet tall plus the height of the base it stands on, but much more realistic looking.

The plaque next to it named it not primarily Bigfoot, but as "Oh-Mah," the local Native American name for the creatures. It stands in a small park in which several people were milling around, mostly young college-age people with backpacks and rain ponchos, and as I studied them, I wondered who they were and why they were there. They seemed to be a widespread presence in the town, people equipped for camping out in the elements rather than with indoor lodging.

Homeless, migrant workers, Bigfoot enthusiasts gathering for the anniversary? I didn't know, but I asked one of them to take my picture next to McClarin's wonderful statue and joined the ranks of so many other Bigfooters over the years who have done this obligatory photo op. It was truly a precious highlight in my life and a major Bigfoot nerd moment.

The author with the famous Willow Creek Bigfoot statue.

I did not see anyone I recognized hanging about as I had hoped, so I stopped into the local public library and asked the pleasant young woman working there if she had any information on events going on for the anniversary.

After a quick computer check, she informed me that there was going to be a free public meet-and-greet the next day in the town center with Bob Gimlin, and then later in the day a formal anniversary celebration where Gimlin and other Bigfoot luminaries would be appearing at the local VFW hall, an event one needed a ticket for and was most likely sold out.

If I had known far in advance about this event, I would have definitely tried to get a ticket, but I was only there in response to Daniel Perez's invitation to meet at the film site. I had tried to call Daniel upon arriving in Arcata, and the call had not gone through. I would find out why in due course, but for now, I was just glad to learn that the next morning I was at least going to get to go to the meet-and-greet and see Bob Gimlin, the legend, the surviving figure that had been present with Roger Patterson when the world-famous film was shot.

My inner nerd was truly palpitating. So what to do with the rest of my Thursday? It was now early afternoon, with the skies still solid gray, but the rain still holding back. I had with me very good directions to the film site provided on the website for the Bluff Creek Project, a group that maintains the site, keeps trail cameras active around it, and regularly guides interested parties to it.

After pondering my options for a few moments, I finally decided, what the hell, I'm going for it. So off I went, north along the Bigfoot Highway. Highway 96 proved to be even narrower and more winding than the road from Redding, and I came to regard the area as the absolute most gorgeous scenery I had ever driven through without getting hardly a chance to actually look at it because I was too focused on trying not to die in a fiery crash. In this shockingly beautiful vista surrounding the Klamath and Trinity rivers I passed through the small Native communities of Hoopa and Weitchpec, names I was very familiar with after years of reading about them in Bigfoot books.

I crossed from Humboldt County into its northern neighbor, Del Norte. And then, at some point, before I arrived at the equally tiny town of Orleans, which is nearly 40 miles up that winding road from Willow Creek, the skies finally opened. The rain began as a drizzle but steadily increased as I turned off the highway at Orleans according to the directions I had and found myself on a road that was ascending the mountains, a road that, to my absolute surprise, was paved and would continue to be for about 15 miles as I drove up and up and up with huge majestic pines towering all around me. At one point, I just had to get out of the car and get a little wet to collect a souvenir that lay in the middle of the road, a pine cone the size of a pineapple that had fallen from above.

Eventually, I came to the point where the directions led me off the comfortable paved road and on to a couple of rough gravel roads that led to the film site and after years of taking vehicles down such treacherous trails in Minnesota, I have to say that those last few miles along this route were quite possibly the worst forest roads I have ever driven. They were extremely rocky, the nearly brand-new Nissan Versa I'd rented in Sacramento bouncing violently up and down as I slowly made my way and as the rain continued to pour down, I couldn't help but worry about what it would be like to break down up in this wild place. Knowing that I was within striking range of the Patterson film site, however, was a powerful motivator.

In retrospect now, I think it was crazy. I should not have had that car in that place under those conditions, and it's only by the grace of God that disaster did not strike. I did have the thought in my head that I just might not make it to the film site in spite of getting so close, and that if that turned out to be the case, I was just going to have to be ok with it. Finally, though, ultimately, I came to the end of the trail. There was a spot where the rocky gravel road just ended in a slight clearing, and to my surprise, several vehicles were parked there.

There was only one other car such as I had, all the rest being pickup trucks better suited to the terrain. The rain was an absolute miserable downpour now, and as I was starting to gather that these must be Bigfooters who were already here a day in advance of the anniversary, despite the weather, I started to awkwardly put on the rain gear I had with me, never easy while sitting in a car.

As I did, I saw a couple of other men in similar gear eyeing me and seeming to wonder who I was. When I finally got out of the car and popped open my umbrella, I felt a bit silly, just marveling at this outrageous setting that I found myself in. But then, unbelievably, out of the blue, I suddenly saw none other than Cliff Barackman from TV's "Finding Bigfoot" right in front of me. Hooray! I had a brief conversation with Cliff as the rain pelted us.

He remembered who I was from the correspondence we'd had online and was completely friendly and engaging, just as he seems on the show, but he was in the midst of preparing to leave the site and head back to Willow Creek. He pointed out to me the trail that led steeply downhill from this parking spot and gave me a brief description of what was to be found at the bottom, that the trail "spits you out" at Bluff Creek and that one must then wade across it to reach the film site. He said that Daniel Perez and a few other people were down there and that some good Bigfooter fellowship had already occurred at the site, but he himself was on his way out.

Before he left, he cautioned me that with the vehicle I had, I might not want to stay long as the rain was going to make the road conditions even worse than they already were. After Cliff left, I went to check out the trail and walked just a short distance down it. It was very steep and very rocky, big jagged rocks protruding all over the place. It was at that point that I started to consider an unfortunate detail about myself. I was a month away from turning 50, and as I'd aged, I had developed an inflammatory condition known as plantar fasciitis in my feet. Flareups of it were sporadic and of varying severity, at its worst, has actually put me on crutches a few times.

As I looked down that trail that led to the spot, I had traveled hundreds of miles to reach, I had to consider that, especially with the rain making that rocky ground wet and slick and dangerous, and Cliff's warning about the road out getting worse and worse was also a big factor. I did not want to end up injuring myself or getting my rented car stuck. I was at a turning point. Was I really this close to my goal and yet faced with the prospect of turning back? As I stood there pondering, this another figure appeared, clad in rain gear and walking up the trail from down below. With him was a little dog wearing saddlebags to help carry provisions.

This turned out to be none other than the well-known publisher of the Bigfoot Times newsletter, Daniel Perez. Daniel often gets tough with people in print when he disagrees with them, but in person he turned out to be a downright jovial guy and our years of occasional correspondence insured that our first face-to-face meeting was quite fun. He explained that my attempted call to him when I'd gotten to my hotel had not gone through because he was already up here beyond the range of cell service.

He introduced me to some other people that were there with him for the occasion and made a joke out of it, "Hey guys, this is Mike Quast from Minnesota, and he's here for reasons that have absolutely nothing to do with Bigfoot and just happened to run into us!" He urged me to head on down the trail, echoing the voice in my head telling me that I'd come all this way and how bad it would be to have to turn back now, but when I asked him how far it was from here to the film site, he said it was about a mile. I think that was the deciding factor for me, that a full mile hike that I would have gladly done in good weather was just too much for me under these conditions.

Highway 96 where it heads north out of Willow Creek.

Just outside Orleans, headed south back toward Willow Creek.

We also talked about the following day's activities in Willow Creek, and though the event at the VFW was sold out, he suggested that if I wanted to go, I should still try and get in. He, however, was going to stay here in the soggy woods surrounding the film site because that was the most important thing for him within the anniversary.

I reached the point where I had to make the decision to leave rather than attempt the hike down, and my god, did it sting. I knew that I would have only the flimsiest of chances the next day to try and link up with someone in Willow Creek who was going to come up to the film site, but in the present moment, I just had to get out of there. I told Daniel that I was going to go up to where my car was parked to turn it around and get it ready to head out, but when I did so someone in a pickup started waving me forward to go ahead of him, presumably, I thought so that he could follow behind me in case I got stuck, so off I went without saying goodbye to Daniel, which I felt bad about.

As I made my way back down the rough trails leading out of the area, I suddenly noticed that they somehow did not seem as bad as they had on the way in. After some thought I realized that probably meant that they had softened so much in the rain that all the rocks that had made the car bounce before were being pushed down into the ground by the tires. If I had stayed much longer, that car would most likely have gotten stuck. In spite of how bad it felt to come so close to my goal and fail to achieve it, I knew that I had made the right decision.

When I made it back to the long paved road that led back down the mountain to Orleans, I had a sighting that helped ease my mind. It was not of a Bigfoot, but a black bear that suddenly appeared in the road a short distance ahead of me after climbing up an incredibly steep slope to reach it. Upon seeing my car approaching, the bear seemed to go "Oh no!" and spun around to head right back down the slope.

If I had attempted to make the hike to the film site, I would not have had the pleasure of seeing that bear, and that helped me to feel a little bit better. (I'd just like to interject here a little jab at skeptics who say that peoples' minds can play tricks on them and that seeing a bear can lead one to imagine that they've seen a Bigfoot. Well, I was in one of the most "squatchy" places on Earth, but when I saw a bear, I immediately knew it was a bear! 'Nuff said.)

I made it safely back to my hotel in Arcata, and the next morning found me back in Willow Creek for the meet-and-greet. It was still raining on and off, not a downpour but not showing any sign of stopping, and the first thing I noticed upon reaching the town was that the China Flat Museum that had been closed the day before now had a full parking lot. As it turned out the event that was supposed to have taken place outdoors in the park surrounding Jim McClarin's Bigfoot statue had been moved to the museum because of the weather.

I was thrilled about this because it meant that I got to see the collection of Bigfoot artifacts that the place was famous for. The museum is officially dedicated to the whole history of the community, but Bigfoot definitely dominates, taking up probably three-quarters of the space.

It was exciting to see the collection of footprint casts from areas I had read about for so many years, old preserved newspaper articles and photographs, paintings, movie posters, wooden carvings and other models of Bigfoot, and many other displays showcasing the creature and its special relationship with the Willow Creek area. It also pretty much had a monopoly on the gift shop area, with Bigfoot track casts displayed in the China Flat Museum.

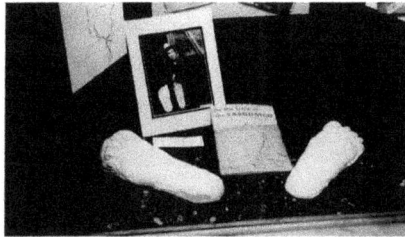

Bigfoot track casts displayed in the China Flat Museum.

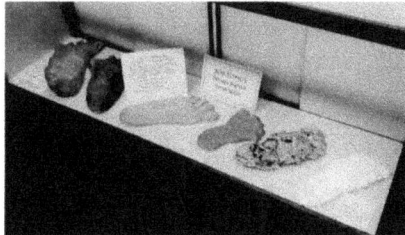

More Bigfoot displays in the China Flat Museum.

Bigfoot books and figurines and coffee mugs and everything else under the sun for sale. And while I was exploring it all, the man of the hour arrived. Bob Gimlin, the only living witness to what had happened on October 20, 1967, at the spot I had failed to reach the day before, entered the museum surrounded by a small entourage of much younger people. Bright-eyed, silver=haired and with a thick mustache framing his mouth, he had recently celebrated his 86th birthday.

He was clad in a black hooded sweatshirt with a red bandana around his neck. There was such a large crowd in the museum by that point, with everyone wanting to be near Bob and including many people that he knew, that I never actually got to approach him and shake his hand and speak with him, but I was glad to be able to take some good pictures of him and just be in his presence and observe the kind of man he is. He seemed completely friendly, gracious, and overjoyed to be there among his admirers on the 50th anniversary of the event that had ended up defining his life.

I knew that for a long time he had avoided the spotlight and just tried to live his life in Yakima, Washington, working with horses, but as he had entered his golden years and became less active physically, he had taken time to reflect on his role in the Bigfoot field and realized that there were many people out there that valued not only the words he might have to say but also valued him as a person. Thus, he had started to appear quite often at Bigfoot conferences and other public events like this one. The respect for him in the air was palpable.

At one point, I heard some people in the crowd remarking about him, and a woman saying, "There aren't too many of the old, genuine cowboys left, but that's one of them right there." Bob's great sense of humor showed through in a moment when the crowd gathered around him at a laptop computer that was set up in the museum, programmed to play the Patterson film every time one would hit "enter."

I gathered that it was his first time in a while seeing it, and everyone seemed so excited just to watch him watching the film, but rather than him saying something profound about it, he made a wonderful joke. At the point in the film where the creature turns to look directly toward the camera. Bob turned to the crowd and said, "Did you see her wink at me?" And, of course, that got a big laugh from all. (Joking aside, I have seen other comments from Bob in which he asserts that that particular moment in the film happened not because the creature was giving Roger a warning glance, but because it was at that point that Bob had dismounted his horse with his rifle in hand in case he needed to shoot and that the creature was reacting to him, not Roger.)

Bob has his detractors among the skeptics who still insist that the film is a fraud, but within the Bigfoot field, he is absolutely beloved, and I feel a little guilty every time I refer to it as merely the "Patterson film," which is easy to do. Rightfully it should be referred to as the Patterson- Gimlin film, as I have titled this chapter. I may not have gotten to actually meet Bob personally, but I did get another chance to talk with Cliff Barackman at some length, and I also got to meet another of the biggest celebrities in the field in the modern era, Prof. Jeff Meldrum of Idaho State University.

He is considered by many to be the successor to Grover Krantz, the most prominent scientist today who researches the Bigfoot phenomenon and professes to believe the creatures are real. I was well familiar with him from his many television appearances and his 2006 book "Sasquatch: Legend Meets Science." Surprisingly, he turned out to be very tall. I'm six foot two myself, and he towered over me as Cliff introduced me to him, and I shook his hand.

After that brief meeting, the two men who were both so-known as Bigfoot stars on TV kind of sequestered themselves in a corner of the museum examining the exhibits and talking in-depth about the subject, and I am embarrassed to admit that I kind of shadowed them and waited for the opportunity to ask them for their autographs, which they politely gave me. "I hate to sound like a fan," I said, but honestly, I was being a total Bigfoot nerd.

The great Bob Gimlin had a fine time at the China Flat Meet and Greet.

I have the piece of paper with Barackman's and Meldrum's autographs on it in a frame now next to the computer on which I am writing this book. The event began to wind down, and after Bob and his people left, and there were still several people milling about, something quite unexpected happened.

I noticed a man in the crowd wearing a black and green Minnesota Bigfoot Research Team t-shirt and suddenly realized that it was Abe DelRio, the investigator I'd seen speak at the Remer, Minnesota Bigfoot Days festival a few months before but hadn't had the time to actually meet with him. When I introduced myself, he let me know that he was well familiar with who I was, and we both shared a bit of a laugh over how two fellow Minnesota Bigfooters had had to come all the way to California to actually meet each other.

As we were chatting, he said that he and his partners were about to head up to the film site to meet with Daniel Perez and the others who were still up there in the rain. I pondered asking if I could tag along, but the VFW event was coming up later and I really wanted to try and go to it, so I decided against it. Just before I was about to leave the museum as the remnants of the crowd were dispersing, I heard an unmistakable voice, and when I turned toward it, I found that I was correct. It was James Fay, "Bobo" from "Finding Bigfoot."

He was standing on the deck just outside the museum entrance talking to another man, and I tried to introduce myself and tell him I was a Bigfoot researcher from Minnesota. He told me, "Well, I'm talking to this guy right now, but I'll catch up with you as soon as I'm done, ok?" Ok, I thought and went back into the museum to browse their gift shop and wait for him. While doing so, I actually bought a copy of a rather flamboyant "Finding Bigfoot" book that the show produced to help promote itself and which the museum sells among several other books.

I waited for a bit, but the next time I looked out the door, Bobo was walking away across the parking lot, walking his dog and heading toward the nearby Bigfoot Motel. Well, I thought, so much for that. When it comes to the "Finding Bigfoot" cast, Cliff Barackman is friendly, but perhaps Bobo tends to keep more to himself. I cannot say what Matt Moneymaker or Ranae Holland would be like in person because they were not there.

I did note, however, that as the person so often used on "Finding Bigfoot" to reenact Bigfoot sightings, Bobo is even taller than Jeff Meldrum. It was lunchtime by then, and I went and enjoyed a sandwich at the Willow Creek Subway, and then turned my attention to the VFW event, which was scheduled to take place in a few hours. Daniel Perez had urged me to try and schmooze my way into this affair, so I thought I would at least give it a try.

It was to be a formal gathering with presentations made by a few prominent Bigfoot researchers but most importantly, a talk by Bob

Gimlin. The host, as I was told, was researcher Tom Yamarone, whose name I had heard before but whom I had very little familiarity with and knew almost nothing about.

With time to kill, I went and parked near the VFW and waited for people to show up, thinking that someone must surely come in advance to set up for the gathering. I was right, as an SUV with several people in it eventually pulled into the parking lot, and I approached them to ask about the event.

As it turned out, there was controversy brewing that I had no idea about, and just blundered into. As people who got out of the SUV started to unload equipment, I asked one man if there was any possibility of getting into the event at this late hour and said that, I was totally willing to pay for a ticket.

Unfortunately, he told me no, that the event was sold out and that the local fire department was adamant about a maximum number of people allowed into the building. He also kind of chided me for not buying a ticket months before, but I explained that I hadn't known about the event and was only in Willow Creek in response to Daniel Perez's invitation to meet at the film site.

I then became aware that Tom Yamarone was sitting in the front passenger seat of the SUV and that he was not in a good mood. When he heard me mention Perez, he opened his door and spoke with me rather harshly, asking if I'd been in touch with Perez and complaining about how the anniversary should have been all about honoring Bob Gimlin and how anyone who felt that way should be down here with Bob instead of camping up in the mountains.

He seemed a very angry man but told me "good luck" before shutting the door and continuing to just sit inside the vehicle. So I did not get to go to the VFW event and hear Bob speak, but as I would read later, it was a successful and ..well-received event during which Yamarone, a musician in addition to being a Bigfoot researcher, performed a song he wrote about the film entitled "Roger and Bob Rode Out That Day."

However, there was further controversy to follow the next day on October 21st, when a bigger event was held in the city of Eureka to commemorate the film that was also under the charge of Yamarone. Bob Gimlin was again scheduled to speak, but as I would read later in Daniel Perez's Bigfoot Times newsletter his time slot was instead given over to an auction of Bigfoot memorabilia and the assembled audience who had hoped to hear him went away disappointed.

Yamarone's position was said to be that he was a total supporter of Gimlin but that he disliked the agent that represented him. I have no personal position on this big mess and am only relating what went down in the public record. Bob, however, appeared in YouTube videos saying that he was quite disappointed in how things turned out for the anniversary.

The Ace Hardware store in Willow Creek displays a wonderful mural depicting Bigfoot inserted into various points in the community's history.

The least known of three Bigfoot statues that graces the town.

When it came time for me to leave my great California excursion, I had to travel that winding mountain road back to Redding in the dark starting at three in the morning because of the time of the flight I had to catch from Sacramento.

The one thing that stands out the most about that drive was the moment when there was a sheer vertical rock wall on my right and a deer suddenly crossed the road in front of me from the left and then incredibly started to climb straight up that wall in a way that did not seem physically possible. I swear to God I saw that.

After Sacramento, I had a layover at LAX in Los Angeles before finally returning home, and the gate I left from happened to be pointed straight toward the Hollywood Hills, and I was told that a tiny white streak that was visible on the horizon was actually the famous Hollywood sign. Combined with everything else I'd experienced on this trip, it made for an adventure I'll never forget.

Daniel Perez called me the day I got home to make sure that I was safe and that I had gotten to at least see Bob Gimlin. I apologized to him for taking off from the mountain without saying goodbye, but he said there were no worries. I think that is a good place to conclude the account of my adventure to California. I very much wanted to go again before long and succeed in making it to the film site.

The film exists today in the public consciousness in a peculiar and frustrating way. Only a very small percentage of people have done the research to know the full story. The majority of people these days get their information from quick sound bites they pick up online and on social media, or occasionally remember some TV special they once saw that they can't remember whether it was on the Discovery or the History Channel.

People who doubt the film's authenticity will have heard something in passing about how it has long since been proven to be a fake and that the person in the suit has confessed, sometimes to the point of using this information to make fun of those who still believe in it, saying, "Don't you know what old news that is?" even though they can't begin to recall the actual details of what they're talking about.

Others are certain that they heard somewhere that Roger Patterson made a deathbed confession to having faked the film, and that this is common knowledge. Even those on the other side of the fence who believe in the film are often unaware of all the facts behind it. Some point to an interview Bob Gimlin once did in which he alluded to the fact that after many years of contemplation, he now thought there was a chance that Roger just might have managed to pull a fast one on him. It was on the 1998 BBC series "X Creatures" in which producer Chris Packham did a phone interview with Bob. In response to the question "Do you still think what you saw was an animal?"

Bob answered: "I've thought about this many, many times over the years. At one time in my life, right shortly after the film footage, I was totally convinced no one could fool me. And of course, I'm an older man now, and I see a lot of things, and I think there could have been a possibility. But it would have to have been really well planned by Roger.

And I feel that they would have had to've been very, very careful because I had a 30.06 loaded with 180-grain bullets, and had that thing have turned and rushed me I woulda' shot it. So I feel that if that was a hoax, somebody was taking an awful big chance with his life." Many have blown that out of proportion as an admission on Bob's part that the film was a hoax, but that is not what it was.

It was a passing thought, making it clear that he considered it only a remote possibility and a one-time comment that must be weighed against his many, many vehement statements that he has always been telling the truth about the film, even turning down money to "come clean."

And as for a deathbed confession by Roger, Bob made a statement while addressing an audience at a Q & A put on by Portland Oregon Bigfoot Community organizer Guy Edwards in January 2016 that refuted that idea in a powerful way. It had to do with the last conversation the two men ever had, addressing the fact that in spite of his important role in the filming, Bob had never shared in any of the profit from it and had felt quite slighted about that.

With deep emotion in his voice, Bob told the crowd: "I'll never forget what Roger kind of rallied up and said, 'Bob, I know that Al (DeAtley, Roger's brother-in-law) and I did you wrong.' And he said, 'As quick as I get well, I've got the equipment, money that I've made on this... I've got track dogs...' He said, 'As quick as I get well' he said, 'we'll go down to northern California and we'll capture one.'

And I said yeah, Roger, you get well, and we'll think about it. He died the next morning. So you see, I forgave him for all the dirt that he handed me out. And when a man's dying and looks as bad as Roger did, there ain't no way that you hold a grudge if you got any Godly in your heart at all." In fairness, I must mention that there is another account of the day before Roger's death in Greg Long's 'The Making of Bigfoot" in which the author spoke with Roger's older brothers Les, Loren, and Glenn about their visit with Roger at his deathbed.

They said Roger reminisced about how even though he was the youngest brother, he had always been able to beat the rest of them at arm wrestling and how he wanted to do it one last time because he knew he was dying, so they all humored him and let him beat them at the bedside. The difference between the two accounts is that Bob Gimlin said that Roger spoke as if he believed he would beat his cancer, while the brothers said he knew he would not.

I personally would put that down to Roger feeling contrite toward Bob and wanting to leave him with something positive rather than fatalistic talk even though he knew it was the last time they would ever speak. He was staring death in the face, with a history of far less than perfect integrity, so I don't think contrition is hard to imagine. With the emotional difficulty Bob seemed to have in giving his account of his last meeting with Roger, I have trouble believing that was not genuine.

There was one anecdote in "The Making of Bigfoot" that really made me laugh -- not mockingly, but with genuine humor -- and that was in a section in which Greg Long described his contact with some of the more prominent Bigfoot researchers about the Patterson film, including the legendary Rene Dahinden. Rene was always known as someone who fired from the hip and was never afraid to offend people, a human storehouse of knowledge after his decades spent in pursuit of sasquatch and having done more work on the Patterson film than any other Bigfooter but having no patience for novices who hadn't done a fraction of the work he'd put in or the money he'd spent on it, estimated at $30,000. He was cantankerous, funny, and downright awesome.

Though there was no doubt as to his impressive level of intelligence and learnedness he was infamous for going off on people in his very thick Swiss accent with torrents of angry profanity, and what made me laugh was just knowing that Greg Long had been one of the victims of those torrents. They spoke over the phone only about two years before Rene passed away from cancer at age 70, and six years before Long's book finally came out. I suppose I have to give Long credit for having put that many years into preparing the book, but I have a wicked satisfaction in knowing that he experienced the Dahinden treatment along the way. (I actually experienced it myself once, but only in writing.) In the transcript of their conversation he pestered Rene with questions about Patterson's character, trying to pin him down into admitting that Roger was dishonest.

They debated back and forth, comparing the terms "dishonest" and "irresponsible" until Rene lashed out at Long with one of his famous tantrums. It began with him saying that it wouldn't matter to him if Patterson was found to be a pedophile, what mattered was the study of the film, not the man. And it ended with the rant (censored here): "Just examine the (blanking) film! (Blank) Al DeAtley! (Blank) Roger Patterson! And (blank) Bob Gimlin! Ok? Ignore the human element. Look at the (blanking) film!" It's funny, but God bless Rene because he was right. No matter what is found to be true about the people involved, and no matter how damning it might seem, none of it really matters if the film in question is subjected to scientific analysis by acknowledged experts and it's found that it is simply literally impossible for the creature in the film to be a human being in a costume.

As I stated earlier, with the older analyses of the film that were done in places like England and Russia, there was once a complaint amongst the Bigfoot community that no serious scientific study had been done in America. Today, however, with the proliferation of cable tv shows that routinely cover the paranormal, "Ghost Hunters," "UFO Hunters," "Monster Quest," "Finding Bigfoot," etc., there have been a plethora of studies done on it by various experts, aided by modern computer technology that was not yet available when the older ones were done.

Though the researchers in those early days did come up with important findings about the film, modern studies have gone much farther. For instance, "Sasquatch: Legend Meets Science" aired on the Discovery Channel on January 9, 2003, and was later followed up by a companion book of the same title in 2006 by Professor Jeff Meldrum.

In this presentation, Meldrum had enlisted forensic animator Reuben Steindorf of Vision Realm Entertainment Inc. to analyze the film. Steindorf did a complex computer analysis in which he plotted a skeletal structure on to the creature's body and determined that its gait, in addition to having a much more bent kneed posture than humans, also showed a peculiar inward and outward rotation of the hips and knees with each stride absolutely non-typical of humans.

Through enhancing the film and looking at it thoroughly and perhaps with a bit of luck, Steindorf also noticed something very significant that all previous researchers had somehow missed. The creature's right thigh had a strange golf ball or perhaps even tennis ball-sized bulge in it that would protrude outward with each step, appearing to be a possible injury, a rupture of the muscle that might have been a reason why the creature only walked away from Patterson and Gimlin rather than running.

There is no apparent limp in its gait, but this detail seems unlikely in the extreme to have been worked into a costume if the film was a hoax. There have been other such studies done for tv shows that have ruled the film to be genuine, but the one which I believe to be the most significant and which I am going to end this chapter with was done in 2008 by Bill Munns, a retired special effects and makeup artist, cameraman and film editor who had worked for many years in the Hollywood film industry.

Was he a scientist? No, but as far as qualifying to be worthy of studying the Patterson-Gimlin film he was something just as important- someone whose job had been to design and create realistic looking monster costumes and fit actors into them. He had even worn them himself on occasion, such as in the 1982 DC Comics movie "Swamp Thing." He had also designed and built lifelike models of prehistoric primates to be displayed in museums, so his expertise seemed especially relevant when he decided to take on the world's most famous Bigfoot film.

His analysis was featured in two different tv shows, the 19th episode of Season Three of "Monster Quest" on the History Channel entitled "Critical Evidence," and the Bigfoot episode of a National

Geographic Channel show called 'The Truth Behind," both airing in 2009. "Monster Quest" showed how Munns began his study of the film by subjecting it to photogrammetry, a process that uses measurements gleaned from two-dimensional images to create three-dimensional models, using as part of the math involved the 25-mm lens that had always been thought to have been used on the camera Patterson used.

However in attempting to create the three-dimensional model, he had trouble making all the trees in the film align where they should have, strongly suggesting that a wider angle lens must have been used. In checking old literature on the Cine-Kodak K-100 camera, he found that in addition to the 25-mm lens, it also had a 15-mm available.

When he entered the new data using that lens, everything fell perfectly into place, making Munns confident that that was the lens Patterson had used, but it also made for significant changes in what prior researchers had always believed about the film. Munns reported: "Now, the first thing that caught my mind was that this defies everything that everyone else has recorded for 41 years.

What I did not realize at the time was the ramifications that it would have in the entire analysis of the creature and its height. It was only after I began to revisit the optical formula with a 15-mm lens that I realized that it increases the height for the creature tremendously, for any given frame, for any given distance. And that, in my personal opinion, was the real game-changer, if you will, for this entire analysis... This creature is approximately seven foot four inches tall, and I'm allowing a margin of error between seven-two and seven-foot six, but even within that margin of error, this is something quite extraordinary.

It is highly unlikely to be a human being." At the very least, this completely rules out Bob Heironimus, who stands a mere six-foot one. Munns then turned his attention to studying the different parts of the creature's anatomy and trying to determine if a human body could have fit into them. He continued: "Back in 1967, we didn't have any type of stretch fur technology which became available in the early 8os. The stretch fur technology would have enabled a lot of what we see in the film to be possible. The old standard non-stretch furs of the time, however, behaved very, very much like ordinary cloth, in the way they fold, the way they bend, the way you stretch your seams.

And if we look at the Patterson film, there's a lot of subtle curvatures in the body that are apparent by the highlights and shadows that suggest that either it was masterfully tailored or it's simply not fur cloth at all. That's what basically prompted me to continue to have doubts about whether or not we're seeing simply a character suit in that particular film." He then used a computerized overlay technique that attempted to place a human figure inside the body of the creature. Of special emphasis was the head, which appears to be shaped much like that of a male gorilla with its peaked sagittal crest but looks slightly different in various individual frames of the film, likely the result of motion blur.

To zero in on the truest representation of the head shape Munns built five model heads that ranged in shape from human-like to apelike that were designed to be fitted to a piece of equipment approximating the size of the creature that would be moved along for a certain distance by an assistant while he and another assistant filmed the process both with an old Cine-Kodak K-100 and with a modern video camera. In comparing the footage of these tests to the original film, it was determined that the creature's head truly did have an apelike shape to it, in particular, a radically different forehead shape to that of a man.

In essence, if a man's head were inside the creature's head, the slope of the creature's forehead would mean that the man's would protrude out and above it. As the show's narrator explained: "Munns has concluded that it cannot be a human in a mask unless the wearer's head is buried deep inside the suit, making it impossible for the wearer to see. He is also unable to get a human figure to sit within the proportions captured in the film." Munns further commented, "Then we're getting to the point where it may be a very simple reality that there may not be a human on the face of the

Earth who has the proportions and height necessary to be this creature."

One will hear many superficial arguments by debunkers of the film who insist that because of the upright stance of the creature, its posture, and its walk simply "look human," and that it is therefore very likely to be a human. But the real tipping point comes in the form of the close analysis of each bodily proportion such as the one conducted by Bill Munns, revealing not really blatant but very subtle mathematical discrepancies between the creature's body and that of literally any human, no matter how tall or muscular they might be.

These cannot be denied or ignored by rational thought, but they are anyway by die-hard unbelievers who will hear the data explained to them but then continue to just say, "Well, I still don't believe it." An extreme example of this would be the authors of the aforementioned book 'The Making of Bigfoot," who actually, harshly ridicule anyone who accepts this data. Their stance is based, really, on a stubborn preconceived notion that no matter what evidence there might be to the contrary, there is simply no way in Heaven, Hell, or Earth that Bigfoot exists. Before I go on with Munns' findings, I'd like to address the word "evidence" and how it relates to the word "proof." They are not the same thing.

Most people who insist there is no real evidence for the existence of Bigfoot are really meaning to say that there is no proof. Evidence is observed data, and in the case of Bigfoot, there is a mountain of it. The study of evidence can go in any direction, either positive or negative. Proof is a level of evidence that rises to the point of being able to firmly establish the truth.

Many insist that the only evidence that will ever prove the reality of Bigfoot once and for all would be a body, either dead or alive delivered into the hands of science, and of course, that is what all of us in the field would love to see. But maybe it is possible for proof to be something not quite that dramatic but just as impressive. The National Geographic Channel program 'The Truth Behind: Bigfoot" went into even more detail about Bill Munns' computerized attempts to match a human figure with the body of the Bluff Creek creature.

He zeroed in on the knees, stating unequivocally, 'There's virtually no way with any costume that we could alter where the knee is going to bend on the subject." The narrator then elaborates: "In short, an actor's knees must line up with the knees in a costume. But lining up an actor's knees means that neither his ankles or hips will line up with Patterson's Bigfoot... The torso of the creature in the Patterson film is also longer than a typical human's, and the hip is lower.

If an actor's shoulders are lined up, then the hip is too high on the human. Match the hips and the shoulders fall short. But it's the legs that really seem unusual." Munns picks up the narrative: "The most curious thing that I found is in the leg proportions themselves. We have a very long upper leg and a very short lower leg by comparison. This particular configuration is exceedingly rare on human beings.

The anatomical proportions of the body are extremely unusual and suggest to me that it would be very, very hard to find a human being who has the appropriate anatomy to wear a suit even if you made one." Narrator: "Arms and torso too long. Hips too low. Legs out of proportion with a human. And the joints can't be made to line up with a human in a suit. To Munns, this can mean only one thing-these proportions are more like an ape, not a man." Munns' final assessment: "All of these add up to something which in my mind is biologically real, and not a human in any type of costume."

It doesn't matter who claims to have been the man in the suit because it's impossible. And it doesn't matter how shifty a character Roger Patterson was. Though he had good intentions, he was admittedly a scoundrel. A scoundrel who got very, very lucky on one October afternoon. Study Bill Munns' findings as many times as you need to. In case you missed it, folks... that's proof.

10

ADDENDUM

My failure to reach the Patterson-Gimlin film site in October of 2017 after traveling so far was a hard blow to take, and I vowed that I would return and make another stab at it. That time came less than a year later, in September of 2018. In booking my flight west far in advance in order to save money, I chose a block of four days with the hope that at least one of them would have good enough weather rather than the torrential rain of the year before.

As it turned out I got very lucky because the days I chose happened to be within a weeks-long period of absolutely gorgeous late summer weather in the region, partly sunny and in the low 70s in temperature every day. I stayed in the same hotel in the city of Areata that I'd used the year before, which I liked for its location right next to the Pacific Coast Highway interchange that gets one to Willow Creek.

I still marvel about how sources tell me that the PG film site is only 18 miles from the ocean but that the drive from Arcata to Willow Creek takes 45 minutes, the effect of that narrow and winding mountain road. In studying the excellent directions to the film site on the Bluff Creek Project's website I noted the mention about a forest service gate that is closed for part of the year and blocks access to the site, sometimes beginning in September.

Though it had been open in late October the year before, I was a bit worried about it and contacted both Daniel Perez and one of the organizers of the Bluff Creek Project, Steven Streufert. Steven assured me by e-mail that the gate would only be closed early if there was substantial rain in the area and that it is normally left open until the end of the autumn hunting season. Daniel, meanwhile, responded to my e-mail by wanting to talk to me on the phone and, in addition to repeating the information about the gate, warned me to make sure that I brought some form of protection with me because of the prolific number of bears and mountain lions in the area.

Having met me at the parking area above the site the year before, in the pouring rain, he seemed excited for me in making my second attempt. As it turned out I was not allowed to carry bear spray in my luggage, but a pocket knife was allowed in my checked bag. I also resolved to look around for a good tree branch to use as a walking stick and potential weapon. "Well," Daniel said, "if you're alone and you're quiet, you might just see some action." I had to think to myself, though, that if I was actually to see a Bigfoot at the PG film site, I would not expect anyone - Daniel included - to believe me.

That was not why I was going, it was simply a major goal on my personal bucket list that I wanted to check off to visit this major historical site. On Friday, September 14th, I drove to Willow Creek to meet with Steven Streufert, the owner of a business called Bigfoot Books. From the name of the place, I had had the impression that it was a store specializing in books about Bigfoot, but though it does have some of those it is really just one of the many businesses in Willow Creek that feature the word Bigfoot in their names and is primarily a typical small used book store. Steven only had a small amount of time to give me, but it was a valuable visit as he is an absolute authority on the film site and showed me on a detailed topographic map exactly where the film site was.

He said that the gate I worried about should be open, and that while he'd seen bears in the area several times, they had always acted timid around people and that the mountain lions were more of a concern. I resolved to look over my shoulder regularly. Being in Willow Creek again that day was a fun reminder of the year before, and the China Flat Museum was open, and I visited it again. There was nothing new, but it was nice to view their collection of artifacts a second time. The next day, I decided I would head up to the film site. Saturday, September 15th, the mid-to-late morning drive to the site was now familiar to me.

The gate was indeed open, a huge relief, and now I knew I was going to make it. Those rocky gravel roads, though, were every bit as treacherous in good weather as they had been the year before in the pouring rain and though only going on for a few miles, they seemed as if they would never end, but end they finally did at the parking area where I'd met Daniel Perez and Cliff Barackman. This time I was alone, no other vehicles were there, and the primeval forest all around me was quiet.

A small fire ring made of rocks was on the ground near the tree on which a very small wooden sign simply reads "Trail," and lying on the ground close by was a perfect sanded walking staff about five feet long that someone had left there. An oversight or an act of generosity so that it would be there for visitors to use? I didn't know, but I was happy to find it and made great use of it, as it turned out to be quite necessary. The hike down into the valley that contains Bluff Creek is a rugged one but despite a rock slide covering part of the trail, trickles of water flowing across it in places, and other assorted debris here and there, it only took me about a half-hour.

At the bottom was a tree with a red ribbon tied around it and another rough wooden sign carved with the information "PG Trail" where the trail turned a sharp corner to the right into a thick but flat section of mostly coniferous woods. This went on for a relatively short distance until about 1 pm when I finally reached the object of my journey, the famous body of water known as Bluff Creek. Its width and depth varied but never seemed to exceed about 20 feet across with a depth of anywhere from a few inches to a foot deep, the occasional pool maybe twice that.

When in flood from melting snow in the spring I knew that it was very different, with deep and fast-moving water that carried large amounts of forest debris and even made the channel of the creek shift around a bit, but now in the fall, it was just a gentle stream with a steady current flowing from right to left.

The majestic Bluff Creek wilderness.

By my approximation, this may be about the spot on Bluff Creek where Patterson's and Gimlin's horses panicked when the Bigfoot came into view on the opposite bank.

This is a section of the path that the Bigfoot walked in the PG film.

The author on the spot where Patterson knelt down to shoot the film, marked by the red ribbon.

On the banks, what are described in the literature as "gravel bars" are in fact a covering of medium-sized rocks of various fascinating shapes and sizes, mostly flat and quite easy to walk on. My directions instructed me to head upstream and that there would be some fallen logs to negotiate just before the point where I would have to wade across the creek to reach the filmsite.

Sure enough, everything was accurate. When I reached that point, I took off my hiking boots and socks and put on an old pair of tennis shoes, I'd brought for this purpose. Rolling up my pant legs, I made my way across, the water quite cold but not unbearably so. On the other side, I then knew that my personal bucket list had just earned a major check because I was virtually on top of the Patterson-Gimlin film site.

As far as I could gather, the point at which I crossed the creek must have been about where the two mens' horses panicked when the Bigfoot first came into view. It was about the same spot where Patterson had charged across the creek with camera in hand in his cowboy boots on a slightly injured foot. This exact location had been a matter of controversy and conjecture for years, but the Bluff Creek Project had finally zoomed in on it in the summer of 2012 when certain trees seen in the film that still stood were identified.

In 51 years, the site had changed in innumerable ways. Roads that had once existed that had allowed one to almost drive all the way to the site had long since gone unused and been reclaimed by the forest. Most of the open clearing that one sees the Bigfoot walk through in the film is now covered with new forest growth. The area has gone through immense changes brought about by man, including logging, bulldozing, and I would imagine even replanting. The log jams and stumps and so forth that are seen in the film are decades gone, replaced by new ones and either carried away by subsequent floods or just rotted away as dead wood will do.

I'd been told to look for a large object known as the "root ball" where a big tree had fallen and exposed its roots, and that the exact spot where Patterson knelt down and filmed the creature would be next to it. It was easy to find and as further clarification, a bush that was not there yet at the time had a red ribbon tied to it to mark that spot. I can't really put into words what it felt like to stand there where such a monumental event had occurred, but I will never forget it. I walked what I understood from the instructions to be the path that "Patty," the female Bigfoot, filmed by Patterson, had walked. Much of it was overgrown, but there was somewhat of a clearing for part of the way.

I tried to estimate where the spot would have been where the creature turned to look directly at the camera but have no idea how close I came. What struck me the most about the place was how small and compact it seemed to me in comparison to the impression that is given in the film. I'd always pictured an enormous clearing with the trees seen in the background being far away, and the creature walking along almost forever before it finally disappeared into the forest that led up the valley wall. I can only assume now that my early impressions and probably the impressions of many who view the film are the result of camera angle and film speed.

Seeing it in person, I realized that everything seen in the film is much closer together than it seems, and that the event probably happened much faster than most think it did. But it was such a thrill to be there and a sense of accomplishment that I am so proud of. When I decided that it was time to start back, I had some curiosities occur that turned out to be funny in retrospect. First, I lost track of where the log was on which I had left my hiking boots.

Examples of artificial structures found near the filmsite, probably the work of humans.

I thought I had the right spot, and they were not there. As I was looking around trying to get reoriented, I found another log at the side of the creek on which two small stones had been neatly set. Just for a moment, I actually allowed myself to think, "Ok, this is weird. Did Bigfoot just actually take my boots and then leave me these stones in return?" I was hoping I wouldn't have to wear the wet tennis shoes on my feet for the rest of the excursion, but eventually I back-tracked and found where I'd left my boots.

Give me a break folks, I was in very unfamiliar territory. I also found a couple of spots in which rocks had been stacked up in small but clearly artificially created piles, one right along the creek bank and another inside a hollow stump nearby. I also found where a few small pieces of wood were dangling from a log by long strands of fiber-thin vine, clearly meant to look decorative. I am fairly certain that this was done by humans trying to fool other humans into thinking that it just might have been done by Bigfoot.

I then had a brief moment of panic while trying to relocate the trail that would lead me back up to the parking area, because once you walk away from it, it is not that easy to spot again. But in a few minutes I did find it, and just as I was starting out along it, I heard a deep, gruff rumbling sound coming from a point perhaps 50 yards in front of me, and I'm pretty certain it was the sound made by a large bear exhaling. Oh great, I thought, that's a bear, and I'm heading straight for it, but though I believe it was there, I never saw it or heard it again.

Shortly before I reached the point where I had to start heading back uphill, I also caught sight of a trail camera attached to a tree, and since I knew from the Bluff Creek Project's online presence that they had those there and that they were not just still cameras but were shooting video, I waved at it, and I hope Steven Streufert and the other members of that group have that footage of me. I'd seen a few clips of wildlife activity that they'd captured at the film site on those cameras, including a fascinating shot of two adult mountain lions walking together.

Those cats are known to be such solitary creatures that I knew how precious and rare such a clip was, and I imagined that they must have been a mating pair, but when I met with Steven, he told me that they were actually siblings that his group had been seeing since they were cubs. That's a nice image, but though I'd been excited about the prospect of encountering predators that day I suppose it's lucky that my wildlife sightings were actually limited to one deer and a couple of squirrels, plus the plethora of golden eagles that can regularly be seen soaring over those mountains. The hike back up to the parking area was a hard one and had me out of breath a few times, but luckily my legs and feet, which I have sporadic issues with, held up.

When I got back to the car I left the walking staff beside the fire ring for the next visitor to use and then started my drive back to civilization. On the drive out, one notices much more dramatically how much you are going uphill out of the valley, than you notice the downhill descent on the way in. When arranging for my rental car, I had chosen a Ford Echo Sport because of its reputation for being good on rough terrain, but it turned out that I received a Kia Sorento instead. It impressed me greatly the way it climbed those narrow rocky roads that in many spots are at the edge of steep and deadly drop-offs if one should be unlucky enough to slide off.

The whole way, though, I was hearing and feeling sensations that made me wonder if there was a problem of some kind with the car or if it was just the natural way any vehicle would sound and feel as it bounced over all those rocks. I found out for sure when I made it out of the five mile-plus stretch of rough roads back to the paved road that ascends the mountains from the town of Orleans, which is known as the GO Road, "GO" being an acronym for two small towns that the road was originally meant to connect when it was built, the O standing for Orleans and the G representing a town whose name escapes my memory now.

The rugged mountain road between the GO Road and the filmsite parking area.

A sheer dropoff along the hiking trail from the parking area to the filmsite.

As soon as I turned on to this road, the car was making the same troubling sound it had been making on the rocks, and then I knew something was wrong. Sure enough, when I got out, I found that the right front tire was not only flat but absolutely shredded. It had obviously been flat for quite a while, and I marveled at how I had made it this far.

Whether the Echo Sport I'd originally wanted would have made a difference I will never know, but I owe a great debt to that Kia Sorento for getting me to the more well-traveled GO Road. It was now mid-afternoon, and I was a 17-mile downhill drive from Orleans. As I was beginning to work at changing the tire, a pickup truck came by from farther up the road on its way down and stopped. Inside was a young couple from Orleans who were just out driving around, and as far as I recall, their names were Mark and Deirdre.

In a case of small world, Deirdre was originally a fellow Minnesotan. I want to give my most profound thanks to these people because, as it turned out, they would become my absolute saviors that day, and I hope they might somehow see this book someday, though I know it's unlikely. Mark helped me change the tire, which was difficult on the not quite level grade I was on, and then just as I thought I was about to be able to get back on my way it turned out that the car had an automatic locking system, and suddenly the keys were locked inside the car.

Bad had just gone to worse, and I couldn't believe the turn the day had just taken. We then spent a long time trying to whittle small tree branches down to be thin enough to do the "coat hanger thing" and stick them through the top of the passenger side window and try to trigger the door unlocking button, but sticks that thin are springy and lack the strength to be able to apply enough force, and it was to no avail.

At one point, another vehicle came by driven by an older bearded man who judging by the cased rifle next to him must have been out hunting, and he also stopped to help but only stayed for a brief period and offered the advice of just smashing the window with a rock before continuing on his way, but I decided I did not want the inside of the car to be littered with broken glass. Our efforts turned out to be a waste of time, and it got to be about 5 pm before I asked the young couple to just give me a ride down to Orleans, where I hoped to be able to figure things out. I rode in their truck's back seat with their dog, which was ok since I am an animal lover.

They took me to the only business in the very small town of Orleans, which is a general store called the Orleans Market, where I was allowed to use their phone and call a towing service in Willow Creek, a 36-mile drive away along dangerously winding roads. They told me they would send someone up to unlock my car and that he would be there in about an hour and 15 minutes. It turned out to be closer to two hours, and I was watching for a tow truck to arrive, but when the service person finally arrived at around 8 PM, he was unexpectedly driving a convertible.

It had started to get cold by that time, and he had the heater running, but it was still a bit of a chilly ride back up the GO Road. He got the car unlocked and got me back on my way, and I did not get back to my hotel in Arcata that night until about midnight. It was a day I will never forget, half thrilling with my film site visit and half horrible, with many hours that left me thinking sarcastically to myself, "Oh yeah, this is a great vacation!" It was made even more dramatic by the fact that I had told a couple of my loved ones back home to call my hotel (where I'd left a note about where I was going to be) and check on my safety if they didn't hear from me by a certain time that day.

I was not able to contact them because there is no cell service up in the mountains, plus even if there had been my phone was locked inside the car. My worried girlfriend called me when I was finally driving back between Orleans and Willow Creek, and I was happy to be able to tell her that I was ok. One odd and unexpected thing on that drive was that I noted that making it at night in the dark and just focusing on the lines on the road and not being able to see the high rock walls just inches away along the roadside that I was hoping not to crash into made the drive much less stressful. At one point between Willow Creek and Arcata, I caught sight of some kind of feline creature in my headlights running away from the road toward the trees, something about the size of a bobcat but with very large ears. I think it was a lynx, a very neat sighting as I had never seen one of those before.

A further mishap occurred a few weeks after I had returned home from my California trip when the phone I'd been using was unfortunately lost. I had sent most of the pictures from the trip including all of the Bluff Creek ones to my computer so they were preserved, but a four- minute video I'd shot at the film site was gone forever. That was a tough blow. Perhaps I will return to the site again someday, but if not, my memories and still shots will have to suffice. For anyone who wishes to follow in my footsteps and in those of Roger Patterson and Bob Gimlin and visit the PG film site, I urge you to do so cautiously. Use a hardy vehicle that can handle the roads, be prepared for a rugged hike steeply downhill and then the even harder trudge back up, and keep your eyes open for dangerous wildlife.

It is well worth the difficulties, though, to visit this important historical site and see where the best piece of evidence for the existence of Bigfoot was captured. You will hear that it has been debunked. It has not. On the contrary, it has been proven. The Patterson-Gimlin film is genuine and for real and shows a creature that should thrill and captivate the hearts and minds of everyone.

I have included this chapter in a book that is mostly about Minnesota Bigfoot reports because of my deep interest in all the various claimed photos and films of the creatures from far and wide, and I hope you the readers have enjoyed it.

The filmsite trailhead, with fire ring and walking staff as found. To all Bigfoot enthusiasts, by all means visit this fascinating place if you can!

11

IN CONCLUSION

What can one conclude after spending over 30 years in pursuit of something that the majority of people do not believe exists? The late great Rene Dahinden, one of the most famed Bigfoot researchers of all time, often stated right up until the end of his life that despite all he had seen and heard and learned in his decades of investigation that he was still uncertain as to whether the creatures really existed at all.

I personally think, however, that in his private thoughts, he must have been at the same place where I am today and just didn't want to say it. I am many years past the point of wondering whether Bigfoot really exists.

I know that it does. I am also long past any need I might have once had for my own childhood sighting in 1976 to have occurred, though it is certainly a priceless memory. It was a fairly mundane occurrence as Bigfoot sightings go, dwarfed by many of the reports that will appear in the appendix to this book that will immediately follow this

12

AFTERWORD

When I first started out as a Bigfoot researcher, I remember purchasing 1982's "The Bigfoot Casebook" by Janet and Colin Bord, which covered reports from all across North America and listed Minnesota's grand total as nine. A single digit. I was still in my teens then and used that number as a starting point, traveling to the places listed and beginning to poke around.

The fact that the plethora of adventures I've been on since then has led me to the hundreds of reports I've now cataloged for Minnesota is something I take a great deal of pride in, but at the same time, I feel that in most states, anyone who would commit themselves to doing the same kind of research I've done would come up with similar results. In fact, I believe that if someone were to do that kind of study in the Pacific Northwest states of Washington, Oregon, and California -- not to mention Canada -- they would no doubt come up with not just hundreds but thousands of reports for each state and province.

None of the individual sources that exist even begin to cover the total number of reports that are out there to be uncovered if one truly explores all of them collectively -- books and newspapers, documentaries, websites, conferring with other investigators and just seeking out the word of mouth stories. This is what I have done. One of the most common arguments put forth by skeptics on the existence of Bigfoot is simply, "If these creatures really exist, why aren't they seen more often?"

Any number of responses has been offered by the Bigfoot community in answer to that question, ranging from the relatively low population the creatures must have and the remoteness of the wilderness areas they inhabit to the apparent level of intelligence they seem to have that makes them almost supernaturally elusive, not to mention the hit and miss factor of campers and hunters being in exactly the right place at the right time.

However, though all of these answers have their merits and are completely valid, I would like to offer another much simpler response to the question that I feel should be first and foremost. "If these creatures really exist, why aren't they seen more often?" THEY ARE! Not a year passes without Bigfoot sightings or the discovery of other evidence of their existence in North America, and the numbers are not tiny, easily numbering in the hundreds per year.

While skeptics and debunkers pick apart the details of the dramatic reports that have received widespread media attention, the real strength of the phenomenon lies in the multitude of unknown ones that accumulate and pile up year after year after year. I dare say there are probably areas where Bigfoot is seen more often than such elusive creatures as the mountain lion or wolverine, even though those animals are there. Most of the incidents are never documented, being shared only with the witnesses' close friends and families.

A small percentage of them, however, do see the light of day, enabling the debate to go on and on. The problem, it seems, is that for many people, Bigfoot is stuck in a peculiar mental niche that it seems unable to break out of until final proof is achieved. I think that even if there were ten thousand sightings a year, after every single individual one some skeptic would scoff and repeat the same old tired question - "If they exist, why aren't they seen more often?" A variation of that question is used by skeptics who point out that with the proliferation of logging in our wilderness areas and the number of campers and hunters and wildlife officials that are out there, "It's hard to understand how something like Bigfoot could have evaded detection for so long."

Excuse me? What in the waking world are they talking about? Bigfoot has been detected again and again and again! If not, we wouldn't even be talking about it! Even that is challenged, though, by the skeptics who insist that the average citizen who reports seeing something is not a "trained observer" or a scientific expert that is really qualified to objectively interpret what they have seen and that the entirety of the Bigfoot phenomenon can be brushed off in that way. I'm not going to say that I don't understand that rationale, but I think that it only goes so far and that the length to which these skeptics take it is a huge leap in logic and downright insulting to witnesses.

I am offended personally by it, and I am offended on behalf of the thousands of people that it attempts to marginalize and discredit. Some reports are indeed open to interpretation, but there is a category of Bigfoot sighting in which people see the creatures up close and personal, sometimes in broad daylight, in ways that leave absolutely no room for interpretation as to what they are looking at. There is an analogy I have come to use in response to criticism of how people observe things. Let's say multiple people all witness a car crash at an intersection.

It is common for their descriptions to vary widely in the aftermath as to the description of each car, how fast each was going, which was at fault and who hit who, etc. But the one thing they will all agree on one hundred percent is that they did indeed see a car crash! No one doubts them on that. And it's often been pointed out that eyewitness testimony can not be discounted if it continues to be used as a major facet of criminal prosecution in our legal system.

People are sent to prison for life or even to death based on what others swear under oath to having seen them do. Detectives sit down in interview rooms with frightened and rattled witnesses and say to them, "All right, calm down... tell me what you saw." The argument has even taken the form of saying that people, in general, can not fully trust our brains to interpret the things we see, yet that rationale only seems to get applied to claims of extraordinary things like the sighting of a UFO or a Bigfoot. If true, shouldn't it apply to everything, even the most mundane of observations?

If the skeptics are as confident in their argument as they sound, then they should be telling us that every time we approach a traffic light while driving, we should never be sure whether we should stop or keep going based on whether our brains tell us that the light is red or green. Personally, I think the human brain is a miraculous device and that we ought to have a little faith in it. I have seen one Bigfoot in my over 50 years on this planet.

For what it's worth, at the time of this writing, I have also seen only one wild wolf, one wild coyote, and one wild mountain lion in Minnesota in all that time, and surprisingly despite all my time spent in the wilderness all the wild bears I've seen have been in Yellowstone National Park and northern California. (I should mention that I've been close enough to Minnesota bears to hear them a couple of times, but they've managed to keep out of sight.) Deer are seen in droves (though even they seem to vanish ghostlike on the first day of hunting season), and smaller critters like raccoon, skunk, beaver and porcupine turn up semi-regularly, but the larger predators have always been elusive in my travels, as is Bigfoot despite its frequent appearances to people who are not looking for it.

A catch phrase has been coined, "You don't find Bigfoot, Bigfoot finds you." But even with that being the case and with how frustrating the search usually is, I have to say that even if I were to quit the pursuit right now, I would hardly come away empty-handed, and that's with what feels to me to have been a minimum of effort on my part in comparison to many other Bigfoot researchers. Beginning with next to nothing, I have traveled to areas of my state in pursuit of rumors and have found the people that have told me, "Yes, that happened to me," and then gone into great detail about the huge hairy manlike creatures they have seen.

These people had nothing to gain by talking to me, a total stranger, and in some cases, had something to lose in fear of ridicule, but they shared their stories because they could tell that I was treating them seriously. I have had them get emotional and extremely animated in telling their stories, and one man who was willing to share but didn't want to be recorded pointed at my equipment and said, "Is that thing on?" before he would talk.

In addition, in randomly searching areas in which reports have occurred, I have been lucky enough to find Bigfoot footprints well over a dozen times over the years and have even had the rare and priceless experience of listening to what I believe to have been the sounds of two Bigfoot creatures screaming and howling to each other in the dark of night. I can't lie about that incident- I panicked and felt about two inches tall even though I had a gun close at hand.

That was decades ago, and while I hope for something that significant to happen again, I find myself having to advise people interested in getting into the Bigfoot field that if you commit to it and if you diligently seek out reports and witnesses and are willing to put miles on your vehicle driving to far away wild places that are out of your comfort zone, and if you find the courage within you to go out there and brave all the conditions that come with it, there truly is the potential for you to have your own experiences.

If there is an area where several people have claimed to see Bigfoot, it probably has Bigfoots in it. Search that area, and you just might find evidence. I find myself wanting to say that it is really not that simple, but that it really is that simple at the same time. No guarantees, of course. I've been asked what is the strongest physical evidence I've personally found to support the existence of Bigfoot in my years of searching.

I could cite the many eyewitnesses that I have so much respect and admiration for and the accounts they've given me, or the footprints I've found, or the blood-curdling sounds I've heard, or even the tree break evidence and other weird stick structures that are so controversial, but when it comes to evidence that can really be put under the microscope scientifically, I have to point to what myself and Ed Trimble found in Itasca County in May of 1992.

We were investigating a series of claims by a man who said he had been monitoring the presence of Bigfoot in a particular area where he had found tracks, broken branches that seemed to indicate the creatures swinging through the trees, and he'd also had a small number of visual sightings of them. He was a drinker, however, and honest enough to admit that for one of his sightings, he would have gotten a better look if he hadn't been drunk at the time. I realize that skeptics will take that admission and run with it, seeing it as the sole detail they need to debunk the entire story.

Alcohol, however, is a depressive drug, not a hallucinogen, far more likely to blur memories as the man admitted than it is to create them out of thin air, and there was more to the story. He also stated that the creatures had responded to bait he had left for them, and that there was damage to a series of old inactive highline poles that turned out to be the most compelling evidence of Bigfoot that I have personally found to this day. It was a chilling experience when Ed and I found those poles in fading daylight. They had had splintered strips of wood torn off of them and scattered about all over the ground, pieces ranging in size from a few inches to a few feet long.

Some of the poles were torn into so deeply that they were in danger of falling over. In addition, there was a series of twin slashes embedded in the wood all over the poles that just screamed "teeth marks," the impressions of eye teeth, "fangs" or "tusks." They ranged all the way from just a few inches above the ground to seven feet up. I carefully measured the distance between these marks, and in all examples, they were 3 1/2" apart.

Skeptics, of course, will say that the damage was done by bears, which are well known for marking their territory in such ways. However, there are reasons why that absolutely can not be the case. Nowhere on either the poles or any of the pieces torn from them was there any hint of claw marks, suggesting that the larger pieces had to have been pulled off with hands.

Furthermore, when my partner in this investigation Ed Trimble showed me black bear skulls collected in his long history as a tracker and trapper, it turned out that even large black bears -- the only species of bear native to Minnesota -- have eye teeth only about 1 1/2" apart, less than half the width displayed on the damaged poles. To my mind, this left only three possibilities. One, a bigger species of bear such as a grizzly or polar bear that do not exist in Minnesota. Two, some hitherto unknown species of large animal never encountered before. Or three, Bigfoot, which had been reported to exist in the area multiple times.

It called to mind the principle of Occam's Razor, which states that in a general sense the most likely answer to any question is usually the correct one. This does not ever rule out the most likely answer being something paranormal. My trusty sidekick Dean did suggest a fourth possibility, just to be thorough, the idea that what appeared to be teeth marks might have actually been some kind of tool marks from some metal implement, but that seems highly unlikely.

These were old and long unused highline poles, and the pieces scattered on the ground were so haphazard it looked for all the world like something an animal would do rather than human activity with some rational purpose. Ed's theory was that the creatures enjoyed the taste of the creosote that the poles were coated with, and that they might even rub it on themselves as an insect repellent. (Incidentally, just to be even more thorough, I investigated the width between a grizzly bear's eye teeth by doing a measurement on a particularly large taxidermy mount in a local sporting goods store in my home area.

It was three inches, exactly twice that of a large black bear but lacking the extra half-inch of the alleged Bigfoot teeth marks. It's irrelevant anyway, since a grizzly turning up in Minnesota would be unprecedented.) The phenomenon and the experience of what has come to be given the almost cartoonish name of "Bigfoot" is very real and affects the lives of countless real people.

Does it have its share of crackpots, kooks, and conmen? Yes, without a doubt, but so do virtually all fields, including politics, science, and religion. The heart, soul, and strength of the Bigfoot field lies in the multitude of people out there of all walks of life who, in the course of just going about their daily business have occasionally experienced something absolutely incredible, an encounter with a huge wild creature that society at large tells them should not and does not exist.

These people are often mocked and ridiculed for sharing the experience, sometimes even by people they have always loved and trusted. Have a clear sighting of a Bigfoot, and one can never unsee it. The list of people who have gone from being total unbelievers and blown right past the level of believer to the level of an absolute knower in one dramatic moment is a long one.

Those people are privileged to have come to know what they now know, but many of them have suffered for it too. My work is for them, this book is for them, and if I can one day contribute in any way to proving to the world once and for all that their experiences were real and that they are not liars or idiots or maniacs, I will be more than satisfied.

What follows now is a list of nearly 700 Bigfoot reports for the state of Minnesota. And that's what I call a grand total. Enjoy.

Forest cover in Minnesota.

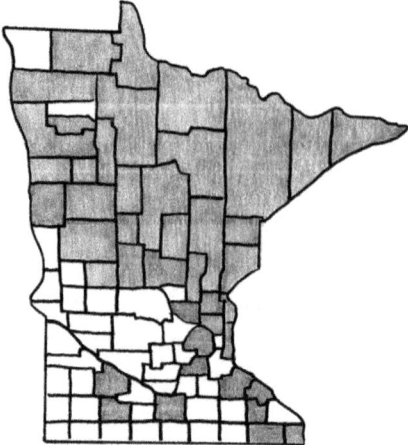

Counties in Minnesota in which Bigfoot reports have occurred.

13

APPENDIX

MINNESOTA BIGFOOT REPORTS BY REGION

I ndividual incidents are counted as single reports. "Episodes" of activity in which a specific number of incidents is unclear are counted as single reports. People whose names have been published before or who have given permission are named in full, otherwise by initials or as "anonymous."

Abbreviations used include:

- BFRO - Bigfoot Field Researchers' Organization
- GCBRO - Gulf Coast Bigfoot Research Organization
- SRA - Sasquatch Research Association
- DNR - Department of Natural Resources

ARROWHEAD/SUPERIOR

1. Names unknown, "northern tip" of state, 1911- Two men hunting came across strange tracks and followed them until they saw a "human giant" covered in short light hair. A posse was collected to track down the creature, but it had disappeared. *"Things" by Ivan T. Sanderson.*

2-4. Gwynne H. Boucher and "Richard," Duluth area, March 1946 -

A tale exists of U.S. Navy men who
purchased two captive "yetis" in
China after the end of World War 2
and brought them back to America.
After docking in Washington state,
they planned to sell the creatures to
Ringling Bros., Barnum & Bailey
Circus, which was based in Baraboo,
Wisconsin, so they transported them cross country by truck. In
Minnesota, they encountered a fierce winter storm which caused
them to overturn just west of Duluth, and the creatures escaped into
the woods. They tracked them for a week to ten days as far as the
Finland area, then lost them. Boucher related that in subsequent
years he and his wife had twice had encounters that he thought
might have involved the creatures or their offspring. While canoeing
at Homer Lake, they heard a large animal crashing through brush
and making a strange uttering, and while bicycling near Pancore Lake
he briefly glimpsed something chasing a moose calf that gave off the
same odor he remembered the yetis having. Cook County News-
Herald. May 13, 1991; Scott Benson.

5. Frank Hansen, Whiteface Reservoir, Fall 1963 - The well-
known keeper of the Minnesota Iceman related an experience unre-
lated to that exhibit. During a deer hunt while on leave from the Air
Force in Duluth, he saw a strange creature that frightened him
greatly at the same time a UFO landing was known to have taken
place in the area. As to description, he simply said, "Maybe it was
from outer space, maybe it was Bigfoot, I don't know." Personally
related by witness.

6. Kerry Peterson, Two Harbors area, February 1972 - A youth
enjoying the Presidents' Day weekend off from school was snowmobiling in the woods near Two Harbors when he saw a large manlike
creature emerges from the trees onto the trail he was using. It was
covered in chocolate brown hair with a lighter-colored face and
considerably taller than a man. As he was nervously wondering how
he might get past it, he turned on the snowmobile's headlight which

seemed to make it go back into the woods and disappear. "Monsters of the Midwest" by Jessica Freeburg and Natalie Fowler.

7-8. Debbie, Michael, and Bob Trucano, Billy Jarve, David Galaski, near Tower, early July 1972 - A white-haired bipedal creature about four and a half feet tall and three feet wide was seen twice on the Trucano property, first by 13-year-old Debbie and her boyfriend while they were playing badminton near the house at dusk, then less than a week later when four people saw it emerge from some woods into a sandpit, again at dusk. The Tower News. July 21, 1972.

9. Anonymous, northwest of Big Sucker River near Two Harbors, August 1973 - A couple having a romantic encounter in the woods, heard screams and howling approaching them and fled. Years later, the man heard a recording of alleged Bigfoot vocalizations on a radio program and it was identical to what he had heard previously. BFRO website.

10-11. Anonymous, near Brimson, late June or early July 1976 - A child at a gathering of family and friends at a rustic farmstead were inside a tent at 11 PM when bipedal footsteps approached, then the silhouette of two legs was seen walking around the tent. All persons were accounted for at the time, and no one else lived in the area. A Bigfoot sighting was known of in the same area that same year. Bigfootencounters website.

12. Anonymous, Dark Lake near Buhl, Summer 1977 - For an entire season, a family had a Bigfoot lurking around their home, making various sounds, chasing a horse, splashing in a lake, and being chased off with shots fired. A grandmother had a clear sighting of it eating raspberries, and noticed it was large and reddish colored. BFRO website.

13. Anonymous, near Cloquet, September 1977 - Six teens sitting around a campfire at around 9-10 PM heard footsteps approaching them from the woods and smelled a strong odor like human sweat, then saw the silhouette of a bipedal figure about eight feet tall walking and swinging its arms. It did not come near enough for a clearer view. BFRO website.

14. Chris Machmer, Long Lake east of Cotton, July 1977 or 1978 - A

five or six-year-old boy saw a Bigfoot looking in the door of a cabin. BFRO website.

15. Anonymous, near Lake Superior, 1978 - A young man on a rural property went out at night to investigate dogs barking and a foul odor coming from a chicken coop. By flashlight beam, he saw a dark-colored Bigfoot with a human-like face holding a chicken. When it made a deep toned chattering sound, he panicked and dropped the rifle he was holding, which went off and blew a hole in the chicken coop and caused the creature to scream and run away. The next day a hole was found ripped in the chicken wire around the coop with tufts of hair snagged in it, and footprints 18-20" long were found crossing a muddy meadow. The Track Record. Ray Crowe, January 1992.

16. Anonymous, Fall Lake in Boundary Waters Canoe Area, 1980 - Limited information on a man from Ely who was said to have had a Bigfoot sighting. Tim Olson.

17. Anonymous, Lax Lake area near Silver Bay, Fall 1985- Two teens out grouse hunting near dusk heard a frightening howling and could hear a large animal moving a couple of hundred yards away. It was in the path they needed to take to get out of the area, and they tried to cautiously move past it, catching a glimpse of it when they came closer and seeing that it was a dark bipedal creature about nine feet tall. Once they had passed it, it followed them for a bit and then finally moved off. BFRO website.

18. Anonymous, Ramshead Lake in Boundary Waters Canoe Area, late May 1986 - Three Air Force men on leave from their base in Grand Forks, North Dakota, and one child were on a canoeing and camping trip when loud wood knocking was heard near their camp. One man went into the woods to try and track down the source but came back when he began to feel he was being led into a trap. They built a large fire during the night and prepared to leave at first light, and when morning came, they found a large wet footprint about 14" long on rocks beside their canoes. Whatever made the print had to have swum across 100 yards of lake to reach them. BFRO website.

19. Anonymous, north of Two Harbors, 1987-1990 - An episode occurred at a rural home used as a cabin by several relatives and

friends wherein over a few years, a Bigfoot was seen and heard many times. It was six to seven feet tall, light brown in color, and made growling sounds. Eventually, when it was seen prowling around some junked cars behind the house, two men went after it with a shotgun and fired at it, certain they'd hit it. It fled with much roaring and crashing of brush and was never seen again. Minnesota Bigfoot website, Joe Heinan.

20-21. Bill M., near Two Harbors, late August 1990 or 1991 - At dusk, a man heard heavy bipedal footsteps approaching his home along a creek and fired a shotgun in the air, which caused whatever it was to run away and utter an intense scream that began like a donkey bray or pig squeal but then merged into a yodel-like call. Then after a pause, it started to come back, but a second shot made it flee for good. The witness knew of loggers having Bigfoot encounters in the area. Related by witness by phone.

22. T.S., near Gilbert, Fall 1991 - A person driving home from a sports event saw a human-like creature eight or nine feet tall covered in shaggy hair running along the side of the road that veered off into the woods when the car passed by. It left a foul odor in the air. BFRO website.

23. Jesse B., near Eveleth, 1995 - Limited information on a person who saw a Bigfoot standing beside some railroad tracks. Related by witness by e-mail.

24. "Steve," near Embarrass, September 1996 - A man driving at about 11 PM saw a Bigfoot walk across the road ahead of him and then down into the ditch. His wife was beside him, but she missed seeing it. BFRO website.

25. Anonymous, Oberg Mountain near Tofte, mid-October 1996 - A tourist found odd droppings near Lake Superior that were large, black and green, and somehow unusual which caused them to be suspected of being associated with Bigfoot. R.A. Gilbertsen.

26. "Dave," west of Ely, January 1997 - A man out snowmobiling and trapping in the Lucky Boy Mine area at dusk saw what he at first thought was a bear in some reeds ahead of him. As he watched, he realized it was an upright apelike creature with brownish hair. It

looked at him, showing eyeshine, then moved off into the woods. Minnesota Bigfoot website, Joe Heinan.

27. "Steve," near Ely, 1999 - The witness from the 1996 Embarrass report was deer hunting at about 6 PM in poor light when he heard grunting and the sound of a small tree being broken off and thrown in his direction, causing him to flee. He went back later and saw that the tree had been thrown about 25 feet. BFRO website.

28. Kris Johnson, north shore of Lake Superior, 1999 - A Minnesota rep for the BFRO states that she became interested in Bigfoot when she found a footprint and scat somewhere on the Superior north shore.

29-30. Christopher P., near Island Lake, May 14, 2000 - A man went outside to smoke a cigarette and heard the sound of barking dogs and howling wolves about 1/3 mile away which was not unusual, but it was accompanied by a powerful wailing sound he had never heard before and the sound of crashing brush and then ice breaking as if something large had tried to cross the frozen lake. He had heard stories of Bigfoot from the area, including one of a man who saw a creature running through swampy terrain while he flew in a helicopter over the Cloquet State Forest. BFRO website.

31. Anonymous, north of Virginia, May 2000 - A person bicycling on a dirt road saw a lanky human-like creature covered in black hair and at least as tall as a man watching from a hillside. After a moment, it turned and walked in a crouch up the hill and into the woods. BFRO website.

32. Anonymous, near Wolf Lake between Tower and Ely, November 2000 - A person found a supposed Bigfoot track 10-11" long in freshly fallen snow near the lakeshore. Minnesota Bigfoot website, Joe Heinan.

33. Anonymous, near Eveleth, 2000 - A man had just gotten off work and was relieving himself by a propane tank in the parking area when a Bigfoot stood up from the other side of the tank and walked off into the woods. The witness noted that it was known locally as the "4 Mile Creature." Bigfootinfo website.

34. Andrea Z., Gunflint Trail near Grand Marais, late April or

early May 2001 - A woman who had a dog kennel business was walking with her dog at 9:15 AM on an overcast morning when she saw a six to seven-foot-tall hairy creature standing about 150 feet away. Described as a "hominid," it had long gray mottled hair, long arms, a hairless face, and it was standing in profile for about 15 seconds before it moved away. This happened only about a half-mile from the woman's house near the George Washington Memorial Ski Trail and Elbow Lake. She also noted that her dog did not seem upset but was wagging its tail during the sighting. Don Sherman.

35. Anonymous, near Embarrass, May 4, 2001 - A person living at a place where sled dogs were raised woke up at night and heard a series of gibberish-like howls unlike anything he had ever heard before, followed by the dogs erupting in howls of their own. Later, while looking for tracks, he found the carcasses of three beavers (which were used to feed the dogs) that had been stripped and stacked, all facing the same way. BFRO website.

36. Anonymous, near Duluth, September 2001 - Two friends driving at night toward Wisconsin stopped to check their map and saw an animal in the ditch they at first took to be a bear, but when they shined the high beam of their headlights at it, it looked directly at them and looked more like a gorilla. It then "staggered" into the woods on two legs. Bigfootinfo website.

37. "Steve" and son, near Aurora, late May 2002 - The witness from the 1996 Embarrass and 1999 Ely reports and his son found a Bigfoot footprint and made a cast of it. BFRO website.

38. Anonymous, Superior National Forest, Fall 2002 - A man called the author to report an incident during a hunting trip some-where in the national forest the previous year in which a trailer he and another person were staying in was grabbed and shaken by something with a horrible smell, which he believed was a Bigfoot. Related by witness by phone.

39-40. Andrea Z., Grand Marais area, May 2003 - The witness from an earlier 2001 sighting had another Bigfoot encounter when she saw a creature standing at the edge of a road on a sunny morning at 6:45 AM. It was standing in the shade, but as it was only a tenth of a mile away she could see that it was six to seven feet tall and covered with light brown hair. On a later occasion the woman found Bigfoot tracks along the edge of the road that she photographed. Don Sherman.

41. Anonymous, near Chub and Geddess Lakes in Carlton County, June 2004 - A person very familiar with bears saw a large dark figure standing beside a clearing about a mile from the nearest road and could tell it was not a bear. It looked at the witness and then ran into the woods. Bigfootinfo website.

42. Richard Sade, near Ely, January 26, 2006 - A man driving at about 4:30 AM heard an owl-like cry coming from some woods. When he slowed down to see what it was, a six-foot-tall Bigfoot, with brown hair and a black face, stepped into the road in front of his car. After looking at him through the windshield, it walked to the other side of the road as he grabbed his video camera and began to film. The video shows the creature with its back to him, "doing something," near a pine tree, then walking uphill into the woods. He believed it was picking up a baby creature which was what he first heard. Cryptomundo website, Loren Coleman.

43. Anonymous, near Mountain Iron, 2006 - Someone is alleged to have spotted a Bigfoot through an infrared device. It ducked behind a tree and disappeared when they yelled at it. Bigfootencounters website; Calvin Goggleye.

44. Anonymous, Little Iron and Poplar Lakes in Cook County, March 9-11, 2007 - Friends were snowmobiling in the Boundary Waters area and found sets of supposed Bigfoot tracks over three days, 16" long with a six-foot stride even in heavy deep snow. BFRO website.

45. Mrs. Bycofski, Mountain Iron, October 2009 - A woman driving to church in Virginia spotted a large silver-gray creature with a cone-shaped head in a clearing just about to enter some woods, moving its arms in a peculiar way. She only saw it for about three seconds but noted there was another car pulled over on the opposite side of the highway with the driver apparently watching it. BFRO website.

46. Anonymous, near Lutsen Mountain, July 6, 2010 - A man was doing some hiking and camping along the Superior Hiking Trail and was using a tarp enclosure as a shelter. After lying down to go to sleep, he heard two loud footfalls but ignored them. He was awakened suddenly at about 2:30 AM by something reaching into the tarp and violently shoving him by his left shoulder to the back of the enclosure and also knocking it down. Whatever it was then ran off with heavy bipedal footfalls and had a foul stench like rotten eggs or milk. It was heard crossing a nearby bridge across the Poplar River. Campers on the other side of the river heard the man scream and the footfalls running away. Bigfoot was suspected. Sasquatch Research Association website.

47. Anonymous, near Grand Marais, January 29, 2011 - A brother and sister at the back of a group of snowmobilers in the Superior National Forest at about 3:30 PM saw a tall manlike creature standing in a clearing watching them about 200 yards away. It was about seven feet tall with dark brown hair, darker in the face and chest areas. After about a minute, it grabbed a tree branch and then walked off into the woods. Bigfootencounters website.

48. Anonymous, near Two Harbors, May 7, 2011 - Two men and the wife and children of one were hiking around scouting out locations for a Bigfoot expedition when they encountered an outburst of screams and chatter such as a group of apes would make when startled, followed by a series of wood knocking coming from different locations. About two miles on, the men split up to explore separate areas while the woman and children rested, and the single man had a sighting of a dark upright creature estimated at twice the size of a man running about 65 yards ahead of him, in sight for only three strides which were very wide. The men then found tracks 18" long with a seven-foot stride that made it look like the creature had been following the people for a time. Sasquatch Research Association website.

49. Anonymous, Lake Jeanette near Orr, August 22, 2011 - A woman in a tent heard heavy bipedal footsteps approaching at about 4 AM When she yelled, "Who's there?" a rock was thrown and hit the

tent just before the footsteps hurried away. Another woman with her was asleep at first but heard the rock. Later they tried to recreate the sound of the footsteps but were unable to sound that loud. BFRO website.

50. Anonymous, Bassett Lake near Brimson, October 26, 2011 - A man with a cabin on the lake was in a boat fishing when he saw a tall, bulky tan-colored figure walking through bullrushes in shallow water near the shore about 300 yards away. It seemed larger than a man, with longer arms and no apparent neck. After watching it for about a minute, he started his boat motor to try and get a closer look, but the noise caused the figure to disappear. GCBRO website.

51. "J" and parents, St. Louis County, 2011 - A man who made his livelihood hunting and trapping was walking on a logging trail with his parents when they found a bed of blueberries where something very large had been rolling around. There was a thick, foul odor in the air worse than anything J had ever smelled before. BFRO website.

52. "J" and brother, St. Louis County, November 2011 - The witness from the previous report and his brother were out setting bobcat traps when they came across several pine trees that had been twisted and snapped off, some strewn across the trail they were walking and others suspended above ground woven between other trees. They would later see a t.v. show on Bigfoot that described the creatures making similar structures. BFRO website.

53. Name unknown, near Aurora, 2011 - While in camp at night during a hunting trip a member of the Minnesota Bigfoot Research Team heard noisy chipmunks go silent and then something approaching the camp, making grunting sounds. He also noted a foul odor and thought it was a bear at first until it threw a rock in his direction, at which point he suspected a Bigfoot. A popular theory among the members of his research team is that Bigfoot uses low frequency infrasound as a defense mechanism, and he thought later that that might have been what gave him the anxiety that caused him to decide not to shoot at the creature. Related by the witness at 2017 Remer Bigfoot Days festival.

54. "Mike," southern St. Louis County, March 15, 2012 - A

Minnesota Bigfoot researcher placed a recording device that ran continually for 20 hours on boggy woodland where the landowner said he had been hearing strange unidentified howls for years. At around 4:30 AM, it picked up 20 minutes of howls sounding as if they were from more than one creature, one within probably 100 yards of the recorder. There were also several other sounds, including knocks and slapping or popping noises. Sasquatch Research Association website; YouTube.

55-58. Anonymous, Lake County, July 2012 - A group of scouts and their scoutmaster were on a 10-day camping and canoeing trip along a series of lakes. On the fifth night, the man was sleeping in a hammock and awoke to a sound like a woman crying that was approaching him. When he sensed that it was right next to him, he moved, and his hand struck the large hairy body of something that then ran off into the woods before he could get a good look at it. The next day three miles down the lake, they were at a new campsite when the man heard two loud "primal," sounding screams while out collecting firewood. The day after that, they decided to go on a night time canoe excursion at about 10 PM. While they were negotiating a narrow passage between two lakes, something on the shore threw a very large rock 15 yards into the water directly in front of them. It was too heavy for them to pick up. GCBRO website.

59. "J," St. Louis County, August 12, 2012 - The witness from two previous reports was out picking mushrooms just after sunrise and heard a series of loud wood knocks nearby, three knocks at a time that seemed to be following him as he went further into the woods. He grew nervous left, wondering if his brother might be playing a prank, but when he got home, he found that his brother had gone off to work and could not have been responsible. BFRO website.

60. "George" and friend, near Skibo, Labor Day 2012 - Two men were out in late afternoon scouting for hunting locations when one saw a bipedal creature 7-7 1/2 feet tall and covered in long scraggly reddish-brown hair walking through the woods about 20 yards away. Its head was cone-shaped and had shorter hair than the body. George saw it for four to five seconds and his friend did not, but both heard

its heavy footsteps and smelled a strong, musty odor like that of a wet dog. They then fled the area. BFRO website.

61-62. Anonymous, near Virginia, September 12, 2012 - A man had just arrived at a bear hunting location at about 7:20 AM and was about to walk to his bait station when he saw a bipedal creature eight to nine feet tall with a stocky build and covered in whitish-gray hair walk across a path 50-60 yards ahead of him. He saw it for three to four seconds and then heard its heavy footsteps retreating into the woods. He then abandoned his hunting plans and did not come back to retrieve his gear for a few weeks. He had also had a possible Bigfoot experience at age 16 while hunting when he heard what sounded like two individuals communicating with wood knocking and something large walking near him in the woods, which frightened him. BFRO website.

63. Anonymous, near Cloquet, December 7, 2012 - An episode of Bigfoot activity that had begun in September with a family hearing howls and tree knocks and finding a tree knocked down as well as large unidentifiable droppings culminated in a sighting by a bowhunter. On his way to his tree stand before sunrise he found a tree twisted about 6 1/2 feet up and bent down to block the trail. As he continued on, he then heard footsteps on the frosty ground following him, stopping when he stopped to listen. Once in his tree stand, he heard a very loud wood knocking and crashing 20 yards behind him, shined a flashlight toward it and glimpsed the upper body of a Bigfoot about seven feet tall with shaggy dark hair as it was turning to walk away. After this sighting the witness and "SRA Jim" of the Sasquatch Research Association continued to find tree breaks, tracks, and other evidence of Bigfoot in the area. Bigfoot Research Association website.

64. "Charlie" and friend, Lake Jeanette near Orr, June 28-29, 2013 - A two-day camping trip was marked by episodes of wood knocking in which the witnesses answered back with knocks of their own and got responses, and by a loud grunting sound heard very nearby. BFRO website.

65. "Jesse" and friend, Arrowhead Trail area in Cook County,

August 18, 2013 - While canoeing in the Boundary Waters at about 10 PM, two friends had a rock thrown at them from shore, which they estimated came from 150 yards away. About 20 minutes later, while negotiating a canal between two lakes, they began to hear a strange sound like a cross between a gorilla and a duck which persisted for about 10 minutes, but when they would shine their flashlights at it they could see nothing. BFRO website.

66. Anonymous, Gary-New Duluth, September 14, 2013 - A 9-year-old girl playing outside her house with a friend at about 8:30 PM in the section of the city of Duluth known as Gary- New Duluth near the St. Louis River saw an upright hairy creature standing near the garage which then walked away toward the river on two legs. It stood about 7 feet tall, was covered in brown hair that was long above the face and hung in its eyes, and it made a huffing-breathing sound as it walked away swinging its arms with heavy flat-footed footfalls that made loud impact sounds in strides of three to four feet. The girl said she knew that bears have a protruding muzzle and that what she saw could not have been a bear because it had a flat face like a human, but not exactly like a human. She told her mother, who then found tracks impressed into the grass that were 12" long by 10" wide, unusually wide for Bigfoot tracks. The next day the mother called Lady Ocalat's Emporium of Duluth, a metaphysical shop that investigates paranormal events, and they sent two people -- Lady Ocalat herself and Bill Couture. As Ocalat spoke with the family Couture was looking around outside when he found another track in gravel, just outside the mother's bedroom window, which was cast in plaster. The conclusion was that the creature had been attracted by the sound of the children playing and had curiously checked out the home. Lady Ocalat's Paranormal Investigations website.

67. "SRA Jim," near Cloquet, December 9, 2013 - An investigator with the Sasquatch Research Association was driving at about 8:30 AM in the area of the previous Cloquet report and saw a line of tracks 18-20" long crossing the road from one section of forest to another. Judging by snow conditions, they had been made between two and five that morning. Sasquatch Research Association website.

68. "Andrew," south of Buhl, September 2014 - A man heard howling he could not identify, intriguing in retrospect with a Bigfoot encounter he would have a month later. BFRO website. 69-70.

69-70. "Andrew," south of Buhl, October 23-24, 2014 - The same man from the previous report was hunting along old railroad tracks when he heard howling in a spruce swamp nearby that would stop whenever he stopped moving. He then saw a black figure on the road about a half-mile ahead of him that he first took to be a bear until it stood up and ran into a ditch on two legs. It was seven to eight feet tall with long arms and legs, very fast, and seemed to be nervously watching him. By the distance involved, it had to have been a different creature than the one responsible for the howls. The next day at about 9 AM, he heard wood knocking in the same area about 500 yards from him. BFRO website.

71. Names unknown, near Duluth, Christmas 2014 - A video posted on YouTube depicts a family at a rural home in a wooded area near Duluth filming their holiday celebration when the camera catches a brief glimpse of a Bigfoot skirting the property through a window. Male and female family members go outside to try and get a better look as the creature flees into nearby woods. A dog called by the name "Rif" then goes running after the creature but then quickly retreats as if spooked and takes a position near the house where it stands, barking into the woods. After a moment, the camera catches another glimpse of the creature - just a vague and small black upright bipedal form - still striding through the woods, after which the people retreat back into the house. YouTube.

72. Mark Nicklawske, Duluth area, January 20, 2016 - Internet blogger Nicklawske or "Nick Up North" discovered a large lean-to stick structure at the end of Minnesota Point on the shore of Lake Superior that he believed was created by Bigfoots, though it could have also been of human construction. YouTube.

73. Joe Parkhurst and wife, Two Harbors, December 24, 2016 - While on a trip to the Superior north shore to visit his father's rural residence Bigfoot researcher Joe (best known for his work in Fort Snelling State Park near St. Paul) and his wife were staying at a hotel

in Two Harbors and saw a line of human-like tracks in the snow just outside the hotel that seemed curious, as they were in a perfectly straight line rather than side by side like normal human tracks. They led off the hotel grounds toward Lake Superior, which was about 5,000 feet away. Joe seemed to imply that he wondered if they were Bigfoot tracks. YouTube.

74. Joe Parkhurst, Two Harbors area, December 24, 2016 - On the same day as the previous report, Joe was exploring a remote area around his father's residence where several tree breaks had been noted at about six feet above ground, and where a sound had been being heard that Joe had also heard during Bigfoot searches at Fort Snelling in the southeast section of the state, a sound like the croaking of a frog that could obviously not be an actual frog during wintertime. He spotted what looked like a fresh tree break, but when he looked closely, he found that it was actually parts of two different trees, a length of white birch that had been sawed off flat by man that had been carried from somewhere else and placed next to a snapped off the trunk of a darker tree. There was also a pathway of old and indistinct tracks that were clearly bigger than the several deer and dog tracks in the area, and Joe wondered if Bigfoot might be responsible for all these signs. YouTube.

75. Names unknown, Ely area, dates unknown - Witness "Dave" from the 1997 Ely report told of stories of unearthly screams in the night heard in Ely's early years as a logging town. Minnesota Bigfoot website, Joe Heinan.

76. Waino Sarri, High Lake near Ely, date unknown - Witness "Dave" from the 1997 Ely report told of a man claiming to have seen an ape-man on a frozen lake eating the remains of a moose that had been killed by wolves. Minnesota Bigfoot website, Joe Heinan.

77. Chris D. and father, west of Ely, early December, year unknown - A boy and his father saw a bipedal creature about the size of a bear, dark brown in color with long arms and a flesh toned apelike face, as they were driving home from looking for a Christmas tree in the Lucky Boy mine area. It turned to look at them and then continued on into the woods. Related by witness by e-mail.

78. Anonymous, Twin Lakes Road near Ely, date unknown - Two classmates of the boy in the previous report were driving on a forest road trying to reach another vehicle that was stuck in the snow when a large bipedal creature crossed the road in front of them, frightening them into turning back. Chris D. by e-mail.

79. Brian B. and family, North McDougal Lake near Isabella, date unknown - While sitting outside their cabin at about 9 PM, a man and his wife, mother-in-law, and three-year-old son heard a series of odd whistling calls as of two unknown creatures calling to one another, the first sounding less than 150 feet away and the other farther away. They did not sound like birds. The family's dogs were also acting very nervous and refused to go for walks. Bigfoot was considered as a possibility. Minnesota Bigfoot website, Joe Heinan.

80. "Gretchen," Cromwell Swamp west of Park Lake, date unknown- A woman reportedly saw an upright walking white creature either riding or attempting to ride her horse from a distance of 100 yards. The horse was understandably spooked and eventually ran away. The woman first thought the creature was either a bear or a man in a white coat, but her brother relayed it as a possible Bigfoot report. Bob Olson.

81. Anonymous, Cloquet Valley State Forest in Saint Louis County, dates unknown - The brother of the woman from the previous report relates that he worked as a forester for many years and had numerous occasions of finding Bigfoot tracks in the Fish Lake area. Bob Olson.

82. Names unknown, Cook area, dates unknown - Limited information - the same man from the previous report also knew of Bigfoot sightings in the Cook area. Bob Olson.

83-84. Anonymous, Isabella area, dates unknown- A woman claimed her father had a photo of a Bigfoot at a bear bait taken by a trail camera. It was said to look like a gorilla on all fours, with a cone-shaped head, flat face, and long arms with huge hands. The father was unwilling to circulate the picture, but the woman said she showed it to her daughter's school bus driver who had seen a Bigfoot while snowmobiling in the area, and she said it looked the same. Pam E. by e-mail.

85. Anonymous, Ely area, date unknown - A very shaky video depicts two young men running across a frozen lake trying to get closer to a Bigfoot, continually exclaiming, "What the (expletive) is that?" The supposed Bigfoot only appears as a small black dot in the far distance. YouTube.

86. Names unknown, Lake Vermilion, date unknown - An Internet video posted on March 4, 2018 by "Minnesota Bigfoot" shows a photograph taken by people fishing on Lake Vermilion north of Tower showing a supposed Bigfoot standing on the shore surrounded by foliage in bright daylight. The photo is enigmatic but shows a powerfully built figure standing upright in profile, seemingly covered in gray hair, its left arm at its side and its right arm held out in front of itself with a bent elbow and a very wide hand and the face in dark shadow. The video stresses how the proportions of the figure indicate that it can't possibly be a bear. YouTube.

NORTHWEST

1-4. Mickinock and Nelson fami-lies, Roseau County, 1898-1904 - The Windego, known to Mandan Indians as a spirit that would appear as an omen of impending death but described physically as a giant white figure 15 feet tall with a bright star on its forehead, was seen four times by members of two families. After each sighting, someone died soon after. The Windego is often associated with Bigfoot folklore. "Haunted Heartland" by Beth Scott and Michael Norman.

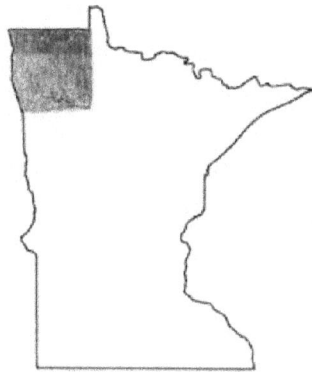

5. Ed Trimble, Lake of the Woods area, 1940s - Prolific Bigfoot track finder Trimble of Clearwater County had an early experience

while driving near Lake of the Woods when he saw red eyeshine in his headlights, not the usual color for nocturnal animals. The eyes were fairly high off the ground. Personally related by the witness.

6. "Jerry, Gary, and Rick," Lake of the Woods area, Summer 1976 - Three men camping near the Canadian border saw a 6 1/2-foot bipedal hairy creature standing by a tree that ran off when they tried to get a better look. It left behind a smell like bad foot odor. A little later, as they were walking down an old railroad track that passed through swampy terrain, a rock the size of a football came flying at them, and a moment after that, they saw the creature again running across the tracks about 100 yards ahead of them. When they reported what they'd seen to local townspeople, some there said they had seen it too. BFRO website.

7. Anonymous, near Graceton, 1976 - Limited information on a boy who reportedly saw a Bigfoot in his front yard. The Track Record. Ray Crowe. David Patrick Bulzomi, near Graceton, 1978- A witness saw a Bigfoot crossing a crossroads and noted that it was taller than a road sign. Two weeks later, a tracker was brought to the scene and found footprints. This was three to four miles from the location of the previous report. The Track Record. Ray Crowe.

8. Anonymous, northwest of Middle River, November 4, 1978 - A man hunting deer at about noon, had just had a misfire attempting to shoot a deer when he entered a clearing and glimpsed what he first thought was a man turning away from him 60 to 70 feet away, not wearing orange hunting clothes. Upon a second look, he realized it was an upright hairy creature about 6 1/2 feet tall, very heavily built, and dark brown to black in color. He saw it for about five seconds as it walked away in a hunched posture. He did not stay to look for tracks since his gun had just malfunctioned, and he did not feel safe. BFRO website. Anonymous, near Crookston, early Spring 1981 - Possible Bigfoot tracks were found in the snow, just north of a house near the Gentilly Bridge, with narrow heels and possibly about 18" long. Display at RBJ's Restaurant in Crookston. Anonymous, Lake of the Woods County, October 15, 1990 - Some grouse hunters found an odd oval-shaped bed fashioned out of long grass in a densely wooded

area. It was about 20" high and five feet by four feet in area. Their dog acted nervous around it and wouldn't go near it, and the grass had been carried some distance. Bigfoot was suspected. BFRO website.

9. "Brad" and friends, Roseau area, January 18, 1992 - A young man reported that the legend of the Windego was still known around Roseau, and that he and some friends had seen it themselves from a car and captured it on video. However, he believed it to be a spirit being as the Indians do and not a physical animal. Personally related by the witness.

10. Anonymous, Warroad/Swift area, June 1994 - Two people driving to work saw a Bigfoot running along the roadside beside a lake in swampy terrain, bobbing in and out of the ditch. They knew it was not a bear or a human. BFRO website.

11. Jeff T. and others, Thief Lake in Marshall County, 1995 - A party of hunters in a vehicle were approaching the lake in the early afternoon when they saw a very tall, dark bipedal creature walking along a woodline 400-500 yards away, swinging its arms. It walked for 30-50 yards and then went into the woods. Related by the witness through e-mail.

12. Name(s) unknown, Wannaska area, 1996 - A Bigfoot encounter is reported to have taken place. Loren Coleman at Paracon, Shooting Star Casino Mahnomen, October 14, 2017.

13. Name(s) unknown, Beltrami Island State Forest, 2007 - A Bigfoot encounter is reported to have occurred. Loren Coleman at Paracon, Shooting Star Casino Mahnomen, October 14, 2017. 17-18.

14-15. "Priscilla," north of Badger, April 9, 2013 - A woman driving to work at 6:30 AM was passing between two farms when she saw what she first took to be the operator of a snowmobile emerging from a ditch, but instead, it turned out to be a large black creature that ran across the road with larger strides than a human and disappeared into the woods behind a farmhouse. The farm was vacant at the time, but when she later contacted its owner, she learned that his son had had an experience there two years previously in which he saw someone or something watching him through a living room window that was about eight feet off the ground. BFRO website.

16. Name unknown, west of Lower Red Lake, Summer 2014 - A woman driving east on Highway 19 turned on to Highway 1, and after a half-mile, she saw a figure at the roadside, thinking at first that it was a man in an overcoat. Since the temperature was 85 degrees, she wondered why someone would be so dressed, but then she realized it was not a human but a "hairy man" which then turned and went into the woods. Don Sherman.

17. Jen Kruse, Nikki Jourdain, Jennifer Grover, northwest of Lower Red Lake, April 13, 2017 - Members of the SheSquatchers Bigfoot research team (all of whom claim various levels of psychic ability) were on an excursion to look for evidence, and while riding in their vehicle member Jen Kruse was filming with a low-quality video camera. Upon reviewing her footage later, it appeared that a blurry image of a Bigfoot may have been captured as they passed it. Shortly thereafter she got a sudden psychic urge to pull over and check out a gravel pit area, where they found a high hill with a line of Bigfoot tracks ascending it. The prints were huge, 18-24" long, with some of them longer from the feet sliding in the gravel, and showed toe impressions and considerable stride length while ascending a slope so steep that the women had trouble walking up it. At the top of the hill, they found rings of concentric circles scratched into the ground, a symbol that Jen believed to be representative of dimensional portals, strengthening her belief in the paranormal nature of Bigfoot. SheSquatchers website; Personally related by the witnesses. 21-22.

18-19. Names unknown, Swift area, dates unknown - A woman in the audience at a presentation by the SheSquatchers research group at an expo in Thief River Falls on April 8, 2017 reported that she knew of two separate sightings of Bigfoot by two men she knew in the Swift area south of Lake of the Woods, both of which had occurred "within the last few years." "Bigfoot Banter" event at the Home, Sport, and Family Show at the Ralph Engelstad Arena in Thief River Falls. SheSquatchers group led by Jen Kruse, Stephanie Ayers, and Kimberly Juarez.

20. Names unknown, near Fourtown, date unknown - Limited information on an elder Native American woman and her son seeing

two Bigfoot creatures on the road leading to Fourtown on the west side of Upper Red Lake. Bob Olson.

CENTRAL NORTH

1. William P. Remer, Remer area, early 1900s - A postmaster for whom the town of Remer was named in 1904 is said to have found Bigfoot tracks around the time of the town's inception. Councilman Mark Ruyak on "Finding Bigfoot" episode "Bigfoot Town," Animal Planet.

2. Names unknown, International Falls area, around 1910 - A tale exists of loggers who captured a Bigfoot, kept it in a cage of poles, and fed it for a week until it escaped before an expert that had been summoned could arrive to examine it. The loggers named the creature "Jocko," which makes the story either confused with the famous British Columbia story of "Jacko" from 1884 or a case of the loggers naming their creature after that one. Ed Trimble.

3. George Wilson, north of Ball Club, 1920s and 30s - A man who worked at logging with horses had an episode in which he would hear a horse in his barn raising a commotion, but when he went to check on it, the horse was calm again. Then in the morning, he found the horse's mane and tail intricately braided. This repeated a couple of times. Bigfoot researcher Don Sherman equates this with similar stories associated with the yeti in the Himalayas. Don Sherman.

4. Name unknown, Remer area, 1942 - Limited information on a male picking blueberries near a wild rice bog that was frightened away by a gorilla-like creature. The witness' granddaughter related the story many years later. Related by the host of the presentation at the 2017 Remer Bigfoot Days festival.

5. Anonymous, near Bovey, mid-1950s - A young girl was picking

blueberries when she saw a figure watching her through the bushes. Thinking it was one of her family members, she went toward it, and it bolted for the nearby woods with a great crashing of brush, making her think it was a bear. As she then fled the area, she looked back and saw a very tall creature looking like a man covered with hair following her, moving in a stooped posture with its arms at its sides. When she reached home, she spoke about what she had seen, and her brothers went armed to the site and found a patch of brush matted down with a bad smell to it. BFRO website.

6. Nancy Mostad, north of Chisolm, 1959-1965 - As a child, a future acquisitions director for New Age publisher Llewellyn Publications regularly saw a 'big white gorilla" that would stand at the edge of a tree line and watch her whenever she would play in a particular meadow. She viewed it as a protector. Related by witness by letter; telephone interview by Tim Olson.

7. K.R., Bemidji, pre-1969 - A man with a bait shop awoke one night to a commotion and the howling of his dogs. When he turned on his porch light and shouted, he saw a "big, black hairy monster" run from his minnow tank and head for some nearby woods. "The Abominable Snowmen" by Eric Norman.

8. Name(s) unknown, Six Mile Lake Road east of Bena, 1960s - A report posted to the BFRO website about the famous Bigfoot tracks found at this site on June 7, 2006, mentions that "The prints look exactly like the molds from the 1960s on this site," but does not elaborate. BFRO website.

9. Michael Hexum, near Nashwauk, November 1, 1970 - A teenage hunter in a tree stand heard a strange chirp/grunting sound and saw an object emerge from brush about 150 yards away that he first took to be a moose. When it reached a clear area 50-60 yards from him, he had a better look and thought it was a man in a brown fur coat. When he yelled at it, it turned to look at him, and he realized it was a manlike hairy creature with a sunken face, walking in a hunched manner and swinging its arms. The sighting lasted about a minute, and when he and his father examined the scene later, they realized by the height of nearby tree branches that the creature had to be around

eight feet tall and weigh 500-600 pounds. Also noted was the fact that a friend of theirs' also saw the creature from a nearby passing truck. His father told him not to talk about the sighting and that it would embarrass the family, but years later, in adulthood Michael would have another sighting and become a Bigfoot researcher. BFRO website; MPR News, John Enger; "Finding Bigfoot" episode "Bigfoot Town," Animal Planet.

10. Cheryl Riggs and boyfriend, between Leech and Cass Lakes, early November 1971- A young couple was driving on a very winding gravel road at about 10 or 10:30 PM when they saw a manlike creature six feet tall or taller and covered in white hair run across the road in front of them in a very smooth gait. It paused at the edge of the woods and looked at them, its eyes not reflecting their lights, and after they passed by them, they stopped to try and get another look but by then it had disappeared into the woods. Ed Trimble.

11. Larry G., Rapid River area north of Upper Red Lake, late Fall 1974 - A man was camping with his four-year-old son, and they were in a tent, the boy asleep when a high-pitched scream began to be heard at intervals, getting closer and closer until breaking brush was also heard and it was upon the camp. Something large went running past the tent 10 to 12 feet away with heavy bipedal footfalls, and then the sounds got farther and farther away until they faded out. The man had a pistol out and ready to defend himself and his son, who did not wake up to hear the sounds. They left in the morning, but the man returned heavily armed later with his brother, and they found footprints three or four inches longer than a size 13 boot and deeper than they were able to duplicate. Personally related by the witness.

12. Alan Hyatt and father, north of Remer, 1975 - A father and son were by a small lake in a swampy area when a yellow lab dog they had with them became excited and took off into the woods. Twenty minutes later it came back, at which time they heard something large moving through the woods that gave off a foul odor "like a garbage truck." Related by the son at a presentation at the 2017 Remer Bigfoot Days festival.

13. Larry G., wife, Doug H., one other, Rapid River area north of

Upper Red Lake, Spring 1976 - The witness from the previous Rapid River report and three others were canoeing on the river and stopped to examine an old ruined cabin, then noticed similar footprints to the ones seen before with flattened grass that was just starting to pop back up as if the creature had just been there and heard them coming. Nothing else was seen. Personally related by the witness.

14. Lee Cluff, northeast of Waskish, late Spring or early Summer 1976 - A man riding in a semi-truck being driven by his father hauling a load of logs saw a Bigfoot 6 1/2 to seven feet tall and weighing three to four hundred pounds with thick black hair beside a logging road. It appeared to be watching a tractor working in a nearby field and didn't notice the truck approaching until it was very close, and when it did, it made direct eye contact with the passenger and then stepped quickly across a four to five-foot wide ditch in one stride and fled into the woods. The father was concentrating on driving and missed seeing it. Also noted that the creature's arms reached to its knees and that it had a sort of tuft of hair on top of its pointed head. Personally related to and recorded by Ed Trimble.

15. Larry and Henry G., Doug H., Rapid River area north of Upper Red Lake, January 1977 - Larry from the two previous reports in this area and his brother and friend went to look for more of the tracks they'd previously seen in the snow. They failed to find any, but while camping out at night, Doug heard a scream that frightened him out of wanting to go any farther. Personally related by Larry G.

16. Larry and Henry G., Rapid River area north of Upper Red Lake, Fall 1978 - The brothers from the previous reports were hunting a distance apart when Henry came across two apparent Bigfoot tracks, one on either side of a wide ditch, that made him panic. He fired shots in the air and his brother fired shots in return to help him navigate his way out of the area. Personally related by Larry G.

17. Richard Johnson, south of Margie, November 1978 - A man searching for Bigfoot had a sighting of one with reddish hair entering a swamp. He noted that it was not as heavily built as he had expected. International Falls Daily Journal. July 13, 1979.

18-19. Harvey Cole, others, Big Bog area in Koochiching County,

Winter 1978 - A DNR forester and two others were cruising timber on snowshoes on a small island in the bog when they found a line of footprints 12-16" long in deep snow. Cole followed them for a distance and found a tuft of hair snagged on a black spruce tree but didn't keep it and regretted it later. He later talked to another timber cruiser who had seen the same tracks about three miles to the north at about the same time. Personally related by the witness to and recorded by Tim Olson.

20. Chipper Lowe, one other, near Marcell, Summer, pre-1979 - Two men were working in the woods when they thought they saw a bear on a lakeshore. That night something shook the trailer they were sleeping in. The incident became associated with Bigfoot reports in the area. International Falls Daily Journal. July 13, 1979; Harvey Cole.

21. Richard Johnson, south of Margie, March 1979 - The same man searching for Bigfoot from the previous Margie report found footprints in the area, remarking that they were narrower than he had expected. International Falls Daily Journal, July 13, 1979.

22. Anonymous, Big Bog area in Koochiching County, 1979 - When a powerline was being constructed through this remote area, helicopters were used to carry the huge steel support towers and one pilot reported seeing upright creatures running through the swamp below his chopper. Harvey Cole; Tim Olson.

23. Kerry Meyers and John Seitz, near Little Fork, September 1, 1979 - A man and his father-in-law found strange tracks passing through a series of mud holes while out scouting for deer hunting locations. There were five of them, 12" long with a stride of 3 1/2 to four feet, and they showed six toes. It was near dusk, but Meyers returned the next day and made a plaster cast of one print. International Falls Daily Journal. September 14, 1979.

24. Anonymous, Big Bog area in Koochiching County, Fall 1979 - A beaver trapper was deep within the bog, traveling by canoe in the ditches that intersperse it, when he encountered a Bigfoot that stood up from the opposite side of a beaver dam. The creature had reddish-brown hair and displayed a prominent male sex organ, something

not normally noted in Bigfoot sightings. Both the man and the creature were startled and fled in opposite directions. The man reported his sighting to the DNR office in Waskish, and two agents - Vince B. and Steve H. - went to investigate and found the creature's tracks. They poured a plaster cast, but since it was late in the day, had to leave it to dry and then were not able to return. Forester Harvey Cole did go out to locate the cast much later but found that the acidic soil in the bog had degraded it, and it was unrecoverable. Harvey Cole; Tim Olson.

25-26. Anonymous, Northome area, 1970s - A man saw a dark brown Bigfoot run across the road in front of his truck that scared him so badly that he didn't even slow down to try and get a better look. At a later time, he was hunting in the same area when he found a patch of pine trees that were twisted off in a circular pattern, with the bodies of some eviscerated grouse nearby. This scared him, and he equated it with his earlier sighting. Minnesota Bigfoot website, Joe Heinan.

27. Don Sherman, west of Ball Club, 1970s - Bigfoot researcher Sherman reports that when he was in his early 20s, he was walking on Forestry Road 2164 off of Highway 2 at about 3 PM when he saw a tall reddish-brown hairy figure ahead of him. He noted that it had hair, not fur, but that he couldn't make out much detail in his quick observation. There was then a loud tree knock to his right in an area that was clear enough that he should have been able to see the source, but he saw nothing, and when he then looked back to where the tall hairy figure had been it was gone. Personally related by the witness.

28. Stanley Sunderland, west of International Falls, May 3, 1980 - A man was in a pickup truck with his two sons returning from an annual Canadian fishing trip at about two PM and was sitting on the right side when he looked out the window and saw an upright hairy creature about six feet tall and weighing about 250 pounds running across an open field, covered in long brown hair. Of special note was that the air on its head and neck was up to 18" long and streamed out behind it as it ran. It was about 300 feet away, and he assumed it must

be an escaped gorilla, not knowing that gorillas walk on all fours. He alerted his sons, who did not see the creature, and they turned around to try and get another look, but it had disappeared into nearby woods. Personally related by witness; Ed Trimble.

29. Anonymous, near Goodland, November 14, 1980 - A youth who was part of a hunting party became lost at around midday and while trying to find his way back to the group he entered an area completely devoid of any animal sign, whereas everywhere else, it was plentiful. There he found a line of bipedal tracks 12-14" long with a stride longer than a man's with tree branches broken off above them at a great height. When he found his way to camp, only one friend would come back with him to see the tracks, and by the next day, melting conditions had made them impossible to find again. BFRO website.

30. "William" and friend, Remer area, about 1980 - A longtime Remer resident told of how when he was 13 years old, he and a friend, in a moment of delinquent youth, went to raid another boy's play fort to steal comic books at night, and on their way back from the raid they heard footsteps, thumping, and grunting in the woods nearby that seemed to be following them. William threw a rock into the woods and thought he hit whatever was doing it, which made it flee. The next day the boys came back to the spot and found 18" Bigfoot tracks in mud 20 feet off the trail they were on. Related by the witness at 2017 Remer Bigfoot Days festival.

31. Charles Prichard, northeast of Swan River, mid-November 1982 - A man on a deer hunt in the early morning with his father and brother was alone when he saw a black upright "ape-faced" creature standing in some short pines watching him. When he saw it, he saw the mist of breath being blown out of its nostrils, and it then moved back into some thicker woods where he heard the sound of it moving away through the brush. As he was looking for tracks to back up his sighting, his father and brother came along and did not believe what he had seen. Later he found a trail in the snow that looked like something had been dragging an object to erase its tracks. Bigfootencounters website.

32. Anonymous, Moose Lake near Little Fork, Fall 1982 or 1983 - Two men hunting grouse near the lake saw a Bigfoot cross their path very close by without seeming to notice them. BFRO website.

33. "William" and friends, Remer area, 1983 - The same longtime Remer resident from the previous 1980 report told of how when he was 15 or 16, he was on a county road near a lake with some friends at dusk when a freak thunderstorm struck. Lightning set fire to a bog, and as fire engines were arriving to fight the fire, the boys saw a female Bigfoot that looked like it was pregnant fleeing from the fire with a frightened look on its face. This happens to be the only report this author has ever heard of from anywhere that describes an apparently pregnant Bigfoot. Related by the witness at 2017 Remer Bigfoot Days festival.

34-35. Jerry Andersen, Squaw Lake in Itasca County, January 1984 - A man doing some logging 11 miles off a main road saw a figure quite a distance away that at first looked like a big man in a black overcoat but turned out to be a Bigfoot six to seven feet tall and weighing over 300 pounds with broad shoulders. It moved quickly into the woods and disappeared. The man believed he may have had another Bigfoot sighting near Outing Mountain. Bigfootencounters website.

36. Mrs. V.P., between Wildwood and Effie, mid-1980s - A woman standing by her garage heard a high-pitched wavering cry that couldn't have been more than a mile away in an area where Bigfoot encounters would become known. Personally related by the witness.

37-38. Troy and Clark Parson, between Wildwood and Effie, Spring 1987 - Troy stopped by a bridge on the Caldwell Forest Road to look for old bottles, which he collected, and found large manlike tracks four to five inches longer than a man's and fairly deep. At around that same time his brother Clark showed him a place along the nearby Cutfoot Forest Road near Bigfork where there had once been an outpost that manufactured highline poles. There were broken tree branches there and a single manlike track on the ground, looking like a creature had been swinging through the trees and accidentally touched the ground just once. Ed Trimble, related to him by the witness.

39. Lisa Deiderich, near Bemidji, August 1987 - A 15-year-old girl attending El Lago del Bosque (Lake of the Woods) Spanish Language Camp was walking to the restrooms one night when she saw a huge manlike figure walking just off the path, up to seven feet tall, with a powerful build, but in the darkness, it was just a silhouette. No one at the camp was of that size and the encounter frightened her. When she spoke of it the next day, she was told it must have been a Bigfoot, as there were stories going around of the creatures being in the area. Personally related by witness.

40. Anonymous, Nett Lake in Koochiching County, 1987- A man was hunting during the day and thought he saw a bear, but when he looked at it through his rifle scope, it stood up on two legs and walked away like a man, and he couldn't shoot it. Duluth News Tribune, October 13, 2007.

41. Walter F. and family, Side Lake area near Chisolm, late July 1989 - While driving between 7 and 9 PM, a family saw an upright creature seemingly larger and faster than a bear, run across the road 50-75 yards ahead of them. Related by the witness by letter.

42. T.P., between Wildwood and Effie, late 1980s - A man found big scratches on a tree nine feet up about three miles north of his home. There was also golden or reddish hair snagged on the tree and a well-worn trail deeply impressed in the ground as if by something heavy. This was not put off as a bear sign due to Bigfoot reports in the area. Personally related by neighbors Mr. & Mrs. V.P.

43. Anonymous, Cass Lake area, 1980s - A Native American woman was driving a new baby home when the child began to cry, so she pulled over to give it a bottle. Suddenly something pounded on the back of the car and frightened her, and as she drove away, she saw a tall, manlike creature covered in brown hair. BFRO website.

44. Anonymous, Moose Lake near Little Fork, early 1990s - Limited information on some people who saw a Bigfoot while swimming in the lake. BFRO website.

45. Anonymous, western Red Lake Indian Reservation, October

22, 1990- A group of cousins were outshining deer at about 10 PM when they saw yellow eyeshine in a small field, whereas deers' eyes shine blue. When they looked through their rifle scope, they could see the eyes belonged to something very large and wondered if it was a moose. As they were debating it the animal stood up from a sitting or kneeling position and turned out to be a Bigfoot, dark in color and eight to nine feet tall, that stood there for a minute and then ran into the woods on two feet. In all, it had been in their light for about three minutes. Their report states that Bigfoot has been known on the reservation for decades and their elders tell about such things as leaving plates of food out for them in years past. GCBRO website.

46. "Mr. Lammers" and son, near Mizpah, November, 1990 - A man and his 12-year-old son were hunting and had returned near dusk to their pickup truck to wait for two companions still in the woods. Suddenly a gorilla-like creature appeared, very heavy and muscular and around six feet tall with dark brown hair. It grabbed the back of the truck and shook it, making angry grunting sounds. After a few moments of this behavior, it crossed the road along which the truck was parked and picked up a rock about 30" wide and threw it into the truck bed from 15 feet away, denting the metal six inches deep. Finally, it ran away, leaping almost effortlessly over a pile of brush in its path. Marion Senn.

47. A.K., Big Falls area, about 1990 - Limited information on a man who ran a timber operation where Bigfoot activity was experienced.

48. Names unknown, between Gemmel and Mizpah, about 1990 - A sighting of a Bigfoot crossing the road between these two towns by two women in a car was said to have appeared in local print media. Personally related by Mrs. Troy Parson.

49. Clark Parson, near Bigfork, early 1990s - The man who had previously seen Bigfoot evidence in the area of an old abandoned outpost where highline poles were once manufactured along the Cutfoot Forest Road had a long episode of Bigfoot experiences there. He discovered that the creatures seemed to be rubbing, chewing on, and tearing pieces from poles in the area. He had two brief sightings of them, including one in which a creature sitting on a log was said to

be built like a football player, but bad brakes on his vehicle prevented him from getting a better look at it. At one point, he left a bag of produce, including sweet corn and rutabagas for them in a hole beneath a log and later found that they'd taken it a distance but then dropped it. He had never heard the creatures' vocalizations but knew of a neighbor couple that had. Ed Trimble and this author investigated this story in May of 1992 and found the damage to the poles both in the place indicated by Clark and on a trail near his brother Troy's home nearby. Pieces of wood ranging in size from tiny to a couple of feet long had been ripped from these old inactive highline poles with no claw marks evident, and they were covered in teeth marks all the way from a few inches above ground to seven feet up, the twin marks of eye teeth that measured 3 1/2 inches apart. Clark had found reddish-brown hair snagged on some poles that were tested and identified as being that of a bear and indeed bears were in the area, but the teeth marks were much too wide apart to have been made by a Minnesota black bear and definitely came from something else. Report originally received by Ed Trimble from Clark Parson after a tip from Clark's father.

50. Harvey Cole, Gemmel Ridge Road in Koochiching County, Spring 1991 - DNR forester Cole, known for finding Bigfoot tracks in 1978, had another discovery. While checking on some newly bought woodland to see how it was being developed, he found tracks 17" long, distorted somewhat by melting snow but still very large. Personally related by the witness.

51. Candy Bealieu and children, east of Rigby on Red Lake Indian Reservation, 1992 - A Native American woman took her three children and two of their friends for a supper break from a pow-wow. While driving she saw what she thought was a brown bear, so she slowed down for a good look since brown bears were a rare sight, with most bears in the area being black. Then it stood up on two legs and ran into the nearby woods, turning out to be a bipedal creature with a hairless human-like face and rather skinny build, standing five to six feet tall and weighing an estimated 130 pounds. Its arms dangled like those of an orangutan, and it seemed to be trying to get a

good look at the witnesses as it ran off in a rather hunched-over posture. She would later learn that one of her neighbors had seen the same creature. Beverly Brandenburger.

52. G.B. and two friends, Moose Lake in Itasca County, September 4, 1993 - Three friends fishing in a boat near dusk about 100 feet from shore heard something in the nearby trees suddenly make a high-pitched scream much like a woman screaming and also heard branches breaking and heavy bipedal-sounding footsteps. BFRO website.

53. "Mr. Plautz," north of Bemidji, November 1993 - A man on a hunting trip with his two sons was sitting in their pickup truck waiting for them near dusk when he was startled by something lifting the entire back end of the truck off the ground, then shaking it violently. He looked back to see a manlike creature eight to ten inches taller than the cab covered with chocolate brown hair. It shook the truck angrily for about three minutes with him inside, then finally dropped it and fled into the woods, leaving tracks 17-18" long and five feet apart. Marion Senn.

54. Lance R., west of Cotton, August 15, 1995 or 1996 - A man was driving at 6 AM one to two miles west of Cotton on Highway 52 and had just crossed the Whiteface River and was nearing a hill when an upright dark bipedal creature crossed the road, about 7 1/2 feet tall and fairly thin. In profile its face appeared rather canine, protruding outward a bit. Bob Olson.

55. Josh M., near Remer, Fall 1996 - A man hunting grouse with his father saw a Bigfoot cross a trail about 25 feet in front of him. He thought it looked like Chewbacca from "Star Wars," but was black, with long arms below its knees. After crossing the trail, it ran toward him in a slightly hunched posture but very fast, then veered off into the woods. He knelt and looked low down to try and get a glimpse of its feet as it fled and did so for just a moment. His father was nearby but did not see or hear the creature as he was hard of hearing. Related by the witness by e- mail.

56. "Faith and Larry," near Margie, 1996 - A woman driving a handicapped-equipped van and a disabled person in a wheelchair

saw a very small and presumably young Bigfoot only a few feet tall cross the road in front of them, looking at them as it did, then climb a ridge on the other side. Related by Terry Portinga by e-mail. 57-58.

57-58. Anonymous, near Togo, May 1998 - Two people in a vehicle on their way to visit a girlfriend saw a very large and human-like Bigfoot leap from a steep wooded hill on to the road, landing in a crouch on both legs and one arm and then immediately jumping back into the woods when it saw them. One of the witnesses had seen what he believed to be the same creature earlier about four miles away in wintertime, the temperature 15 to 20 below zero. It acted similarly, emerging from woods into a ditch and then straight back into the woods again. GCBRO website.

59. Cameille N. and friend, Cass Lake area, 1990s - Limited information on a woman and her friend seeing a Bigfoot in a swampy area. Alan Weaver.

60. Anonymous, northwest of Margie, 1990s - Three to five men were camping in a swampy peat bog area when they heard screams that were like a combination of a woman screaming, a baby crying, and a horse whinnying. They fled immediately. R.A. Gilbertsen; Harvey Cole.

61. Shane D., Remer area, late 1990s - A minister who had once done some logging work told of having seen a Bigfoot up to 12 feet tall running quickly beside a river while operating a skidder in cold wintertime conditions. Related by proprietor of Icecube Coins & Antiques in Remer.

62-66. Anonymous, near Grand Rapids, July 1998-August 3, 2000 - A family experienced several Bigfoot incidents. First, the mother was in her garden when she heard bushes rustling and looked to see a human-like leg covered in brown hair disappearing into the woods just 15 feet from her. Second, at around the same time, her sons were claiming they had seen Bigfoot tracks in the woods, not huge but barefoot human-like tracks. Nothing happened in 1999, but thirdly in April or May of 2000, the oldest son was out collecting maple sap on a four-wheeler when he had a quick sighting of a brown Bigfoot about six feet tall or shorter run across a trail about 60-65 yards in front of him. At this time, the father knew of his wife's sighting, but they had not shared it with the boys yet, the father trying to remain skeptical. Fourth, in July 2000, both parents and the oldest boy heard an odd howl or scream at about 11 PM that sounded like a Bigfoot vocalization they heard a recording of on the BFRO website. As a fifth and final experience, on August 3, 2000, both boys were riding a four-wheeler in the woods when the younger one thought he saw their father, but the older one knew it was the creature they had by now named "Big Paw" and beat a hasty retreat. At this point, the father dropped his skepticism, and the family held a meeting in which they shared all the experiences with all members, and it was agreed to share them with the BFRO and allow investigators on to their property. BFRO members found scat and depressions in the ground but nothing that could be definitely linked to Bigfoot. BFRO website.

67. Anonymous, northeast of Cass Lake, Summer 2000 - A Native American family on the Leech Lake Reservation was having a spiritual gathering at their home when a sound like a woman screaming was heard nearby. Afterward, a boy saw a large animal he could not identify a short distance up the road from the property. About a half-hour later, he was in a pickup truck with some cousins being driven home in the opposite direction from where the animal had been, and all of them saw a creature crouching beside the road with green eyeshine in their headlights. As they passed by it then stood up and revealed itself to be a Bigfoot about six feet tall with dark shaggy hair about three inches long, long arms, and broad shoulders. If it was the same creature seen both times, it had to have crossed the family's property during the half-hour between sightings. BFRO website.

68. Mike Quast and Alan Weaver, near Gemmel, October 7, 2000- While searching for Bigfoot evidence this author and a friend found strange bipedal tracks ascending the side of a gravel pit beside the Gemmel Ridge Road. They resembled the impressions of a human walking on only the foreparts of the feet with some toe impressions evident and with a slight bit of snow on the ground, it was clearly not the season for going barefoot. At one point off to the right was a handprint with a clear thumb as if the climber had steadied himself.

Most interesting was that at the top of this line of tracks, just below level ground at the top of the pit, was a horizontal hole dug into the slope with loose gravel still evident cascading down where it had been dug out. This hole was exactly the length of a human arm as this author could just touch the back of it. Another handprint was found on level ground near the pit but with no footprints around it. Personal experience.

69. Amanda K. and Lisa G., near Bemidji, July 2001 - Two friends were picking up some possessions at a house owned by one of their fathers in the wooded area along Town Hall Road. As they were leaving the house, they noticed that all of the usual animal sounds in the area had gone silent, but then a crashing in the brush in a swampy area downhill from them caught their attention, and they saw a huge bipedal creature covered in long light brown hair standing in the swamp and shaking some trees as if agitated. After a few seconds both, the creature and the witnesses fled. Two men were also present at the house but did not see the creature. Of note is the fact that when this author later explored the site, several dogs in the area were barking loudly, something not happening at the time of the sighting. Curt Nelson.

70. Steve W., north of Remer, Spring 2002 - Limited information on a Bigfoot sighting about two miles north of Remer. Bob Olson.

71. William Bobolink, daughter and son-in-law, west of Bena, Fall 2002 - An elder and spiritual adviser for the Leech Lake band of Ojibwa living one mile west of Bena along with his daughter and her husband saw a Bigfoot 30 feet west of their house. They watched from inside as the creature was out in the yard apparently curious about a clothesline, spinning clothespins in circles with a finger of its right hand. The clothesline was at about the height of its stomach. When it realized it was being watched, it walked away. Bob Olson; Lady Ocalat's Paranormal Investigations website.

72. Craig James Myran, Pennington area, Winter 2002 - In a comment posted to an Internet video a man related how he saw possible Bigfoot tracks in snow while working on a trail in the winter in the Pennington area. YouTube.

73. Darrel Rodekuhr, west of Walker, 2002 - A man in a rural home was awakened at two AM by a high-pitched welping/wailing cry and went outside with a flashlight where he saw a Bigfoot about seven feet tall, standing between two poplar trees. When he ran back into the house the creature followed and stood outside his bedroom window continuing to issue its wailing cry for about 30 minutes. It then moved on to a nearby neighbor's house, where it did the same thing, but no one happened to be home there. Don Sherman; Comment posted to "The View from this Side of the Lake," blog featured on areavoices.com, March 22, 2009.

74-76. Darrel R., Walker area, 2002 or 2003 - A man living in a wooded area heard loud human-like screams outside his house at about 2 AM, sounding pained and sorrowful in one-minute increments lasting for half an hour. At 2:30, he went outside, and the screaming sounded almost directly in front of him. In the beam of a light he'd brought, he saw a dark-colored creature about seven feet tall and covered in long hair, standing 20 feet in front of him. He noticed no smell. In fright, he ran back to his house and hid under his bed, listening as the creature kept screaming for another half hour, then moved on to a neighbor's house and continued to scream for a time there. The man knew of two other sightings in the area that same year. Bob Olson.

77-78. Laura L. and two friends, west of Togo, August 5, 2003 - Three women driving home from work at about 7:30 PM were approaching the Flaming Pine Youth Camp when they saw a creature beside the road looking into the woods about 400 yards ahead of them. At about half that distance, it looked at them and then crossed a seven-foot wide ditch in one step and disappeared into the woods. When they reached the spot a moment later, they stopped and watched for five minutes but did not spot the creature again despite the sparse tree cover and seeming difficulty it should have had to conceal itself in the time allowed. It was about eight feet tall with an athletic build and covered with dark brown or black "poufy" hair. They also related that someone else from the area had reported seeing a similar creature earlier in the year. Joe Heinan; Carrie and Allen Donais.

79. Anonymous, south of Hibbing, July 17, 2004 - A man had just gotten up for the day when he heard a low cry or calling sound outside that he had never heard anything like before. He went outside to investigate and saw a figure six to seven feet tall in a grove of pines, upright and hair covered. When it noticed him, it ran away. He went to the spot and could see its foot impressions in the grass. Later that day, the man's father-in-law found droppings in the area that were not from deer or bear. BFRO website.

80. Anonymous, Red Lake, February 6, 2005 - Bigfoot tracks were found in snow within the city limits of the town of Red Lake on the Red Lake Indian Reservation. Over 100 tracks measuring 17" long with a stride of over five feet came from a swampy area and crossed the grounds of the school as well as passing through several peoples' yards. A sound like a woman screaming as well as dogs barking were heard at around 2 AM. This incident would come to be regarded spiritually as an omen of ill-fortune as several tragedies occurred on the reservation soon afterward, including a hunter dying of hypothermia, two children falling through ice and drowning, and a mass shooting at the school with multiple fatalities. BFRO website; Red Lake Net News, Michael Barrett; Cryptomundo website, Loren Coleman.

81. Thelberta Lussier, near Bena, June 2005 - An elderly woman and her adult daughter were driving at about 4:30 PM, the daughter asleep, when a large creature, first taken to be a deer, was seen at the side of the road ahead of them. In a moment, as the woman slowed down the creature stood up, raised its arms, and turned out to be a Bigfoot about seven feet tall with dark brown hair and a pointed head. At about 60 feet from the vehicle, it took one large stride away from the road and disappeared into the woods. The witness screamed and awoke her daughter, who failed to see the creature. Bigfoot Times, Daniel Perez; Bob Olson.

82. Anonymous, near Bena, June 2005 - Limited information on a woman driving near Bena, who saw a brown-haired Bigfoot walking near some railroad tracks. She said when it looked at her she felt it

was looking into her soul, and she began to cry. Duluth News Tribune. October 17, 2007; Lady Ocalat's Paranormal Investigations website.

83. Anonymous, Hibbing area, Summer and Winter 2005 - Teepee structures believed made by Bigfoot were discovered near a couple's cabin. Bigfootencounters website, "J.P.H"

84. Name unknown, Knutson Dam area on Cass Lake, September 2005 - Limited information on a Bigfoot sighting. Bob Olson.

85. Mary M., Deer River area, 2005 - Limited information on an elderly woman seeing a Bigfoot in her yard. Bob Olson.

86. Anonymous, near Boy River, 2005 - A woman told Bigfoot researcher Don Sherman that as she was driving and turned onto Highway 8 near the Boy River, she saw a Bigfoot in the ditch. She was scared and took off, and when she looked in her rear-view mirror, she saw that the creature was chasing her until she outdistanced it. Don Sherman.

87. Name(s) unknown, near Bena, 2005 - Limited information on a deer that was reportedly found torn apart four miles west of the Bug-O-Nay-Ge-Shig Indian school and associated with Bigfoot. Don Sherman.

88. Name(s) unknown, northwest of Deer River, early 2006- Limited information on a Bigfoot sighting in a location known for other sightings eight to ten miles up Highway 46 from Deer River, listed in March 2006 as very recent. Bob Olson.

89. Anonymous, near Bemidji, April 8, 2006- A woman and her son and boyfriend experienced various happenings around their rural home for a few years culminating in a Bigfoot sighting. A variety of vocalizations were heard in the woods, including screams, howls, and what sounded like words but in no identifiable language coming from behind their garage which stopped as soon as the boyfriend came out to try and record it. On another instance, they heard something hit their door and went out to find a three-foot poplar branch lying there, which was odd since there were no poplar trees in the area, and the branch appeared twisted off, not broken. The sighting occurred when the couple was in their car about to pull

out of the driveway on an overcast and foggy morning when they saw a black hairy creature 7-7 1/2 feet tall walking on two legs along the road about 35-40 yards away. They watched it for about five minutes until it was out of sight, then found several tracks 16 1/2-17" in length. BFRO website.

90. Cory Frazer, near Bena, June 7, 2006 - A road grader operator was grading the Six Mile Lake Road when just off of Highway 2, he noticed large human-like tracks in the gravel at the roadside. There were about 30 of them, 15" long, two to three inches deep, and with 15-18" between them. It was Frazer's second sweep of the road, and when he'd first gone up it in the opposite direction, the tracks were not there. These tracks became quite famous, attracting curious crowds and launching a career in Bigfoot research for local auto body repairman Bob Olson. Bigfoot Times. Daniel Perez; Bob Olson; Cass Lake Times. June 22, 2006.

91. Anonymous, near Ball Club, June 20, 2006 - An elderly Native American woman was driving to the White Oak Casino in Deer River at about 11 PM when she saw a man-like creature about eight feet tall and covered in brown hair standing beside Highway 2, looking like it was preparing to cross the road toward Ball Club Lake. She was positive it was not a bear. A BFRO investigator went to the site and found a well-worn trail in the grass as if something large often used it. BFRO website; Duluth News Tribune. October 17, 2007.

92. Darlene F., near Ball Club, July 17, 2006 - Another Native American woman driving to the White Oak Casino in Deer River saw a Bigfoot standing over eight feet tall beside Highway 2 two miles east of Ball Club. She stated, "It gave me the creeps." Bob Olson; Lady Ocalat's Paranormal Investigations website.

93. Jacob Suihkonen, Carey Lake area near Hibbing, July 18, 2006- The 14-year-old son of a Hibbing city engineer saw a Bigfoot about three miles from Carey Lake Park and stated that it turned to look at him as a man would do. Western Itasca Review. August 17, 2006; Don Sherman.

Another version of this report states that Jacob saw not just one but a family of three creatures. Lady Ocalat's Paranormal Investigations website; Bob Olson.

94-96. Bob Olson, Tom Biscardi, others, Carey Lake near Hibbing, August 4, 2006- Members of the research team Searching for Bigfoot Inc. led by Tom Biscardi accompanied by Minnesota researcher Bob Olson and a reporter from the Iron Range News went to an area at Carey Lake Park, where there were old concrete structures once used by the DuPont company for manufacturing black powder for the military. When they were near the structures, they noticed a tree moving in a nearby swamp, and Biscardi looked toward it with a thermal imager, seeing the heat signature of a large bipedal figure. Two team members tried to get close to the creature as it hid behind tree cover, its head occasionally bobbing into view on the thermal imager, but when they called out to it they apparently frightened it into fleeing and disappearing up and over a nearby hill. The team came back to the spot later at about 12:30 AM and had a second sighting, again by thermal imager. Four team members tried to circle the creature, but it avoided them and once again disappeared.

The team was in the area in response to a youth telling Bob Olson at a presentation he'd given at the Itasca County Juvenile Center in Grand Rapids about a Bigfoot being seen recently at the DuPont site. Western Itasca Review. August 17, 2006; Don Sherman.

97. Justin M., north of Grand Rapids, late September 2006 - A man saw a Bigfoot 10 miles north of Grand Rapids along Highway 38 between 6 and 7 PM Described as nine feet tall, large and hairy with broad shoulders, it came out of some woods 75 yards from a house, walked briefly in a field on two legs, then went back into the woods. Bob Olson.

98. Everett A., west of Ball Club, September 30, 2006 - A 16-year-old boy was hunting near the Mississippi River when he saw a Bigfoot walking in a low swampy area. It looked back at him when he yelled at it but then just kept walking with a steady gait, while the boy was frightened into running all the way to Highway 2, where he hitched a ride into town to get away, swearing he was never going hunting again. Unfortunately, just one week later, he was killed in an

accidental shooting, perhaps lending weight to the idea held by some Native Americans that to see a Bigfoot is an omen of ill fortune. BFRO website; Bob Olson.

99. Anonymous, Pine Island State Forest, 2006 - A major and controversial story came to Bigfoot researcher Don Sherman at a speaking event in Remer in 2016. A fellow researcher approached him to describe how he'd been present ten years earlier in the Pine Island State Forest near the Canadian border when a man he knew was deer hunting from a tree stand. The man saw a doe come out of the trees acting nervous, and he suspected a buck would be coming close behind, so he raised his rifle and aimed through the scope, but when a Bigfoot then appeared instead, he was so shocked that he accidentally pulled the trigger and shot and killed the creature. The man reporting the incident to Sherman said that he observed authorities come in and seal off the area as well as a helicopter lifting something believed to be the body of the Bigfoot and then flying off in the direction of Duluth. Don Sherman.

100. Kathy Sheffield, Ball Club area, 2006 - Researchers from the group Searching for Bigfoot Inc., led by researcher Tom Biscardi collected Bigfoot stories while attending a wedding on the Red Lake Reservation, including limited information on a sighting of a creature by witness Sheffield in the neighborhood where she lived. Searchingforbigfoot.com website; Don Sherman.

101. R.O., Gull Lake near Hackensack, 2006 or 2007 - Limited information on a Bigfoot sighting at the northeast corner of Gull Lake. Bob Olson.

102. Natalie L. and mother, Andrusia Lake area in Beltrami County, May 12, 2007 - A woman driving with her mother had just passed the Palace Casino when a large upright creature covered in dark hair crossed the road in front of them. Bob Olson.

103. Anonymous, near Akeley, Memorial Day weekend 2007 - Limited information on a Bigfoot sighting six miles from Akely on the west side of Highway 64. Bob Olson.

104. Jody Hansen, Carey Lake near Hibbing, June 12, 2007 - A Bigfoot enthusiast searching for evidence in an area of past reports

found a track 16-18" long in an anthill at 9:30 AM. Half an hour later, he heard two grunts come from a small wooded valley beside an ATV trail. Bob Olson.

105. Jody Hansen, Carey Lake near Hibbing, June 19, 2007 - The witness from the previous report found two old tracks at 3:30 PM along the same ATV trail, both from a right foot and 16- 18" long. Bob Olson.

106. Jody Hansen, Carey Lake near Hibbing, July 6. 2007 - The witness from the previous reports found several animal trails in the Bauer Road area at around 2:30 PM that he believed may be Bigfoot related, including one that gave him his second experience of finding a Bigfoot track in an anthill. Another had a kidney-shaped bed in the grass next to it that was not similar to deer beds. Bob Olson.

107. Jody Hansen, Carey Lake near Hibbing, July 8, 2007 - The witness from the previous reports found more animal trails, possibly Bigfoot related that had not been there two days earlier, again in the Bauer Road area, while searching at around 3:15 PM Bob Olson.

108. Jody Hansen, Carey Lake near Hibbing, July 27, 2007 - The witness from the previous reports was in the same area when he found several piles of branches oddly stacked up for no apparent reason, then heard a loud, deep growl close behind him in the woods followed by heavy breathing lasting for a few seconds. He did not see what made the sounds but thought it was too loud to be a bear. He felt the branch piles might be a form of communication between Bigfoot creatures. Duluth News Tribune. October 17, 2007; Bob Olson.

109. Brad H., Child Lake between Longville and Hackensack, Summer 2007 - A man living on the northwest side of the lake heard loud screams and thought at the time it might be a mountain lion but would change his mind after a later experience and suspect Bigfoot. Bob Olson.

110. Name unknown, near Nary, 2007 - In this area southwest of Bemidji, a woman saw a Bigfoot eating apples off a tree outside her home. In complete panic, she insisted that she refused to "live in a state that has monsters in it" and refused to go back, with her son eventually having to help relocate her to North Dakota. Bob Olson.

III. Anonymous, north of Cass Lake, 2007 or 2008 - Bigfoot researcher Don Sherman met a woman who confided in him a story involving people she knew that took place in the area near Mission Bridge. A woman living in a trailer with her five or six-year-old son scolded the boy for throwing half his sandwich out the door to feed the area dogs. He told her, "No, I'm feeding Scary Man." This happened at least twice over a few days. Then one night, the woman saw a shadow move across the kitchen window by the glow of a yard light, and the next day she realized that with the elevation above ground of the trailer, whatever it was had to have been ten feet tall. Sometime later, the child called out, "Come see Scary Man!" and when the mother came to look, she saw a small juvenile Bigfoot behind a tree. The next day they saw a family of three Bigfoot creatures at dusk, which they were able to watch for about ten minutes until it got dark. Don Sherman.

112. Alan Hyatt, west of Remer, 2007 or 2008 - A man who had a previous report in the Remer area in 1975 was deer hunting in an area of cedar swamps when he heard two loud wood knocks and then felt watched that night, activity he equated with Bigfoot. Related by the witness at presentation during 2017 Remer Bigfoot Days festival.

113. Brad H., Child Lake between Longville and Hackensack, February 29, 2008 - The same man from the previous report in this location heard loud tree knocking coming from very close behind his house in the evening. The sounds gradually moved off and faded out. He looked for tracks in the snow but found none. This made him reconsider the screams he had heard the previous summer as being probably Bigfoot related. Bob Olson.

114. Bob Olson, others, Inger area, April 17, 2008 - In response to hearing of Bigfoot tracks in the area researcher Bob Olson was driving slowly along Pine Grove Road scanning the roadsides to see if he could spot any when at 7:35 PM, he found what appeared to be the track of a crippled and misshapen foot 14" x 7" in size. Bob Olson.

115. Anonymous, near Laporte, June 21, 2008 - Six girls were camping at Gulch Lake Campground in the Paul Bunyan State Forest, and after sitting around their fire late into the night, they bedded

down at about 3:45 AM with four in one tent and two in another. The four fell asleep, but the two remained awake and heard two strange calls consisting of high pitched screaming and grunting that sounded less than 100 yards away. They were afraid and moved to the tent with the other four girls who were still asleep. After a while, they sounded what sounded like bipedal footsteps moving through the camp and their cooler being opened. Once everyone got up, they found all the bottled water gone from the cooler, but beer and food were untouched. BFRO website.

116. Anonymous, Lake Winibigoshish in Itasca County, June 28, 2008 - This author was with a female friend on Tamarack Point on the lake at about 2:30 PM in drizzly conditions on an excursion to search for Bigfoot evidence. We had just decided not to stay the night at the campground due to the weather and were driving out in her van with myself looking down at my lap studying a map when she suddenly slowed to a stop. I looked up at her, not forward out the windshield, and asked what was wrong. Staring straight ahead with a numb expression, she said that something had just crossed the road a short distance ahead of the van and proceeded to describe a large dark manlike figure built like a football player in full pads moving from right to left across the road in only a couple of strides and swinging its arms, moving from a trail on one side into solid woods on the other. I had missed seeing it by seconds. Personal experience.

116-117. Name unknown, Cass Lake, July 2008 - Limited information on a Bigfoot being seen running across the road near the Bingo Palace and Mission Bridge in Cass Lake. A UFO was also reported seen in the form of an orange orb over the lake in the same area on that same date. Don Sherman.

118. Name unknown, west of Ball Club, November 19, 2008 - Limited information on a female college student who saw a Bigfoot on the shoulder of Highway 2 just west of Ball Club at about 6:30 PM while driving from Bemidji to her father's home in Duluth. She immediately texted her father, who contacted a relative who relayed the report to Bigfoot researcher Don Sherman. Don Sherman; Cass Lake Times. January 15, 2009.

119. Kip Blum, Lillian Lake area near Deer River, November 19, 2008 - By coincidence, this report occurred on the same date and at the same time as the previous one not far away. A man had just left his father's house at 6:30 PM when a large upright hairy creature crossed Groth Lumber Road only about six feet in front of his car. It was 7 1/2 to 8 feet tall with brown hair about the color of a Chesapeake dog, longest on its upper arms where it was up to a foot long. It had no neck and a dark hairless face with wrinkled skin, a small nose, and human-like lips. It moved rapidly across the road in the direction of the nearby lake, swinging its arms rapidly. The man returned immediately to his father's house, whereupon he heard a loud drawn-out scream come from the lake. While investigating the sighting, researcher Don Sherman is said to have found a deer carcass hanging high in a tree in the area. Bob Olson; Don Sherman; Cass Lake Times. January 15, 2009; Lady Ocalat's Paranormal Investigations website.

120. Greg W. and Jody H., Carey Lake near Hibbing, October 30, 2008 - Two men were walking on a lighted ski trail in western Carey Lake Park at 5:00 PM when they sat down on a bench to rest and heard a rustling behind them in the woods. After resuming their walk, they went about 50 yards and then heard what sounded like a heavy exhaling sound, repeated a second time about three minutes later. Then as they were rounding a curve, Greg saw a large dark upright figure run quickly across the trail 150 to 200 yards ahead, crossing the 15-foot wide trail in three strides. It was about seven feet tall and looked silvery on its back, clearly not a man or a bear. They hurried to where it had been, and Jody tried to follow it but found only a few small broken branches. He had been keeping track of other sightings in the area and searching for evidence, finding many tracks, a possible nesting area, and once heard a loud growl and heavy breathing. Bob Olson.

121. Dean T., one other, between Bena and Deer River, November 2008 - Limited information on two men seeing two Bigfoot creatures somewhere between these two towns. Bob Olson.

122. Anonymous, Inger area, 2008 - A woman living in a trailer

house heard noises outside, went out and saw a small juvenile Bigfoot sitting in a tree with an adult creature reacting to its cries and standing there with outstretched arms reaching for it. When the adult noticed the woman, it turned toward her and emitted an angry vocalization described as "Hissssss Hah!" She was frightened to the point of falling down on the ground. Bob Olson; Lady Ocalat's Paranormal Investigations website.

123-124. Anonymous, near Calumet, July 2009 - Two friends were sitting on a porch talking when they noticed a manlike figure atop an iron ore hill about 60 yards away. It was walking along in an odd hunched way with long legs and long swinging arms and at some point, during the 40 seconds it was in view, they realized no human being could be as large or cover as much ground so fast as what they were seeing. The figure was four feet taller than the trees atop the hill, trees that were measured later by a BFRO investigator as being 8-12 feet tall after two years of growth. The witness who lived at the site reported that she had also been hearing wood knocks from time to time. She also said that a next-door neighbor had had a similar sighting while driving by the same hill early one morning, seeing a brown manlike figure standing on the hilltop gazing out at the valley below. BFRO website.

125. Anonymous, north of Bovey, August 2009 - A couple was driving back from swimming at their lakeshore property at 4:30 PM with the husband in the passenger seat when they saw what they took to be a man in the ditch 200-300 yards ahead of them, but it moved like an animal as it went toward the woods behind it, then seemed to change its mind and darted across the road instead, by which time the car had slowed down and was only about 20 paces away. The creature was six to seven feet tall and covered with dark brown hair, had a broad nose and a little hair on its forehead and cheeks, and long hair on its feet like a Clydesdale horse that trailed behind it. Welts were noticed on its chest that were taken to be insect bites. It swung long arms as it leaped the width of the opposite ditch. The husband stated he could see fear in the creature's eyes. BFRO website.

126. Tim, Peter, and Casey Kedrowski, north of Remer, October 24, 2009 - A father and two sons had a trail camera set up in a hunting area near Shingle Mill Lake that captured a mysterious image at 7:20 PM on a rainy night, appearing to show a tall, dark hairy figure walking from left to right. Its upright stance and a clear right arm and hairless hand rule out it being a bear, and its height compared to trees in the photo appears to be around seven feet, but many have commented that it resembles a hunter in a gilly suit or other such hunting camouflage, though it does not appear to be carrying any weapons or other gear. The father, Tim, had hunted the area for 43 years. The sons, Peter and Casey, investigated and found that two elderly hunters had been staying in a shack in the area on the night the picture was taken, and they had not known there was a camera nearby and insisted they had not gone anywhere near where it was, however they did say that at about 2 AM on that night, they had gone out to their outhouse and had heard strange squealing noises. Forum Communications Co., Molly Miron, December 11, 2009.

127. Helen B., Hibbing area, Winter 2009 - A woman was asleep at about 3 AM on a bitterly cold night when she was awakened by growling noises outside her window. She looked out to see a Bigfoot, sensing its wildness, and perceived that in a deep baritone voice it was growling her name. It then walked away with heavy crunching footsteps in the snow, leaving tracks that were 14" long by 8" wide with a stride of about 5' 5" that she found the next morning. Investigator Bob Olson commented that though the witness sounded believable, he was skeptical of the report since she claimed the creature could talk. Bob Olson; Lady Ocalat's Paranormal Investigations website.

128. Anonymous, three miles west of Bena, 2010 - Limited information on three bank examiners driving to Bemidji on Highway 2 who saw a dark-colored Bigfoot cross the road in front of them. Lady Ocalat's Paranormal Investigations website.

129. Roger Johnson, between Bena and Winnie Dam, April 30, 2011 - A man from Inger driving four to five miles down Highway 9 or the Winnie Dam Road north of Highway 2, saw a Bigfoot with reddish-brown hair running upright through a swamp just off the road. He

was too afraid to stop. Lady Ocalat's Paranormal Investigations website.

130. Randy B., one other, south of Grand Rapids, June 17, 2011 - A young Native American man who worked at a Holiday gas station near Pokegama Lake was on his way to work at 2:30 AM and was speeding because he was late. As he turned on to Southwood Road, he saw a black upright creature seven to eight feet tall with a cone-shaped head, no neck, and a flat face just 30 feet in front of him. In the same moment, a Highway Patrol car came up behind him with lights flashing to pull him over for speeding, and as both cars came to a stop, both the young man and the patrolman had a full view of the creature in their headlights. It stood still at first in the middle of a turning lane, then walked to the shoulder of the road in three strides. The patrolman, clearly stunned, got out of his car and shined a spot-light on the creature, following its movement as it walked away. The young man, also shaken up, then drove on to the gas station to begin his shift. Soon the patrol car came speeding into the station with its lights still flashing as the patrolman was apparently caught up in dealing with the creature sighting, and the young man did not dare to approach him as he did not want to get a ticket for his speeding. Rumor has it that the patrol car's dashboard camera captured video of the creature but all attempts by investigators to see the footage have gone unanswered. Lady Ocalat's Paranormal Investigations website; Bob Olson; Don Sherman.

131-132. "Carl," Lydick Lake near Cass Lake, August 11, 2011 - A Fire Management worker for the U.S. Forest Service was checking out a site for a proposed training burn at the site of an old baseball diamond that was being reclaimed by the forest when he heard strange calls in the woods that sounded like two creatures about a mile apart communicating with each other. The calls were a mixture of high and low pitches, a guttural whooping. The witness was certain they were not wolf calls though wolves were known to be in the area, in fact, a recent wolf kill was found at the scene with deer bones scattered about. About a week later, he returned to the site with his wife and while driving she thought she saw a tall, dark manlike figure walk across the road about a half-mile ahead of them. BFRO website.

133. Marie and Mike Cloud, Boy Lake area, October 11, 2011 - Two residents of Inger were working on a road in an area of Leech Lake Reservation Housing Authority homes two miles from the Boy River Bridge off Highway 157 when they heard tree knocking and then saw a Bigfoot standing nearby staring at them. One took a photograph, but it turned out blurry. A housing crew was also said to have found hairs at the scene. Don Sherman.

134. Name unknown, Remer area, 2011 - Limited information on an elderly Native American man telling of hearing the sounds of a Bigfoot. "Finding Bigfoot" episode "Bigfoot Town" on Animal Planet.

135. Names unknown, east of Bena, 2011 - Two Native Americans driving on Six Mile Lake Road came around a corner and saw a Bigfoot standing in the middle of the road. Instead of fleeing the creature stood its ground, and the terrified witnesses had to drive around it, so close that it was right beside the driver's door as they passed by. They immediately to nearby Bena where they reported the sighting at the gas station there. Lady Ocalat's Paranormal Investigations website.

136. Name unknown, six miles northeast of Togo, 2011 - Limited information on a deputy sheriff who had gone into some woods to do an inspection and then saw a Bigfoot standing near his pickup truck. Lady Ocalat's Paranormal Investigations website.

137. Jack Barnes & Jeff Andersen, between International Falls and Fort Frances, Ontario, March 10, 2012- What was alleged to be the longest Bigfoot trackway ever found anywhere at the time was found crossing the Canadian border in deep snow. There were three miles of tracks numbering between 3,000 and 6,000 individual prints that measured 17" long. They were estimated to have been made three to six days previously as they had a quarter-inch of snow in them. At one point, several deer and moose carcasses are said to have been found stacked up. YouTube.

138. Names unknown, east side of Leech Lake, April 6, 2012 - Two Native Americans driving on Sugar Point Road spotted a Bigfoot with

black hair and green eyes. It became aggressive and started to chase their car, keeping up for a time even though they were going forty miles per hour. Lady Ocalat's Paranormal Investigations website.

139. Anonymous, 15 southwest of Bemidji, April 11, 2012 - A male school bus driver was just beginning his morning run at 7 AM, the bus still empty of passengers, when he noticed movement 75 yards off the road to his left and then saw a dark-colored Bigfoot that seemed to be about seven feet tall sitting on a pile of logs. It appeared to notice him, but he then sped away in fear. Lady Ocalat's Paranormal Investigations website. 140-142.

140-142. Sherie Rodriguez, Mike Tibbetts, Don Sherman, north of Ball Club, May 2012- Sherie Rodriguez heard her dog barking wildly, looked out her kitchen window, and saw what she described as looking like a "polar bear" on all fours. Mike Tibbetts was in the same area on the same day and found typical looking Bigfoot tracks, which he reported to Bigfoot researcher Don Sherman a couple of days later, but by then, rain had erased the tracks. Sherman did an investigation along East Bank Road near Rodriguez's house in which he did wood knockings and got responses that came steadily closer to him between 11 PM and 1 AM. This episode is intriguing since a major sighting four years later in the area - that of Sammy Cleveland - would feature a white Bigfoot. Don Sherman.

143. Names unknown, Nevis area, Spring-Summer 2012 - Videos posted by "MinnesotaEric" described how Bigfoot sightings had been occurring "from County Road 23, west of Huntersville State Forest, to north of Kabekone Lake through Paul Bunyan State Forest" and showed a man and woman north of Nevis examining broken cherry trees that they believed to be the work of Bigfoot. YouTube.

144-145. Anonymous, Beltrami County, Summer 2012 - A man went outside his house to turn off a spigot and heard a low growl about ten feet behind him that didn't sound like any animal he had ever heard. Oddly, he immediately went into a relaxed state of mind and felt as if he was telepathically communicating to whatever it was to calm down and keep its distance, then made his way back into the house, consciously keeping his back to the source of the sound so as not to look at it. The man's daughter had complained of something looking in her window on that side of the house, and he hadn't treated it seriously, but now he equated that to the growl and also to stories he'd heard from Native American friends about beings similar to Bigfoot being in the area, feeling that there was a spiritual or psychological element that came along with the physical presence of the creatures. Two years later, he would have a sighting at a golf course a mile from his home. BFRO website.

146-147. Anonymous, Marcell area, Fall 2012- Limited information on Bigfoot sightings said to have occurred, including one very near town, then shortly thereafter another on a highway a short distance from town. "Bill," friend of resort owner in the following report.

148. Bob Olson, between Inger and Little Ball Club Lake, 2012 - Bigfoot researcher Olson found a grouping of tracks in three different lengths- 18", 14", and 7. The largest and smallest were together, but the mid-sized track was ten feet from the others and more oddly shaped, causing Olson to theorize that that creature might have been different from the others in some way and kept at arm's length from them. Bob Olson.

149. Bob Olson, one other, northwest of Deer River, 2012 or 2013 - In response to a tip by a woman saying she had found Bigfoot tracks beside a creek off of county road 44, researcher Olson went to the site and found one track, 10" x 5 1/4" in size, with five toes. Bob Olson.

150. Names unknown, Hungry Gulch Forest near Walker, 2012 or 2013 - Limited information on sightings of UFOs that seemed to coincide with sightings of Bigfoot by people riding four-wheeler ATVs and also someone finding Bigfoot tracks. Bob Olson.

151. Names unknown, Lake Andrusia northwest of Cass Lake, 2012 or 2013 - Again UFO and Bigfoot phenomena seemed to intertwine when a large orange orb was seen over the lake and there were Bigfoot sightings in the area that night. Bob Olson.

152. Lyle Enger, Hatch Lake near Bigfork, March 3, 2013 - The owner of Maple Ridge Resort came outside with his dogs at 10 PM after they scratched to get out, but they wanted back inside after only a few seconds. He then looked around and found bipedal manlike

tracks in the snow 16" long and seven to eight feet apart. The trackway was about a half-mile long, crossing the frozen lake and coming ashore at the resort where the tracks meandered among the cabins and then went through the woods to Turtle Lake Road, where it stopped. A friend named Bill reported that there had been other Bigfoot incidents throughout the fall and winter, including a sighting near his cabin. The TV show "Finding Bigfoot" made these tracks famous when they came and filmed an episode at the resort. BFRO website; "Finding Bigfoot" episode "Bigfoot Basecamp" on Animal Planet.

153-161. Other reports covered - most with limited information - in the area around Maple Ridge Resort on the "Bigfoot Basecamp" episode of "Finding Bigfoot" which all occurred prior to filming in Fall 2014:

*Two young girls canoeing on the opposite side of the lake from the resort had something throw rocks at them.

**Near Federal Dam east of Leech Lake, "Scott and Janice" had a shed next to their house with a large glassless window in it. Scott was taking out the garbage at 9 PM when a Bigfoot jumped through the window from inside the shed, a standing broad jump that ended in a crouch 10 feet from the shed, which would have been a 12-15 foot leap. The creature, 8 1/2 to 9 feet tall. with arms down to its knees, casually walked away in a hunched manner. (Bigfoot researcher Don Sherman informed the author that he investigated at this site and found some strands of hair inside the shed that he intended to have analyzed, but they were accidentally lost. He also related that a year before this sighting, a woman saw a Bigfoot crouching beside a mailbox at the same location.)

**Melissa Berg was driving from work to her home south of Leech Lake at dusk in late September or early October when she saw what she at first took to be a large beaver in a small lake but then realized it was a Bigfoot wading toward an island, head and shoulders above water. She watched it for three to five minutes. The "Finding Bigfoot" crew found the depth of the water to be six feet, making for a creature about nine feet tall. Berg also reported that later, over time, 27 chickens disappeared from her property with only feathers being found.

*A trapper saw a Bigfoot shaking a tree, then saw trees "folding" in its path as it fled. He had no gun at the time but had a machete and was so frightened he said he was ready to use it to defend himself.

*A man heard a loud crack 30 yards away along a tree line, followed by a deep guttural growl, which he associated with Bigfoot.

*A girl saw a Bigfoot a little bigger than a man squatting down by a tree.

*A man saw a Bigfoot nine feet tall standing up to its crotch in deep snow. (Bigfoot researcher Don Sherman reports that this witness is likely Kenny Grife, who was snowmobiling in the Mud Goose Lake area near a boat landing and saw the creature walking easily through three feet of snow.)

162. Anonymous, north of Marcell, August 2013 - A young man with a garden along Turtle Lake Road had been having trouble with something raiding his turnip patch and set up a trail camera to find out what it was. The next morning the camera had captured images of a Bigfoot bending over eating out of the patch, its back at least five feet above the ground. The man reported this to local Bigfoot researcher Bob Olson. Lady Ocalat's Paranormal Investigation website.

163-164. Jody Hansen, Carey Lake near Hibbing, September 9-11, 2013 - A Bigfoot enthusiast who often looked for evidence in this area known for past reports was at the lake and heard something large moving in the woods nearby him. He threw three small rocks into the trees in the direction of the sound, but nothing further happened. Two days later, he was at the spot again and was looking for tracks along the lakeshore when he heard a splash and realized something had just been thrown into the water and that it had to have come from a considerable distance away. He thought the two incidents were possibly related. Bob Olson.

165. Anonymous, near Bemidji, mid-December 2013 - A mother and adult daughter were driving along Lake Bemidji at night, the daughter driving and another car approaching in the opposite lane,

when a large bipedal creature ran across the road between the two cars illuminated in the headlights of both. Its arms were pumping like a man running, and it crossed the entire road in only 2 1/2 strides. The mother saw it clearly, but the daughter was not sure of what she saw. BFRO website.

166. Names unknown, between Inger and Cutfoot area, 2013- Some Native Americans cutting wood for a pow-wow near a site called the Turtle Effigy Mound saw a Bigfoot with black hair and standing eight feet tall run across the edge of a meadow without ever looking at them. Investigators Bob Olson and Don Sherman were able to arrive on the scene of this sighting within 45 minutes. Bob Olson.

167. Names unknown, near Boy River, 2013- A Native American road maintenance crew using heavy equipment working on Gazegan's Road saw a Bigfoot leaning against a birch tree watching them work, with its arms folded in a posture just as a man might do. When it saw that it had been spotted, it walked away. Bob Olson; Lady Ocalat's Paranormal Investigations website.

168. Anonymous, Beltrami County, May 24, 2014 - The man from the previous 2012 Beltrami County report had a sighting occur while working at a golf course a mile from his home. At about 7 AM, he saw a creature about seven feet tall with a lanky build and covered in reddish tan hair walking in dense woods just off a paved golf cart path about 10 feet into the brush but moving easily. It passed behind a building housing restrooms and did not emerge on the other side, meaning it had turned off into the woods while out of sight. The man had the creature in sight for about 20 seconds and was too stunned to mention it to a coworker who was facing him. BFRO website.

169. "Steve," near Bemidji, mid-June 2014 - A man living in a wooded area smelled a strong musky odor about 100 yards from his house, where he had a tree stand. During this time his wife was also sensing something watching her three to four times a week as she worked in her garden in the morning and deer that had used to congregate in their driveway were no longer being seen. It was the

start of what would become a series of Bigfoot experiences on the property. BFRO website; Bob Olson.

170. Anonymous, near Bemidji, first week of July 2014 - The wife of the man in the previous report was in their back yard in the morning when she heard three loud "shush" like sounds coming from the nearby tree line, sounding like they were coming from something with a big set of lungs and not human-like. She was frightened by the sounds. BFRO website; Bob Olson.

171-172. "Dave," near Bemidji, July 15, 2014 - The 9-year-old son of the couple from the two previous reports was helping his mother with yard work at 10:30 AM when he wandered about 20 yards into the woods and saw a dark, hairy figure about seven feet tall with its back to him. It turned to look at him and he saw that it had a hairless face gray and brown in color and a head that hung forward without an apparent neck. He then ran back to his mother after a few seconds to tell his mother, but when they looked again, the creature was gone. The boy's father Steve examined the scene and found a vague track in some moss as well as a tree branch 1 1/2-2" thick that had been twisted and ripped off 5 1/2-6 feet above the ground. That evening at 8:30 or 9 PM, Steve was sitting in his tree stand about 40 yards from where the sighting occurred when he heard two "heavy but quiet" footfalls and a low growl behind him. BFRO website; Bob Olson.

173. Anonymous, near Bemidji, July 23, 2014 - Steve's wife from the previous reports was in their backyard when she heard three heavy footfalls in the woods, sounding bipedal and as if they had a long stride. She tried to see what was making them but saw nothing. BFRO website; Bob Olson.

174. "Steve" and wife, near Bemidji, July 27, 2014- The couple from the previous reports were outside their house at 11:15 AM, Steve in the front yard and his wife in the back, when they both heard a loud moan come from the trees behind the house. The wife also heard two or three soft footfalls and felt like she was being watched. BFRO website; Bob Olson.

175. Anonymous, near Bemidji, July 29, 2014 - Steve's wife from the previous reports was again in the back yard at 10:15 AM when she

heard wood knocking in a 2-3-2 pattern at five second intervals, and then two very soft footfalls about ten seconds later. She was frightened and returned to the house. Bob Olson.

176. "Steve," near Bemidji, July 31, 2014 - Steve from the previous reports found another track in the moss in the area where his son's sighting had occurred, and also smelled a skunky odor though no skunk was detected. Bob Olson.

177. Jerome Grussel, north of Deer River, Summer 2014 - A deputy sheriff found Bigfoot tracks 16" long in a gravel pit. Bob Olson.

178. "Steve," near Bemidji, September 10, 2014 – Steve from the previous reports, decided to broadcast a supposed Bigfoot scream/howl vocalization from the Internet through a bullhorn at about 8 PM He received an answer from the woods, a low moan followed by 10-12 wood knocks in a rapid and almost frantic manner. Bob Olson.

179. "Steve" and "Dave," near Bemidji, September 11, 2014 - The father and son from the previous reports were at their tree stand at about 7:30 PM when they heard a series of heavy footfalls and breaking branches interspersed with pauses of 20-30 seconds and sounding as if it was getting closer to them. They withdrew to their house. Bob Olson.

180. "Steve" and "Dave," near Bemidji, September 12, 2014 - The father and son from the previous reports went to their tree stand again at about 7 PM and again heard heavy footfalls nearby. They went toward them with a camera, hoping to get photos but saw nothing. However, they also found a cave-like structure that had been fashioned from a fallen tree about ten feet long, 4-5 feet wide and four feet high. Bob Olson.

181. "Steve" and "Dave," near Bemidji, September 13, 2014 - The father and son from the previous reports returned to the cave-like structure they'd found the evening before at four PM and found a large piece of bark inside it that had not been there previously, three feet by two feet in size and placed in a vertical position. They photographed it and left an offering of an apple and some carrots. This was the last recorded report by the family. Bob Olson.

182. James "Bobo" Fay, Leech Lake area, Fall 2014 - While filming an episode of the tv show "Finding Bigfoot" researcher Bobo was on a night time solo foray in an area of known Bigfoot reports when he did a wood knocking and got a response in the form of a possible Bigfoot vocalization. "Finding Bigfoot" episode "Bigfoot Basecamp" on Animal Planet.

183. Matt Moneymaker, Cliff Barackman, James "Bobo" Fay, Ranae Holland, south of Leech Lake, Fall 2014 - While filming an episode of the tv show "Finding Bigfoot" the crew was investigating a cedar swamp by night near the Melissa Berg sighting location when they did some wood knocks and got responses in the form of another wood knock and a whooping sound. "Finding Bigfoot" episode "Bigfoot Basecamp" on Animal Planet.

184. Michael Hexum, near Nashwauk (presumably), 2014 - Minnesota Bigfoot Research Team member Hexum was operating an ATV and cutting wood when he turned off his chainsaw and heard mumbling and chattering sounds in the woods nearby that went on for 20 minutes. He believed the sounds to be Bigfoot vocalizations. Personally related by the witness at 2018 Remer Bigfoot Days festival.

185. Anonymous, near Alvwood and Bigfork, June 3, 2015 - A man was photographing 350-year-old white pine trees in the Lost Forty scientific natural area near Dora Lake when his father, who was waiting for him in a car a quarter-mile away, became impatient and honked the horn. This seemed to trigger an outbreak of wood knocking in the woods that the witness described as sounding like "a 500-pound woodpecker." He continued taking pictures until he heard the sound of a very large birch tree only 20 to 30 feet away cracking and falling over, then saw the tree flung back into its vertical position. He did not see what was doing it, but this act obviously required such enormous strength that he immediately felt himself in mortal danger and ran back to the car in a panic. After telling the story to others and being directed to watch the TV show, "Finding Bigfoot" he came to believe a Bigfoot was involved. BFRO website.

186. Names unknown, Sugar Point area near Leech Lake, Summer 2015 - Three men were in a car headed slowly north in an area of

Native American housing when they saw to their right a Bigfoot coming toward them with green glowing eyes. They were scared and took off without looking back.

187. Don Sherman. Don Sherman and girlfriend, south of Wini Dam, September 2015 - Bigfoot researcher Sherman reports that he and his girlfriend got tape recordings of Bigfoot vocalizations on West Bank Road off of Highway 9 about two miles south of Wini Dam at around one AM The sounds were mixed in with the howls of wolves and coyotes, consisting of low growls and whistling sounds as well as howls that did not match the sound of the canines. The sound of heavy footsteps were also recorded, and Sherman thought the sounds originated from as close as 60 yards away. Some sounds responded to him doing his impression of a Bigfoot howl himself. This incident contributed to Sherman forming the theory that Bigfoot might communicate with wolves and use them for hunting as primitive man did. Don Sherman.

188. Michael Hexum, Remer area, Fall 2015 - Bigfoot researcher Hexum told of a cedar swamp area in which he heard two Bigfoot vocalizations and also several wood knocks that would respond to his own knocks after about one minute. The vocalizations sounded like two creatures mumbling to each other from about 20 yards apart and lasted for about 20 minutes. "Finding Bigfoot" episode "Bigfoot Town" on Animal Planet; Related by the witness at 2017 Remer Bigfoot Days festival.

189. Mattie Bowstring, Bowstring Lake near Inger, 2015 - A man heard what he thought sounded like two Bigfoot creatures talking to each other. He returned later at night with Bigfoot researchers Bob Olson and Don Sherman and fellow witness Ken Grife. The men saw what they at first thought was someone walking with a flashlight but then it turned out to be a mysterious ball of floating light, which some believe to be a paranormal phenomenon that occurs in association with Bigfoot. Don Sherman.

190. Chele White & one other, Red Lake Indian Reservation, April 5, 2016 - A YouTube video featuring audio-only features a man and woman repeatedly reacting to supposed Bigfoot howls in frightened

wonderment and "What the (blank) IS that" type comments. YouTube.

191. Michael Hexum, Abe Del Rio, north of Nashwauk, June 11, 2016 - While being covered by a news crew Bigfoot researchers Hexum (who had had two sightings in the Nashwauk area) and Del Rio (who is from St. Paul and had had Bigfoot encounters in Ohio) found a possible Bigfoot track about 20 miles north of Nashwauk. It appeared to be a right foot impression 13 1/2 inches long, six inches wide, with a possible midtarsal break. MPR News, John Enger, June 22, 2016.

192. Sammy Cleveland, Six Mile Lake near Bena, July 5-6, 2016 - A Native American man was bass fishing in the evening along the southwest shore of Six Mile Lake just offshore from a spot where he cached a canoe when he saw a Bigfoot covered in white hair and estimated to be ten feet tall (though the size of its tracks indicates this was probably an exaggeration), moving about in the shallows along the shoreline, doing something in the water with its hands, perhaps washing something or perhaps foraging for food. He had an impressively lengthy view of the creature from a distance of only about 20 yards, watching it from his canoe for up to two hours, and darkness fell before the sighting was over. He yelled at it in an attempt to make it go away but it would not leave, seeming to want to block him from coming ashore. It finally fled into the woods at the sound of his cousin arriving onshore in a vehicle. The next day he returned to the site with a video camera in the company of Bigfoot researcher Don Sherman, who was a friend of his, to see if he could find any physical evidence, narrating as he filmed the swampy woodland surroundings, and was astounded to find several clear five-toed manlike tracks with up to 5 1/2 feet between them. He expressed fear of the creature and finished the video by saying, "I better get out of here before I get eaten alive." A relative of his then posted the video on the Internet. I, the author, examined the site in both August and September and found extensive mudflats along the shoreline with water only a few inches deep, plus large numbers of frogs that led me to theorize that the creature was likely feeding on them. I also found ferns smashed

down flat to the ground near the spot where the tracks had been. A careful examination of the video reveals that two different footprints that Sammy put his hand down next to news crew Bigfoot researcher Hexum show their size are of completely different shape, suggesting that two creatures might have been present. YouTube; Bob Olson and Don Sherman; "Finding Bigfoot" episode "Bigfoot Town" on Animal Planet.

193-197. Other reports covered - most with limited information - in the area around Remer on the "Bigfoot Town" episode of "Finding Bigfoot," which all occurred prior to filming in July 2016:

* A man told of seeing and hearing a tree being shaken by a Bigfoot about 50 yards into the woods from him.

* A woman told of seeing a large and tall figure she believed to be a Bigfoot.

* A man told of seeing a Bigfoot he likened to a "walking outhouse" in its build.

* A man told of hearing the call of a Bigfoot so powerful that it moved the air around him.

*Siblings Isaac and Emily Birchem told of a sighting at their home near Backus 35 miles southwest of Remer in which they'd been looking across a lake at a deer on a hillside when suddenly a Bigfoot came running down the hill, grabbed and strangled the deer, then dragged its body back up the hill with one arm. They said the deer seemed frozen like a typical "deer in headlights" and the "Finding Bigfoot" crew theorized about how Bigfoot might use a type of infra-sound to immobilize its prey. When crewmember Cliff Barackman was taking part in a recreation of the event, he found that in running down the hill, he was not able to quickly stop at the spot where the deer was grabbed as the Bigfoot had, and overshot it.

198. Matt Moneymaker, Cliff Barackman, James "Bobo" Fay, Ranae Holland, Michael Hexum, Abe Del Rio, Remer area, July 2016 - While filming an episode of the TV show "Finding Bigfoot" a team of researchers checking out a cedar swamp area by night where Hexum had told of hearing Bigfoot vocalizations and wood knocks the previous fall had a new encounter. While walking in, they found the

trail blocked by an x-formation of small trees crossing it from opposite directions. They then did a wood knock and received an answering knock about a minute later from about a half-mile away, then briefly heard what sounded like something approaching through the woods. "Finding Bigfoot" episode "Bigfoot Town" on Animal Planet.

199. James "Bobo" Fay, Remer area, July 2016 - As a follow-up to the previous report Bobo checked out an area a few miles to the north at night and got another response to a wood knock, as well as two soft whooping sounds. "Finding Bigfoot" episode "Bigfoot Town" on Animal Planet.

200. Matt Moneymaker, Cliff Barackman, James "Bobo" Fay, Ranae Holland, Six Mile Lake near Bena, July 2016 - While continuing to film their latest episode of "Finding Bigfoot," the crew did a nighttime stakeout at the site of the Sammy Cleveland sighting with two people on land and two in a boat on the lake with a thermal imager. No sightings were made, but the two on land did a wood knocking and seemed to get a response in the form of a large branch snapping nearby. "Finding Bigfoot" episode "Bigfoot Town" on Animal Planet.

201. Name unknown, north of Deer River, late July 2016 - Limited information on a Bigfoot encounter that occurred along Highway 6 north of Deer River. Don Sherman.

202. Stephanie Ayers, Jen Kruse, Kimberly Juarez, Katie Sonmor, Mario Schmidt, Six Mile Lake area near Bena, August 20, 2016 - Members of the newly formed SheSquatchers Bigfoot research team (who all claim various levels of psychic ability) were on their first overnight wilderness excursion searching for evidence. During daylight, they found possible Bigfoot tracks in one location, but at night their intuition led them to check out another spot where they heard something large approaching them in the woods. They never saw it, but it threw rocks at them which were clearly not meant to hit them but just to land near them, flying up and over the treetops. They also recorded some distant sounds that night that they regarded as possible Bigfoot vocalizations but couldn't be sure, sounds that

could have also been those of owls. "The Calling" radio show on Para-X.com; SheSquatchers website; Personally related by the witnesses.

203. Dean Opsahl, Six Mile Lake near Bena, August 20, 2016- An associate of the author visited the site of the Sammy Cleveland sighting on the lake's southwest shore to retrieve a trail camera that had been left there a week before, but heard what sounded like a large animal moving in the brush nearby. It was not a bounding sound such as a deer makes, and it worried him enough that he left the scene without retrieving the camera. We both returned to the site the next day and looked for tracks but found none. Personally related by the witness.

204. Abe DelRio, two others, Remer area, 2016- DelRio, head of the Minnesota Bigfoot Research Team, was on an excursion searching for evidence with a couple who worked as hunting guides and had had a previous Bigfoot sighting near Leech Lake. They were sitting at a campfire by a lake at night near a spot where they had had some bait disappear when DelRio was suddenly stricken by what felt like a heart attack or anxiety attack. At the same time, the couple heard two whoops - one high and one low - come from across the lake. DelRio went to a hospital where he was found to be fine. His team has the theory that Bigfoot uses low-frequency infrasound as a defense mechanism, and he believes that is what may have given him the sudden attack. The day after the incident, he returned to the area and found an arch formation in the woods. Related by the witness at 2017 Remer Bigfoot Days festival.

205-206. Michael Hexum, (presumably) near Nashwauk, 2016- Hexum, a member of the Minnesota Bigfoot Research Team, had something throw sticks at him while in the woods one morning, and a similar incident occurred the next day with rocks thrown at him. Related by the witness at 2017 Remer Bigfoot Days festival.

207. Name(s) unknown, Werner area west of Turtle River, 2016 - A Bigfoot sighting was reported. Loren Coleman at Paracon, Shooting Star Casino Mahnomen, October 14, 2017.

208. Names unknown, Talmoon area, May 2017 - Limited informa-

tion on two women who had driven north out of the town of Deer River saw a Bigfoot cross the road in two leaps. Bob Olson.

209. Daniel Carlson, Boy Lake area, June 18, 2017 - In an Internet video, Carlson describes how a recent temperature drop and change in barometric pressure has resulted in increased Bigfoot activity around Boy Lake and records tree knocking in response to his own knocks and attempts at imitations of Bigfoot howls at night. YouTube.

210. Mike Quast, north of Talmoon, June 26, 2017 - The author found two possible Bigfoot tracks, both about eight inches long and not quite complete but both showing clear toes and rather pointed heels, about two feet apart, along a muddy trail off of Highway 6 two miles north of Talmoon in a section of brush and wildflowers just past a heavily logged area. Also, in the area were noted broken tree limbs that seemed to have been placed deliberately across trails and a teepee-like stick structure around a tree about 80 feet off the trail containing the tracks. Personal experience.

211. Name(s) unknown, Boy River area, late June or early July 2017 - Limited information on Bigfoot tracks being found. Related by the host of presentation at 2017 Remer Bigfoot Days festival.

212. Name(s) unknown, Remer area, late June or early July 2017 - Limited information on a Bigfoot sighting at a local lake. Related by the host of presentation at 2017 Remer Bigfoot Days festival.

213. Names unknown, near Remer, July 6, 2017 - Limited information on a woman hearing screams near her house thought to be those of Bigfoot, and dead spots in her lawn thought to possibly be caused by a creature relieving itself. Related by the host of presentation at 2017 Remer Bigfoot Days festival.

214. "Camden," Remer, July 7, 2017- A little boy at a presentation on Bigfoot information at the Remer Bigfoot Days festival briefly related how on the previous night, a Bigfoot had come into the campground where his family was staying and left a scratch on his stepfather's truck. Personally related by the witness at 2017 Remer Bigfoot Days festival.

215. Names unknown, near Remer, July 7 or 8, 2017 - A group of men found and filmed impressive Bigfoot tracks during the Remer

Bigfoot Days festival and reported it to the SheSquatchers research group, but they failed to note the proper directions to the site preventing any followup, and then it rained, presumably erasing the tracks. Related by Jen Kruse and Jena Grover of the SheSquatchers at the 2018 Remer Bigfoot Days festival.

216. Mike Quast, north of Talmoon, July 8, 2017 - On a follow-up visit to the site of my previous report, the author found a possible Bigfoot track 17" long in deep sawdust in the logged area near the spot where the previous tracks had been found. It was not distinct enough to show toe impressions. Further strange tree structures in the surrounding woods were also noted. Personal experience.

217. Mike Quast, north of Talmoon, October 28, 2017 - On another visit to the scene of my previous finds this author found another possible Bigfoot track of the same size and shape of the ones seen in June, about eight inches long and showing clear toe impressions, on the same trail and only about 50 feet from where the previous ones were seen. More mysterious stick structures and tree breaks were also noted, this time including healthy pine trees snapped off a few feet above the ground and looking like they'd been carefully placed, and branches bent down on either side of the trail in opposite directions as if to try and block traffic, obviously not the result of wind. Personal experience.

218-219. Names unknown, Itasca County (?), November 11, 2017 - An experience occurred with two men deer hunting, one of them a member of the "Search 4 Spirits" team, and based on this team's reporting on other experiences in Itasca County, it is presumed this one occurred there as well though it is not specified. One man sitting on a log decided to do some "grunt calls," which resulted in a response of three loud yelps followed by wood knocking coming from a swampy area less than 50 yards away. The sounds were also heard by the second man who was 100 yards away and were said to have "no human element" to them. The second man commented that he had heard something big moving past him breaking brush in the area more than once, and also that a Bigfoot sighting had occurred in the same area back in logging days "many years ago." While investigating the area and shooting video the next day on November 12th, the two men found no Bigfoot tracks but did find large branches that seemed to be pulled down to block trails. YouTube.

220. Name unknown, Remer, 2017 - A Bigfoot sighting reportedly occurred within the city limits of Remer when a 16-year-old girl was on her way to a bonfire party at night and a creature crossed the road in front of her a block away from the Remer Motel. Related by Abe DelRio during presentation at 2018 Remer Bigfoot Days festival.

221. "Randy," north of Blackduck, 2014-2017 - In an area along Hornet Road (County Road 41) a man is reported to have been finding stick structures as well as the skeletons of both deer and bears believed to be associated with Bigfoot, reported in 2017 as having been going on for the "last three or four years." Don Sherman.

222. Names unknown, south of Remer, February 19, 2018 - Two men driving on Draper Tower Road south of Remer reported encountering a Bigfoot that was evidently in an agitated state and tossing large logs into the air, some of which were becoming caught up in the surrounding treetops. The men took photos of some of the logs in the trees but did not manage to photograph the creature. Accounts vary as to whether the men actually saw the creature or just heard it and saw the logs being thrown up. Pine Cone Press-Citizen, March 31, 2018; Abe DelRio.

223. Mike Quast, north of Talmoon, May 6, 2018 - On yet another exploration of the site of this author's previous finds at this site, another possible small Bigfoot track was found in sawdust in the open logged area near where the previous small tracks had been found in the more wooded area, this time measuring nearly ten inches as opposed to the earlier length of only eight inches, suggesting that it was either not the same creature or that the earlier young creature had grown in the nearly year-long interval since the first find. The toes seemed more widely splayed than before with a more prominent big toe. Personal experience.

224. Mike Quast, north of Talmoon, May 26, 2018 - Three weeks after the previous report this author found further evidence at the same site in the form of three possible Bigfoot tracks measuring 18"

long in the trail through the open logged area as well as more odd tree structures, trail blockages, and a small hollow stump that had two hand-sized clumps of deer hide placed inside it. Personal experience.

225-226. Abe DelRio and "Bill," others, near Remer, July 6-7, 2018 - While attending the 2018 Remer Bigfoot Days festival Abe and another member of the Minnesota Bigfoot Research Team went to an undisclosed location at night to do Bigfoot calls and wood knocking and got a response in the form of one wood knock. The next day they heard from another group of people who had heard wood knocks in the same place between 2 and 5 AM Personally related by Abe DelRio during a presentation at 2018 Remer Bigfoot Days festival.

227. Michael Hexum, near Nashwauk, date unknown - A man who had had an earlier Bigfoot sighting as a teenager in 1970 was living in a primitive cabin in the winter and would go down to a frozen lake each morning to gather water. One morning he had a second sighting of a tall hairy creature walking on the ice far across the lake, an experience which made him dwell on his earlier sighting and decide to become a Bigfoot researcher. MPR News, John Enger, June 22, 2016.

228. Michael Hexum, three others, (presumably) near Nashwauk, date unknown - Another incident involving Hexum - now a member of the Minnesota Bigfoot Research Team - occurred when three women he knew pestered him into taking them Bigfoot hunting, and when he did, so they got an answer to wood knocking, which frightened them. Related by Hexum at 2017 Remer Bigfoot Days festival.

229-230. Michael Hexum, location unknown but within this region, dates unknown - Hexum also reports having twice been affected by low-frequency infrasound, which his team believes is used by Bigfoot as a defense mechanism. One of these times resulted in him feeling as if he nearly had a heart attack. Related by the witness at 2017 Remer Bigfoot Days festival.

231. Names unknown, Leech Lake area, date unknown- A couple who work as hunting guides, known to the head of the Minnesota Bigfoot Research Team Abe DelRio reportedly had a Bigfoot sighting

near Leech Lake. Related by Abe DelRio at 2017 Remer Bigfoot Days festival.

232. Anonymous, International Falls area, date unknown - A young boy reportedly saw a Bigfoot cross a country road "many years ago" (reported in 1996). He told his elders and showed them the place. Some hair was found on a barbed-wire fence. Ed Trimble.

233. Anonymous, International Falls area, date unknown - Some friends reportedly had a hunting cabin where something would make noises outside the door and leave strands of hair behind. One time they jerked the door open in time to see the backside of a Bigfoot running away upright into the woods. "Loped" was the word used to describe its movement. Ed Trimble, related to him by brother of witness.

234-235. Anonymous, Red Lake County, July, year unknown - A five-year-old child and a friend were inside a house working on a jigsaw puzzle when he or she (gender unknown) looked out a window and saw a black creature seven feet tall with a bulky build walking between two bushes, locking eyes with the child for just an instant. Panic ensued, and after falling over from a chair, the child glanced out one more time to see the creature running away into nearby woods. Family members told the child it was probably a bear, although an aunt had reported seeing a Bigfoot eating from her apple trees about seven years earlier. GCBRO website.

236. Joseph L., near Walker, date unknown - Limited information on a North Dakota man who had a Bigfoot sighting in that state and also possibly heard one of the creatures while fishing near Walker in Minnesota. Related by e-mail by Rona Johnson of the Grand Forks Herald.

237. Mel A., Cass Lake-Turtle River area, date unknown - A man found a huge footprint in mud far back along a logging road, very long and very fresh and showing such details as the toes and the fine lines in the sole of the foot. He brought a friend in to show it to and intended to come again and to take pictures and make a cast, but it rained before he got a chance. Ed Trimble.

238. Anonymous, Lake Winibigoshish area in Itasca County, date

unknown - Some people were driving at night on County Road 9 or the Wini Dam Road when a Bigfoot crossed the road in front of them, causing them to slow down to avoid hitting it, moving at a slow pace, and looking at them as if unafraid, taken as a menacing attitude. Of special note was that its eyes did not reflect light and that it had huge legs. Bigfootencounters website.

239. Don Sherman, Nushka Lake near Bena, date unknown - Limited information on Bigfoot researcher Sherman making a cast of a Bigfoot track 15" long found at Nushka Lake. Don Sherman, Bob Olson.

240. John Green and son, Boy River, date unknown - A man and his son fishing from the Boy River bridge on Highway 8 thought they saw a large black tree stump until it suddenly turned out to be a living upright creature that took off running to the south faster than any football player. Don Sherman.

241. Names unknown, Cass Lake area, date unknown - An anonymous source told Bigfoot researcher Don Sherman that he knew of an elderly Native American woman and her daughter who found the body of a dead Bigfoot and buried it. The source refused to give Sherman any further details. Don Sherman.

242. Don Sherman and friend, near Inger, date unknown- Limited information on Bigfoot researcher Sherman and a friend finding a large impression in the ground they believed to be Bigfoot related along Pine Grove Road (#158) near Inger and seeing a large tree shaking nearby. Bob Olson.

243. Name(s) unknown, near Inger, date unknown - Limited information on another Bigfoot track being found along Pine Grove Road (#158). Bob Olson.

244. Name(s) unknown, near Inger, March 22, year unknown - Limited information on a family finding Bigfoot tracks along County Road 146 near Inger. Bob Olson.

245. Anonymous, Red Lake Indian Reservation, date unknown - Jeff Weise, perpetrator of the deadly Red Lake school shooting on March 21, 2005, had previously written about Bigfoot existing on the reservation, including a sighting by a man who worked in tribal

government with a cousin of his. The man was out in the wilderness doing a spiritual fast when he saw a Bigfoot in a swampy area picking plants out of the water and slinging them over its shoulder, plants that were used for medicinal purposes by Indian shamans. Cryptomundo website, Loren Coleman; Above Top Secret Forum.

246. Name unknown, Red Lake area, date unknown - Researchers from the team Searching for Bigfoot Inc., led by researcher Tom Biscardi collected Bigfoot stories while attending a wedding on the Red Lake Reservation in May 2007, including one involving a young man who was out in the woods shooting video after receiving a camera as a gift and was filming some eagles when he followed them swooping down toward the ground and then caught a Bigfoot coming out of some woods dragging some kind of dead animal behind it. His family reported the incident to the DNR and claimed that they confiscated the film. They had made a second copy that they kept secret, but repeated viewings of it had caused it to become quite blurry. The researchers contacted the DNR about the film and were told that they had no knowledge of it, but reportedly also contradicted themselves and admitted to having made another copy of it. Searchingforbifoot.com website; Don Sherman.

247. Name(s) unknown, near Walker, date unknown - Limited information on casts of two Bigfoot tracks being made in the Hungry Gulch area. Bob Olson.

248. Name(s) unknown, near Inger, date unknown - Limited information on a Bigfoot encounter occurring along Pine Grove Road near Inger. Bob Olson.

249. Jesse Hirschback, south of Bovey, date unknown- A 14-year-old boy was walking along Highway 70 when he began to hear something walking and shaking trees moving in the nearby woods keeping pace with him, stopping when he would stop. Eventually, it came out of the woods into a field, and he saw that it was a creature of typical Bigfoot description which was shaking a tree but then went back into the woods when it realized it was seen. Bob Olson; Lady Ocalat's Paranormal Investigations website.

250. Jim Monk, Big Sandy Lake area near Jacobson, date

unknown - A man on a canoeing and camping trip pitched camp along the Mississippi River near Big Sandy Lake smelled a horrible odor just before bedding down for the night and thought there must be a dead animal nearby. The smell went away, and about 45 minutes later, he was lying in his tent when he heard grunts and screams right outside the tent. He grabbed a flashlight and pistol and opened the tent flap but could see nothing, hearing the sounds repeat from farther away. He got no sleep that night and left the area at first light. Bob Olson; Lady Ocalat's Paranormal Investigations website.

251. Name(s) unknown, Cass Lake, date unknown - Limited information on Bigfoot researcher Don Sherman investigating a Bigfoot incident at the Knutson Dam Recreation area on Cass Lake.

252. Bob Olson, Carey Lake near Hibbing, date unknown - Bigfoot researcher Olson reports that while on an investigation at Carey Lake, he attempted to communicate with area Bigfoot creatures with wood knocking and got five knocks in response to his five knocks. Bob Olson.

253. John C. and son, Carey Lake area near Hibbing, date unknown - Limited information on a Hibbing city engineer and his son having a Bigfoot sighting. Bob Olson.

254. Jody Hansen, Carey Lake near Hibbing, date unknown - Among other experiences in this area by Bigfoot enthusiast Hansen were deer carcasses found with the rib cages torn open and the hearts and livers missing, believed to be fed on by a Bigfoot. No other animals would scavenge on them. Bob Olson.

255. James W., Ball Club area, date unknown - Limited information on a man hearing a scream and the sound of crashing brush. Bob Olson.

256. Aaron R., Deer River, date unknown - Limited information on a man seeing a Bigfoot while standing guard at the White Oak Casino. Bob Olson.

257-262. Names unknown, Bemidji area, dates unknown- Limited information on a family having approximately six Bigfoot sightings in the area of Power Dam Road in northeast Bemidji, the head of the family being a Medivac helicopter pilot out of Bemidji. Bob Olson.

263. Jody Hansen, Carey Lake near Hibbing, date unknown - Limited information on a Bigfoot enthusiast who often searched for evidence in this area of past reports trying to communicate with tree knocking and getting an extensive series of knocks in response. Bob Olson.

264. Names unknown, northwest of Deer River, dates unknown- Limited information on sightings in a location eight to ten miles up Highway 46 from Deer River, related by a tipster. John P., Bob Olson.

265. "Tom" and wife, between Akeley and Walker, date unknown - A husband and wife were camping along Howard Lake Road when a Bigfoot reportedly came up to their tent, let out a scream then ran off and screamed a second time. Bob Olson.

266. Anonymous, between Big Falls and Deer River, date unknown - A Bigfoot sighting was reported somewhere between these two towns, which are connected by Highway 6, involving a dark brown creature with eyes that glowed red or orange. Bob Olson.

267. Names unknown, Bena area, date unknown - Limited information on Bigfoot tracks said to have been observed near the Bug-O-Nay-Ge-Shig Native American school, which triggered talk amongst the students about other Bigfoot reports they knew of in the area. Bob Olson.

268. Shari M. and Karen R., Blackberry area in Itasca County, winter, date unknown - Two women walking in woods near the Blackberry Store discovered Bigfoot tracks along a road and field and were able to follow them for about half a mile. The tracks were in deep snow, and five to six feet apart. Bob Olson.

269. Larry T., Gillette Lake in Hubbard County, date unknown - A man was camping at a DNR campground near Steamboat Road when a Bigfoot stuck its head in his tent. He also later saw and heard it in the nearby woods. Other reports were known involving people leaving this campground in the middle of the night due to Bigfoot encounters. Bob Olson.

270. Name(s) unknown, near Hibbing, date unknown- Limited information - A forester who provided information for some Bigfoot reports in the Arrowhead region also knew of someone claiming to

have seen a family of Bigfoot creatures near Hibbing. Bob Olson. 272-273.

271-272. Erica F., one other, north of Walker, March 5-6, year unknown - A woman was driving to her job at the Northern Lights Casino in Walker and was about eight miles from town when she saw a Bigfoot come out of the woods briefly on the opposite side of the road from her, then step back in. There was also a farm at the spot. The previous day another woman a quarter mile away had seen large tracks in snow while walking along a tree line. Bob Olson.

273. Names unknown, Walker area, date unknown - A YouTube video posted on November 9, 2011 depicts a couple driving between Walker and Nevis at night, documenting road conditions after a first snow, with the man humorously mentioning that that night they had met a man who told them that Bigfoot was being seen in the area and that he and his father had abandoned their plans for a duck hunt at some point after having a sighting of one of the creatures. YouTube.

274. Name unknown, Hungry Gulch area near Walker, date unknown - A man was camping when a Bigfoot stuck its head into his tent. He smacked it in the face and reported that it was like hitting a rock. The creature then had an altercation with the man's Black Lab and threw the dog over the tent. Don Sherman.

275. Tom S. and wife, Howard Lake between Akely and Walker, date unknown - A couple was camping at about three AM when something approached their tent and let out a scream, then ran off and screamed again. They believed it was a Bigfoot. Bob Olson.

276. Sally S., Togo area, date unknown - Limited information on a woman having a Bigfoot sighting. John S., Bob Olson.

277. Name unknown, Bena area, date unknown - A waitress at the cafe in Bena told the SheSquatchers Bigfoot research team when they were there for a town meeting to gather information on Bigfoot that they should come to her home because she saw Bigfoot often. She added that her sightings were always accompanied by the presence of glowing green balls of light floating in the air. She was quoted as saying, "When green lights appear, Bigfoot is near." SheSquatchers led by Stephanie Ayers, Jen Kruse, and Kimberly Juarez.

278. Anonymous, Laporte area, date unknown - A female witness from the previous 2008 Laporte report added that her father had a friend who had claimed to have seen a manlike/apelike creature run across a road early in the morning on his way to work at a logging camp. This was said to have been over 20 years before, so sometime before 1988. BFRO website.

279-284. Limited information cases from the Central North region mentioned briefly in the files of Bob Olson, dates unknown: *A Bigfoot encounter of some kind involving a man named Josh from the Bovey store.

*Jim W. heard a scream and cracking branches. *Cam J. heard a "hooty scream."

*Marrel D., Bigfoot encounter in Bovey area.

*A snowmobiler saw a Bigfoot on a trail.

*A Bigfoot crossed West Bank Road near Deer River just behind a car, making an instant believer out of the driver.

285. "Avery," Remer, date unknown - A little girl at a presentation on Bigfoot information at the Remer Bigfoot Days festival related how after lunch one day at her school, her class went outside to try and spot animals, and she saw a large creature bigger than a bear and without a protruding muzzle stand up nearby and walk away. She believed it to be a Bigfoot. Related by witness at 2017 Remer Bigfoot Days festival.

286. Russ Heinz, Boy Lake area, date unknown - A person posting a comment to an Internet video about Bigfoot sounds stated that he had heard the same sounds while staying at a friend's cabin on Boy Lake. YouTube.

287-288. Names unknown, Itasca County, dates unknown - An Internet video by a group called "Search 4 Spirits" featured an interview with a woman who stated that she and her ex- husband had both had Bigfoot sightings in the same location at a lake somewhere in Itasca County at unspecified times. Her sighting was while riding a horse along the shore and involved a creature about eight feet tall covered in brown hair standing on the far shore about 200 yards away just looking at her for a moment before it waked into the surrounding woods and disappeared. She said she rode over to that area to look for it but never saw it again. Her husband's sighting from about the same spot she placed as around the same time or perhaps a year later and happened while he was fishing at the lake, again involving a creature just watching him from the far shore. He did not tell her about his sighting until much later. YouTube.

289-290. Names unknown, Itasca County, dates unknown - In the same video as the previous reports, the "Search 4 Spirits" group featured another interview with a man who knew another couple who had had two separate Bigfoot experiences. The wife's experience was a close sighting of a creature crossing Highway 38 from west to east while driving, close enough that she could clearly see its face and an experience that scared her enough to not want to drive that road for months. The husband's experience was of finding Bigfoot tracks somewhere in the county, details unspecified. YouTube.

291. Name unknown, Togo area, date unknown- In the same video as the previous reports the same man who related the previous reports also stated that he knew about a Bigfoot sighting at an unspecified time by a man who had run the "Junction Bar" in Togo along Highway 65 in the 1970s and early 80s, and that "authorities" had come and "compression tested" tracks that were found and determined that the creature he saw must have weighed about 500 pounds. YouTube.

CLEARWATER COUNTY

(This section contains many reports by Ed Trimble, an experienced woodsman who found himself in the midst of Bigfoot activity for an extended period and documented it in meticulous detail as well as collecting other peoples' reports.)

1. Anonymous, Buckboard Hills, 1920s - A rumor tells of a hunter who

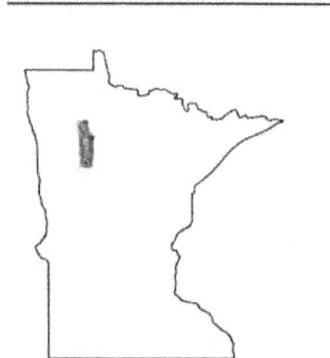

shot and killed a Bigfoot and then
buried it to avoid legal trouble because he feared it might be human.
Personally related by anonymous witness in another report.

2. Ed Trimble, Zerkel area near Mud Lake, November 1957- Ed's
first possible finding of Bigfoot tracks occurred when he was out trapping in a snowstorm and came across very large bipedal-looking
tracks with a long stride in deep snow. Personally related by the
witness.

3. Ed Trimble, Zerkel area near Mud Lake, September 1960 - Ed
and his wife had been visiting neighbors, and as she drove home, he
decided to walk through the woods. Along the way he came across a
clearing full of tall grass that was all wallowed down flat as if very
large animals had been rolling around, but he found no hoof tracks
to indicate it was done by deer. Personally related by the witness.

4. Anonymous, McKenzie Lake area in Buckboard Hills, late
October 1960 - While off duty from logging, a man was doing some
hunting at about 4 PM when he suddenly smelled a foul odor that he
compared to the waste lagoons on a chicken farm. He then saw a
bipedal creature sitting on a log about 200 yards away, about seven
feet tall, weighing around 400 pounds and covered all over with short
brown hair. It was eating a fish, holding it in both hands, and when it
saw him, it let out a screech like that of a lynx, dropped the fish, and
ran away into the woods. When he went to the spot, he saw its tracks
in patchy snow, 14-16" long, the stride shorter in thick brush but
longer in open areas. He also found the partially eaten fish which had
a fishing lure in its mouth, as if it had broken free from someone's
line and then died and washed ashore where the creature presumably found it. Personally related by the witness; Ed Trimble.

5-6. Daniel Tweten and mother, between Leonard and Shevlin,
January 1963 - A 13-year- old boy was out gathering firewood with his
mother when they saw four-toed tracks about 12" long in the snow.
The mother got very afraid and insisted they leave the area immediately, not tell anyone about the tracks, and ordered her son to stay out
of the woods. This lasted for a week to ten days, but then the boy was
out squirrel hunting and came across more four-toed tracks, this time

14-16" in length and traveling in a very straight line with a stride of up to five feet. At one point, they crossed a barbed-wire fence without breaking stride. He was fascinated and followed them for two to three miles until he lost them atop a hill where the snow was sparse. It had grown late, and he had to bed down there, returning the next day to a very upset mother who hadn't known where he was. Personally related by the witness to Ed Trimble.

7. Ed Trimble, near Zerkel, Fall 1965 - In response to a sheep being killed by what he thought was a mountain lion, Ed was armed and staked out in a tree at night when he heard mysterious bipedal-sounding footsteps in the crunchy leaves at around three AM They approached, paused, then departed in a path that took them over a barbed wire fence without breaking stride and with no thud as would be made by jumping over. Years later, after becoming convinced that Bigfoot was in the area, he thought this was probably an early encounter with one. Personally related by the witness.

8. David Sunderland, near Zerkel, mid-October 1968 or 1970 - A young man was in a field by a wooded area waiting for some companions who were duck hunting nearby when he noticed a large bipedal figure walking across the field toward the woods and swinging its arms a quarter to a half-mile away. He could not figure out why a man would have been in that spot, and when the figure passed by a particular tree; he realized it was much bigger than a man. The tree was around 20 feet tall, and the figure was about half that. In light of Bigfoot experiences in the area in later years he came to believe that was probably what he saw, and a truly gigantic one. Personally related by the witness; Ed Trimble.

9. Gerald & Edna Wraa, near Leonard, 1970-1972 - An episode occurred in which something visited a couple's property on a regular basis for two years, always at night and never seen but uttering a high-pitched scream and leaving very strange bipedal three-toed tracks, 11" long, four inches of which was the toes. The depth of the tracks could not be duplicated even by a heavy man, with the heel and the tips of the toes sinking in the deepest, and the stride was one yard. Also, of note was a sickeningly foul odor that would accompany

the creature's visits, so strong that it would permeate the house, and there seemed to be nowhere they could get away from it. Strange lights were sometimes seen flitting about at treetop level during this period as well which made the couple suspect there might be something other-worldly about their visitor. Personally related by the witnesses to Ed Trimble.

10. Wayne Thompson and Bill Rutherford, near Zerkel, Fall 1971 or 1972 - Two friends were grouse hunting and had just gone about 75 yards down a logging road when they smelled a strong skunky odor and then noticed some bushes rustling about 75 feet away for 10 or 15 seconds. Then they heard whatever it was walking away with distinct bipedal footsteps and did not think it could be a bear. Personally related by the witness; Ed Trimble.

11. Leslie Olson and wife, near Zerkel, August 1974 - On a pig farm, something happened while the resident couple was away that caused a panic among the pigs, with 78 of them ranging in weight from 150 to 190 pounds crowding their way into a small enclosed room inside their barn and piling on top of each other and dying of suffocation. When found, the survivors were huddled in the barn shaking with fright. This was such a bizarre incident that Bigfoot involvement was considered when reports of the creatures in the area became widely known years later. Personally related by the witness; Ed Trimble.

12. Ed Trimble, near Zerkel, early Fall 1977 - Ed was out on one of his frequent walks in the woods with his dog when they heard something large crashing through the brush approaching them, so they crouched down to watch. Whatever it was moved in a straight line, smashing its way through thick brush where it could have gone around, which was not behavior typical of a bear. Before it reached their hiding place, it veered off toward a nearby blacktop highway. Ed was thinking it might be a moose, but when it crossed the highway, he heard no hoofbeats. Years later, when he became convinced that Bigfoot was in the area, he thought this was probably an early encounter with one. Personally related by the witness.

13. Terry Johnson and wife, Falk Lake northeast of Clearbrook, mid-June or early July 1980 - A couple was doing some cement work

at a newly built house when they heard a large animal moving in the brush along the lakeshore about 150 feet away, accompanied by a strong smell like "the lion house at the zoo." A heavy breathing sound was also noted. They heard the sounds for about four minutes but never saw the animal. Personally related by the witness to Ed Trimble.

14. Anonymous, Alida-Becida area, early 1980s - During a widespread organized search for a missing person, a local farmer and woodsman taking part in the search reported seeing a human-like figure at the edge of some woods near the Mississippi River about 40 acres away in fading light. When questioned later in light of area, Bigfoot reports, he said he could not be sure if he'd seen a human or a human-like creature. Personally related by the witness to Ed Trimble.

15. Alf J. Berg, Lindberg Lake area south of Clearbrook, Summer 1984 - An elderly man driving in daylight hours saw an upright creature six or seven feet tall covered in long dark gray hair running through a meadow about 50 yards away. Of special note was the hair on its neck and shoulders which was at least 14" long. He had it in sight for less than a minute before it ran into nearby woods. Personally related by the witness to Ed Trimble.

16. Lela or Lila L., near Nay Tah Waush, 1987 - A Native American woman is said to have seen a Bigfoot while driving, running on or near the road ahead of her. In looking at her speedometer, she noted that she was going 30 miles per hour and was not gaining on the creature. Related by uncle and aunt of witness by Ed Trimble.

17. Ed Trimble, near Zerkel, December 1988 - Just after a bad storm, Ed found a strange animal bed beneath a fallen pine tree, five feet long, three feet wide and recently used. It was unlike anything he had seen before in his years of woodland experience. Personally related by witness.

18. Terry Johnson, Falk Lake northeast of Clearbrook, 1989 - The witness from the earlier 1980 report had another experience with strange sounds, this time coming from about a half-mile away from his home. It sounded like three coon dogs running a very large animal which was crashing through brush, with tremendous power,

snapping what had to be two to three-inch thick saplings. Personally related by the witness to Ed Trimble.

19. Kim Fultz, near Zerkel, early 1990 - A woman was cross country skiing near her home when she came across "huge and scary looking" tracks in the snow that frightened her into returning home immediately. After seeing drawings of probable Bigfoot tracks found later the same year by Ed Trimble, who lived two miles from her, she concluded the tracks she saw were probably made by the same thing. Personally related by the witness; Ed Trimble.

20. Ed Trimble, near Zerkel, June 1990 - In his years of experience in the woods, Ed had seen many times the effects of loggers, campers, etc., leaving food in plastic bags tied to branches in an effort to keep it away from animals, and animals' attempts at getting at it anyway in various ways. Just once, six months before his first major find of Bigfoot tracks, he saw such a bag that had been gotten at in a way he had never seen before that seemed to rule out bear, raccoon, squirrel or anything else he could think of, and in retrospect, he suspected Bigfoot. Personally related by witness.

21. Ed Trimble, near Zerkel, July 1990 - Ed, an avid beekeeper, occasionally dealt with raids on his beehives by bears. At this time, he found that something had knocked over and fed upon some old honey boxes and seemed to avoid the fresh hives which were only a few feet away as if wanting to avoid the bees, which bears generally do not have a problem with. Again, in light of discoveries a few months later, he suspected Bigfoot in retrospect. Personally related by witness.

22. Ed Trimble, near Zerkel, December 9, 1990 - What convinced Ed beyond doubt that Bigfoot-type creatures lived in the local woods were two sets of bipedal tracks he found in shallow snow on a frozen man-made pond about 100 yards from his house. They were not human-like tracks typical of Bigfoot, which led to speculation of a possible subspecies. The larger tracks were 8 5/8" inches long and nearly circular, while the smaller were more oval-shaped and 7 3/4" long. Both had two large toes and three tiny ones that only left dime-sized impressions, apparently with hair growing underneath the

small toes. Oddly, the large toes were on the outside corner of the feet instead of the inside as with human and most animal tracks. They were on the ice for a distance of about 47 yards, the larger creature staying very near shore and not striding over 24" as if being careful, but the smaller one venturing a bit farther out. They could not have been bear tracks as there were no claw marks and no separation between the toes and the rest of the foot. Ed reported the find to the DNR, who referred him to this author. The experience caused him to delve deeply into the subject of Bigfoot and to begin to research the history of other reports in his area. Personally related by the witness; Bagley Farmers Independent. March 27, 1991.

23. Anonymous, northern Clearwater County, 1990 - Limited information on the son of the witness from the October 1960 sighting having had one of his own while herding cattle. The Bigfoot he saw was said to have reached out to a dog as if to pet it, causing the dog to cringe and run away, and the creature then doing the same. The father apparently called a hotline run by the California Bigfoot Organization at that time to report this, which was odd as he did not mention his son's sighting to this author when I interviewed him. Bigfoot Co-Op newsletter; Ed Trimble.

24. Mike Powers, between Mud Lake and Long Lake Park near Zerkel, March 1991 - A man was checking on some newly acquired property near Mud Lake, and as it was a nice day he decided to walk to the lake itself. On the way, he found a line of tracks crossing the dirt trail. Most were not distinct, but the one in the center of the trail was perfectly clear, human-like and 18" long or longer. He thought it was a prank until he heard of Ed Trimble's track find three miles to the north. This report indicated that the two possible types of Bigfoot inhabited the same area at the same time. Personally related by the witness to Ed Trimble.

25. Ed Trimble, near Zerkel, March 25, 1991 - At 3 PM, Ed found tracks that had been made during the night, indicating that the smaller of the creatures that had visited his property in December had returned, and he was able to follow them for a great distance through the snow. The creature had come very close to his house,

where it crossed a barbed wire fence and also kept a couple of rings of tracks where it had turned itself around looking in all directions, then moved off into a pasture area, possibly because of the barking of Ed's dog, which he had noticed that night. In the pasture were some large water-filled potholes which the creature approached but would not cross as if it didn't want to get wet. The tracks also indicated that there was a lump or scar on the bottom of the left foot. From the pasture area, the tracks continued on into the thick woods, and Ed estimated that he saw well over 1,000 tracks that day, probably closer to 2,000. It was at this point that he dubbed the smaller of the two creatures "Junior" and the larger one "Mama." Personally related by the witness.

26. Mike Quast, Rock Lake in Buckboard Hills, June 15, 1991 - This author was searching for evidence, and while staying at Arrow Point Campground on Rock Lake, I was checking the shoreline for tracks when I came across some in the deep wet mud where the land met the water, roughly human-like in shape in a spot where a person would not have been likely to have been walking. They were in two sizes, ten inches and eight inches long, the smaller ones showing just a hint of toe impressions. About 30 feet beyond the tracks lay the remains of a large dead turtle, with no flesh remaining and the top shell missing as if something had torn it off. Personal experience.

27. Ed Trimble, near Zerkel, August 1991 - Further damage occurred to Ed's beehives, such a shad occurred in July 1990, perpetrated by something that did not act like a bear, attacking old unoccupied hives instead of the fresh ones. This time the damage was more pronounced, and it was clear that there were no claw marks in the wood, indicating something with hands had grasped it while eating out the old honeycomb. Personally related by the witness.

28. Ed and Nova Trimble, near Zerkel, August 1991 - While staying up until three AM typing up some of his information, Ed heard three occurrences of a high-pitched call outside spaced 30 to 45 minutes apart and lasting only a couple of seconds. His wife also heard them. They did not sound like any animal Ed was familiar with. Personally related by the witness.

29. Anonymous, McKenzie Lake area in Buckboard Hills, Fall 1991 - Limited information on a man and his uncle in a pickup truck, having been doing some logging having a sighting of an upright brown hairy creature about seven feet tall crossing a road. Ed Trimble.

30. Ed Trimble, near Zerkel, April 12, 1992 - While on one of his regular walks, Ed came across what looked like the tracks of the more traditional Bigfoot with human-like feet near his pasture area, but small ones only eight inches long with very narrow heels. They were in patchy snow that did not allow for following them very far. This was the first indication of both types of creature setting foot on his personal property. Personally related by the witness.

31. "P.J.M." and family, outskirts of Clearbrook, May 8, 1992 - At about dusk, a family that was renting a farmhouse noticed two normally docile dogs as well as several cattle in a pasture were acting agitated and thought a bear must be prowling about. The next day as they were walking on a nearby wooded trail they found strange tracks in mud approaching the house, about 10" long and somewhat manlike but with only three toes. During the early summer, there were other such disturbances as well as people smelling a manure or sulfur-type odor, and once some children who had climbed up on to the roof thought they saw something dark lurking in some bushes. Bigfootencounters website.

32. Name unknown, Shevlin area, Summer 1992 - Limited information on an elderly hermit-like man who kept a tame deer as a pet, was fond of whiskey, and claimed to see Bigfoot around his home regularly. Related by a relative of this author, heard as a rumor.

33. Ed Trimble, near Zerkel, January 27, 1993 - Ed was out on snowshoes near his property when he found footprints in the snow with a three-foot stride, but they were old and melted and he couldn't be sure about them. Personally related by the witness.

34. Ed Trimble, near Zerkel, April 7, 1993 - Ed found another footprint crossing a muddy pickup truck track on a trail near his property, about 11 1/4" long. It was the first he found in mud rather than snow. Personally related by the witness.

35-36. Ed Trimble, near Zerkel, late May-early June 1993 - Twice within three weeks, Ed found tracks in the same location as the previous report, about 11" long with a four-foot stride and the same narrow heel as seen in his April 1992 find of eight-inch tracks as if a young creature had grown that much in a year. Personally related by the witness.

37. Ed Trimble, near Zerkel, June 17, 1993 - Two of the 11" tracks turned up while Ed was working on building up the clay dike by his manmade pond, less than 24 hours old when found. One was in the new clay on the dike, and the other was 15 1/2 feet away at the edge of some swamp grass. Ed thought the creature had been startled and had made a standing broad jump of that distance. Personally related by the witness.

38. Mike Quast, near Zerkel, June 21, 1993 - While camping near Ed's property at about 10 PM, this author heard a sudden outburst of loud "Woop Woop" type vocalizations coming from about a quarter-mile away, like an Indian war cry with the voice of a police siren. It lasted for 20-30 seconds, then repeated for about 15 seconds three or four minutes later a little farther away. I was unsure if it was one creature or two calling back and forth. Personal experience.

39. Ed Trimble, near Zerkel, June 24, 1993 - While continuing to work on his clay dike Ed found that something had broken off a stick that he had placed upright to show the depth of the water and left the broken-off end on some rocks.

40. Ed Trimble, near Zerkel, mid-July 1993 - The tracks of "Junior" returned on the clay dike, not seen since 1991 and the size they had been then. In one spot, just some toe prints had smeared the clay, but nearby was a whole print. This was confirmation that the two types of creatures did not just share the general area but visited the exact same spots. Personally related by witness.

41. Ed Trimble, near Zerkel, July 23, 1993 - More "Junior" tracks appeared on the dike, one left and one right, with a stride of 38" if made at the same time, but Ed could not be sure of that. Personally related by the witness.

42. Ed Trimble, near Zerkel, August 5, 1993 - Just before dark, Ed

heard a call he was unfamiliar with, a low-pitched cry followed by a series of whoops, sounding not far off from his home. Personally related by the witness.

43. Ed Trimble, near Zerkel, August 11, 1993- Just after 8 PM, Ed heard the same sounds again in about the same place, and this time what sounded like a second creature joined in with the first. Personally related by the witness.

44. Ed Trimble, near Zerkel, early September 1993 - Ed found another of the small manlike tracks in mud crossing a ditch he'd dug to bring water to his pond. Personally related by the witness.

45. Ed Trimble, near Zerkel, early September 1993 - Yet another of the small man-like tracks turned up. Personally related by the witness.

46. Mike Quast, near Zerkel, October 7, 1993- While exploring Ed's property, this author found possible partial tracks in two different spots. Personal experience.

47. Ed Trimble, near Zerkel, late March 1994 - Ed heard another strange call, four long cries, each lasting seven or eight seconds and almost overlapping, without the usual whoops. Personally related by the witness.

48. Mike Quast and Kathy Keating, near Rock Lake in Buckboard Hills, June 4, 1994 - This author found a possible Bigfoot track 11" long crossing a trail, the toes indistinct, shaped completely different from tracks of the same length found on the Trimble property, the heel being wide. A friend camping with me also saw it. Personal experience.

49. Ed Trimble, near Zerkel, early September 1994 - During a time when cattle were pastured in the area where many of the tracks had been turning up, Ed continued to explore it. On a pleasant afternoon, he found three small tracks in a muddy area that the cows had not disturbed, and then heard a mysterious half-second whistle come from about 60 yards away that he described as sounding like a person blowing across a shell casing. Personally related by witness.

50. Ed Trimble, near Zerkel, late April 1995 - Ed found another narrow-heeled manlike track in the pasture area, now measuring 11

7/8" in length suggesting continued growth of the young creature. This would turn out to be Ed's final discovery of Bigfoot evidence. Personally related by witness.

51. Mike Quast and Alan Weaver, Buckboard Hills, May 20, 1995 - While exploring logging trails this author and a friend found a possible Bigfoot track 14" long and hourglass-shaped, partial toe impressions separated from the rest of the print by a pressure ridge at the edge of a deep trench gouged across trail presumably by logging equipment. About five feet down near the bottom of the trench, what appeared to be a heel mark, was impressed into the nearly vertical slope. This was not far from the June 1994 track find. Personal experience.

52-53. R.A. Gilbertsen, near Zerkel, May and June 1997 - During two visits to Ed Trimble's home a Bigfoot enthusiast reported finding three possible Bigfoot tracks and also "territory markers." The tracks showed two toes, one large and one small. Personally reported by witness.

54. C.L.C., southwest of Clearbrook, late November or early December 1997 - A friend of Bigfooter R. A. Gilbertsen saw a very large creature with black and white hair running very fast across a frozen slough 50-75 yards away and thought he saw four legs. Gilbertsen investigated a few months later and found what appeared to be Bigfoot tracks 17" long and showing four or five toes frozen beneath the ice. In other places, a second set of smaller tracks was visible. The two men tried to follow the tracks and found them sporadically for about a mile and a half before the terrain became impassible. The thought was of an adult Bigfoot running with a juvenile one concealed behind it, but the legs of both being visible. Related by R.A. Gilbertsen by letter.

55. Mike Quast and two others, Buckboard Hills, October 3, 1998 - While exploring a spot with two friends where a hillside had been dug away to harvest gravel, forming a nearly vertical cliff, this author found three human-like tracks about 13" long and showing vague toe impressions in the soft gravel at the base. It appeared that the track-maker had started to climb up, then found the slope too steep and

jumped back down - not stepped down, as the tracks only went in one direction. Personal experience.

56. Anonymous, Tulaby Lake area, 1990s - Limited information on a possible Bigfoot sighting by a young boy near the Tulaby Lake village. Ed Trimble.

57. Anonymous, Buckboard Hills, mid-winter, 1990s - Limited information on a young logger who saw possible Bigfoot tracks by a small deep lake somewhere in the area. Ed Trimble.

58. Anonymous, Waptus Lake area in Buckboard Hills, late 1990s - A man reported knowing about an incident involving two snowmobilers in which one saw a hairy arm reach out of the woods and try to grab the other as they passed by. Anonymous source.

59. Mike Quast and two others, McKenzie Lake area in Buckboard Hills, June 20, 2000- While searching for evidence with two friends, this author found two tracks at the edge of a gravel road where it passed a cabin that used to stand near McKenzie Lake, one whole and the other blurred and partial. They greatly resembled the roundish tracks seen by Ed Trimble in the early 1990s and would have been the larger of the two sizes, or the creature Ed called "Mama," making this the only time those tracks were seen in the Buckboards or anywhere else away from the area around Ed's property. Personal experience.

60. Miff S., near Shevlin, Fall 2001 - A man driving saw a bipedal creature six to seven feet tall and covered with chocolate brown hair beside a highway. When it saw his vehicle, it crossed down into the ditch and back up the other side with a few quick strides, impressing the man with its fluid and agile movement. Curt Nelson.

61-67. Names unknown, Cox Lake area, Summer and Fall 2011 - After Bigfoot activity seemed to stop in the Buckboard Hills for several years, a man reported about seven reports of screams and tracks in the Cox Lake area less than ten miles away to the east. A police officer was said to have taken a track photo. Chad S.

68. Name(s) unknown, Lengby-Ebrow area, 2014- A white Bigfoot was reportedly sighted, marking a further continuation of activity in

this region. Loren Coleman at Paracon, Shooting Star Casino Mahnomen, October 14, 2017.

69. Name(s) unknown, southeast of Zerkel, 2016 - Another or the same white Bigfoot is reported to have been sighted south of Highway 200, further indicating a return of Bigfoot activity to this area. Loren Coleman at Paracon, Shooting Star Casino Mahnomen, October 14, 2017.

70. Anonymous, Zerkel area, date unknown - A woman picking berries smelled an odor like a wet dog and heard something very large moving in the nearby brush. The experience was viewed in the context of Bigfoot reports in the area with some thinking a bear was involved but the woman saying she could not confirm that. Ed Trimble.

71. Mr. & Mrs. L., La Prairie Township, date unknown - A Native American couple related to the witness in the above 1987 report told Ed Trimble that they had heard a strange call very similar to the ones he heard but higher pitched and years earlier. It consisted of a drawn out call about eight seconds long followed by whoops, only the word they used was "roop." Ed Trimble.

VERGAS TRAILS

(This is an area between the towns of Vergas and Detroit Lakes in Otter Tail and Becker Counties which spawned the legend of the "Hairy Man," a saga which did include fanciful made up tales as well as some hoaxing but appears to have had a real Bigfoot presence as its origin. Only reports thought to involve the real creatures are included here.)

1. "Bruhn" and others, 1967 - Some people driving through the trails on a curvy and rocky road at around ten PM saw something

leap out from a cleft in a high bank beside the road and land on the hood of their car. As it blocked most of the view out the windshield, they could only describe it as a big hairy thing, and after the driver sped up and swerved back and forth, it fell off and the car kept going. Detroit Lakes Tribune. October 31, 1991.

2. Ken and Duane Zitzow, Pam Cook, October 1969 - A dramatic episode began with a night time sighting by three youths in a car out driving at about ten PM, with Ken driving while his brother sat in the back seat with his girlfriend. An upright creature seven to eight feet tall, weighing around 300 pounds and covered with dark brown or black hair suddenly leaped from the ditch into the center of the road, a jump of about 20 feet as if it was "spring-loaded." It had a man-like body with shoulders about four feet wide and arms down to its knees, and its face was like a gorilla's but with a thick beard. It held its arms in the air as if to try and stop the car, but jumped aside at the last second. The two in the back seat had not seen it, so Ken turned the car around for another look, at which time they all saw the creature attack the car as it passed and strike the trunk with its hands, putting a large dent in it. In the weeks that followed, they started driving through the area looking for the creature and saw it a few more times, running through fields in the moonlight. Sightings ceased in the winter, and they wondered if it might be hibernating. Then in the spring of 1970, they found what they believed to be its den near Trowbridge Lake, a space beneath an old wooden shack containing an old mattress and thick with wild animal smell. They burned the shack and then never saw the creature again. Personally related by witness Ken Zitzow.

3. Cheryl and Jolyn Hanson, winter 1972 - Two young cousins were snowmobiling in the afternoon in the Lost Highway area off County Road 130 when they decided to check out an old cabin they came across. As they circled it, a large manlike creature covered with hair suddenly emerged from the cabin with an object in one hand described in one account as a stick and in another as a hatchet and lunged at them as if to chase them away. They fled in fear on their snowmobiles, trying to rationalize what they had seen and thought

that though the creature was man-like it had been barefoot in the snow and couldn't be human. In adulthood, Cheryl Hanson would become a vocal public witness, including tales of the Hairy Man as she acted as a local historian and promoter of tourism in the area. Becker County Record, July 1, 2012; YouTube.

4. Names unknown, 1978 - Limited information on some teenagers who reportedly saw the creature and left to get a shotgun, but when they returned, it could not be relocated. Paul Lindstrom.

5. Name unknown, 1978 - Limited information on a farmer who moved away from the area after having trouble with the creature raiding his cabbage patch and killing his dog. Paul Lindstrom.

6. Mike Quast, March 31, 1989 - While exploring the area after hearing tales of the Hairy Man this author found what appeared to be a footprint about 12" long with a narrow heel and showing only two toes in the snow near a powerline corridor on the Detroit Lakes end of the Trails. While attempting to photograph it, the snowdrift on which I was crouching collapsed, which caused me to fall on the track and destroy it. Personal experience.

7. Anonymous, Spring 1989 - Limited information on a woman near Vergas who was sweeping her front porch, then began to shake the dirt out of some rugs. When she picked up the first rug and gave it a snap a Bigfoot suddenly scurried out from beneath the porch and ran away. Marion Senn.

8. Mike Quast, August 31, 1989 - While exploring the powerline corridor near the site of my earlier find in drizzly conditions, this author found a 16" track with the toes blurred together by rain. About three feet in front of it were two possible heel impressions, and about 135 feet behind it, another 16" track was found that showed three clear toe impressions and in which the foot had bent around a little rise in the ground. Personal experience.

9. Mike Quast and Tim Olson, August 10, 1990 - While searching for evidence in the afternoon this author and researcher Tim Olson found huge bipedal tracks in fresh deep gravel at the roadside at the top of the powerline corridor where my previous track find had occurred. Toe impressions did not show in that soft surface, but the

tracks were 20 1/2" long with a stride of 84" and went on for a few yards. Personal experience.

10. Mike Quast, May 27, 1992 - This author found another track at the top of the powerline corridor just below the level of the road in a patch of soil in between patches of tall grass where it made sense that only one track would have been left. It appeared to be the same one seen in March 1989, 12" long and showing only two toes. Whereas the three-toed tracks found looked like they were designed with only three, this one looked like it was missing a toe and was also bent somewhat as if from a badly injured foot. The three distinct sizes of tracks found in this area now seemed to suggest a family group of creatures. Personal experience.

11. Mike Quast and Alan Weaver, June 11, 1993 - This author and a friend found more tracks in the powerline corridor area. First, I found a scuff mark 21" long descending the corridor at a steep angle, looking as if a large foot had slid a bit. Next, a short distance up the road from the corridor, Alan spotted more tracks in a low sandy spot beside the road. There was one 16" long, possibly with three toe impressions though they were indistinct. Facing in the same direction, 52" to the right were two tracks measuring 20 1/2" long, the left foot quite clear but the right somewhat deteriorated and with anthills in it, indicating that the tracks were not fresh. Both these tracks had very clear toe impressions, four in number rather than three. These tracks would turn out to be the last pieces of evidence for the Hairy Man known to be found, and as tracts of once wildland were being developed and built upon the creatures seemed to finally leave the area. Personal experience.

12. Anonymous, date unknown - A skull exists, shown to Vergas gas station owner Kim Doyle by a man who said a local family he knew had found it in a boggy area in the Vergas end of the Trails several years before. The man's identity is unknown, and the skull has never been made available for analysis. It is superficially human-like in appearance but has several features that are not quite human, such as a smaller braincase, smaller eye sockets, and no nasal cavity bone. A short length of spine is attached to its base. Photos of it were

allowed to be taken which appeared in a newspaper, but its authenticity or whether it is even a real skull or a fabrication, is unknown. Becker County Record. July 1, 2012.

MID-STATE

1. Anonymous, Lake Mary near Alexandria, late 1940s - A group of ice fishermen reportedly saw a very ugly naked woman covered in hair walk casually out on to the ice where they were fishing and steal their catch of eelpout. Bigfootencounters website; Cletis Dubois.

2. Uno Heikkila, north of Floodwood, November 12, 1968 - A deer hunter sitting on a stump saw a creature about 4 1/2 feet tall jump from a balsam tree about 125 feet away and walk off into the woods on two feet. He tried to follow it but lost it after about 200 feet. "Sasquatch: The Apes Among Us" by John Green.

3. E.G. and others, Mantrap Lake in Hubbard County, pre-1969 - A scoutmaster and a group of young scouts canoeing on the lake saw a creature emerge from the woods on the shore and drink from the lake. It was about seven feet tall with broad shoulders and covered with black hair. The scoutmaster first thought it might be an escaped gorilla but changed his mind when he realized its build was much more human-like. The scouts stopped paddling and had an extended look at the creature, which would look up at them sporadically while drinking. "The Abominable Snowmen" by Eric Norman.

4. LaRae J. and grandfather, northwest of Hawley, late 1968 or early 1969 - A woman who lived as a little girl on a farm with her grandparents remembered one morning when her grandfather came in from doing chores and talked about seeing very large footprints in the snow that frightened him. Personally related by e-mail.

5. Anonymous, McGregor area, pre-1970 - Limited information on

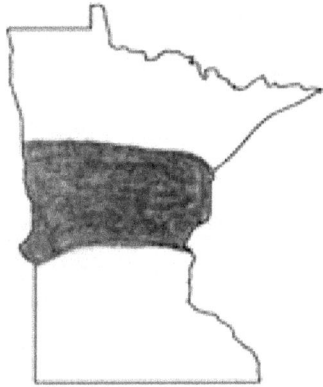

roadworkers around McGregor frequently having Bigfoot sightings along the local roads. Mark A. Hall.

6-7. Anonymous, east of Willow River, August 1972 - A young man driving saw two upright creatures in a clearing about 30 yards away, both of them covered in white hair. He took them to be male and female, the female seven feet tall and gorilla-like and the male nine feet tall and more brutish in appearance with a weathered gray face. They had been walking but froze when they saw his vehicle. After passing by, he quickly turned his car around for another look but was surprised to find that the creatures had apparently made it 60 yards into some woods and disappeared in the moment it took him to do so. The witness also reported having had a possible sighting once before of a small dark Bigfoot sitting cross-legged in some woods eating that scared his dog, but it was in dark shadowy conditions, so he hadn't been sure about it. BFRO website; "The Minnesota Road Guide to Mysterious Creatures" by Chad Lewis.

8-9. "Rick" and others, near Brainerd, March or April 1974 - Around Easter time, eight young men were enjoying a night of partying and camping. In the morning, one of the first to awaken went to a nearby creek to wash his hands and saw a clear human-like footprint in the mud in the shallow water, too large to be that of a human. There was still snow on the ground, the water very cold. The witness also reported that the girlfriend of one of his friends inherited land in the same area on which people would go four-wheeling and have keg parties, and they would sometimes see what was thought to be a pine tree in the distance, but later it would be gone, the idea being that it was a Bigfoot watching them. Minnesota Bigfoot website, Joe Heinan.

10. Ron Morris, between Isle and Wahkon, Summer 1974 - A future police officer had a Bigfoot sighting as a teenager. While driving near Mille Lacs Lake at about 1 AM, he saw a fairly small bipedal creature five to six feet tall, weighing about 150 pounds, and covered in light to medium brown hair two to three inches long standing beside the road in low swampland. Its arms may have been somewhat longer than a human's. Personally related by the witness.

11. Sheila A., near Onamia, Summer 1974 - Limited information on a woman who claimed to have been chased by a Bigfoot in the same general area and time as the previous report, near Izatty's Resort. Ron Morris.

12. Verna Kyrkyri, near Heinola, early or mid-1970s - An elderly woman who lived alone on a small farm was alerted by some noisy chickens to a disturbance in her barn in which she kept some tame rabbits in a hutch. Upon investigating, she saw the back end of a large animal that was stooped over beneath the six-foot-high ceiling in the barn, scrambling around trying to catch a wild cottontail that had wandered in. Thinking it was a bear and concerned for her rabbits she grabbed a broom and smacked the animal on the hindquarters, whereupon it turned out not to be a bear but a Bigfoot that then fled from the barn and ran on two legs toward a nearby swampy wooded area. Marion Senn.

13. Brian P. and Rick G., Aitkin, Summer 1976 - Two young teenage boys were riding their bicycles on an earthen dike along the Mississippi River within the city limits of Aitkin at about 8:30 PM when they saw a large brown animal in a swampy area between the dike and the river that appeared to be digging in or pulling up swamp grass. They thought it was a bear, but when one yelled at it, it stood up erect and turned to look at them, revealed as a bipedal creature between 5 1/2 and 6 1/2 feet tall and weighing about 300 pounds with a husky build, with arms that seemed to reach almost to the ground and a fully bearded face. Upon seeing them, it ran toward the river, moving easily through very rough swampy terrain. The boys were frightened and fled, but returned the next day to look for tracks. However, they found the area the creature had run through was so thick it was impossible for them. Related by witness Brian P. by letter.

14. Mike Quast, Strawberry Lake area in Becker County, Summer 1976 - As a child of eight while on a recreational afternoon drive in a forest area with my family, this author saw a black vertical object beside the road about a hundred yards ahead of our car, which I at first thought to be a burned, blackened tree trunk around seven feet tall. In a few seconds, it turned out to be a living bipedal creature

which stepped away from the roadside and walked into the nearby woods with a smooth, even stride. No arms were visible, so presumably, they were hanging motionless at its sides, and at that distance, there was little other detail apparent. Though my parents were in the front seat of the car, and my older sister was in the back seat next to me, I was the only one who saw it. This was the sighting that played a major role in my eventually becoming a Bigfoot researcher and investigator. Personal experience.

15-16. Anonymous, Outing area, mid to late 1970s - Two boys from Edina who put out a Bigfoot newsletter reported that two Bigfoot sightings occurred in the Outing area but were short on detail. They went to explore the area on June 2, 1978 but did not find any evidence. Minnesota Bigfoot News. Ted Steiner and David Warner.

17. Anonymous, Ogilvie-Cambridge area, early August 1978 - Two sisters aged 13 and eight attending a family reunion at their aunt's farm were playing tag in a cornfield at about dusk when they came out of the field beside a swampy area and saw a large manlike creature standing only about 20 feet away. It was about seven feet tall with matted and dirty brown or black hair, showed electric blue eyeshine in the fading light and had a strong sulfur-like odor. After about a minute of staring, the creature made a noise in its throat, which startled the girls, and their sudden movement seemed to startle the creature, and it stepped toward them. They then fled and ran to tell their family, but when their mother and an uncle came back to the spot with them the creature was gone. BFRO website.

18-19. Anonymous, near Emily, September 1978 - Just after a couple had gotten into bed at 10:30 PM the wife noticed there was something outside their bedroom window, so the husband flipped on the light. Three sets of eyes ringed with orange, and each five to eight inches apart with the outlines of heads around them were then seen pressed up against the window. One of the beings seemed to be bending down to see in the window, which was six feet above the ground. The light coming on made one of the beings utter a frightening scream, and then the couple could vaguely see three bipedal forms running away. The couple also had frequently heard strange animal sounds coming from the nearby woods described as sounding like a wolf's voice howling in backward-spoken German, starting in a low pitch then rising to a high one. A mention was also made of some of their neighbors having experiences but not wanting to talk about them. BFRO website.

20-21. Anonymous, Becker County, October 20, 1978 - A young person out grouse hunting between nine and ten AM noticed that the woods were dead quiet with no apparent animal activity. While sitting on a stump, he then heard bipedal footsteps approaching along a nearby creekbed and smelled a skunk-like odor. Thinking it might be his father, he called out, at which point the footsteps stopped, there was a loud crack like a tree breaking, then the footsteps retreated in the opposite direction, the smell went away, and the woods erupted with bird and squirrel activity. The witness fled but returned in the afternoon with his father (who had been nowhere around at the time of the incident) and they found a freshly broken tree three to four inches in diameter. The witness also recalled hearing howling while waiting for the school bus that he had always assumed was from wolves or coyotes, but in light of this experience, he wasn't sure. GCBRO website.

22. Susie S., near White Earth, Summer, 1970s - An 11 or 12-year-old girl was sitting at the end of her driveway at about dusk waiting for a ride when a skunk came out of some woods on to the road. Moments late,r as she was watching the skunk, a large upright creature also stepped out onto the road a distance of about one city block away. It was a little bigger than a man, slightly hunched over with a face like a gorilla's and all covered with dark hair, making eye contact with the girl as it crossed the road in an odd side-stepping manner. It scared her into being afraid to be in the woods from then on, whereas she had always enjoyed it before. Related by witness by phone; Witness's brother Ken S.

23-24. Grant H., west of Gowan, 1970s - Limited information on a man having two separate Bigfoot sightings. R.A. Gilbertsen.

25. L.R., north of Floodwood, 1970s - Limited information on a

man hearing possible Bigfoot screams near his home. R.A. Gilbertsen.

26-28. Names unknown, Floodwood-Gowan area, 1970s, 1980s, 1990s - Witness Grant H. from the previous report told of hearing rumors of Bigfoot sightings and screams being heard in each of these decades. R.A. Gilbertsen.

29. Name(s) unknown, southeast of Fergus Falls, 1980 - A Bigfoot encounter is reported to have occurred. Loren Coleman at Paracon, Shooting Star Casino Mahnomen, October 14, 2017.

30. Anonymous, south of Brainerd, Fall 1981 - The father of the witness from the 1996 Remer area report in the Central North section, who was present for his son's sighting but did not share it, had had an experience of his own while deer hunting with a friend. He heard his friend firing his rifle repeatedly, and when he reached him, he found him in a frightened state, reporting that he had seen a Bigfoot eight feet tall and covered in white hair and that he had tried to shoot it in the head but had missed. Related by the son of the witness by e-mail.

31. Anonymous, near Long Prairie, April 1989 - Two college-age friends were at the farm of the parents of one of them working at clearing refuse out of a garage and burning it when at about 9 PM, they started to hear sounds like something running around the perimeter of the fire and large tree branches breaking in the nearby woods. Over time it began to sound like multiple beings running powerfully at athletic speed, and as the men grew more and more nervous they then glimpsed the silhouettes of two creatures seven to eight feet tall, the first about 100 yards away, moving along the edge of the woods, and the second about 70 yards away peeking out at them from behind an old trailer. They were continuing to nervously work at their rubbish fire as these things happened but eventually had enough and left the area on the tractor they'd been using to haul things out of the garage. The next day they looked for tracks but the ground was too leafy. The man who reported the incident and whose parents owned the property also noted that over the years, dogs have acted very nervously in the area, and some have gone missing or turned up dead with broken bones, and at least one odd tree break

was found near a hunter's tree stand with a three-inch thick tree twisted and torn down. BFRO website.

32. "Brad and Greg," Mille Lacs Lake in Aitkin County, early July 1989 - Two men camping were walking back to their campsite from the lakeshore at about 5:30 AM when they heard something following them along a high wooded ridge and thought it was a bear, but when they reached camp, it became visible between two trees 75 to 100 feet away and turned out to be a large human-like creature standing about eight feet tall and covered with dark brown hair. It had long legs, narrow hips, arms that hung to its knees, and a huge chest and shoulders. There was little to no neck, and the hairless face had large round eyes and a flat nose. The men thought the creature seemed curious as it stood watching them for about three minutes before disappearing back into the woods. One of the men commented that it resembled the Bigfoot in the movie "Harry and the Hendersons." Tim Olson.

33. Anonymous, northeast of Audubon, November 4, 1990 - A young man deer hunting was sitting in his pickup truck at about 6:30 AM atop a hill beside some woods when he heard movement in the brush and saw what he described as an object "about six feet long with many legs" moving along. When this "object" emerged from the woods at the bottom of the hill about 100 feet below him, it turned out to be three manlike creatures moving together in tight formation in a stealthy stooped-over posture. They were about man-sized, the one in the middle slightly smaller, and covered in dark hair. Their heads were rounded, not peaked, and their arms were held almost at ground level in their stooped position. They traveled along the bottom of the hill for a short distance, then turned and headed off across a field of tall grass, eventually disappearing back into thick brush on the other side beyond which lay a swampy area, never standing up to their full height. The witness thought the creatures did not notice him but were being stealthy to avoid being seen by another hunter stationed about 100 yards away. This author was shown the spot-on November 30th, at which time the paths the creatures made in the tall frozen grass were still to be seen. I searched it

again on December 16th, and at the exact spot where the creatures had emerged from the woods, found branches up to an inch thick snapped off and hanging at three distinct heights- 65", 74-76", and 83". Personally related by the witness.

34-35. Anonymous, north of Wadena, August 1992 - A mother and her two sons aged eight and 12 went to visit family friends, and a number of children playing in the yard built a fort/tent out of sheets under a clothesline which they were instructed to dismantle before the visitors left just after sunset. As this was going on, a dark figure 6 1/2-7 feet tall was seen in flashlight beams standing in some trees only 20-30 feet away watching the kids. They quickly and nervously finished their work, and then as the mother and her sons were leaving in their van the brothers saw the creature running after them. It was covered in dark fur, with a large crested head, flat face, and no apparent neck, and it ran swinging its arms gracefully as it chased them coming as close as ten feet from the van as it drove at about 30 miles per hour. It continued the chase for half to three-quarters of a mile before finally breaking off and heading into an open field. About a week before, the mother and the younger son were driving toward the same property when they saw what they thought was a skunk crossing the road at the top of a hill, but when they crested the hill, they saw a cornfield with rows of cornstalks knocked down four to five feet wide, forming a corridor through the field as if something large had gone through, and after their later creature sighting, they thought in retrospect that what they had thought was a skunk at the top of the hill might have been only the head of the large creature with its body concealed behind the slope of the hill about to enter the cornfield. BFRO website.

36. Anonymous, west of Sebeka and north of New York Mills, 1994 - The family in the previous report related that a man they knew of had seen a large hairy bipedal creature running quickly across a field on his property about two years after their experience. BFRO website.

37. Marion Senn, Heinola area near New York Mills, April 28, 1994 - A publicly known UFO researcher with many personal UFO and E.T. experiences was driving home from New York Mills at about 9

PM and as she neared her home, she saw a seven-foot manlike creature in the road ahead, covered in rust-colored hair such as she had never seen on any other animal, darker on the limbs, with a big upper body, a very short neck, and a fairly rounded head. It took two steps from the center to the edge of the road bent at the knees with its arms back, and jumped down into a small wooded boggy area where it disappeared, a freefall of about 20 feet. The spot happened to be right next to the home of an elderly neighbor couple Marion knew so she turned into their driveway and told them what she'd just seen. The next day the husband went to look around and found impressions of flattened grass 16-18" long (not true footprints) at both ends of the bog, both below the road and at the opposite end where they emerged into an alfalfa field skirted the tree line for about 20 feet, then re-entered the bog where there were small branches snapped downward in opposite directions four to five feet up as if parted by the creature. This author examined the site on July 16th, and the snapped branches were still to be seen, with apparent fingernail prints pressed into them. Personally related by the witness and by neighbors and by Ed and Florence Kasma.

38. Chuck N., Big Sugar Bush Lake in Becker County, late October 1995 - A man at a fishing camp was standing on the lakeshore at night when he heard something very big approaching in the woods. He thought it was a moose, but when he shined a light in its direction, it let out a horrendous and very un-mooselike screech and ran away, never showing itself. After he was directed to this author a couple of years later, I played him some recordings of Bigfoot vocalizations from Washington state, but though he thought he may have heard a Bigfoot, he said it was not similar to those. Personally related by the witness.

39. Guy N., two others, northeast of Hawley, October 1995 - Two men out duck hunting before noon in an area of mostly open fields and pasture with a few scattered groves of trees saw a black upright creature over six feet tall at a distance of about four city blocks away. It began to run on two legs, swinging its arms, moving easily through thick high grass that the men would later find to be difficult for them

to walk through. The creature then ran across a gravel road down which a car was coming, the driving having to slam on his or her brakes to avoid hitting it. The car then drove on, and the hunters never discovered the identity of the driver. Related to witness Guy N. by letter.

40. G.L., southwest of Ulen, November 1995 - A man out deer hunting near dusk saw what he at first thought was a large man about 50 yards away but noticed he was not wearing orange hunting clothes. Then he noticed that the figure seemed too big to be a man and that the head didn't look right, and the shoulders were too sloped. He looked away for a moment and then the figure was gone. After later learning of the previous report in the same area, he thought he may have seen a Bigfoot. Related by witness' wife by e-mail.

41-42. L.R., north of Floodwood, Summer 1996 - A man who heard possible Bigfoot screams in an earlier 1970s report had two occasions of something knocking over a bird feeder that was seven to eight feet above the ground. A grunting sound was heard, but the culprit was not seen. Once when this happened, the man's dog was in his garage and barked and scratched frantically to get out. R.A. Gilbertsen.

43. J.B., west of Itasca State Park in Hubbard County, Fall 1996 - A man reported that while hiking about 3/4 of a mile down a trail just outside the western border of the park, he heard a heavy animal panting sound and smelled a powerful rotten-type odor. He fled, thinking it might be a Bigfoot. He hinted that he had had a few other experiences over the years with Bigfoot evidence but seemed reticent to talk about it, saying he would e-mail about it later but never doing so. Related by witness by phone.

44. Anonymous, near Menahga, September 14, 1997 - Two people out for a walk at about 4:30 PM heard a loud groan in some trees, then saw just a glimpse of a hairy, apelike creature jumping from the trees into a field next to a swamp. Bigfootinfo website.

45. Ken S., Strawberry Lake area in Becker County, Spring 1997 or 1998 - A man saw very big tracks in melting snow with branches broken above them nine feet above the ground in more than one

spot. He was undecided over whether it was a sign of moose or of Bigfoot. This man was the brother of Susie S. from an earlier 1970s report near White Earth. Related by witness by phone.

46. Anonymous, near McGregor, November 1999 - A man hunted deer in an area for five years, having two normal years and then two years in which he felt something was watching him and noticed that the woods were strangely quiet. In the fifth year, while sitting in his tree stand in the late afternoon near dusk, he heard two horrendous screams coming from about 300 yards away. He fled to his nearby four-wheeler, hearing another scream on the way that ended in a growl, then quickly left the area and felt fear about the area from then on. Minnesota Bigfoot website, Joe Heinan.

47. Anonymous, near Wadena, December 1999 - Two friends were snowmobiling on a pleasant winter day when they saw what they first thought was a man walking along the edge of a swamp. When they went closer, they saw that it was actually a hairy, apelike creature that then fled into the swamp. Bigfootinfo website.

48. Name unknown, Hinckley area, early 2000s - Limited information on a member of the Minnesota Bigfoot Research Team having a Bigfoot sighting. Related by team leader Abe DelRio in presentation at 2017 Remer Bigfoot Days festival.

49. Dave Gunderson, Strawberry-Sugar Bush Lakes area in Becker and Mahnomen Counties, July 2000 - A man was driving from the Strawberry Lake Store toward a cabin on Big Sugar Bush Lake at about noon in bright daylight when he saw a man-sized dark upright figure cross the road about a quarter-mile ahead, in view for a few seconds. There were no structures or any other vehicles anywhere in the area, and he believed what he had seen to be a Bigfoot, but was laughed at by his companions upon reaching the cabin and telling them. Personally related by witness.

50-51. Anonymous, Mille Lacs Lake area in Mille Lacs County, Summer 2001- A cryptozoology researcher visited the Mille Lacs Band Indian Museum in 2002 to inquire about strange creatures in local folklore and was told by a female staff member that she thought she'd had a quick sighting of what she believed to be a Bigfoot the previous summer, just a dark figure running, and her brother had also had a sighting that year of a bipedal creature running across a road. Nick Sucik.

52. Name(s) unknown, near Little Falls, Winter 2000-2002 - Limited information on a possible Bigfoot sighting in this area, the exact time uncertain. Nick Sucik.

53-54. Anonymous, Norman County, April 2002- A couple purchasing a home in a wilderness area that had been vacant for a couple of years were sitting in their pickup truck in front of the garage talking about how to fix the place up at 10 PM when they heard an extremely loud sound "like an Indian war cry or screeching monkeys" that seemed to emanate from directly behind them, but nothing was seen. They fled but came back 15 minutes later to look around and again a few days later to look for tracks, but no evidence of any kind was found. However, the husband had recently seen something odd while driving at night in the area, a briefly glimpsed an upright figure in the dark next to a pine tree, but he thought it could have been a moose or bear standing upright. After hearing the sound later, they considered the possibility of Bigfoot. GCBRO website.

55. Anonymous, south of Carlton, July 4, 2002 - At about 10 PM, a half-hour after setting off some fireworks, a couple and a friend heard loud screaming like that of a woman lasting two to three minutes and coming from an area of woods, ravines, and rolling hills. Minnesota Bigfoot website, Joe Heinan.

56-57. Anonymous, south of Carlton, September 2002 - A friend of the couple from the previous report living ten miles south of them heard a strange howl that he could not identify coming from near his home. Later he was telling a DNR officer about it when the howl sounded again, and the officer couldn't identify it either. Minnesota Bigfoot website, Joe Heinan.

58. Anonymous, Richwood area, Fall 2002 - Something seen in a tree made a man flee in fear from a hunt in the woods, scaring him so badly that he refused to talk much about it with his family, but it

would become associated with later Bigfoot experiences had by other family members. Personally related by family members.

59. Names unknown, near Little Falls, 2002 - A member of Bigfoot researcher Bob Olson's church congregation reported to him years later that he and another man had been in a pickup truck with the other man driving when they spotted a mysterious black object next to a stop sign ahead of them. Not knowing what it was, they began to slow down, and when they came to a stop they were only a few feet in front of it. It was a Bigfoot standing eight feet tall with a shorter juvenile creature standing directly in front of it with its back leaning against the adult. As the men stared at the creatures, dumbfounded; the adult then made one fluid motion in which it pushed the juvenile behind it with one arm, took one step forward, and with the other arm brought its flat palm down hard on the roof of the truck, denting it. The men took off in a panic. Bob Olson.

60. Anonymous, Richwood area, 2003 - A 12-year-old boy related to the witness in the previous Richwood report heard wood knocking in the woods on his grandmother's property which would become associated with Bigfoot activity occurring there later. Personally related by witness.

61. Anonymous, near Carlton, June 2004 - A person very familiar with bears living near Chub and Geddes Lakes saw a dark upright figure near a clearing about a mile from the nearest road and was certain it was not a bear. It looked toward the witness and then ran off. Bigfootinfo website.

62. Anonymous, near Hinckley, June 2004 - A man living on a farmstead in a wooded area was lying in bed at about 3 AM when he heard a loud whooping howl coming from north of his house. BFRO website.

63. Anonymous, Richwood area, August or September 2004 - The same boy from the previous Richwood report, now 13, was with his mother at a small farmstead not far from the sites of their family's previous encounters when they heard their dog barking frantically from where it was tied to a tree just outside the house at around 2 or 3 AM. They looked out to see a Bigfoot about eight feet tall, covered in

dark brown or black hair and with orange glowing eyes, standing behind a larger tree about 30 feet from the house looking at the dog. Believing it meant to kill their pet, the boy went outside to untie the dog and bring it inside while his mother was too afraid and remained in the house. Personally related by the witnesses.

64. Anonymous, near Hinckley, early to mid-November 2004 - The same man from the previous Hinckley report was talking on the phone in his kitchen at about 10 PM when he looked out the window and had a two-second glimpse of a dark furry manlike creature running past his barn. It was 7-7 1/2 feet tall with a stocky build, a domed head with no apparent neck, and long arms that hung below mid-thigh. The man went out the next day to look for tracks but ground conditions were not right for them. BFRO website.

65. Anonymous, Richwood area, Summer 2005 - A niece of the mother from the previous Richwood report saw an upright hairy creature about six feet tall emerge from some evergreen trees and cross a road as she was driving past a rural church after dark. She turned around for another look and saw it enter a cornfield. This creature was believed to be the same type as one not like a typical Bigfoot that would be seen later within the city limits of nearby Detroit Lakes. Personally related by the witnesses from the previous Richwood reports.

66. Name unknown, near Crosby, about 2005 - Limited information on a woman who was driving when she saw a deer running with a Bigfoot close behind chasing it. Don Sherman.

67. "J.P.H." and friend, Eagle Bend-Parker's Prairie area, October 2006 - An episode of suspected Bigfoot activity occurred around a hunting cabin in a remote area when two friends were there, one the cabin's owner and one a guest. The first three sets of tracks were found in a potato field, lengths 15", 13", and 11". Across a pond from the field in some woods, they heard what sounded almost like human voices speaking to each other in short choppy sentences rather like some Asian language, a phenomenon called "samurai chatter" by Bigfoot researchers in other areas. Next, as they were passing by a barrel of corn left out for deer, they heard a loud grunt, compared

both to someone clearing their throat and to sounds made by the velociraptors in the movie "Jurassic Park." They looked through the brush and saw nothing, but then found a 15" print in the mossy ground next to the corn barrel, as well as two arched tree structures nearby that they believed were made by Bigfoot, logs placed on the ends of the bent-over trees to keep them down. Later that day, the guest heard something following him down a hiking rail but could not catch sight of it. The cabin's owner reported that he sometimes heard strange noises while coming back from his deer stand after dusk, and once found a large pile of scat with nuts and grains in it. Bigfootencounters website.

68. Joanne S. and family, Wild Rice River west of Ulen, January 2007 - Large human-like footprints began to appear on a rural property directly beside the river, turning up about every two weeks. This was the beginning of a series of Bigfoot incidents on this property. BFRO website; Personally related by the witness.

69. Anonymous, near Sturgeon Lake, February 23, 2007 - A man driving through woodland saw a black man like figure in the road about a quarter-mile ahead of him, seeming larger than a man with long arms and legs and a head that seemed to sit atop the shoulders with no neck. He drove down a slight dip in the road and lost sight of it for a moment, and when he came out of the dip, it had disappeared. As the trees were 50 feet back from the road, he was surprised that it had gone out of sight in such a short time. He had had the creature in sight for about ten seconds. When he passed the spot, he noticed that there was garbage at the roadside including grapefruit peels. BFRO website.

70. Dan P., Washburn Lake area in Cass County, 2007 - A man was hauling a load of lumber when a Bigfoot crossed the road in front of him, crossing from east to west in three or four strides. Its hands were as big as baseball mitts, and the sun glinted off the hair on its back. The man was very shocked and struggled to keep calm for days afterward. Forum Communications Co., Molly Miron, December 11, 2009; Bob Olson.

71. Amanda Schluttner, Kirk & Matt Orr, west of Staples, July 2008

- A young girl driving to her boyfriend's house was going about 35 miles per hour when she suddenly struck a dark bipedal hairy creature, she estimated to be about seven feet tall that rolled across the hood of her car and fell into a ditch. She described it as looking both bearlike and human-like, but bigger. This was witnessed from the house just a few hundred feet away by her boyfriend and his brother, who put the creature's height at as much as 8 1/2 feet and likened it to a football player in full pads. They thought it was a bear at first but noticed that its body twisted in a way that a bear would not. They both armed themselves and went after the creature as it fled toward nearby woods, steadying itself with a hand on its leg and grabbing a tree branch, apparently injured. The boyfriend fired twice at it with a .30-30 rifle and was sure he had hit it in the chest, but it continued on into the woods and disappeared. Later a team of investigators consisting of Bigfoot researchers Bob Olson and Don Sherman and animal tracker Gene Hagen conducted a search studied the dents left in the hood of the car and located one of the bullets lodged in a tree. The bullet was extracted and analyzed for DNA since it was believed to have passed through the creature but there were no conclusive results. "Monster Quest" episode "Monster Close Encounters," The History Channel.

A somewhat different description of this incident from other sources states that the incident actually occurred at the residence of Bruce Harne in rural Staples, where Schluttner had been visiting with the Orr brothers and that she was actually leaving the property when the collision occurred. This version states that the creature came toward them after being shot so they retreated into the house, from which they heard howling outside. Upon going back outside they found their two dogs cowering in fear and also noted that a ladder that had been lying in the back yard had been placed up against the house and that the creature was now up on the roof. When Kirk took the ladder back down, the creature grabbed a tree branch, jumped down from the roof and ran off into the woods, where further howling made it sound as if there might actually, be more than one creature present. Curiously Kirk Orr was also alleged to have reported that the dark brown creature had a head "almost like that of a wolf," which might equate it not with Bigfoot but with another mysterious creature that has been documented in America commonly referred to as the "Dogman" or "Werewolf." Bruce Harne and his wife Marietta were reported to have heard more howling in the woods in following days, but no further sightings had occurred. "Stranger in the Night" by Mike Tracy, Sebeka/Menahga Review Messenger. July 30, 2008; Cass Lake Times. September 18, 2008; Don Sherman.

72. Anonymous, near Nimrod, August 2008 - A group of friends went regularly at night to a spot where they believed they could hear Bigfoot sounds, including vocalizations and wood knocking, at least once to the point where they thought the creatures were trying to intimidate them into leaving. On one particular night, they had their closest and best encounter with the creatures coming as close as 75 yards from them at one point. They made recordings with a digital camera and submitted them to the BFRO, which concluded that the calls sounded like those of a primate but were mixed in with others that sounded like atypical cattle calls, cows being known to be in the area. BFRO website.

73. Dale & Kristy Aho and kids, north of Kettle River, September 2008 - A man out bird hunting was in a patch of trees and spooked up a crouching Bigfoot estimated at eight to nine feet tall with black hair that ran past his wife and children who were seated on ATVs nearby. Its footfalls were so heavy they made the ground shake. "Finding Bigfoot" episode "Peeping Bigfoot," Animal Planet; Bigfootevidence Blog; Moose Lake Star-Gazette. Dan Reed.

74. Anonymous, Wild Rice River west of Ulen, late Fall 2008 - A grandson and nephew of Joanne S. from the January 2007 Ulen report saw what would come to be called a "teenage" Bigfoot, about 5 1/2 feet tall with dark brown hair, moving through Joanne's front yard in the early evening. Personally related by Joanne S.

75-81. Other reports from the Ulen location that occurred in the next weeks and months, dates and sequence uncertain:

* Joanne also saw the "teenage" creature running across her front yard and driveway.

** Twice, Bigfoot tracks appeared in a ravine behind Joanne's trailer house where squash rinds had been disposed of, which disappeared.

** Twice, tracks also appeared in the front yard where Joanne's sighting had occurred, crossing a small fence without breaking stride. (Tracks were five-toed, made a size 14 shoe look small, and had a bulge by the big toe like "bunion problems.")

* Joanne heard a whooping call at dusk and into the evening echoing through the trees, like "WhoooOOO!" a distance away but not "miles and miles."

* A neighbor to the south had a water-filled gravel pit that he stocked with bass, and all the fish mysteriously disappeared.

All Personally related by the witness Joanne S.

82. Names unknown, Crosby/Deerwood area, 2008 - A woman and her son were driving on Highway 6 heading south near the golf course south of Deerwood when a Bigfoot suddenly appeared on the left side of the road rushing straight at them. The woman said she first thought it was a man wearing Carhartts but soon realized it was an inhuman creature standing eight feet tall with long arms and covered with long brown hair. She had to swerve to avoid hitting it as it ran between her car and another that was approaching behind her, narrowly missing her fender. Don Sherman.

83. Dale Aho, north of Kettle River, 2008-2009 - While appearing at a town meeting, put on by the TV show "Finding Bigfoot" to discuss area Bigfoot sightings, Kristy Aho stated that her husband had seen what was probably a family of creatures in the area several times but that he was not present at the meeting to discuss it. Moose Lake Star-Gazette. Dan Reed.

84. Anonymous, Wild Rice River west of Ulen, March 4, 2009 - The daughter of previous Bigfoot witness Joanne S. and her son were coming for a visit and were approaching the driveway when they saw a Bigfoot standing in the middle of the road, seven to eight feet tall with long arms illuminated in their headlight beams. They sat and

watched it for two to three minutes during which time it never moved and never looked at them, looking instead toward the river about 150 feet away, which was in severe flood at the time. They then continued on down the driveway to tell Joanne what they'd seen. There are some inconsistencies in the story. In a report the daughter made to the BFRO she stated the creature's hair was two-tone brown, that the sighting occurred at around midnight, and that she and her son never felt any fear as the family had accepted the presence of the creatures in the area. However, the version given personally to this author by Joanne said the hair color was silver, the time 6 to 8 PM, and that the pair were visibly frightened when they told her what they'd just seen to the point of keeping her from going outside to see it for herself since the creature was so big. Joanne formed the theory that this creature was the mother of the smaller one she and others had seen earlier and that with the river flooding, it may have been looking for its child to make sure it was safe. BFRO website; Personally related by Joanne S.

85. Dale & Kristy Aho and kids, north of Kettle River, July 2009 - The same family from previous reports had another sighting while in their pickup truck at night. They first saw red eyeshine about 200 feet away which approached them until they could see the creature clearly, swaying back and forth as it walked in what they perceived as a threatening manner. They thought this creature looked even bigger than the first one they'd seen while hunting. The children, exposed in the back of the truck, were frightened to the point of crying, so the family fled. Bigfootevidence Blog.

86. Anonymous, Detroit Lakes, Summer 2009- A female friend of the mother from the 2004 Richwood report was driving at night along west Willow Street where it passed through a large marshy area and beside a water treatment plant when she saw an upright hairy creature around six feet tall, come out of the wooded marsh and on to the road, and then leap up on to a wooden light pole and cling to it. Though an upright hairy biped, this creature did not resemble a typical Bigfoot but walked in a very gangly hunched over manner and had two prominent hooked claws on each hand and foot, its feet

being circular in shape. Personally related by witnesses from the previous Richwood reports.

87. Andy Peiper, Rich Knofke, Kris Perlock, Kettle River area, September 13, 2009 - Members of the BFRO recorded what was believed to be Bigfoot calls mixed with wolf howls during an expedition organized by Andy Peiper. Known officially as the "Minnesota Howls," the sounds were similar to the wolf howls but clearly louder and deeper in pitch. BFRO website; "Finding Bigfoot" episode "Peeping Bigfoot," Animal Planet; YouTube.

88. Anonymous, near Moose Lake, September 17-18, 2009- Members of the Sasquatch Research Association had several tantalizing experiences at night while on a weekend expedition including berries and other things being thrown at them from the woods, tracks 17-19" long being found, howls being heard 200-300 yards away and heavy footfalls and branches breaking as close as 15-30 feet from their campsite. This was in close proximity to the Kettle River area reports going on during the same time period. Sasquatch Research Association website.

89. Name unknown, 30 miles south of Hill City, 2009 - Limited information on a person seeing a Bigfoot cross the road ahead of him on Highway 169 near a forestry building and some power lines. Lady Ocalat's Paranormal Investigations website.

90. Jenna Wilenius, Kettle River area, June 12, 2010 - A young woman was out jogging with her dog when the dog started acting nervous. She looked back to see a huge Bigfoot with black hair and long arms and legs standing at a tree line beside the road watching her. She kept running until she reached her parents' house where she was living. When working with investigators later and going by the height of a tree branch where she'd seen the creature she estimated its height at a gigantic 11 feet. However, a neighbor who would become involved in the story, John Gran, was of the opinion that a slight slope in the road and the distance between Jenna and the creature resulted in her slightly overestimating the height. "Finding Bigfoot," episode "Peeping Bigfoot," Animal Planet; Bigfootevidence Blog; Moose Lake Star-Gazette, Dan Reed.

91. John Gran, Kettle River area, June 13, 2010 - The day after Jenna Wilenius' sighting neighbor John Gran was driving past her family's house at about 11:05 AM pulling a lawnmower on a trailer when he saw a figure standing beside their garage seemingly watching the house, the same height as the garage eave, about eight feet. It had a black body, a lighter colored face, and long legs. He wanted to stop for a closer look, but it was hard with the equipment he was hauling. The next day he drove by at the same time to make sure it hadn't been some kind of optical illusion, and there was nothing there. This suggests that the creature seen by Jenna had followed her home and taken an interest in her. Personally related by the witness; Moose Lake Star-Gazette, Dan Reed.

92. John Gran, Kettle River area, Summer 2010 - The witness from the previous report had another experience while sleeping on his screened-in porch in the evening and was awakened by a noise coming from down his driveway, like a growl combined with a loud throat-clearing sound. He immediately thought it was a Bigfoot that was looking around the properties on the short road he lived on near the site of the Jenna Wilenius sighting. Personally related by the witness; Moose Lake Star-Gazette. Dan Reed.

93. John Gran, Kettle River area, Summer 2010- After his previous experiences, Gran set up a trail camera in his back yard which was at the edge of the Kettle River, and captured a nocturnal photo of possible Bigfoot eyeshine, several feet above the ground. Personally related by witness.

94. Robert & Roger Siltanen, Kettle River area, September 2010- Two brothers had been hearing growls and whines north and west of the dairy farm they operated together when one night their barks were barking wildly at something in a plowed field. They suspected a bear was to blame, but when they looked in the field the next day, they found about 75 tracks of a huge bipedal creature with a span of 42 inches between them and believed they had become part of the Bigfoot activity going on in the area. However, the BFRO believes the brothers to be hoaxers trying to cash in on all the notoriety. Moose Lake Star-Gazette. Dan Reed.

95. "SRA Jim," others, Hubbard County, September 4, 2010-
Members of the Sasquatch Research Association were camping over
Labor Day weekend in a wooded area where possible Bigfoot tracks
had been found previously and deployed trail cameras around their
campsite, which turned out to be along a trail heavily used by ATV
riders. On their second night there they heard and recorded some
howls coming from nearby that were mixed in with coyote calls but
distinct from them, and later heard footfalls around their camp, some
sounding stealthy and others like something running. At the end of
their stay, they found that one of the trail cameras had picked up an
interesting series of photos while they'd been away from camp at
around 11:30 AM, triggered by passing ATVs but also showing what
they believed to be a Bigfoot about seven feet tall, partially hidden
behind a tree looking toward their camp. They dubbed the creature
"Curious George." Sasquatch Research Association website.

96. Anonymous, Kettle River area, presumably 2008-2010 Bigfoot
episode - During the town meeting put on by the show "Finding
Bigfoot" two boys said they'd seen a Bigfoot watching them from
outside their home and expressed concern. BFRO head Matt Moneymaker assured them that the creatures were not dangerous and that
they were lucky to have seen one. Bigfootevidence blog.

97. Margaret Olson Webster, Kettle River area, presumably 2008-
2010 Bigfoot episode - A woman who was collecting maple syrup had
just brought a load into her camp when she heard a strange noise
that was unlike a person or any animal she knew of. She was frightened, but decided to collect another load. When she returned to
camp, something had dumped over six buckets of sap. Bigfootevidence blog.

98-99. Bud Olson, Kettle River area, Spring, presumably 2008-
2010 Bigfoot episode - Also engaged in maple syrup collecting was a
man who was taking a break from sapping and delivering a newspaper to a neighbor's house when he saw a large black hairy bipedal
creature sitting down beside a railroad, as he crossed the tracks in his
pickup truck. It had long arms and legs, a lighter colored face, and
hair on its head that hung far down its back. He watched it for eight

to ten minutes and could tell that it was nervous about his presence, eventually standing up and walking away on two legs. He went and fetched a camera and came back but could not spot the creature again or find any tracks in the gravelly and grassy surroundings. The day before he and his son- in-law had heard a strange noise they could not identify while gathering sap, and after his sighting he made a connection between the two incidents. Moose Lake Star-Gazette. Dan Reed; Bigfootevidence blog.

100. Loren Mattson, Sturgeon Lake area, presumably 2008-2010 Bigfoot episode - A man saw a tall, dark manlike creature in the middle of a road in his headlight beams while driving at night. With a few strides, it disappeared into the woods. Moose Lake Star-Gazette. Dan Reed.

101. Todd Newby, Kettle River area, presumably 2008-2010 Bigfoot episode - A group of friends were camping in the area and passed around a thermal camera to scan the area while sitting their campfire at night. When it was Todd's turn, he glimpsed eyes and a large head in an area of sparse foliage. He went to examine the spot the next day but found nothing. Moose Lake Star-Gazette, Dan Reed.

102. Anonymous, Kettle River area, presumably 2008-2010 Bigfoot episode - While answering questions in response to the local Bigfoot episode, a waitress in a cafe in the town of Tamarack told this author that a friend of hers' in the Automba-Kettle River area claimed that a Bigfoot would come into his yard and scare his dog. Personally related by a friend of witness.

103. Edie Jokimaki, Tamarack-Kettle River area, presumably 2008-2010 Bigfoot episode - A woman home alone one evening heard terrible, frightening sounds just outside a window that she could not identify. This author suspects this is the same report told to me by a family that operates the general store in Tamarack that included the extra detail of an apple tree being stripped bare outside the house. Moose Lake Star-Gazette. Dan Reed; Personally related by friend of witness.

104. Greg & Lorraine Tomczak, others, Kettle River area, 2010- An elderly couple driving in a van during daylight saw three vehicles

pulled over along a road near a vacant trailer house and first thought it might be a police situation, but then realized that one car contained another old couple, the other two each contained a young man, and they had all pulled over to watch a huge Bigfoot that was peering in a window of the trailer house. Later comparison to the trailer would put its height at just under nine feet. After a moment, it ran across the road and into nearby woods, crossing a barbed-wire fence without breaking stride. Lorraine talked to the other elderly woman, who said she'd seen that the creature was a male by noticing a large male organ. This sighting occurred less than two miles from where the "Minnesota Howls" were recorded. When this author later examined the trailer, I found it to be in badly deteriorated condition and full of mice, a possible food source and reason for the creature to take an interest. "Finding Bigfoot" episode "Peeping Bigfoot," Animal Planet; Moose Lake Star-Gazette. Dan Reed; YouTube.

105. Anonymous, Richwood area, June 2010 or 2011 - The sister of the boy from the previous Richwood reports was at her grandmother's property from the 2003 Richwood report, standing outside the house arguing with her boyfriend over the phone close to dusk, when she glimpsed a seven to eight-foot Bigfoot with glowing orange eyes standing beside a power pole along a nearby paved road. Thinking her mind was just playing tricks on her, she turned away and continued her conversation, but two minutes later, while standing on the house's deck, she saw the creature again full-out, standing just across the yard from her near a small satellite dish with woods at its back, staring at her and making a muffled howling sound under its breath. She screamed and ran into the house to report what she'd seen, and someone with a rifle went outside but the creature had disappeared. Her grandmother did not believe her and laughed at her, a major factor in her not wishing to talk about the experience henceforth, but the believers in the family felt this was likely the same creature that had menaced the dog in the 2004 Richwood report. Personally related by the witnesses from the previous Richwood reports.

106. Anonymous, near Motley, presumably Fall 2011 - A video

uploaded to the Internet on December 11, 2011, depicts two young female cousins shooting footage of autumn foliage and listening to country music on their car radio while driving along a dirt road toward a cabin when a large dark manlike creature darts across the road ahead of them from out of one patch of trees and into another. The girls react with "What the (expletive) was that?" type comments and laughter. YouTube.

107. Anonymous, Wadena County, August 19, 2012 - A driver saw a brown furry upright creature about seven feet tall with long arms and legs and a human-like head run across a highway and then pass through thick brush with ease. GCBRO website.

108. Anonymous, Detroit Lakes, Fall 2012 - The second husband of the mother from the Richwood reports had another sighting of the smaller clawed creature in the same area along west Willow Street while driving near the water treatment plant. This time it crossed the road either chasing or running along with some deer. Personally related by the witnesses from the previous Richwood reports.

109. "SRA Andy" and others, Hubbard County, 2012 - An expedition by the Sasquatch Research Association in an area known for past Bigfoot activity discovered several stick structures all within a mile of each other that they believed may have been created by Bigfoots. There were several tee-pees and arches, a blind-type structure, and an X-formation. There was also a small tree that had broken and was blocking a trail, but there was a clear twist in the break. Sasquatch Research Association website.

110. Anonymous, Richwood area, July 4, 2014 - The boy from the previous Richwood reports, now a young adult, was at his grandmother's home where his sister's Bigfoot sighting had occurred as the family was celebrating Independence Day. At about 8 PM, he ignited some firecrackers out in the yard. As if in response, a large thick tree in the nearby woods began to violently sway back and forth. Personally related by the witness.

111. Tracy S., Buffalo River State Park in Clay County, 2014 - A woman who recognized this author in early 2016 from an Internet article on my Bigfoot research told me about a friend of hers' who

had been doing a night time photography project at the park two years before when she'd heard and then seen a Bigfoot fighting with either a coyote or a wolf. The witness did not respond to a message sent to her Facebook page. Personally related by a friend of witness.

112. Names unknown, near Wild Rice River west of Ulen, 2014 - An unknown number of daylight sightings of a Bigfoot walking in the area of two large gravel pits near the river are reported to have occurred as recently as 2014. Jen Kruse of the SheSquatchers.

113. Anonymous, near Wild Rice River west of Ulen, late Spring or early Summer 2015 - Joanne S. of the 2007-2009 Ulen Bigfoot episode reported that a female neighbor of hers' to the north heard "weird sounds," making Joanne wonder if it might be Bigfoot related. Personally related by Joanne S.

114. Anonymous, Richwood area, late Summer 2015 - At the grandmother's home where previous Richwood area reports occurred, over 20 chickens free-ranged during the day but were locked in a shed at night. In one week, all but two of them disappeared during daylight hours with no blood or feathers found. At this same time, it was noted that wolves that used to be heard in the area were gone, and dogs living on the property seemed afraid to leave the yard. Personally related by witnesses from the previous Richwood reports.

115. Names unknown, near Moose Lake, September 3, 2015 - Some people on a fishing trip put up a trail camera along a road just to see what they might capture on it, setting it to take a picture every five seconds. In one shot, a bear was caught crossing the road in the far distance. At 7:07 AM, a dark upright figure was caught standing beside the road not far from the camera and appeared in only one shot, giving it a ten-second window to appear and disappear. People stood in the same spot later for comparison and established the figure's height at only four to five feet. It does not seem to show the short hind legs of an upright bear, and there seems to be some kind of object sitting at its feet with something long and thin protruding up and forward from it. A human carrying something and rushing quickly in and out cannot be ruled out, but the photo was equated

with the earlier Bigfoot activity in the area. Bigfoot Research News website.

116. Name(s) unknown, Pillager area, 2015 - A Bigfoot sighting is reported to have occurred. Loren Coleman at Paracon, Shooting Star Casino Mahnomen, October 14, 2012.

117. Mike Quast, Buffalo River State Park in Clay County, March 2016 - In response to the 2014 Tracy S. report this author was exploring the park when I found a possible Bigfoot track in a flattened gopher mound just beside a walking trail shortly uphill from the parking area. It showed two toe impressions with the rest indistinct, measuring about 12" long. As all the surrounding ground was covered in tall grass, it seemed odd that the creature would have stepped in the one spot where it would leave a track, and also that it would venture to the more open and developed section of the park which is a distance away from the wooded area that follows the Buffalo River, but the park is only officially open in the summer months and has greatly reduced human presence at other times. Personal experience.

118. Name(s) unknown, Menahga-Huntersville State Forest area, 2016 - A Bigfoot encounter is reporter to have occurred. Loren Coleman at Paracon, Shooting Star Casino Mahnomen, October 14, 2017.

119. Name unknown, near Onamia, Fall 2017 - A man grouse hunting in a wildlife management area found two possible Bigfoot tracks 15" long by 6" wide, one barely visible on a hard-packed trail and the second in soft sand 42" away and 3/4" deep. Reported by SCSO Sasquatch Organization. YouTube.

120-121. Name unknown, Rice area, Winter 2016- December 2017 - The same man from the previous report was driving in a heavily wooded area 21 miles from Rice at 9:30 at night when in his headlight beam, a Bigfoot crossed the two-lane highway he was on in just four strides, moving from east to west, coming from the nearby Mississippi River. The creature was 7 1/2 to eight feet tall, three feet wide, and estimated to weigh around 500 pounds, covered in black matted hair and with long arms reaching nearly to its knees that swung as it walked. The headlights illuminated the creature's legs better than its upper body, which was more in shadow. The man reported to the SCSO Sasquatch Organization that he had also been hearing what he believed to be Bigfoot sounds around his home near Rice for the past year, occurring every couple of weeks and consisting of knocks and vocalizations like howls, growls, and chatter. YouTube.

122. Anonymous, near Menahga, July, year unknown - Two people from a party of campers went into some woods after dark to collect firewood. After about ten minutes, they heard footsteps and brush moving and thought it was one of their friends playing tricks until they heard a grunting sound and shined their flashlights into the brush, whereupon they saw a large hairy upright creature stand up, utter a half-roar and run away. Bigfootinfo website.

123. Anonymous, near Menahga, October, year unknown - Two duck hunters taking a break while on the way back to their truck saw a bearlike creature with an apelike face. They thought about shooting it but decided against it because they didn't know what it was. After it went away, they followed its tracks until they disappeared into a stream. Bigfootinfo website.

124. "Neil," White Earth Reservation, date unknown - Limited information on a young part-Native American man seeing a Bigfoot standing about eight feet tall, which he watched for about a minute. This was included in a longer narrative about various spiritual experiences he had had on the reservation. Personally related by the witness.

125. Anonymous, Buffalo River State Park in Clay County, date unknown - Limited information on a person who reported hearing a possible Bigfoot vocalization in the park. Related by witness by e-mail.

126. Anonymous, Syre, date unknown- The same person from the previous report stated that their brother-in-law "who never lies" had seen a Bigfoot standing at the intersection of Highways 32 and 39 at the tiny community of Syre while driving. Related by a relative of witness by e-mail.

127. Anonymous, Huntersville area, May, year unknown - Two

friends were riding ATVs and stopped at the Huntersville Outpost to get something to eat. As they were about to leave they saw what they at first thought was a man walking along the road but then realized it was a Bigfoot. Shortly thereafter, one of the vehicles broke down, and the owner went home with his friend, where they saw the creature again sitting within the cover of some woods watching them, implying that it had followed them there. It then let out a high-pitched scream and ran off. Bigfootinfo website.

128. B.J.P., Big Pine Lake in Otter Tail County, date unknown - A person living on the lakeshore heard a loud noise coming from the top of a nearby wooded hill, sounding a bit like a motor revving but more like the bellow of a large animal. There was no machinery and no people in the area to account for it, and later the person heard an alleged recording of a Bigfoot on a t.v. show and thought it sounded very similar. Related by witness by letter.

129. Name(s) unknown, Johnsdale area in Rum River State Forest south of Mille Lacs Lake, date(s) unknown - A creature known as the Johnsdale Bog Monster is reported to have been encountered. Loren Coleman at Paracon, Shooting Star Casino Mahnomen, October 14, 2017.

130. Name(s) unknown, Sewell Lake southeast of Fergus Falls, date unknown - A Bigfoot encounter is reported to have occurred. Loren Coleman at Paracon, Shooting Star Casino Mahnomen, October 14, 2017.

131. Name(s) unknown, Ponsford area, date(s) unknown - A Bigfoot-type creature known locally as the Bagwajiwinniwug is reported to have been encountered. Loren Coleman at Paracon, Shooting Star Casino Mahnomen, October 14, 2017.

132. Name(s) unknown, southeast of Mahnomen, date(s) unknown - A Bigfoot-type creature known locally as the "Klik-Klak" is reported to have been encountered. Loren Coleman at Paracon, Shooting Star Casino Mahnomen, October 14, 2017.

133. Name(s) unknown, Fergus Falls area, date unknown - A Bigfoot encounter is reported to have occurred. Loren Coleman at Paracon, Shooting Star Casino Mahnomen, October 14, 2017.

SOUTHWEST

1. Names unknown, Windom area, Winter 1966 - Limited information on several sightings of a white-haired Bigfoot. Mark A. Hall.

2. Anonymous, near Milroy, March 1978 - Two children arriving home from school saw a manlike figure by a grove of trees that framed their farm. They first thought it was their father but it darted into the trees in a hunched posture when they approached, and they could hear it breaking branches as it fled. That night something pounded on the front door of their house when everyone was in bed. In addition, there was often heard a sound like pigs around the farm which was an animal they did not have, and once when they rushed outside in response to the sounds there was nothing seen. Bigfootinfo website.

SOUTHEAST

1. J.L., near LaCrescent, Fall 1968 - Two men were duck hunting in a blind in the early morning when one returned to their car to retrieve a pocket warmer. While the other was alone in the blind he thought he heard his blind returning with very heavy footsteps and stuck his head out of the blind to scold him for being so loud, but found that it was actually a huge upright black hairy creature walking along in a stooped manner as if looking for food along the ground. When it saw and heard him it stood fully upright, and he found himself even in

height with about the center of its chest. In a panic, the man accidentally fired his shotgun, causing the creature to let out a scream and
run away. "The Abominable Snowmen" by Eric Norman.

2. Anonymous, south of Rochester, pre-1969 - A trucker who drove
an early morning route from northern Iowa to Rochester took
ribbing from his coworkers for claiming to frequently see "monkey
men" along the road, but he swore it was true and that the creatures
would sometimes stand right in the middle of the road. Then one
morning at about 4:30 AM, the man ran his truck off the road and
was killed, after which his claims were given more credence. Saga,
June 1969.

3. Larry Hawkins, south of Rochester, late 1968 or early 1969 - An
Iowa college student driving from Rochester to Decorah, Iowa, on
Highway 52 near midnight, thought he saw a person crouched at the
roadside and pulled over to help, but then he saw that it was not a
person but a hairy, apelike creature with thick shoulders that immediately leaped up and ran up a steep hillside into some woods. The
student got out of his car and found that the creature had been
crouched over a dead rabbit that had no signs of blood or puncture,
but abandoned his inspection when he heard a harsh roar from the
woods and quickly got back in his car and fled. He went straight to a
police station to report the sighting but was not taken seriously. "The
Abominable Snowmen" by Eric Norman; Saga, June 1969.

4. Anonymous, near Shakopee, late 60s or early 70s - Some
youths were out driving in a rural area at night and parked in a
pasture to sit and talk. They then heard heavy footfalls coming up
behind their car and saw a large bipedal creature approaching them,
which caused them to start the car and flee. The creature chased
them until they reached the road, getting close enough to touch the
car and leave smudge marks on the back windshield. There were
cows in the pasture, but though it was dark and they didn't see the
creature in great detail, they knew it was not a cow. Minnesota
Bigfoot website, Joe Heinan.

5. Names unknown, Minneapolis-St. Paul area, 1971 - A letter to
cryptozoological researcher Ivan T. Sanderson stated that a hairy

human-like creature had been captured while scrounging through garbage cans somewhere in the Twin Cities area and was being kept in the Rochester State Hospital where it refused to wear clothes and was so violent that food had to be thrown to it. This is considered a hoax but was never confirmed or debunked. "Sasquatch: The Apes Among Us" by John Green.

6. Margaret D. and family, near Frontenac State Park in Goodhue County, May 28, 1972- A woman reported that as a seven-year-old child, she and her younger sister were on a walk with their grandfather on a gravel road near their home when they found a footprint in a soft area at the roadside that looked as if its maker had stepped there before ascending a grassy hill. She was fascinated and wanted to study the track, but the grandfather was nervous and got the children back to the house as soon as possible. This was the beginning of a Bigfoot episode that would continue sporadically into the 1980s. GCBRO website; Minnesota Bigfoot website, Joe Heinan; Personally related by the witness Margaret D. by e-mail.

7. Anonymous, west of Big Marine Lake in Washington County, September 1972 - A person sitting in a tree stand while bowhunting saw an upright hairy creature walk by about 75 yards away swinging its arms, never having heard of Bigfoot at the time and so thinking it must be an odd bear. The sighting was not far from the St. Croix River. BFRO website.

8. Anonymous, near Houston, October 1975 - A man was out raccoon hunting on a moonlit night along a picked cornfield uphill from some woods when his two coon dogs became spooked while exploring the tree line and refused to enter the woods. When a low moaning sound then issued from the woods. The man shined his flashlight into the trees, not seeing anything but soon hearing what sounded like a large rock being thrown into a brush pile. When he shouted, "Who's there?" he then heard two loud wood knocks followed by the sound of whatever it was moving away. Later, he talked to a friend who said that deer seemed to have disappeared from the area, and cattle were refusing to venture away from farm buildings. Years later, a TV show on Bigfoot that talked about wood

knocking made him suspect the creatures may have been involved. BFRO website.

9. Name unknown, Fort Snelling State Park near St. Paul, 1975 - Limited information on a police officer who is said to have heard a Bigfoot scream in the Coldwater Spring area of the park. Joe Parkhurst, YouTube.

10. Anonymous, Rushford area, 1976 - A woman was alone in her rural home in the evening when her dogs began fearfully barking and growling, so she took a small-caliber pistol and opened the door a crack to look outside. Two red eyes shone in the darkness, and a foul odor filled the air, so she locked the door but then heard whatever it was rummaging around her house making strange wailing cries. Letter by Terry Burt of the La Crosse Tribune to cryptozoologist Mark A. Hall.

11. Anonymous, Rushford area, 1976 - At around the same time as the above report a Bigfoot sighting reportedly occurred, and two boys from Lanesboro High School made plaster casts of some footprints. Letter by Terry Burt of the La Crosse Tribune to cryptozoologist Mark A. Hall.

12. Mark R. and friend, near Hugo, 1977-78 - An episode of Bigfoot activity occurred around a farm, mostly noticed only by a young boy and his friend. Very large human-like tracks started appearing in 1977, and after discovering some in a clearing in winter 1978, the boys called the Sheriff's Department. Officers responded but branded it a prank. The next day the boys returned to the clearing to see if there were more tracks and found two Bigfoot creatures standing there only about 20 feet away, one about seven feet tall and the other 5 1/2 -6 feet tall, both covered in medium brown hair, including their faces. When the faces turned to see the boys, their faces seemed to register fright, as did the boys who ran back to Mark's friend's home and told his father, who didn't believe them. That evening as the boys were watching t.v. something began beating heavily on the house's back door, and when the boys looked out a window they saw a Bigfoot standing there, which walked away after a minute or two without having been seen by any adults. The next morning, a steel storage

shed about 100 yards from the house was found covered in dents, the door ripped off, and a bobcat tractor inside tipped over on to its side, with Bigfoot tracks all around. The father concluded it must have been a bear, but the boys knew better. Mark added to the story that he sometimes found unusual items beside Bigfoot tracks, such as a fish even though the nearest lake was three or four miles away and half a rack of moose antlers, even though no moose were known to live in the area. Minnesota Bigfoot website, Joe Heinan; Related by witness by e-mail.

13. Anonymous, Rochester, December 14, 1979 - A woman driving home at night with her children aged two and three within city limits were between the Rose Haven and Marvale additions, when her headlights revealed a hairy upright creature. It was seven feet tall, weighed 250-300 pounds, had a huge mouth with a piglike snout and the woman found it to be very ugly. It attempted to cover its eyes from the glare of the headlights with one arm, which did not bend like a normal human arm. She reported the sighting to help ease her children' fears after seeing the creature, but Sheriff's officers found no trace of it. Rochester Post-Bulletin, December 17, 1979.

14. Anonymous, Carlos Avery Game Preserve in Chisago County, mid-to-late 1970s - An episode occurred involving UFOs and animal mutilations as well as a possible Bigfoot presence. Floating lights near ground level began to appear sporadically at a farm in 1971, leading to a spate of animal deaths in which a calf, a deer carcass hung in a tree, and some pigs were decapitated, the heads missing, along with another mangling of the bodies that would have required great strength. Two farm families teamed up to stake out the property in the summer of 1976 when whatever was prowling about appeared on the 19th night of the month for three consecutive months, June through August. On August 19th, no animal was killed, but the men who were armed and on guard heard high-pitched screech-growls typical of Bigfoot coming from all around them and vaguely glimpsed one dark upright form approaching them from a swampy area. It retreated when a frightened dog bolted for cover. The being left no tracks even though the ground had been specifically prepared

for it. Activity seemed to cease then until deer hunting season in 1977 when men hunting in a marsh beside the farm reported being stalked by something that would remain unseen but uttered the same screech-growl heard earlier and would break off three to four-inch-thick saplings. This was recent when the story was made public but in 1990, the Chisago County Sheriff's Department stated in a letter to this author that the activity had ceased. Of note is the fact that the animal mutilations, in this case, are completely non-typical of such cases that are commonly associated with UFOs which normally feature much more precise, even surgical- type damage. Fate. December 1977, Bradley Earl Ayers.

15. Margaret D. and family, near Spring Valley, 1970s - The same woman from both earlier and later, Goodhue County reports related that she had an uncle with a farm where extended Bigfoot activity occurred, including similar noises to what she had heard around her own home, the killing of small livestock and dogs, and a September sighting by a female cousin for which she was also present as a child. They were playing on the floor when the cousin looked up and said she saw her uncle (her father's brother) looking in the window, which was impossible since he was out of the country at the time. That uncle happened to be very hairy. GCBRO website; Minnesota Bigfoot website, Joe Heinan; Personally related by the witness Margaret D. by e- mail.

16. Chris L., one other, near St. Croix River in Washington County, Summer 1979 or 1980 - Two Boy Scouts at Camp Wilder were in some woods just off a trail to a swimming area, searching for a lost pocket knife when they saw what they at first thought to be a tree stump, but then it turned its head and turned out to be a rust-brown creature sitting in a human-like fashion on the ground with its hands resting on its bent knees. The boys then fled. Related by witness by e-mail.

17. Name(s) unknown, Prairie Island Indian Reservation near Red Wing, 1983 - "Cee-ha- tonka" or "The Big Man," the Dakota Sioux tribe's name for Bigfoot, was said to have made an appearance. This was considered to be a spiritual guardian of the people, a big brother figure that appeared when spiritual guidance was needed. Red Wing

Republican Eagle, Jim Anderson, July 23, 1988; Personal discussion with later witness Wayne Running Wolf.

18. Orin Volkman, Anoka County, 1985- A Sheriff's deputy was driving at about 3:30 AM in a northern suburb of Minneapolis, and as he rounded a curve, he saw a set of eyes glowing in his headlights, almost eye level with him in some brush. They were about four inches apart and about five feet above road level, with the ditch bottom being three feet lower, making a height of eight feet. The eyes blinked a few times. He could not explain what he'd seen and allowed for Bigfoot as a possibility. "Jimmy Wilson's Snowman" (film), Jimmy Wilson Company.

19. Name unknown, Prairie Island Indian Reservation near Red Wing, mid-1980s - A young man dating a girl from the reservation was said to scoff at the tribe's belief in Cee-ha-tonka or "The Big Man" until it appeared to him for just a few seconds and then disappeared into thin air. Personally related by tribal elder Ray Owen.

20. Wayne Running Wolf, Prairie Island Indian Reservation near Red Wing, July 21, 1988 - A tribal priest was sitting in his living room at night when he saw a shadow or shape out a window and thought someone was trespassing around his car, but when he later found 18" human-like footprints in his driveway with eagle feathers in them, he knew that "The Big Man" had paid another visit. At this time, the tribe was in mourning for a man killed in a car accident and some were abusing alcohol in their grief, and it was thought that they needed their spiritual big brother to appear to put them back on track. Dwight Wells, a neighbor and brother of the deceased man, added to Running Wolf's account by reporting that his dog had been barking excitedly in his house at the same time. Red Wing Republican Eagle. Jim Anderson, July 23, 1988; Personally related by the witness.

21. Anonymous, Hidden Lake near Circle Pines, Winter 1988 - Two ten-year-old girls were in some snowy woods when they saw what they described as a beige or blonde-colored gorilla that looked at them and frightened them into running to one of their homes and telling her mother, who wanted them to take her back to where it

happened so she could look for tracks but the children were too scared to return. When reporting this online 15 years later, the mother noted that over the years, loud screams had been heard in the area, and large tracks had been seen in the snow as well as foul odors noticed and also shelters found made of logs and sticks. BFRO website.

22-27. Margaret D. and family, near Frontenac State Park in Goodhue County, 1970s-1980s - The woman who reported the previous childhood experience on May 28, 1972, at this location related that a general knowledge of Bigfoot being in the area lasted for several years, marked by her family's dogs, always acting very terrified of something. Once in the 70s her mother reported seeing a black figure "loping" across the back yard, but she was reluctant to talk about it afterward. At around that same time, Margaret was awakened by something that sounded like it was imitating the sound of a rooster crowing but louder than a rooster could possibly do, and the family did have chickens at that time. Another time she heard what sounded like voices but not human ones at the edge of the property at two or three AM, and yet another time something passed by her bedroom window while she was in bed that growled and smelled like wet leaves. Finally, in the 80s, once the woman had grown to adulthood and was married she and her husband lived at the property for a time, during which a howling noise was heard several times that much like an alleged Bigfoot howl captured on tape that they heard online. Her daughter also had a sighting while walking in the woods of something large, brown, and bipedal moving away from her. GCBRO website; Minnesota Bigfoot website, Joe Heinan; Personally related by witness Margaret D. by e-mail.

28. "Rick," near Blue Hill and Zimmerman, November 1998 - A deer hunter in the Sherburne National Wildlife Refuge was sitting in a tree stand when he saw a Bigfoot walking about 400 yards away. It was brown or black in color, very large, and walked with a rather exaggerated swinging of its arms. It seemed to notice him, stopped briefly, and then turned 90 degrees and hurried away into the woods.

The hunter had it in sight for about four minutes. Minnesota Bigfoot website, Joe Heinan.

29. Anonymous, near Minneapolis, January 2000 - Some people were doing some winter camping and ice fishing over a weekend and on Friday night heard a "weird noise" and thought it was someone trying to scare them, so they ignored it and went to sleep. On Saturday, they found some tracks and still thought it was a prank until that night when they heard the noise again and went after it with guns, at which point they saw a figure in the darkness which their report does not give a good description of but it convinced them that it was not a human being, and after it ran away, they never saw it again. Bigfoot-info website.

30. Anonymous, near Centerville, February 21, 2000 - A couple walking with their dogs by a small lake with an island in it saw a manlike figure walking quickly out on the ice about 350 yards away, black in color except for the head, which looked brown with long hair hanging down to its shoulders. When the figure was about 175 yards away, it went into some cattails and two geese flew out, the figure watching them by turning its entire upper body instead of just its head as if it had no neck. After the figure went out of sight, the man wanted to go out to examine the scene, but his wife was too afraid to accompany him, and strangely his normally fearless hunting dogs also refused to go. He went out to the cattails and found that no tracks showed in the ice and hard-packed snow, but most significant was that the cattails were six feet high, and the figure had been visible head and shoulders above them. BFRO website.

31. Anonymous, near Rock Creek and Grantsburg (Wisconsin), July 21, 2001 - Two friends were camping on an island in the St. Croix River, and late at night, they began to hear strange noises around them. They ignited some firecrackers, but the noises continued all night until about 8 AM They then heard something charging through the brush on another island nearby, moving quickly in their direction and accompanied by a foul odor, but they could not see what it was. After looking around the island they were on, they found many human-like tracks 17-18" long and some slightly smaller, as well as a

pile of clam shells that had not been there the previous day. At that point, they were intimidated into leaving. The evidence seemed to suggest a family of creatures swimming back and forth between the two islands during the night, and the crossing brush on the neighboring island in the morning, being a bluff charge meant to scare them off. BFRO website.

32. Name(s) unknown, near Pine City and Rock Creek, Summer 2001- Limited information on tracks of what seemed to be a Bigfoot family that was found near the St. Croix River. There were four sizes, two larger and two smaller. Curt Nelson.

33-34. Anonymous, near Spring Valley, September 2001 - A man preparing to walk to a hunting stand from his truck before dawn heard a noise in a ravine and shined a light toward it, then saw two red eyes eight to nine feet above the ground 60 to 70 yards away. They appeared to be staring back at him, and he saw them blink, then turn away and disappear. He went on with his hunt and nothing further unusual happened, except that when he examined the spot where the eyes had been there was no tree there, which meant they belonged to something that was actually, that tall standing on the ground. One week later, when he was preparing to hunt again in the same spot, the exact same sequence of events happened a second time. BFRO website.

35. Anonymous, near Spring Valley, May 19, 2002 - The man from the previous report was camping on his property with his family, hiking and dirt bike riding in the afternoon, when his 11-year-old son saw a creature he described as a "caveman" crouched over their fire pit 35- 40 yards away and called his father's attention to it. It was partially concealed behind some straw bales so that by the time the father saw it, it had stood and began to hurry away toward nearby woods, a bipedal creature five to seven feet tall and weighing around 300 pounds, covered in reddish-brown hair. Its face was hairless with brownish skin, its head roundish with no apparent neck, its arms hanging to below its knees and its muscles evidently massive as it ran away at high speed pumping its arms. After calming down from the sighting, the father and son followed the creature's path and found

three or four five-toed footprints in a creek bed slightly larger than the father's size 13 boots. Later that afternoon, while taking a break from dirt bike riding to do some maintenance on it, the father heard a high-pitched scream coming from a quarter to a half-mile away, opposite the campsite from him. That night at about 11 PM, the family could hear a dog belonging to their neighbor who lived 1 1/2 miles away start barking crazily, sounding as if it was chasing something, which is kept up for a few hours. At about 3:30 AM, the dog chased its quarry into their campsite, and as the family lay in their tent, they heard crashing brush and heavy bipedal footsteps passing right by the tent and shaking the ground. The pursuing dog then let out a yelp, followed by silence. After a time, the father got up to light a fire for security. No word was given in the report as to the fate of the dog. BFRO website.

36. Margaret D. and family, Wabasha County, August 2002 - The woman from earlier Goodhue County reports also reported that in adulthood, she was now living in a neighboring county and was again hearing noises in the area similar to those she had associated with Bigfoot in her younger years, and that her 17-year-old son had had an experience late at night in which area dogs that normally barked at wildlife were instead crazily howling at something and then heard what sounded like a large human being running. GCBRO website; Minnesota Bigfoot website, Joe Heinan; Personally related by the witness Margaret D. by e-mail.

37. Anonymous, Houston County, September 21, 2002 - A father and son were hunting small game on wooded bluffs just after sunrise when they started to hear a snorting sound that persisted for a few minutes. The father fired a shot in the air that seemed to scare off whatever it was, and the pair continued hunting, but then a small herd of deer suddenly came running along and charged straight past them as if spooked by something, missing them by only a few feet. Eventually, they came to a pile of logs where they normally sat down to rest, and as they did so something on the opposite side of the logs took off running into the brush, breaking large branches as it went and not bounding like a deer but sounding like a heavy bipedal run.

They never saw what it was, but the branches it had broken were up to five feet above the ground. GCBRO website.

38-40. Anonymous, near Spring Valley, late Summer or early Fall 2002 and later- While preparing to eventually sell their property to a friend, the family from the previous Spring Valley reports were showing him around when they came across Bigfoot tracks described as "ape-like" and measuring about 18" long in a cornfield, crossing the field without any cornstalks being broken. Later in the day, another set of smaller tracks was also seen, and the family explained to their bemused friend what had been going on on the property. A severed deer leg was also found that day. A month later, the man's adult son was being shown around the property and also saw tracks. The friend decided to go ahead and purchase the land, hunting on it and seeing no further evidence but one time hearing a loud vocalization that sounded very similar to a recorded Bigfoot call on the BFRO website. BFRO website.

41. Anonymous, near Spring Valley, October 8, 2002 - The family from the previous Spring Valley reports were hunting in the area of the previous events near sunset, the father waiting at the top of a ravine with his bow and arrow while his wife and son tried to flush out game from down below, when he heard sounds in some brush about 30 yards to his left that sounded like a small child spouting gibberish. Also about 30 yards away but to his right, something very large started crashing in the brush, pacing back and forth, giving the impression that he was standing in between an adult creature and its young. He nervously went down into the ravine where his wife and son were, finding them in a similar state as they had just heard something large and bipedal go running up the ravine toward him. They then fled the area. This was apparently the last Bigfoot experience had by the family before they sold their property to a friend. BFRO website.

42. Anonymous, near St. Paul, October 2002 - Limited information on a person sleeping in a tent that was awakened by a rubbing type noise, and upon looking out, saw a Bigfoot that appeared to be cleaning itself. Bigfootinfo website.

43. Anonymous, near Spring Valley, October 8, 2005 - A man out squirrel hunting saw what he first thought was a huge black turkey flapping its wings through thick brush, but then he moved to get a better look, he saw that it was a big black bipedal hairy creature about eight feet tall and weighing around 600 pounds that suddenly stood up and started to run away. Immediately in its wake, a second creature then did the same, also eight feet tall but heavier and with longer reddish-brown hair, stumbling a bit as it started to run. Both creatures had flat faces, no apparent necks, wide shoulders, and arms that hung to their knees. The first creature had a peaked head, but the second one's head was more human-like in shape. The man had the impression that the first creature was female and the second male. They quickly disappeared into the woods, making surprisingly little noise. When he went to examine the spot where they had been he realized that when he first saw the black creature's movements, it had probably been picking chokecherries. He decided not to try to follow them since their silent movement made him fearful that they might sneak up behind him. BFRO website.

44. Anonymous, near St. Croix River 30 miles east of St. Paul, July 16, 2011 - A farmer had a new iPhone and was using it to shoot video of everything when he and his wife were walking along the edge of a hayfield beside some woods and heard a low grunting sound in the trees. The man aimed the phone at what they thought at the time was a deer running, but when they viewed the video a few days later, they saw that they had about five seconds of footage of an auburn-haired Bigfoot moving quickly through the brush in a crouch, its shoulders high and its hands gray. YouTube.

45. Anonymous, near Centerville Lake in Anoka County, Summer 2011 - A man thought he saw someone go into an area of woods and swamp where it seemed too thick for anyone to walk, but he disregarded it until a clearer sighting in 2013. GCBRO website.

46. Name(s) unknown, near Afton, 2011 - A YouTube video posted on September 28, 2011 shows a photo of a five-toed Bigfoot track said to have been found "recently" near the St. Croix River outside Afton,

with a person's hands beside it for scale, making it look about 15" long. Eddie Hanson on YouTube.

47. Anonymous, Goodhue County, August 8, 2012 - A woman was driving home from a golf course at 1:35 PM when she saw an upright human-like creature eight to nine feet tall and covered with long reddish hair at the roadside. It walked into the woods with a four-foot stride, swinging its long arms. The woman drove on without looking back, deeply disturbed by what she'd seen. GCBRO website.

48. Anonymous, Olmsted County, November 4, 2012- A young person in a developed area that bordered a wilderness area had just ridden to an empty wooded lot by bicycle, looking for a friend at 10 AM when he heard a rustling near the top of a hill 60 to 80 feet up. Looking up he saw a manlike figure with long arms and covered in dark hair come out of some brush walking in a slightly bent over posture, quickly moving out of sight. At the upward angle at which he saw it, he could not be sure of its height, but it seemed larger than a man. GCBRO website.

49. Anonymous, near Centerville Lake in Anoka County, January 15, 2013 - The same man from the Summer 2011 sighting in this area was at the same spot walking his dog with his wife at about 7:30 AM when he saw a black figure about seven feet tall walk behind a trail sign and disappear into the woods. It seemed slender, but he was sure it was not a human being. He went to the spot but found no tracks or other signs. His wife did not see the figure. GCBRO website.

50-51. Joe Parkhurst and wife, Fort Snelling State Park near St. Paul, July 19-22, 2016 - A Bigfoot researcher and his wife were cruising the park by car at night, scanning the woods with a thermal imager when they picked up what they believed to be two Bigfoot creatures crouching down. They also noted a number of heat signatures of deer and smaller animals they saw during their search for comparison and the two supposed Bigfoots were clearly bigger and differently shaped. Three nights earlier, they'd seen another Bigfoot heat signature else-where in the park and also heard whistling sounds. YouTube.

52. Joe Parkhurst, Fort Snelling State Park near St. Paul, August 30, 2016 - While exploring at night with a thermal imager, Bigfoot

researcher Joe filmed the heat signature of an animal climbing down a tree and then moving away on the ground on all fours. Debate ensued over the animal's size, whether it could possibly be just a raccoon or something larger. Joe later did a size comparison having himself filmed next to the tree and the result seemed to indicate that the animal was close to man-sized, suggesting that it may have been a young Bigfoot. "7 Months of Bigfoot," YouTube.

53. Chris Lapakko, Fort Snelling State Park near St. Paul, August 2016 - In an episode spanning a couple of days, online personality Lapakko responded to Bigfooter Joe Parkhurst's YouTube videos by going to the park and checking out the area for himself, filming his ventures with a skeptical but open-minded attitude to see if he could either confirm or refute the claims of Bigfoot in the area. He found some of the reputed tree and stick structures Parkhurst had reported and "destroyed" them, then came back later and noted that some seemed to have been at least partially put back together. He also found some footprints in the mud along a riverside that were human-like in shape and slightly shorter than his own size 13 shoes but much wider, in a spot where people were not likely to have been walking. Overall, his findings were inconclusive. "The Chris Lapakko Investigations/Experiment," YouTube.

54. Joe Parkhurst and family, "Neal" and "Robert," Fort Snelling State Park near St. Paul, June-December 2016 - Bigfoot researcher Joe noted several examples of evidence while exploring this area but without a careful accounting of exactly how many, making for a Bigfoot "episode" in addition to the other specific incidents he reports. In the general area of Fort Snelling State Park at the confluence of the Mississippi and Minnesota rivers, including Pike Island, Coldwater Spring, Crosby Farm Park, Hidden Falls, Minnesota Valley National Wildlife Refuge and the Sibley Historic Site, many kinds of evidence were noted, including widespread tree breaks and structures, sounds like screams or howls and growls, skunklike odors, partial tracks, and toeprints, broken pieces of ceramic plates with a bare footprint amidst them the size of a six-year-old child's, and one of Joe's daughters seeing something brown and furry that she first

thought was a bear shaking a tree. Two other researchers associated with Joe named Neal (out of St. Paul) and Robert (out of Bloomington) found similar evidence in the area. "7 Months of Bigfoot" and another video, YouTube.

55. Name(s) unknown, "southern Minnesota," 2016- A brief YouTube video shows two photographs were taken at a farm in what appears to be fall as there are no leaves on the trees with a vague dark Bigfoot-like figure appearing in the distant brush beyond the farm buildings. A person posting a comment asked if the site might be near Mankato. Benjamin Halvorson on YouTube. Joe Parkhurst and daughter Emma, Fort Snelling State Park near St. Paul, January 2, 2017- Bigfoot researcher Joe and his daughter were exploring the area of all their family's previous finds, this time in winter snow conditions, when they finally found a set of complete Bigfoot tracks. It was in a spot where what were thought to be two tents of homeless people had been previously found abandoned, including one that was torn apart. The tracks were in a straight line instead of side by side like human tracks and were partially melted with some distortion, but some showed clear toes, the length not noted but appearing on the video to be significantly larger than Joe's boot, and seeming to approach and investigate a discarded bag of garbage and then lead into a large hole in the ground beneath some fallen logs. Joe noted that the tracks had slippery ice in them while the ground around them was just snowy, suggesting that body heat from the feet that made the tracks had melted the snow, which had then refrozen. Joe quickly documented the scene on video and then got himself and his daughter out of the area, appearing to be show some fear and refusing to explore the hole in the ground, having previously expressed the theory that the creatures in the area might live below ground. "7 Months of Bigfoot," YouTube.

56. Mike Quast and Katelynn Morgan, Fort Snelling State Park near St. Paul, April 30, 2017 - This author and a friend went to the park to look into the observations of Joe Parkhurst and Chris Lapakko there and confirmed that many mysterious stick structures were to be found in the woods between park headquarters and Picnic

Island, including small bundles of sticks carefully placed, teepee-like structures both large and small with some big enough to accommodate a human being, a wall or lean-to type structure, a long branch snapped off at a precise length to allow it to be wedged in horizontally between two trees about 18" above ground and a healthy tree at least six inches thick snapped over at a height of about five feet. One of the teepee structures had flat stones laid out at its entrance as if to form a walkway, taken from the bank of the nearby Minnesota River. Near one of the smaller teepee structures we noticed a pathway through the carpet of leaves on the forest floor and were able to make out a few partial footprints in the dirt beneath featuring both toe and heel prints and measuring 11" in length. Personal observation.

57. "Joe," Rice County, July 9, 2018 - A man was with a child looking for rock formations in a wild area when they saw three Bigfoot creatures about 100 yards away, standing shoulder to shoulder and measuring 9 1/2 feet, 8 1/2 feet, and 7 feet in height. They were covered in light brown hair, long and matted and similar to sheep's wool. No smell was noted. The sighting was investigated the next day by the Minnesota Bigfoot Research Team headed by Abe DelRio. YouTube.

58. Tony R., Hidden Lake in Anoka County, date unknown (2000s) - Very limited information on some kind of Bigfoot report.

59. Edward lyankapisukawaka, Rice Creek Regional Park in Anoka County, date unknown- A series of YouTube videos posted in March 2016 shows a man shooting an extensive video of an area in which he says he had a Bigfoot sighting that he refers to as a paranormal encounter. YouTube.

60. Name(s) unknown, Fort Snelling State Park near St. Paul, date unknown - Blogger Kaitlin Salter posted on her website on September 28, 2016, that she had heard about a sighting of Bigfoot in the park "a few years back" but was short on details. She expressed skepticism that Bigfoot could live there. "Mysterious MN" website.

LOCATIONS UNKNOWN

1. Name(s) unknown, "River Creek," 1972 - Limited information on a reported Bigfoot encounter said to have occurred at this location, but as to its very general name, it cannot be specifically located in any area of Minnesota. Loren Coleman at Paracon, Shooting Star Casino Mahnomen, October 14, 2017.

2. Bill Miller and friend, "northern Minnesota," 1980 - Two men on a fishing trip were doing some night fishing in a feeder stream at 12:30-1:00 AM with the night still and quiet when they started to hear a pounding sound like someone thumping their chest with their fist. It came gradually closer until they could also hear heavy breathing, obviously a large animal that made the unarmed men nervous. Soon it passed by them along the shoreline, a large creature running on two feet with a steady stride like that of a jogger. Then the sounds receded into the distance until they faded away, and the men didn't think the creature even noticed them. Miller would go on to become a Bigfoot researcher. "Bigfoot's Reflection" film, 2007. 3-4.

3-4. Rod R., 1990 or 1991 and earlier - Limited information on a man reported having found Bigfoot tracks in either 1990 or 1991 and also to have had a sighting several years before. Mark Francis of NABIN (North American Bigfoot Information Network).

5. Anonymous, "northern Minnesota," early 1990s - A Native American father and son were fishing on a river when they saw an animal in the water with just its head above the surface and wondered if it was a bear or moose, but when the father yelled, it stood up and turned out to be a Bigfoot that had been crouching in fairly shallow water that then ran up the steep brushy riverbank with ease and disappeared. After leaving, they stopped in a nearby town, saw some Sheriff's officers and decided to make a report. The officers were armed with rifles and told them there had been sightings of "skunk ape" in the area, and they were going hunting for it. Minnesota Bigfoot website, Joe Heinan.

6. Anonymous, "north woods of Minnesota," October 15, 2000 - A person camping with their dog was walking around their camp at 5:13

AM when they saw a Bigfoot 30 feet up in a tree staring at them. They turned to run but were confronted with another creature on the ground that picked up but then dropped the person when the dog attacked it. The person then turned to look back while running away and saw the first creature descend the tree, then join the second creature in grabbing and pulling the dog apart, killing it. GCBRO website.

7. Anonymous, "northern Minnesota," January 2001 - A person out for a walk after fishing between midnight and two AM saw a large manlike creature seven or eight feet tall. In response to a shout, it started looking from side to side as if curious, and not knowing what to do, the person hid behind a bush. When the person came near the bush sniffing the air, the person nervously fired a .44 Magnum in the air, causing the creature to let out a vicious roar, cover its ears and run away. The person tried to take a picture but was out of film, then lit a road flare and followed the creature's path for a bit, finding large footprints in the snow. Bigfootinfo website.

8-9. "SRA Andy," "northern Minnesota," September 2008 - A member of the Sasquatch Research Association was exploring a boggy area and found the tracks of what appeared to be a young Bigfoot only about nine inches long and was able to follow them for about two miles. Occasionally the tracks of a larger creature about 18" long would appear as if the young one was roaming about, and the adult was sporadically checking on it. Later that weekend, a second find was made of the larger track. Sasquatch Research Association website.

10. "SRA Jim," "northern Minnesota," September 28, 2008 - During an expedition a member of the Sasquatch Research Association had a trail camera set up in the swampy area where the tracks in the previous report were found, and it captured an image of what was thought to be two young Bigfoot creatures about the size of small children. The two figures looked as if they were standing in a quadrupedal apelike posture. It was dubbed the "Minnesota Twins" photo. Sasquatch Research Association website.

11. "SRA Andy," "SRA Jim," others, "northern Minnesota," 2009 - While preparing to begin an expedition, the Sasquatch Research

Association had a scout camping in their target area. On the morning the expedition was to begin, he drove out along a trail, after which another researcher found a ten-foot log that had been thrown across the trail that was not there when the scout's truck passed by. On close inspection, the marks of fingers about 1 1/4" thick were found in the mud, the log had been pulled from, and as it had been buried up to two feet deep in the mud, it would have taken enormous strength to pull it out. Sasquatch Research Association website.

12. "SRA Andy," "northern Minnesota," 2009 - During the expedition in the previous report in an area known for Bigfoot activity a member of the Sasquatch Research Association found scat that was about two inches thick and filled with chokecherry pits. Grass around the nearby chokecherry trees were all flattened down as if by flat feet, and the trees had been pulled down and stripped of berries without any claw marks evident, suggesting that bears were not responsible. Sasquatch Research Association website. 13-14.

13-14. Jen Kruse and others, "northern Minnesota," August and October 2017 - Members of the SheSquatchers Bigfoot research group used the psychic process of Remote Viewing to locate a large and intricate tree structure they believed to be Bigfoot related at an undisclosed location in August, containing what they referred to as "towers" and also woven fencing eight to ten feet high, all made out of branches. They returned to the site on a night in October, at which time they heard loud sounds in the woods they felt might have been made by a Bigfoot. SheSquatchers website; Personally related by the witness by text message.

15. Anonymous, date unknown - Limited information on a man who claimed to have seen a Bigfoot while grouse hunting in "one of the state parks" of Minnesota, said to be believable because of how he was never one to want to bring unwanted attention upon himself. Nick Sucik.

16. Anonymous, date unknown - A forester who provided information on some reports in the Arrowhead and Central North regions also related how he had once seen an aspen tree pushed over with strips of outer bark pulled off and tossed all around it, with the inner

bark being missing and apparently eaten away but with no teeth or claw marks anywhere. The inner bark is known to be sweet tasting, and the man thought Bigfoot was a possibility. Bob Olson.

17. Don Sherman, date unknown - Limited information on Bigfoot researcher Sherman once capturing footage of a Bigfoot on a thermal imaging camera and hearing its "warbling call." Forum Communications Co., Molly Miron, December 11, 2009.

18. Name unknown, unknown Indian reservation in northern Minnesota, date unknown - Limited information on a member of the Minnesota Bigfoot Research Team formed in 2000 being punched by a Bigfoot. Related by team leader

19. Abe Del Rio in presentation at 2017 Remer Bigfoot Days festival. Abe DelRio and others, date unknown - The head of the Minnesota Bigfoot Research Team reported that his team had experienced heavy footsteps approaching them in response to call blasting during a search, once during the day and once at night. Related by team leader Abe DelRio in presentation at 2018 Remer Bigfoot Days festival.

TOTAL NUMBER OF MINNESOTA BIGFOOT REPORTS

- ARROWHEAD/SUPERIOR - 86
- NORTHWEST - 23
- CENTRAL NORTH - 292
- CLEARWATER COUNTY - 71
- VERGAS TRAILS - 12
- MID-STATE - 133
- SOUTHWEST - 2
- SOUTHEAST - 60
- LOCATIONS UNKNOWN- 17
- TOTAL - 696

ABOUT THE AUTHOR

Born in 1967, Michael John Quast is a lifelong resident of Minnesota who grew up on a dairy farm, achieved a degree in Commercial Art, and is employed in a maintenance position for a school system. He makes his home in the city of M,oorhead, across the Red River from Fargo, North Dakota.

Since childhood, he has had a deep interest in the paranormal, especially cryptozoology, which was bolstered by his own sighting of a Bigfoot in 1976. Since graduating high school he has traveled extensively throughout Minnesota seeking out and investigating Bigfoot reports and exploring wilderness areas in a physical search for the creatures.

He is the author of four prior books on the subject as well as the editor of the former newsletter "Sasquatch Report."

www.ingramcontent.com/pod-product-compliance
Lightning Source LLC
Chambersburg PA
CBHW070051030426
42335CB00016B/1849